Africa Now

Africa Now is published by Zed Books in association with the internationally respected Nordic Africa Institute. Featuring high-quality, cutting-edge research from leading academics, the series addresses the big issues confronting Africa today. Accessible but in-depth, and wide-ranging in its scope, Africa Now engages with the critical political, economic, sociological and development debates affecting the continent, shedding new light on pressing concerns.

Nordic Africa Institute

The Nordic Africa Institute (Nordiska Afrikainstitutet) is a centre for research, documentation and information on modern Africa. Based in Uppsala, Sweden, the Institute is dedicated to providing timely, critical and alternative research and analysis of Africa and to co-operation with African researchers. As a hub and a meeting place for a growing field of research and analysis the Institute strives to put knowledge of African issues within reach for scholars, policy makers, politicians, media, students and the general public.

www.nai.uu.se

Forthcoming titles

Stephen Marr and Patience Mususa (eds), *Practice and Politics of DIY Urbanism in African Cities*

Cecilia Navarra and Cristina Udelsmann Rodrigues (eds), *Transformations of the Rural Spaces in Mozambique*

Diana Højlund Madsen (eds), *Gendered Institutions and Women's Political Representation in Africa*

Laura Stark and Annika Teppo (eds), *Power and Inequality in Urban Africa*

Titles already published

Fantu Cheru and Cyril Obi (eds), *The Rise of China and India in Africa*

Ilda Lindell (ed.), *Africa's Informal Workers*

Iman Hashim and Dorte Thorsen, *Child Migration in Africa*

Prosper B. Matondi, Kjell Havnevik and Atakilte Beyene (eds), *Biofuels, Land Grabbing and Food Security in Africa*

Cyril Obi and Siri Aas Rustad (eds), *Oil and Insurgency in the Niger Delta*

Mats Utas (ed.), *African Conflicts and Informal Power*

Prosper B. Matondi, *Zimbabwe's Fast Track Land Reform*

Maria Eriksson Baaz and Maria Stern, *Sexual Violence as a Weapon of War?*

Fantu Cheru and Renu Modi (eds), *Agricultural Development and Food Security in Africa*

Amanda Hammar (ed.), *Displacement Economies in Africa*

Mary Njeri Kinyanjui, *Women and the Informal Economy in Urban Africa*

Liisa Laakso and Petri Hautaniemi (eds), *Diasporas, Development and Peacemaking in the Horn of Africa*

Margaret Lee, *Africa's World Trade*

Godwin R. Murunga, Duncan Okello and Anders Sjögren (eds), *Kenya: The Struggle for a New Constitutional Order*

Lisa Åkesson and Maria Eriksson Baaz (eds), *Africa's Return Migrants*

Thiven Reddy, *South Africa: Settler Colonialism and the Failures of Liberal Democracy*

Cedric de Coning, Linnéa Gelot and John Karlsrud (eds), *The Future of African Peace Operations*

Tobias Hagmann and Filip Reyntjens (eds), *Aid and Authoritarianism in Africa*

Henning Melber, *The Rise of Africa's Middle Class*

Anders Themnér (ed.), *Warlord Democrats in Africa*

Paul Higate and Mats Utas (eds), *Private Security in Africa*

Mimmi Söderberg Kovacs and Jesper Bjarnesen (eds), *Violence in African Elections: Between Democracy and Big Man Politics*

Atakilte Beyene (eds), *Agricultural Transformation in Ethiopia: State Policy and Smallholder Farming*

About the editors

Jesper Bjarnesen is a Senior Researcher at the Nordic Africa Institute working on regional and war-related mobilities in West Africa, with a focus on intergenerational relations and urban youth culture in Burkina Faso and Côte d'Ivoire. Bjarnesen has published articles in *Migration Letters*, the *Nordic Journal of African Studies* and *Anthropology Southern Africa* and edited a theme section of *Conflict and Society*. He also co-edited a special issue of the journal *Africa* and was co-editor of *Violence in African Elections* (Zed 2018).

Simon Turner is Associate Professor at the Centre for Advanced Migration Studies, University of Copenhagen. He works on forced displacement, diaspora, conflict and humanitarianism in the African Great Lakes region and on Europe. He has worked on a project on anticipating violence in the Burundi conflict and another on carceral junctions in European refugee policies. He is the author of *Politics of Innocence: Hutu Identity, Conflict and Camp Life* (2010), the editor of journal article 'Diasporic Tensions: The Dilemmas and Conflicts of Transnational Engagement' (2008) and the co-editor of journal article 'Agents of Change: Staging and Governing Diasporas and the African State' (2013).

Invisibility in African Displacements

From Structural Marginalization to Strategies of Avoidance

Edited by Jesper Bjarnesen and Simon Turner

Nordiska Afrikainstitutet
The Nordic Africa Institute

ZED

Invisibility in African Displacements: From Structural Marginalization to Strategies of Avoidance was first published in association with the Nordic Africa Institute, PO Box 1703, SE-751 47 Uppsala, Sweden in 2018. This edition first published in 2020 by Zed Books Ltd, The Foundry, 17 Oval Way, London SE11 5RR, UK.

www.zedbooks.net
www.nai.uu.se

Typeset in Minion Pro by River Editorial Ltd, Devon, UK
Index by Rohan Bolton
Cover design by Alice Marwick

A catalogue record for this book is available from the British Library

ISBN 978-1-78699-919-1 hb
ISBN 978-1-78699-920-7 pb
ISBN 978-1-78699-918-4 pdf
ISBN 978-1-78699-916-0 epub
ISBN 978-1-78699-917-7 mobi

Contents

Figures

Acknowledgements

This book is the result of a productive and stimulating collaboration between all the contributors over the course of two years. From the first steps towards articulating a common interest in the dynamics of migrant in/visibilization, we have been overwhelmed and inspired by the commitment and generosity of our fellow authors, and the final outcome is not only shaped by their case studies but also by their reflections and inputs regarding the overall conceptual framework of the collection.

With that in mind, we wish to thank the Swedish funding agency Riksbankens Jubileumsfond (RJ) and the Independent Research Fund, Denmark (DFF) for their financial support of the author workshop that enabled most of the contributors to meet and create the aforementioned synergy. Maria Frantzoulis provided indispensable logistical support during the preparations for the workshop.

We also wish to thank the Nordic Africa Institute (NAI) and the Centre for Advanced Migration Studies, University of Copenhagen, for providing us with the support and conditions to pursue this venture. NAI's Head of Communications, Victoria Engstrand Neacsu deserves particular mention for facilitating the initial submission and subsequent contact with the publishing team at Zed Books, and also in offering feedback on early versions of the synopsis that developed into this book. Finally, the anonymous peer reviewers provided invaluable critique and encouragement at various stages that forced us to push our ideas forward.

Simon Turner and Jesper Bjarnesen
Copenhagen and Uppsala, February 2020

Contributors

Adamou Amadou is a PhD candidate at the Institute for History, Leiden University.

Andrea Behrends is Professor of Anthropology in Africa at the Faculty of Cultural Sciences, University of Bayreuth.

Clayton Boeyink is researcher at the Centre for African Studies, University of Edinburgh.

B Camminga is Postdoctoral Fellow at the African Centre for Migration and Society at University of the Witwatersrand, Johannesburg.

Mirjam de Bruijn is Professor of Contemporary History and Anthropology of Africa at the Institute of History, Leiden University, and Professor of Citizenship and Identities in Africa at the African Studies Centre Leiden.

Roos Keja is Postdoctoral Researcher at the Department of Cultural Anthropology, Utrecht University.

Loren B. Landau is Professor and South African Research Chair on Migration and the Politics of Difference at the African Centre for Migration & Society, University of the Witwatersrand, Johannesburg.

Ingrid Palmary is Professor of Sociology at the University of Johannesburg.

Lotte Pelckmans is a Post Doc at the SAXO-Institute, University of Copenhagen.

Oriol Puig Cepero is Researcher at CIDOB (Barcelona Centre for International Affairs) and Associate Professor at the Autonomous University of Barcelona (UAB).

Andrea Purdeková is Senior Lecturer in Conflict and Security, Department of Politics, Languages and International Studies, University of Bath.

Line Richter is a Post Doc at the Department of Anthropology, University of Copenhagen.

Joyce Takaindisa is a PhD candidate at the African Centre for Migration Studies, University of the Witwatersrand.

Ida Marie Savio Vammen is a Post Doc at the Danish Institute for International Studies (DIIS).

Trond Waage is Associate Professor in Visual Anthropology at the Department of Institute for the Social Sciences. The name of my university is: UiT The Arctic University of Norway.

Introduction: the production of invisibility in African displacements

Jesper Bjarnesen and Simon Turner

Introduction

African migrants have become increasingly demonized in public debate and political rhetoric over the past decade, and particularly in the aftermath of the 2015 European refugee crisis. There is much speculation about the incentives and trajectories of Africans on the move, and often these speculations are geared implicitly or overtly towards discouraging and policing their movements. But what is rarely understood or scrutinized are the intricate ways in which African migrants are marginalized and excluded from public discourse, not only in Europe but in migrant-receiving contexts across the globe. This book offers a series of in-depth case studies that explore these dynamics of structural invisibilization. What also tends to be either ignored or vilified in public debates on African migration are the deliberate strategies of avoidance or assimilation that migrants make use of to gain access to the destinations or opportunities they seek; or simply to remain below the radar of restrictive governance regimes. Such strategic invisibilizations feature prominently across the empirical cases in this collection and offer insights into the determination and ingenuity of people under conditions of extreme precarity and duress.

On this disconcerting backdrop, human mobility and its governance will continue to set the global political agenda in the years to come, with African refugees and other migrants claiming a central, yet ambiguous, role. From concerns over human trafficking and politicized immigration towards the world's richest countries, to the increasing numbers of refugees and internally displaced persons (IDPs) in the poorest parts of the world, mobilities are often associated with matter-out-of-place; with social anomalies and symptoms of global malaise. Governments, UN agencies, private security companies, NGOs and religious institutions are involved in managing and categorizing these diverse movements, thereby rendering some migrants visible and others invisible, administratively or in the eyes of a global public. Visibilization and invisibilization may also occur simultaneously when, for example, refugees are placed in remote camps, and simultaneously made invisible to the public eye while being rendered visible to international humanitarian actors (Turner 2016b; Agier 2011). Meanwhile, migrants may also seek to remain invisible in particular situations, avoiding the gaze of states and other authorities, in their search for safety and their quest for better lives. This collection explores such processes of simultaneous empowerment and disempowerment empirically, asking what are the specific effects and outlooks created by invisibility and invisibilization? From the viewpoint of people on the move, or involuntarily kept in place, what are the effects of becoming or being made invisible? How does invisibility create vulnerability or precariousness, and under which circumstances can invisibility be used strategically as a desirable position? These questions offer fresh analytical perspectives on migrant and refugee mobilities, and feed into larger debates on agency and social being.

The contributions to this volume offer empirically grounded analyses of the (im) mobilities that take place outside the purview of state bureaucracies and humanitarian agencies, thereby shifting the focus from the reified administrative categories of 'economic migrants', 'refugees' and 'internally displaced persons' towards ethnographies of *processes of invisibilization in displacement*. Whether as a consequence of institutional blindness or non-recognition, or as a result of deliberate strategies by migrants themselves, we explore these diverse processes of invisibilization in order to understand how they affect the vulnerabilities and mobility strategies of the migrants and institutional actors involved. By exploring processes of visibilization and invisibilization across societal levels, the case studies provide new insights into stratified processes of displacement, with particular emphasis on the capacities of migrants to negotiate, manipulate and circumvent the roles ascribed to them by external actors such as state bureaucracies and humanitarian agencies. The contributors analyse the dynamics of invisibilization in displacement on the basis of empirical case studies of African transnational spaces which may either be delimited within a sub-region, as people move through and across borderlands; regionally along well-established paths of labour migration or through temporary corridors of escape; across longer distances as certain states attract labour from all corners of the continent or migrants linger en route to destinations elsewhere; or, finally, trans-continentally, as African migrants to other continents invest in practices and exchanges that tie their countries of origin and their countries of residence together.

The dynamics of invisibilization in relation to migration are not a new phenomenon. New and old forms of labour migration provide corporations with an affordable and unaccountable workforce, whose invisibility as labourers is reproduced by vested interests in keeping migrants undocumented or illegal: outside the order of workers' rights and other forms of legal and administrative recognition. Whether formally categorized as refugees or not, migrants thereby experience varying degrees of vulnerability and insecurity in relation to their mobilities. These vulnerabilities constitute subjective experiences of displacement and may be more pressing for groups of migrants unlikely to be considered formal refugees, such as return migrants or deportees; people stuck in places and positions of extreme vulnerability; as well as migrants who are forced to leave their homes due to lack of livelihood options. While such mobility-related vulnerabilities rarely register for external interventions, they are also kept below the surface within communities and even within families, either by people turning a blind eye or by migrants themselves choosing to lay low (Bjarnesen 2016).

Invisibility may, however, also provide possibilities for physical and social mobility. Migrants may choose to leave the protection and predictability of refugee camps in order to seek their fortune in precarious situations of illegality, going below the radar in Africa's growing cities (Turner 2016a). While invisibility is pursued as a deliberate choice through these diverse and overlapping strategies, the experience of displacement may also involve being rendered invisible against one's will. We therefore explore the institutional strategies and practices of creating administrative and/or normative categories of visibility for migrants, which almost inevitably tend to imply a parallel process of invisibilization. Most obviously, at the level of the state, the distinctions between legal and illegal migrants may be pivotal for the ways migrants are able to move and dwell (De Genova 2002). For example, categorizing a migrant as illegal, or 'irregular' in current parlance, may force people into hiding in order to avoid deportation or other legal penalties.

Non-state actors also contribute to the invisibilization of different categories of migrants. UN agencies and humanitarian NGOs apply the taxonomies of international law in order to select their beneficiaries, thereby rendering the vulnerabilities of those labelled as 'economic migrants' relatively invisible. Religious institutions often reach out to those who have been deemed illegal by states, and with whom established NGOs and UN organizations therefore cannot work. In these cases, dynamics of invisibilization are clearly found in the state's insistence on non-recognition, and the compliance with these norms by the most influential humanitarian actors. But, more subtly, the outreach initiatives of religious actors may also serve to reinforce these dynamics by institutionalizing their formalized invisibility in relation to the state.

The main argument of the book as a whole, therefore, is that understanding migration strategies and governance through an attention to the specific invisibilities that are produced and negotiated by the social actors involved enables new perspectives on the highly politicized field of African migration. By emphasizing the vulnerabilities that are thus produced and, in some cases, overcome, the book offers a more balanced approach to analysing the ways migrants adapt to, engage with or avoid the governing structures that are increasingly geared towards policing and containment.

Approaches to invisibility and displacement in Africa

This is not the first book to explore invisibility and migration in Africa. In the following we outline two main strands of literature that have inspired us in our approach to exploring this phenomenon. We will outline their main arguments, and how they draw on and feed into larger debates on migration governance in Africa on the one hand and conceptual debates on social invisibility on the other. Finally, we will show how our approach departs from these discussions and what we expect to gain from this departure.

Alexander Betts and Paul Collier's *Refuge* (2017) has received much attention as a research-informed agenda for refugee policy reform. Betts and Collier's analysis is, however, premised on the bureaucratic categorizations that we aim to unsettle in this book (most centrally the 'refugee' category). While it may be necessary to engage in a dialogue with actors outside academia, such categorizations contribute to the perpetuation of selective visions of whom and what such a category signifies, unintentionally leaving blindspots and creating invisibilities. The same goes, to some extent, for the relatively over-saturated field of more structural analyses of irregular migration and refugee policy (including Bloch and Donà 2019; Fassin and Pandolfi 2013; Martin et al. 2014; Greenhill 2010; and Lindley 2016), which facilitates exchange between research and policy making but tends to reproduce some of the conceptual 'blind spots' we address here.

One source of inspiration has been a trend in refugee studies that explores the 'blind spots' in policy categories in relation to refugees and other migrants. The argument in this literature is that policy categories – and much policy-oriented academic literature – create and shed light on certain categories such as refugees, IDPs, transit migrants – often with the best of intentions to highlight the needs of particular groups. The problem, according to this strand of critical refugee scholarship, is that by making specific categories visible such policy categories also invisibilize other groups who fall beyond the categories (e.g. Polzer and Hammond 2008). Another relevant strand of literature on invisibility and displacement emerges out of migration studies, exploring the clandestine manoeuvres of undocumented migrants or 'sans papiers' – usually in European cities. These studies take their point of departure in the hardening of migration control and border regimes, arguing that these regimes create their own opposite: human smuggling (Perkowski and Squire 2018), irregularity and illegality (Andersson 2014; De Genova 2002). In the following, we outline these two sources of inspiration.

As a counterpoint to humanitarian discourses, anthropological analyses of refugee regimes and camps have demonstrated how people who have been formally categorized as refugees manoeuvre this administrative label but also experience the limitations of being administered by humanitarian agencies (e.g. Agier 2011, 2016; Andersson 2014; Turner 2010).

Much of the effort of critical refugee studies has been to question categories and demonstrate how they invisibilize certain groups. The concept of 'invisible displacement' featured in a special issue of the *Journal of Refugee Studies* (Polzer and Hammond 2008), with a strong emphasis on the academic ethics of disclosure and concealment in the representation of illegal migrants. The issue provides a precedent for the study of structural processes of invisibilization, and the potential incentive of migrants to become or remain invisible in the eyes of formal bureaucracies. As the editors summarize, invisibility is 'fundamentally relational; its impacts depend on the power relations and interests connecting those who see and those who are to be seen (or not)' (Polzer and Hammond 2008: 417).

Ethnographic research on the overlaps between labour migration and forced displacement has argued that the conceptual boundaries between these two categories are far from self-evident, focusing instead on subjective experiences of displacement in contexts of long-established labour migration (Bjarnesen 2013; see also Bakewell 2008), and on the productive potential of displacement (Hammar and Rodgers 2008). Amanda Hammar's collection in the *Africa Now* series, *Displacement Economies in Africa* (2014), has been an influential publication in this line of research, yet with a different conceptual framework and case selection than the one we present here. Other books on this theme include Stephen Lubkemann's *Culture in Chaos* (2008a); Jansen and Löfving's *Struggles for Home* (2009); and Maja Korac's *Remaking Home* (2009). What these works share is, primarily, a combined attention to the ethnographic specificities of empirical cases and a theoretical engagement with the concept of displacement. Challenging the legalistic connotations of the term, this theoretical engagement implies a conceptual move away from understanding 'the displaced' as a population to analysing displacement as a continuous and differentiated process (cf. Bjarnesen 2016: 57).

These contributions have taught us not to assume that the categories of states or humanitarian actors reflect the lived realities of migrants who blur the distinctions and/or become invisible to statecraft and humanitarian governance. Bakewell's (2008) contribution in Polzer and Hammond's collection, with the thought-provoking title 'Research beyond the Categories: The Importance of Policy Irrelevant Research into Forced Migration', nicely illustrates how policy categories tend to be imported into studies on forced migration with the effect of obscuring or invisibilizing the kind of displacement that he witnessed 'on the ground' in the Zambian–Angolan borderlands. Neither should we assume that displacement leads to loss per se, as argued by Lubkemann in the same issue (Lubkemann 2008b). Since these insights are well-established, at least in the literature we build on, we take them as the starting point of our enquiry. We proceed to ask what the effects are of these processes of categorization and invisibilization. We enquire how migrants, stayees, states, NGOs, families and other relevant actors and institutions operate within and beyond these categories. In other words, while much of this literature in refugee studies has been helpful in deconstructing categories and exposing their blind spots, our aim is to go beyond pointing out the discrepancy between policy/political categorizations and the 'real world' and instead to explore the *processes* of invisibilization in contexts of displacement and the societal and existential effects of such processes. In this manner, we see invisibility as productive, thus challenging the implicit dichotomy between constructed (false) policy categories and lived (authentic) experiences/categories on the ground. We elaborate our way of approaching this later.

Our other overall source of inspiration has come less out of refugee studies and more out of migration studies (to the degree that one can make such a distinction). In recent years, a number of studies of irregular or clandestine migration have emerged. Scholars such as Sylvie Bredeloup and Michael Collyer have explored transit migration across Northern Africa, questioning the concept of transit (Bredeloup 2012, 2013; Collyer 2007; Collyer and de Haas 2012). Others have followed migrants who use human smugglers or fixers to get to Europe (Lucht 2012; Richter 2018; Vigh 2009; Andersson 2014). A central argument in much of this literature is to question common assumptions about human smuggling from Africa to Europe. They show how border regimes and migration control in general, and 'anti-smuggling' policies in particular, contribute to producing illegality (Perkowski and Squire 2019). Furthermore, their ethnographic studies question the binaries between smuggler and smuggled, demonstrating that the roles shift, as migrants may become smugglers for a while (Richter 2018; Lucht 2012) and most irregular migrants rely on a mixture of ad hoc networks, rather than highly organized criminal networks, to make it across the desert and the sea (Andersson 2014). Other studies follow the irregular migrants once in Europe (MacGaffey and Bazenguissa-Ganga 2000; Kleinman 2019), emphasizing their efforts to remain invisible to the authorities. While many of these studies question the administrative and political categories along similar lines as the refugee studies literature mentioned above, they tend to focus more on the migrants themselves. Across these disciplinary fields, scholars have increasingly emphasized how the administrative categories guiding migration governance tend, not only to overlook or ignore certain groups of migrants (cf. Bakewell 2008), but also to impose and reproduce themselves in public discourse, thereby reinforcing the limited and limiting views they represent (De Genova 2002).

It is on the basis of this contextualizing ethnographic approach to displacement that invisibilization provides a prism for understanding migrant experiences across conventional categorizations. The concept of 'social invisibility' has been explored in qualitative research but primarily with the national state bureaucracy as the main counterpoint to migrants' invisibilities (Turner and Vigh 2007; Carleheden et al. 2012; Scotland-Stewart 2007; Vigh 2011). In this way, the concept of invisibility is closely linked to notions of informality, illegality and marginality (Löfving 2005; Carter 2010) and to studies of social exclusion or persecution (Tucker 2008; Carleheden et al. 2012). The aim of this book is, however, to go beyond the predominant cases of young men travelling from West Africa to Europe, via the Sahara and the Mediterranean, or rather to resituate these overexposed cases within a broader view of African mobilities.

Invisible and irregular migration takes place in many directions, at many locations and at different levels and scales. In order to understand its dynamics and effects, we must go beyond the most familiar case studies and operate through different analytical perspectives. To evoke the conceptual exploration of in/visibilization presented in this volume, it is important to appreciate that this current overexposure of specific irregular border crossings into Europe also entails a series of new invisibilities, whereby the cases that are assumed to be the most familiar severely limit the scope for articulating alternative understandings of their complexities. In her chapter on Malian irregular migrants in Paris, Line Richter explores their avoidance strategies as they carve out their own 'path spaces' in a city that primarily defines them through their lack of legal documents, as implied by the label *sans papiers*. Rather than focusing on the policing of irregular migrants from a state-centred point of view, or on irregular migrants as a (threatening, disorderly or criminal) collective in the Parisian public space, which tend to be the predominant media and political narratives, Richter emphasizes the aspirations and orientations of individual migrants, evoking the personal experiences of displacement and endurance that are often forgotten or wilfully ignored. Oriol Puig Cepero's contribution describes how Nigerien migrants are caught in systematic exploitation in Libya on their way towards the North African coast. As a counter-image to the CNN-driven narrative on Libyan 'slave markets', which flourished in late 2017, Puig Cepero's chapter offers a detailed account of the mutual interests of migrants and their captors, as well as of the space for manoeuvre that sub-Saharan African migrants in Libya make use of to negotiate their own exposure. The over-exposed cases of irregular migration to Europe, and involuntary immobilization in Libya, thereby, present themselves in new light in this volume.

In addition to research on migration management and its diverse and differentiating effects, our empirical case selection also engages with other scholarship focused on the specificities of African contexts of migration. Here, some important themes include the attention to how state and humanitarian governance affects the outlooks and possibilities of different categories of migrants; the historical depth of mobility patterns; the adaptability or resilience of migrants in the context of radical social change; and the social and cultural significance of migration to intergenerational relationships. For example, recent studies on child migration in African contexts (Hashim and Thorsen 2011; Razy and Rodet 2016) challenge the categories and assumptions implicit in the Eurocentric constructions of children that inform interventions by international organizations such as the ILO and UNICEF by considering how many children play important roles as breadwinners and agents with their own itineraries, rather than exclusively being in need of (adult) protection. A recent volume on *Hope and Uncertainty in Contemporary African Migration* (Kleist and Thorsen 2017) highlights the ways in which migrants rely on historically reproduced narratives as well as their idiosyncratic readings of ever-changing landscapes of opportunities and restrictions, to orient their aspirations and enact their strategies for mobility. Finally, we also find inspiration in Africa-centred research on irregular migration (e.g. Beauchemin 2018; Bensaâd 2009; Alpes 2017; Jeffery 2011; and Nyamnjoh 2013), which offer empirical cases and analytical perspectives that are less entangled with the current European migration regime. For example, in *Insiders and Outsiders* (2013), Francis Nyamnjoh offers a timely and engaging analysis of mobile domestic workers in Botswana and South Africa in the context of the rise of xenophobia in South Africa, which illustrates the socio-political construction of otherness and its effects. Joyce Takaindisa and Ingrid Palmary, in their contribution to this volume, offer their reflections on this phenomenon on the basis of an ethnography of Zimbabwean irregular domestic workers in Botswana.

Making in/visibility work

Important to our approach is the insistence that visibility and invisibility are intertwined, and that the binary is fractured. By exploring the interplay and oscillation between visibility and invisibility, we go beyond understanding invisibility simply as a taxonomic term that we can use to categorize empirical phenomena. In other words, the theoretical contribution of the collection as a whole is to explore what in/visibilization *does*, or what we term the productive aspects of in/visibilization. This conceptual framing is specifically intended to allow for nuanced analyses of the diverse effects of in/visibilization in the lives of migrants, bringing together the key themes of avoidance, exposure, (mis)recognition and marginalization. In prioritizing processes and experiences of displacement, including the perspectives of camp refugees, our common agenda is to move away from, or offer an alternative conceptualization to, the legal definitions and categorizations of displaced people that dominate common perceptions of African migration.

In order to operationalize this conceptual framework, all chapters are tasked to reflect on the relationality of in/visibility through the following question, elaborated from Polzer and Hammond's special issue introduction on 'Invisible Displacements' (2008): 'Who invisibilizes what from whom and for which purposes?' Invisibility is not a phenomenon independent of a specified and contextualized subject, even if the subject may be an institutional actor. In the lives of irregular migrants in particular, the central subject with whom in/visibility is negotiated tends to be large institutional actors such as states, UN agencies or the European Union with the capacity to determine who crosses borders and who does not, who can be assisted in refugee camps and who cannot, etc. Camminga's contribution to this book illustrates how states and the UNHCR in/visibilize LGBTQ+ refugees in Nairobi in highly differentiating ways, with acute consequences for their security and their ability to move freely in the city. At the same time, while state or other institutional actors tend to be seen as the sole or at least primary actors imposing regimes of in/visibilization on particular groups of migrants, several contributions (Bjarnesen, Pelckmans, Waage, Purdeková) illustrate that even close social ties within families or local communities may contribute to invisibilizing migrants. As noted above, furthermore, migrants may, under various circumstances, seek invisibility as a strategy to stay out of trouble or avoid exposure (Waage, Pelckmans, Camminga, Turner, Keja, Amadou and de Bruijn).

In addition to this relational understanding of invisibilization, we must be attentive to the fact that invisibility and visibility are intertwined and overlapping processes, and that both migrant strategies and structural circumstances may shift the impetus between these two poles. Behrends' chapter shows how a group of displaced people in the Chad–Sudan borderlands, having been content with remaining invisible to the state and other authorities over the course of many years, attempt to engage her as the researcher in an effort to become visible to international NGOs and receive the support that they believe they are entitled to. Here, we see the complexity of invisibility as a strategy, as it changes over time and engages with specific goals and audiences, as we will elaborate below.

If an initial question concerns *who* is the subject of invisibilization, the second question we must ask ourselves is *what* is being invisibilized. Much of the literature assumes that whole population groups are rendered invisible, as for example undocumented migrants in the cities of the global North, or that individuals intend to become or remain entirely invisible under these circumstances. Most often, however, in/visibilization is imposed on a category of migrants in much more differentiated ways depending, for example, on the gendered, classed and racialized characteristics of individual migrants. In addition to this unequal distribution, invisibility is rarely a totalizing disappearing act. Rather, whether imposed or actively sought after, invisibilization usually targets particular aspects of a person or a group's identity, most obviously one's legal status, although such statuses are often more negotiable in practice than usually assumed or acknowledged. For example, the irregular sub-Saharan migrants in Libya that Puig Cepero explores negotiate a difficult balance between remaining invisible as irregular migrants, but available and thus visible as labourers. Likewise, Takaindisa and Palmary show that Zimbabwean women working as domestic workers in Botswana are at once visibilized in the media as a collective category of irregular migrants, while they are invisibilized as an important workforce, leaving female migrants to negotiate the terms of their employment individually, and from highly precarious positions.

Depending on the power relations that constitute the terms of in/visibilization in a given context, legal status may not be the most salient target: ethnicity, nationality, sexuality, class or gender identity may be equally contested. Pelckmans shows how Nigerien women who escape their enslavement as 'wives' in harems in neighbouring Nigeria cannot simply slip back into their old positions in their home village. Social stigma and shame force them to hide these backgrounds and lead them to resettle in so-called 'freedom villages' with no ties to their families. Keja, Amadou and de Bruijn also explore the avoidance strategies of a mobile Fulani man, facing the shame of returning home without having realized his migrant aspirations. Bjarnesen's contribution, finally, considers the importance of keeping up appearances in a context where resettled migrants find it important to present an image of integrity and self-sufficiency, rather than being labelled as someone worthy of charity and pity.

In addition to these differentiating understandings of *what* is being invisibilized in particular contexts, the relational nature of in/visibility also warrants a close inspection of the audience of such strategies. In other words; who are the actors who either see or do not see? This line of questioning is central to understanding the underlying politics of in/visibilization. For example, when undocumented migrants in Europe are invisibilized as workers in the informal economy, as farm workers, cleaners, care givers etc., their irregular legal status may be (partially) visible to local and central authorities, but far less visible in media representations and public debate, so as not to alienate the voting public. On the other hand, as a strategy pursued by migrants themselves, invisibilization depends on a close reading of the possibilities for recognition and the risks of exposure. For example, refugees fleeing state violence may wish to render themselves invisible to police and militias while being visible to international human rights activists in order to claim (legal) recognition, as Turner's contribution demonstrates. Camminga's study of transgender refugees in Kakuma refugee camp illustrates such dynamics of simultaneous avoidance of the hostile Ugandan authorities, and claims for recognition towards the camp authorities. The chapter also exposes how such power relations and strategies may change over time, as the transgender refugees are faced with resentment from a new set of actors within the camp, and struggle to revise their strategies in relation to the inconsistent responses from camp authorities. Vammen's contribution vividly shows how African street vendors in Buenos Aires adeptly move in and out of sight, in order to avoid the local police while remaining available to their potential customers. The street vendors are constantly weighing the risks of being caught and having to pay bribes against the profits from attractive vending spots in the city – from where they are highly visible. Interestingly, the police take part in this game from the other side: allowing vendors to remain in public spaces provides a source of income through bribes but if the bribes are too high, the vendors will stay away and they will lose their income.

Finally, in addition to questioning the subject (*who*), content (*what*) and audience (*from whom*) of in/visibilization, we must further explore its *purpose*. Both structural and strategic in/visibilization is meant to achieve something. Migrants may choose invisibility in order to survive (Turner), in order to maintain social relations, for example by concealing shameful acts from their kin (as Keja, Amadou and de Bruijn show in their contribution), or in order to keep their future open (Richter). They may similarly seek visibility in order to gain recognition from authorities or NGOs and hence seek protection (Camminga), access to income (Behrends) or the possibility of onwards movement. States and other public authorities seek to visibilize certain populations, rendering them legible to governance practices (Boeyink, Purdeková, Camminga), and seek to invisibilize some of their own practices in order to maintain their claims to sovereign power (Hansen and Stepputat 2005). Examining the stated or implicit purposes of in/visibilization does not imply a neat causality between such intentions and their itinerant effects. Rather, the conceptual framework we elaborate around the analysis of in/visibilization is geared towards contextual analysis that incorporates the outlooks and practices of multiple actors, and an emphasis on the interplay between migrant strategies and the power relations within which they are enacted.

While the above analysis is concerned with the invisibility of migrants and refugees, the state and other public authorities may also be engaged in strategies of in/visibilization. A central aspect of sovereignty of the state is its ability to reveal and conceal its intentions (Hansen and Stepputat 2005). The relational character of invisibility also implies that the actors involved may be involved in assessments and speculations about what the other might be hiding. The fact that we know that our surroundings are not what they appear to be and that people, states and other actors are keeping certain aspects out of sight, creates rumours, conspiracy theories and public secrets. Purdeková's study of internal displacement in Burundi highlights the ways in which returnees, internally displaced people and stayees all imagine the state and international NGOs as having secret plans. Likewise, Turner's account of Burundian flight narratives reveals how refugees read the actions of state officials for signs of shadowy plans and intentions. Both these cases are concerned with the displaced seeking to understand and uncloak secret plans of public authorities. In a similar manner, public authorities such as states, religious institutions and NGOs also assume that the displaced have hidden identities and agendas and seek in various ways to unveil these secrets. Such suspicions have become increasingly central to European border regimes, which include highly specialized biometric technologies to verify or disprove the accounts given by asylum seekers and other migrants to claim recognition and negotiate access (see e.g. Fassin and d'Halluin 2005).

Structure of the book

The book's structure is intended to investigate the relationships between in/visibility and displacement in three different institutional contexts: humanitarian, state and social, respectively. In each of these contexts the contributions explore the dynamics of *who* in/visibilizes *what* from *whom* and for *which* purposes, in line with the conceptual framework outlined in this introduction.

In *Section 1: Humanitarian in/visibilities*, Andrea Behrends analyses the shifting strategies of Sudanese refugees from the war in Darfur in the Chad–Sudan borderlands, including her own positionality as a possible mediator towards the humanitarian administration in a nearby refugee camp. Straddling strategies of avoidance and advocacy, her interlocutors negotiate a difficult balance between retaining their independence as self-settled refugees on the one hand, and reaching out to a humanitarian actor to claim recognition and assistance, on the other. Clayton Boeyink's case study of migrant and refugee agricultural labourers and renters in Western Tanzania illustrates a similar complexity, as his interlocutors strive towards being 'sufficiently visible' towards humanitarian and state authorities to receive assistance, while remaining 'invisible enough' to avoid the gaze of these institutional actors upon their quasi-legal agricultural practices outside the confines of humanitarian encampment.

B Camminga's contribution takes us inside the Kakuma refugee camp in Kenya, but reveals the highly differentiated distribution of protection and recognition through the lens of transgender refugees. This group of refugees, escaping persecution in Uganda, face renewed persecution from other camp residents, while also negotiating their in/visibilization strategies in relation to camp authorities, who prefer that LGBTQ+ persons invisibilize their gender identities for the sake of public order. Finally, Andrea Purdeková analyses the spatialized in/visibilization strategies of internally displaced people in Burundi, contemplating return and resettlement in the context of renewed political conflict. This contribution also brings out the ways in which humanitarian governance, through its modus operandi, privileges some displacement trajectories while invisibilizing others.

In *Section 2: State in/visibilities*, Trond Waage analyses war-related displacements from the Central African Republic as a process of invisibilization, whereby forced migrants are integrated into the urban informal economy in neighbouring Cameroon. While expressing the shortcomings of the Cameroonian authorities to officially accommodate these forced migrants, Waage emphasizes that the lack of state intervention serves the mutual interests of both authorities and migrants, in that the state escapes accountability for the plight of these irregular urban migrants, while the migrants themselves are capable of devising strategies to integrate into the local economy. Ida Marie Savio Vammen then presents the case of West African street vendors in Buenos Aires, Argentina, and analyses the dynamics of racialized hyper-visibilization and the intricate negotiations over urban space between street vendors and the local police. Vammen's analysis illustrates the incoherence and negotiability of state policies around the criminalization of the urban informal economy, which is shown to serve the interests of police officers on the ground. Line Richter's study of Malian migrants in Paris explores the existential implications of being defined primarily through the legalistic lens of lacking formal documents. The chapter also highlights that within the restrictive legal-administrative context of French immigration policies, Malian migrants find a sense of belonging in their paths through the city, and in the community of other West African migrants.

In their chapter on Zimbabwean domestic workers in Botswana, Joyce Takaindisa and Ingrid Palmary discuss the livelihood strategies of a category of informal workers who are central to the country's informal economy, yet criminalized in public discourse and state policy. In this precarious situation, many domestic workers engage in invisibilization strategies to avoid deportation. Oriol Puig Cepero's analysis of the plight of Nigerien migrants in post-Kadaffi Libya also brings out the effects of migrant-hostile state policies. In this case, the criminalization of sub-Saharan African migrants in Libya creates the conditions for the exploitation of migrants by local criminal networks, who employ Nigerien migrants as a labour force under appalling conditions while the migrants wait for an opportunity to continue their journeys towards Europe. Rounding off this section, Simon Turner analyses the invisibilization strategies of Burundian refugees straddling the border with neighbouring Rwanda in the context of the Nkurunziza regime's increasingly authoritarian tendencies since the 2015 popular uprising. Turner argues that even under state persecution and mass displacements, his interlocutors constantly have to shift between strategies of visibility and invisibility in order to protect themselves and their loved ones from state violence.

Finally, *Section 3: Social in/visibilities* emphasizes the more intimate contexts of family and community, which constitute central arenas for the negotiation of in/visibilization in Africa and elsewhere. Keja, Amadou and de Bruijn analyse the phenomenon of vanishing nomads in the wider Sahel region, focusing on the mobile lifestory of a Fulani man, Amadou, who reunited with his family in Niger after a three-decades-long absence. In this case, rather than being compelled by armed conflict or state persecution, Amadou remained mobile for so long, in part to avoid the shame of facing up to his lack of social mobility. Lotte Pelckmans explores the multiple displacements of young Nigerien women, who are enslaved as involuntary brides in neighbouring Nigeria, in many cases with the consent of their own families. Tragically ironic, Pelckmans illustrates how women who are able to escape their captivity are unable to return to their families, because of the social stigma implied by enslavement. In the final empirical chapter, Jesper Bjarnesen discusses the resettlement of Burkinabe labour migrants, displaced during the armed conflict in neighbouring Côte d'Ivoire. The analysis focuses on the differentiated distribution of vulnerability under these circumstances, and the variable in/visibilization strategies this unequal distribution engenders. While the family is often assumed to represent the most intimate social relationships, Bjarnesen argues that resettled migrants deploy invisibilization strategies within their own households in addition to those directed towards their neighbours.

Loren B. Landau concludes with an afterword reflecting on the conceptual implications and questions raised by the volume as a whole.

References

Agier, Michel (2011) *Managing the Undesirables: Refugee camps and humanitarian government*, Cambridge and Malden, MA: Polity.

—— (2016) *Borderlands: Towards an anthropology of the cosmopolitan condition*, Cambridge and Malden, MA: Polity.

Alpes, Maybritt Jill (2017) *Brokering High-Risk Migration and Illegality in West Africa: Abroad at any cost*, London and New York: Routledge.

Andersson, Ruben (2014) *Illegality Inc: Clandestine migration and the business of bordering Europe*, Oakland, CA: University of California Press.

Bakewell, Oliver (2008) 'Research beyond the categories: the importance of policy irrelevant research into forced migration', *Journal of Refugee Studies*, 21(4): 432–453.

Beauchemin, Cris (ed.) (2018) *Migration between Africa and Europe*, New York: Springer.

Bensaâd, Ali (ed.) (2009) *Le Maghreb à l'épreuve des migrations subsahariennes. Immigration sur émigration*, Paris: Karthala.

Betts, Alexander and Paul Collier (2017) *Refuge: Rethinking refugee policy in a changing world*, Oxford and New York: Oxford University Press.

Bjarnesen, Jesper (2013) *Diaspora at Home? Wartime mobilities in the Burkina Faso–Côte d'Ivoire transnational space*, Uppsala: Acta Universitatis Upsalienses.

—— (2016) 'Between labor migration and forced displacement: wartime mobilities in the Burkina Faso–Côte d'Ivoire transnational space', *Conflict and Society*, 2: 52–67.

Bloch, Alice and Giorgia Donà (2019) *Forced Migration: Current issues and debates*, London and New York: Routledge.

Bredeloup, Sylvie (2012) 'Sahara transit: times, spaces, people', *Population Space and Place*, 18(4): 457–467.

—— (2013) 'The figure of the adventurer as an African migrant', *Journal of African Cultural Studies*, 25(2): 170–182.

Carleheden, Mikael, Carl-Göran Heidegren and Rasmus Willig (2012) 'Editorial: recognition, social invisibility, and disrespect', *Distinktion*, 13(1): 1–3.

Carter, Donald Martin (2010) *Navigating the African Diaspora: The anthropology of invisibility*, Minneapolis, MN and London: University of Minnesota Press.

Collyer, Michael (2007) 'In-between places: trans-Saharan transit migrants in Morocco and the fragmented journey to Europe', *Antipode*, 39(4): 668–690.

Collyer, Michael and Hein de Haas (2012) 'Developing dynamic categorisations of transit migration', *Population Space and Place*, 18(4): 468–481.

De Genova, N. (2002) 'Migrant "illegality" and deportability in everyday life', *Annual Review of Anthropology*, 31: 419–447.

Fassin, Didier and Estelle d'Halluin (2005) 'The truth from the body: medical certificates as ultimate evidence for asylum seekers', *American Anthropologist*, 107(4): 597–608.

Fassin, Didier and Mariella Pandolfi (2013) *Contemporary States of Emergency: The politics of military and humanitarian interventions*, New York: Zone Books.

Greenhill, Kelly M. (2010) *Weapons of Mass Migration: Forced displacement, coercion, and foreign policy*, Ithaca, NY and London: Cornell University Press.

Hammar, Amanda (ed.) (2014) *Displacement Economies in Africa: Paradoxes of crisis and creativity*, London and New York: Zed Books.

Hammar, Amanda and Graeme Rodgers (2008) 'Introduction: notes on political economies of displacement in southern Africa', *Journal of Contemporary African Studies*, 26(4): 355–370.

Hansen, T. and Stepputat, F. (2005) *Sovereign Bodies: Citizens, migrants and states in the postcolonial world*, Durham, NC: Duke University Press.

Hashim, Iman and Dorte Thorsen (2011) *Child Migration in Africa*, London and New York: Zed Books.

Jansen, Stef and Staffan Löfving (2009) *Struggles for Home: Violence, hope and the movement of people*, New York: Berghahn Books.

Jeffery, Laura (2011) *Chagos Islanders in Mauritius and the UK: Forced displacement and onward migration*, Manchester: Manchester University Press.

Kleinman, Julie (2019) *Adventure Capital: Migration and the making of an African hub in Paris*, Oakland, CA: University of California Press.

Kleist, Nauja and Dorte Thorsen (2017) *Hope and Uncertainty in Contemporary African Migration*, London and New York: Routledge.

Korac, Maja (2009) *Remaking Home: Reconstructing life, place and identity in Rome and Amsterdam*, New York and Oxford: Berghahn Books.

Lindley, Anna (ed.) (2016) *Crisis and Migration: Critical perspectives*, London and New York: Routledge.

Löfving, Staffan (2005) 'Silence and the politics of representing rebellion: on the emergence of the neutral Maya in Guatemala', in P. Richards (ed.), *No Peace No War: An anthropology of contemporary armed conflicts*, Oxford: James Currey; Athens, OH: Ohio University Press.

Lubkemann, Stephen C. (2008a) *Culture in Chaos: An anthropology of the social condition in war*, Chicago, IL: University of Chicago Press.

—— (2008b) 'Involuntary immobility: on a theoretical invisibility in forced migration studies', *Journal for Refugee Studies*, 21(4): 454–475.

Lucht, Hans (2012) *Darkness before Daybreak: African migrants living on the margins in southern Italy today*, Berkeley, CA: University of California Press.

MacGaffey, J. and R. Bazenguissa-Ganga (2000) *Congo–Paris: Transnational traders on the margins of the law*, London: International African Institute in association with James Currey; Bloomington, IN: Indiana University Press.

Martin, Susan F., Sanjula Weerasinghe and Abbie Taylor (eds) (2014) *Humanitarian*

Crises and Migration: Causes, consequences and responses, London and New York: Routledge.

Nyamnjoh, Francis (2013) *Insiders and Outsiders: Citizenship and xenophobia in contemporary southern Africa*, Dakar: CODESRIA Books, London and New York: Zed Books.

Perkowski, N. and V. Squire (2019) 'The anti-policy of European anti-smuggling as a site of contestation in the Mediterranean migration "crisis"', *Journal of Ethnic and Migration Studies*, 45(12): 2167–2184.

Polzer, Tara and Laura Hammond (2008) 'Invisible displacement', *Journal of Refugee Studies*, 21(4): 417–431.

Razy, Elodie and Marie Rodet (2016) *Children on the Move in Africa: Past and present experiences of migration*, Suffolk and Rochester, NY: James Currey.

Richter, Line (2018) 'Gaps in a bordered world: Malian men trying to make it to and in Europe', PhD thesis, University of Copenhagen.

Scotland-Stewart, Laurel (2007) 'Social invisibility as social breakdown: insights from a phenomenology of self, world, and other', PhD Thesis, Department of Philosophy, Stanford University.

Tucker, Andrew (2008) *Queer Visibilities: Space, identity and interaction in Cape Town*, Oxford: Wiley-Blackwell.

Turner, Simon (2010) *Politics of Innocence: Hutu identity, conflict, and camp life*, Studies in forced migration, New York: Berghahn Books.

—— (2016a) 'Staying out of place: the being and becoming of Burundians refugees in the camp and the city', *Conflict and Society*, 2(1): 37–51.

—— (2016b) 'What is a refugee camp? Explorations of the limits and effects of the camp', *Journal of Refugee Studies*, 29(2): 139–148.

Turner, Simon and Henrik Vigh (eds) (2007) 'Usynlighed. Globaliseringens blinde vinkler', *Den Ny Verden*, Copenhagen: Danish Institute for International Studies.

Vigh, Henrik (2009) 'Wayward migration: on imagined futures and technological voids', *Ethnos*, 74(1): 91–109.

—— (2011) 'Vigilance: on conflict, social invisibility, and negative potentiality', *Social Analysis*, 55(3): 93–114.

Section 1

Humanitarian in/visibilities

1 | Renegotiating humanitarian governance: challenging invisibility in the Chad–Sudan borderlands

Andrea Behrends

Introduction

In February 2003, the border region between Chad and Sudan became caught up in what was to remain a protracted situation of rebellion, counter-rebellion, refuge, humanitarian aid and international military intervention. As the 'Darfur Crisis' it initially received the world's attention in late 2003 and was eventually framed as the 'first genocide of the twenty-first century', as Colin Powell, then US secretary of state had called it in September 2004. Although tensions had been rising before 2003, violence accelerated to an extreme after a prominently placed and surprisingly successful rebel attack, in which a group of armed men captured a military air base of the Sudanese army in Sudan's westernmost province in the town of Gulu (de Waal 2004; Flint and de Waal 2005, 2008). While, as Prunier (2005) shows, much of the media attention focused on the violence and the need to prevent a second Rwanda, little attention was given to the populations that had been living in the border region for decades and for whom this war resembled others they had experienced before. As *machakil* (arab.: problems) or *harb* (arab.: war), people had developed knowledge about how to deal with such situations. Moving into refugee camps was one of those options. Remaining close to their homes and land another. Both (and other) options were related to factors such as access to land, the quality of land, but also access to national governmental institutions on both sides of the border, or access to humanitarian aid.

This chapter argues that in order to come closer to an understanding of the everyday dealing with violence, flight, aid and survival, it is necessary to look at a larger ensemble of actors and factors that characterize displacement and emplacement (Glick Schiller and Çağlar 2015; Bjarnesen and Vigh 2016) as well as at the knowledge, materials and technologies that accompany such processes. If aid agencies and international media, for instance, highlight only certain specific actors concerned by a so-called crisis, this bears the risk of making visible only parts of a much more complex situation. If the United Nations High Commissioner for Refugees (UNHCR) categorizes certain people as refugees, born out of a need to be able to deal with a complicated situation, a specific group with specific, well-defined characteristics is constructed as real, with real consequences on their everyday lifeworlds. Less visible, but with similar consequences, the registering of people who arrive at the gates of refugee camps as refugees in need of and entitled to aid also creates another category: those who do not address the aid agencies. Instead, they are perceived to belong to the much more vaguely defined category of host populations (those who have lived in areas where refugee camps are installed before the arrival of refugees) but also the categories of rebels (those who presumably cause the trouble and roam about rendering situations less secure) or better-off populations (who are presumed to be in control of their own survival by being in command of the means needed to cater for basic needs and security). High visibility thus creates shadows; spaces, where people and their needs become less visible – for instance to international media or, in particular, to aid infrastructures set up during displacement situations.

Such aid infrastructures are large-scale technologies that comprise historically developed procedures, regulations and categorizations (Glasman 2017, 2019). This technology is braced to address the presumed disorder that results from violence, war and displacement, by making populations 'legible', as James Scott (1998) called it, by counting people and putting labels on them – while others become invisible. Invisibility has been a prominent theme during the European industrialization and its consequences, which engaged a number of philosophers to think about the effects of what they observed to be an increasing technicization. In contrast to other philosophers of his time, the German philosopher Hans Blumenberg (1981) had a rather positive perspective on technicization and modernity. He maintained that in order for technologies to work as they should, a conscious invisibilization of their setup – a 'waiver of sense' (*Sinnverzicht*). Understanding technicization as the human enlargement of the room of creative possibilities, he proposed that it was indeed a positive development – and not, as Edmund Husserl had maintained before him, a 'loss of sense' (*Sinnverlust*) – that humans decided to invisibilize certain aspects of the process of technical innovation, so as to be able to apply them without constantly having to return to renegotiating their setup (Bolz 2012: 44). Translated to the technologies and infrastructures of humanitarian aid, this invisibilization of their technologies – that is, the underlying set-up and rules of each operation –might indeed be a gainful effect in order to calculate and justify aid measures and to be able to act quickly. Gainful, at least, for the aid agencies. When aid organizations focus on the people who are defined as recipients of aid, this may result in an exclusion or neglect of those whom the underlying set-up and rules have made legible as non-recipients. In this chapter I argue that the gainfulness of rendering some populations invisible is a one-sided affair. It is a measure of power, which results from creating legibility by 'seeing like a state' (Scott 1998). The villagers I had first met during the war were conscious of their being rendered invisible, and they lived with it, as they had chosen not to move to the camps. This decision might have been based at least in part on their previous experiences with aid measures in the 1980s, when the origins of people's flight was misunderstood as being drought rather than war, leading to region-wide and disastrous famine (de Waal 1989). When I returned to the border region in 2007 to pay a visit to the people, both within and outside the refugee camps, whom I knew from my long-term research before the war (2000–2001), a spontaneous possibility opened to actively counter invisibilization by making me an intermediate between border villagers and the aid agencies. Arguing from a lifeworldly perspective of individual and collective 'existential' experiences (Jackson 2013, 2017), I maintain that the formalized rendering of people as legible (by applying categorizations) is actually by default relationally and temporally contingent. Elaborating on this example in the following, I aim to show that while aid agencies, in the end, will have had the power to decide whether people who are not categorized as refugees have access to aid measures or not, they could not prevent that the villagers' move led to a higher visibility – in their active challenging of the invisibility enforced upon them.

Being – differentially – displaced in the borderlands

The war in Darfur approached slowly; there had been many signs of warning. While the world's attention picked up on the events only in late 2003, Flint and de Waal (2008) describe how, already in 1995, harassing, sudden brutal attacks on villages, theft and violent assaults on people going to or returning from markets, as well as governmental patronizing and political side-lining had not only enraged, but also left many people desperate. While a number of factors came together in aggravating the conflict at the local level, including the historical situation of war and flight in the larger region (Burr and Collins 1999), its basic tenor was a continuation of the region's political and economic marginalization that had been initiated in British colonial times and perpetuated through various phases of national leadership until today (Harir 1994; Johnson 2003; Mamdani 2009; Prunier 2005). Flight first started in small numbers. In 2000 when I started in my research, about 10,000 people had moved away from Sudan to settle in villages along the Chadian border, assisted by a one-person office of the UN Refugee Agency in Abéché, the largest city in Eastern Chad, and a locally staffed Catholic NGO called SECADEV (Sécours Catholique et Développement) with an office in the border town Adré. I had gone to this area for a study on 'conflict and integration'[1] and had lived for months in the small villages that hosted people from Sudanese Darfur who defined themselves as *Masalit* or *Arabs* respectively.[2]

Before the war in 2000 and 2001, I spoke with those who had recently come to the Chadian side of the border, but who maintained close contact to their former villages. The older women in particular regularly walked several miles across the border to work in the fields where their houses had been. Apart from hoping to reap the fruits of farming, they also wanted to mark their continuing ownership of the land. Their incentive was to temporarily stay on the safer side of the border, where they received aid in the form of food or other household provisions, hoping to return once the situation calmed down. During this phase of my research, I began to understand that villagers with land on the Chadian side of the border differed in their standing from those who owned land on the other side.[3] People whose land and villages were on the other side of the border and out of walking-distance were in yet another. Another difference was between the villagers who defined themselves as *Masalit* (speaking the Masalit language, originating in *Dar Masalit*, the Arabic word for 'land of the *Masalit*', which stretches on both sides of the Chad–Sudan border) and those who defined themselves as belonging to one or the other *Arab* family. At first, I did not grasp the different forms of belonging, as people not only spoke the same languages (a Chadian/Sudanese dialect of Arabic), wore the same kind of dress, shared the same religion (Islam) and generally lived in very similar houses. They became visible over time, as I learned more about people's backgrounds and personal histories – or, for instance, when I understood that the *Arabs* could cross the international border easily and earn money at the markets on the other side, while this option was too risky for people who defined themselves (and were externally recognized) as *Masalit* or *Fur*. These differences became significant when the latent crisis on the Sudanese side of the border suddenly erupted into extreme violence in a deadly counter-insurgency.[4] The difficulty for outsiders to distinguish between the people of the borderlands was a recurring topic. Clear distinguishing lines were often hard to establish. This was partly due to the fluidity of situationally defined forms of belonging, already observed in this area by Fredrik Barth (1967) in his classic thesis on ethnic groups and boundaries. He highlighted the possibility of people to switch categories from farmers to herders (for a longer term) or between speaking Arabic and other languages (in a market situation). His argument, however, concerned the maintenance of boundaries. I would argue that drawing on different registers of belonging by foregrounding and backgrounding certain characteristics during encounters provides for a flexible form of living through difficult circumstances, be they war, famine, family disputes, or restricted access to land or governmental services.

During my pre-war research phase (2000–2001), I also began to understand the different trajectories of people who lived in the borderlands. Adré, for instance, had been a military border post founded by the French colonial power around 1925. Here, the best plots in the city centre were owned by people from around the city of Abéché, the capital of the formerly powerful Wadai Sultanate (Reyna 1990) who defined themselves as Maba, and who had arrived as translators or administrative clerks of the French army. They were significantly better off than the villagers, and less involved in the conflict that was brewing on the other side of the border. In contrast, most of those who defined themselves as belonging to the *Masalit* people lived in the villages around Adré. Although poor in relation to the town dwellers, they considered themselves the owners of the land, called *Dar Masalit*. Some had been born there and had stayed on their family's land, while others only returned temporarily from short or long-term labour migration towards the Sudan or further into Egypt, Libya or Saudi Arabia. Still others had been expelled from cities where they had not been able to make a living, maybe due to a divorce, the death of a family member or a bankruptcy. Almost all of them had moved across the border to Sudan during the famine and wars of the early 1980s, from which some had returned and others had remained in Sudan.[5] In direct vicinity to the *Masalit* villages were a few so-called *Arab* settlements, called *feriks*. *Arab* families, mainly cattle or camel herders, had settled in the area around the 1950s. They told me that they had come down from further north, fleeing, among other factors, the degradation of land and the continuing conflicts in their previous home area. Although their lives did not seem to differ much from that of the *Masalit* villagers, they enjoyed certain privileges in terms of being able to freely cross the border to Sudan: as the Sudanese regime of President Omar al-Bashir had promoted *Arab* supremacy since taking power in 1989, *Arab* villagers from the Chadian side could trade on the market of nearby El-Geneina, return and sell their goods with profit.[6]

By realizing their differing positions before the war, I understood that the war did not affect all people of the borderlands in the same way. Thus, I would like to provide a bit more on the backgrounds of displacement and emplacement before the war. I realized differences among the people who started crossing the border from Sudanese Darfur into Chad to flee increasing harassments, including massive theft of animals and belongings; ambushes during market days; severe insults and, in a number of cases, torture. Some had walked for days to fleeing places quite far from the border, while others could cross the Wadi that demarcates the border between the two countries in one day. One of those who came from closer by was Daldoum, a former head of a village. He told me that he had been repeatedly put in jail and tortured on charges of his people hiding weapons in the bush, which he denied. When Daldoum and his family left as the last people of their village, they joined their daughter Ashta, who had installed herself with her children on the land of distant kin in a village only a few hundred metres away from the international border.[7] They told me that their village was about 30 kilometres away and that Ashta walked back and forth regularly. Ashta and many others like her still tried to maintain scaled-down farming activities in Darfur. For Ashta, Daldoum and his wife Mariam, coming to Chad and moving into the borderland villages had been an obvious move, as they had established long-term relations with the villagers, and since their own villages were not far away. They were usually given parts of their relatives' fields and gardens to sustain themselves and their lives did not differ much from those of the host population.

This differed for the people who had lived further away from the international border, but who also had taken refuge in Chad around 1997, a few years before the war became increasingly violent in 2003. They did not integrate into the villages as easily. Their former homes were out of reach for a day's walk, and they were more dependent on whatever aid they could attract. Their temporary settlements were often built outside or rather next to existing villages as they had not established relationships with the Chadian villagers and tended to remain among themselves. Although they, too, were given land to cultivate, this land was often remote, as they complained to me, and of lesser quality. When the UNHCR refugee camps opened their gates in 2003, they were the ones who first and foremost claimed refugee status. I had first met them in 2000, in Wandalou, one of the borderland villages. Since they became the most visible refugees at the height of the humanitarian intervention during the war, I will dwell a bit on their pre-war situation in the following.

Becoming visible

'They are terrible!' These were the first words that came to Henri Marcel's mind when he spoke to me in N'Djamena at the end of my second visit to Chad in 2001. As the only UNHCR representative in Wadai – the Chadian border province to Sudan – the tall man from Ivory Coast was visibly upset when I told him about my first encounter with the group of Sudanese people living in Wandalou, a village located about 18 kilometres to the south of Adré along the Chad–Sudan border. In 2001, Henri Marcel's task was to manage the care of the about 10,000 people who had fled from Sudan after their villages had been violently attacked by men on horseback. His desperation about the Wandalou group of refugees was due to their manifested unwillingness to integrate. Their experience in Chad stood in contrast to other places where the differentiation between so-called refugees and so-called locals had taken on more of an externally imposed and artificial character, contrasting the feeling of belonging most refugees reported. In Wandalou, a situation of fierce competition erupted between the villagers of Wandalou and the newcomers from Sudan. It was mainly concerning the provision of aid, which was first restricted to those who had settled in the villages recently. As per the terms of the UNHCR's emergency intervention programme, those refugees who had settled in Wandalou were in the most complicated category. According to Henri Marcel, they had continuously complained about the land given to them being too far away, too dry, that their houses had no shade because their settlement was outside the established village, and had, unlike the old village, no nice and shady trees. Furthermore, they needed meat and the aid they were given did not include meat. Because of that, they had initiated a meat market, which quickly became larger than the surrounding weekly markets, leading to jealousy and profit seeking on the side of the autochthonous authorities. Moreover, the established Wandalou villagers had started to complain about the goods the refugees had received from the World Food Program and UNHCR. They claimed to be in need of similar support, as they had stretched their own supplies to help the refugees, and now suffered of shortages themselves. In short, many things were unresolved, and more and more issues kept piling up on Henri Marcel's table. But the Wandalou group achieved a certain kind of visibility – being recognized as 'true refugees' – particularly by not mingling (or emplacing themselves) with the villagers and being compelled to finding their own solutions to their situation. They made themselves visible to the aid structures by claiming and complaining, risking conflict with the villagers instead of trying to find agreements. As it turned out, they remained visible as a maverick group throughout the mounting crisis in 2001.

Challenging invisibility

When the Darfur War started in 2003 I followed it from afar in Germany on Internet fora and through newspaper articles. The main incident that accelerated violence, displacement and the building up of aid structures was the above-mentioned rebel attack on an army garrison in Gulu in North Darfur. The Sudanese government retaliated violently by bombing the area and unleashing local militias who attacked villages on horseback to burn houses, plunder and kill. It became evident that the usefulness of aid structures that had prevailed before this outbreak of extreme violence had come to an abrupt end. Aid was now provided in two phases: from the time the emergency was declared, which was phase one, to taking the first measures for providing people with shelter, food and medical aid, the official phase two. Hundreds of thousands of people, now arriving from Sudan were immediately absorbed into a social technology of aid, which had been hurriedly set up, and was carefully orchestrated in the years to follow. The twelve refugee camps built in 2003 soon held between 20,000 and 40,000 people each – numbering about 200,000 camp dwellers who still remain in these camps at present.[8] The Chadian camps are not in the direct vicinity of the border, but about 50 kilometres inland, the original intention being to prevent attacks and to build up a larger security zone.[9]

The people I had met in 2000 and 2001 reacted very differently to this sudden turn of events. The 'rebellious' group from Wandalou immediately left the village and moved to one of the refugee camps. They literally stood in front of the administrative registration of the camp when it first opened. One of the men I had come to know was Musa, a former teacher and political activist. As soon as he reached the refugee camp in Farchana, he was elected the refugee president and proceeded to formulate claims for aid products, housing, meat and the like. He reached a certain fame among aid staff and camp dwellers alike, until, a few years later, some misunderstandings led him to leave his prominent position and continue working as a teacher for the camp's children. The UNHCR team was now large, with a headquarter in Abéché and satellite offices in all twelve camps. In contrast to Musa and the Wandalou group, those who had formerly been given space and land inside the villages, among relatives and friends – those who, in Henri Marcel's words, had 'integrated into the Chadian villages' and whose Sudanese home villages were closer by – did not move to the camps. Instead, they first remained in the villages, and then, when war and rebellion spilled over into Chad,[10] moved to Adré along with nearly all the autochthonous villagers. Here they continued their modes of marking land ownership by farming, but they now left behind the Sudanese villages and turned their focus to the new Chadian houses and fields they had only recently been given. Ashta, for instance, left her old parents, Daldoum and Mariam, in the Chadian border village while she and her four children moved to Adré. She now regularly walked to the village to support her parents. And Daldoum, who had been the last to leave his former village on the Sudanese side of the border, now refused to leave the new place, at the risk of being killed.

I returned to the Chad–Sudan borderlands during the Darfur War in 2007. At the time, the war had become protracted. Fighting took place on both sides of the border, and both national government regimes supported the other side's rebel groups. The Chadian army made a strong appearance in the borderlands and the UNHCR refugee camps were in full operation. I met the people who had not moved to the camps and whom I had known from my research five years earlier both in Adré and in the villages. When I saw the group who had moved to Adré again, they were destitute. They had lost everything and lived in shacks that would be blown away by the first storm of the upcoming rainy season. I brought them small gifts and food, which they appreciated. But they asked me if I could not do more for them. They needed to start farming again and, through farming, maintain their claims to the land.

The problem was that they lacked seeds. By leaving the villages, all their stock had been destroyed, used up or stolen. Thus, instead of farming, they had left some of their old folks and younger children in the villages (the former Sudanese village headman Daldoum and his wife Mariam were among them) to at least claim their houses and the land surrounding them, and they regularly walked there to bring them food.[11] The old people's lives in the villages were very hard, as they often had nothing more to eat than the wild berries they found in the bush, which were normally considered children's food. But the lives in the outskirts of Adré were not any easier. The former villagers lived in shacks outside town and they now had to pay for basic amenities like water and food. Through heavy day labour for the better-off town dwellers many of the men and women barely made enough money to buy a day's food for themselves and their children. Despite their distress, however, the former *Masalit* villagers made no attempt to move to the UNHCR camps. Their intention was to survive the war and then return to their land – or possibly remain in Adré and establish themselves as townspeople – and they preferred a situation of independent hardship over a dependent life in a camp with no access to land (see Malkki 1995; Spittler 1989). It turned out that by deciding to remain in what was, by international standards, declared a war-zone, the refugee-villagers were rendered invisible to the aid agencies, who now focused aid exclusively on the refugee camps.

When I returned to the border town of Adré during the war in 2007, the same former villagers who now lived on the town's outskirts actively attempted to become visible to the aid infrastructures. With me as their messenger, they wanted to approach the aid agencies, although they knew that they were not eligible to aid outside the camps. They took my visit as an occasion to reach out to the aid organizations, a possibility they had previously ruled out by deciding not to move to the camps. We sat down after the first excitement of reuniting after a long and difficult time. Then they turned to me and asked if I could not help them. I had feared that question, because I had no idea how I could be helpful to better their situation! I sadly admitted this helplessness. To my surprise, it turned out that they knew very well what to do. With the aim of successfully communicating their situation to and inviting assistance from the world of humanitarian aid, they sought to create what Star and Griesemer (1989) have called a 'boundary object'. In this case, the boundary object was a rather simple list of all the people who had fled the villages to now precariously live in the outskirts of Adré. The challenge was to ensure that this object would translate information about their circumstances in a manner that would lead to them becoming visible, thereby renegotiating the humanitarian dictum about them.

The list, in more general terms, represents an accepted institutional practice, which standardizes diverse understandings of how to deal with or 'navigate' crises.[12] As I understood it, the list not only required people's knowledge about the history of individual members within their village communities who had taken flight, but was also intended to comply with the requirements of the international aid structures and the categorizations they had enforced: those of being or not being a refugee, an internally displaced person, or a member of the host population surrounding the twelve camps. The former villagers in Adré were none of the above. They were too far from the camps to count as host population, and were thus categorically excluded from receiving aid in kind. As a bridging concept, the list was therefore supposed to address what they perceived as a lack within the approach adopted by aid institutions, actively seeking to adapt to and change an international institutional practice that had not responded to the realities of the borderland villagers during the war.

So, we sat down and compiled the list – that is, they compiled it and I passively sat down to watch them – and after three days it was completed. It was hand written by a clerk from Adré into a small note book. He put the list into five columns out of which only the first four were used, indicating (1) an ordering number, (2) the name of the head of the family, (3) the number of people in the household and (4) the head of the family's gender. An additional column was created for (5) remarks, but apart from an occasional line – the meaning of which escaped me – this column remained empty. With the help of Djamal, a local employee of the Chadian government agency for rural development, whom I had known from my previous stays, we calculated what I should demand from the aid agencies. As an act of informed translation,[13] Djamal broke down the numbers to reach a moderate sum that he assumed the aid agencies would be willing to give out. Certainly, this attempt to reach the aid agencies was only one of the many pragmatic and everyday practices employed to navigate the crisis. Everyday, because they could flexibly be integrated into a daily routine, even without thinking too much about them when the event took place. The practice was contingent on my visit and on the particular time it took place, at the beginning of the farming season. After it had been completed, I went to Abéché with the list in my bag.

It turned out that in most offices I went to the humanitarian staff was very interested in the document, but had to decline because of their strict safety regulations. As inhabitants of what was defined as a war zone, the borderland villagers were only entitled to a form of aid that is defined as 'emergency'. According to international agreements only very few aid agencies are in a position to intervene in such circumstances, among them the International Committee of the Red Cross (ICRC) and Médecins sans Frontières (MSF). Both operate mainly through medical interventions and are not mandated to hand out seeds, which would be declared development aid and not emergency intervention. While I only learned about these regulations on the spot, list in hand, I could observe the list working as a true boundary object. In line with Star and Griesemer's (1989: 388) thoughts about such objects enabling 'common representation in diverse intersecting social worlds', the list could be interpreted as the line between claiming and accepting or rejecting visibility of the borderlanders' situation. Running from office to office, I could observe very different reactions to both the object and my narrative. Some, while underlining that they could not do something now because 'budgets had been allocated', agreed to make copies of the list, possibly as evidence should they be able to use it, and then treated me to a cup of tea. Others declined even touching the list, as if touching it would mean seeing and thereby accepting the imperative to give aid to people in need, perhaps fearing being seduced to go against their orchestrated and pre-configured forms of intervention. By not touching the list, the villagers' claim to visibility could be denied, just like holding a hand in front of the eyes, not wanting or not being able to see. In the end, one maverick development worker, who had a reputation of going against the rules, pragmatically undid all boundaries and regulations. He simply used some leftover funds, stacked his truck with farming tools and seeds and drove, all by himself, the four hours from the aid headquarters in Abéché to Adré to hand them over to the people. It was far less than Djamal had calculated, but highly appreciated.

Critique and counter-critique of humanitarian governance

The approaches that severely criticize humanitarian aid are by now well established, characterizing aid as 'long-distance' or 'benevolent dictatorship' (McFalls 2010), through which people are forced into (citizenship) structures that deny them their own decision-making power and put them under a new governmental power structure in the event of crisis. In comparison to more recent studies about the ways aid imposes categorizations upon the recipients of aid (Bornstein and Redfield 2011; Fassin and Pandolfi 2010), my understanding of power asymmetries deriving from aid structures among receiving populations contradicts some of the findings cited particularly in McFalls (2010) about the logic of humanitarianism's 'therapeutic domination'. McFalls describes aid as being 'the uncontested and uncontestable radical biopower of our age' (2010: 317). Instead of this extreme view of a one-sided production of new forms of citizenship or even dictatorship on the part of aid agencies, I argue that people attempt to maintain lifeworlds. They do so by knowing and constantly and flexibly crossing the categories which are imposed upon them, thereby, over time, reaching mutual adaptation – even if this adaptation and its effects only become visible in the long term when experiences from 'within the actual social fields and formations in question' can be accounted for (Bjarnesen and Vigh 2016: 9). This lifeworldly perspective focuses on everydayness even in situations of severe crisis and uncertainty. Some criticism of 'humanitarian imperialism' relates to the notion of 'crisis' itself. Roitman (2011, 2014), following Koselleck (2002), holds that it is mainly the declaration of a crisis that conjures its visible forms, while Vigh's (2008) declaration of a 'chronicity of crisis' puts the notion under a temporal perspective of crisis experiences, as at times accelerating and at times slowing down.

Within this discourse, humanitarian agencies are seen as replacing the state and creating new forms of sovereign subjects: the HIV AIDs-infected person, the refugee or the vulnerable person in need of aid thus become visible, but at the same time, they have to fully comply with the powerful aid regime. But again, this is no one-way process. Highlighting the relationality within such interactions, Joël Glasman (2017) foregrounds the historical development of UNHCR classifications, which, in the past, continuously adapted to the agency's interventions during emergencies. With a focus on what emerges during aid interventions, he compares the agency's development to how James Scott (1998) defines state regimes aiming to achieve modernity by rendering citizens legible. Glasman explains that as Scott defines 'categories, formats, processes of standardization and rationalization' as images of the modern state, the UNHCR 'arranges populations according to its mandate to protect'. It does so by translating 'complex, illegible and multiple local claims into standard categories that can be recorded, compared and used' (2017: 4). Comparing the agency thus to the state – instead of viewing its sovereignty as a substitute for the state – Glasman shows how it is similarly split up in its various agencies and situated actors. His analysis claims that the UNHCR 'acts in a decentralized and fragmentary manner through a range of other actors – states of varying sizes and strength, UN agencies with different mandates, NGOs with diverse interests, refugees committees with varying representation and so on' (2017: 18). Instead of postulating a power asymmetry by the creation of aid subjects, Glasman invokes the 'highly connected' character of UNHCR interventions, which result 'not so much in the means of protection as of the quasi-monopoly it holds over the means of classification' (2017: 18). This is not to deny that regimes of aid can lead to forms of oppression, as during the creation of famine, which de Waal (1989) analyses in his impressive ethnography of humanitarianism in the 1980s, in which he describes how aid agencies caused famine through the provision of aid on the Sudanese side of the borderlands. He claims that the agencies operated using a false image: they failed to recognize that the people who came to UNHCR camps in need of help were not refugees of drought, but, in fact, of war – and that they could not return home as soon as the rains came in (a course that de Waal suspects aid agencies had imagined). These approaches allow taking a closer look at how, during such situations, emergent interrelations and connections contribute to new constellations of power, thus 'both reproduce(ing) and transform(ing) ... existing structures, practices, and ideas' (Beckett 2013: 98).

In line with Beckett and Glasman, I hold that while the urgency and traumatizing experiences of war are real, lifeworlds continue on a daily basis during such 'emergencies' as modes of processing uncertainty despite forced mobility and displacement. Processing uncertainty and surviving war necessitates knowledge of the possibilities of access to vital resources such as land, housing, food, work or health services. Displaced populations, host populations, international agencies and other actors involved all rely on this kind of knowledge, which informs categorization practices of who qualifies for access to the needed resources. International practices of categorizing often are not congruent with local practices of identification and (self-)ascription, so that categorizing derives from situational and negotiable social processes. With such a perspective on both providing and claiming access to aid, the political and internationally entangled aspects of categorizing come to the fore.

I do not aim to deny that aid agencies create new social environments, often by imposing structures; by applying the smorgasbord of available control mechanisms and technologies; by erecting and managing refugee camps; setting up eligibility criteria for providing different forms of aid; and leaving out those who do not fit their criteria. And I agree that they thereby introduce new categorizations for people both inside and outside camps, by allocating goods and services and employing people at higher and lower levels of the organizational structure and thus create new hierarchies with a much larger impact on an area's interpersonal infrastructure than simply providing aid. However, in light of the prevailing tendency to regard this form of aid as 'benevolent dictatorship' (McFalls 2010), my point is to show that within the continuing lifeworlds around structures of aid, possibilities exist that transgress the boundaries created by aid structures, both physically and ideologically.

Conclusion

The story of the villagers' list addresses an aspect of humanitarian aid that could be termed as structural invisibilization: an invisibilization that, according to Blumenberg (1981), is indeed 'gainful', for operations within the sphere of providing aid, but at the same time imposes exclusionary power upon those who remain outside this infrastructural technology. I have intended to show that however powerful the structural disadvantage created by aid might be for those left on the outside, it leaves, neither the targeted nor the left-out populations as passive and helpless, as much of the critique against humanitarian aid would imply. Through the process of compiling a list, the villagers demonstrated two things: (1) their careful balancing of future options by deciding to remain close to the land and not abandoning it for a temporary form of security in the camps, and (2) their active challenging of their invisibilization by creating a boundary object that rendered their existence and their claims visible to those who were meant to see it. The boundary object enabled reterpretations and renegotiations of humanitarian governance structures by demonstrating a knowledge of these structures, and about the possible power of written evidence.

My intention is to understand the ways people maintain lifeworlds in situations of rupture, caused by violence, war and displacement; how they survive such situations in which many institutional arrangements no longer hold (Calkins 2013). In contrast to clearly delineated and defined ways of approaching a crisis situation, lifeworlds can be defined by the contingency, the unpredictability and the flexibility that they grant those who live in them, which also translates into sudden or prolonged uncertainties about how to proceed. In this sense, lifeworlds existed in all parts of the aid scenery that I came to know: at the border, but also in camps, villages and towns where people tried to flexibly adapt by actively crossing modes of belonging and self-identification.

In this contribution I have tried to show how a larger set of actors and factors comprising relationalities and infrastructures of survival and aid can be analysed by thinking along the concept of visibility. I argue that the technologies of aid work well with clearly delineated boundaries of who is and who is not entitled to aid. Those who are entitled to aid are rendered highly visible, while those not entitled to it are relegated to an invisible place, one in which aid can only be provided in a limited way. But, as Redfield (2010) has shown, crises and emergencies also have flexible boundaries, the existence of which can be negotiated, both on the part of the aid agencies (on which he focuses), and on the part of those rendered invisible – as this study tries to show. Thinking through the concept of 'emplacement' rather than only that of 'displacement', the activities of a number of actors come to the fore. Here, villagers who decided not to move into aid camps proved their knowledge of the aid structures when they, situationally, emplaced themselves within these structures and used their knowledge to create evidence that would change their position from invisible into undeniably visible. Although their list had an impact of sorts, they were up against a heavily pre-structured set up of aid actors. During the war, their efforts therefore only had limited success (at the hands of one aid worker who went against the rules). But when the definition of a war zone ended a few years later (with a peace agreement between Chad and Sudan in 2010), the villagers' situation also changed: now the aid agencies were interested in setting up integration measures, for which a collaboration with the borderland villagers was highly desirable. In order to leave the intervention site, the aid agencies now negotiated access to land for the camp dwellers, thereby making the formerly invisible peasants an important partner in development aid.

Notes

1 I undertook this research as a post-doctoral researcher at the Max Planck Institute for Social Anthropology in Halle/Saale, Germany. I received further funding from the Volkswagen Foundation and the Deutsche Forschungsgemeinschaft (DFG).

2 As these ascriptions are partly of colonial, partly of local construction and are not to be understood as essential, I italicize them throughout the text.

3 The 'Chadians' had access to land with higher qualities as compared to the 'newcomers' from Sudan (as, for instance, closeness to the village, fertility etc.).

4 Among the numerous publications about this war, see Behrends (2007, 2014), Beck (2004), de Waal (2004, 2005), Flint and de Waal (2005, 2008), Jánszky (2014), Marchal (2004), O'Fahey (2007), Reyna (2010), Tubiana (2008), Tubiana et al. (2012).

5 Rising tensions and the influence of regional warring in the Chad/Sudan borderlands have been analysed by Abdul-Jalil (1984), Burr and Collins (1990), El-Battahani (2004), Harir (1984), Jánszky (2014), Prunier (2005), Ruiz (1987).

6 The contentious relations between so-called Arabs and so-called Africans have been a matter of much debate. See for example Abd Al-Rahim (1970), Aguda (1973), Barth (1967), Beck (1988), Braukämper (1993), de Waal (2005), El-Battahani (2002), El-Tom (2006), Harir (1994), Suliman (2003), Wai (1981).

7 The temporary riverbed of *Wadi Asoungha* marks the border between Chad and Sudan in this particular part of the borderlands, which had been defined by the French and British colonial troops only in 1924 (Khayar 1984: 62).

8 In a relapse of violence, a new camp has been opened very recently in 2020 for several thousands of people fleeing from Sudan. Located around *Wadi Mourra*, this new camp is even further from the border, necessitating transport of people by truck or four-wheel drive vehicles. Local voices speak of an incident at a local market tea stall, in which the *Masalit* tea seller served an *Arab* customer before a *Masalit* one. In the fight that followed, the *Masalit* killed the *Arab* man, causing attacks on *Masalit* villages in return.

9 From 2008 onwards this zone was secured with the help of international military, first the European Union Force (EUFOR) troops and, after 2010, the United Nations Mission in the Central African Republic and Chad (MINURCAT) soon to be replaced by a mixed troop of Chadian and Sudanese soldiers. As reported to me by several eye witnesses, a joint force of rebel fighters had attacked the Chadian capital in February 2008, later to be referred to as the 'battle of N'Djamena'. After a week of heavy fighting, the Chadian government, together with the French army stationed in Chad and the forces from several West African countries, successfully countered the rebels. After this attack, the Chadian president negotiated with the Sudanese regime, so that by early 2010 a peace deal had been signed. With the stationing of a mixed armed force along the border, the Chadian president ordered the UN military to leave the country only a few months after they had been installed.

10 See Marchal (2006) on what he calls the 'merging' of two crises.

11 I describe this situation with more detail in a paper about 'securing livelihoods' (Behrends 2014).

12 On the concept of navigation in relation to crisis, see the work of Vigh (2008, 2010).

13 Regarding translation and mediation in the frame of development aid, see Lewis and Mosse (2006), Rottenburg (2000, 2009) and Behrends et al. (2014).

References

Abd Al-Rahim, Muddathir (1970) 'Arabism, Africanism and self-identification in the Sudan', *The Journal of Modern African Studies*, 8(2): 233–249.

Abdul-Jalil, Musa Adam (1984) 'The dynamics of ethnic identification in northern Darfur, Sudan: a situational approach', in Mohamed Omer Beshir, Mohamed Abdel Rahim Mohamed Salih and Musa Adam Abdul-Jalil, *The Sudan: Ethnicity and national cohesion*, Bayreuth African Studies Series no. 1, Bayreuth: Bayreuth University.

Aguda, Oluwadare (1973) 'Arabism and pan-Arabism in Sudanese politics', *The Journal of Modern African Studies*, 11(2): 177–200.

Barth, Fredrik (1967/1998) 'Economic spheres in Darfur', in Stephen Gudeman (ed.), *Economic Anthropology*, Cheltenham and Northampton, MA: Edward Elgar, 468–492.

Beck, Kurt (1988) *Die Kawahla von Kordofan. Ökologische und ökonomische Strategien arabischer Nomaden im Sudan*. Stuttgart: Franz Steiner Verlag Wiesbaden GmbH.

—— (2004) 'Die Massaker in Darfur', *Zeitschrift für Genozidforschung*, 5(2): 52–80.

Beckett, Greg (2013) 'The politics of emergency', *Review of Anthropology*, (42): 85–101.

Behrends, Andrea (2007) 'The Darfur conflict and the Chad/Sudan border: regional context and local re-configurations', *Sociologus*, 57(1): 99–131.

—— (2014) 'Securing livelihoods: economic practice in the Darfur–Chad displacement arena', in Amanda Hammar (ed.), *Displacement Economies: Paradoxes of crisis and creativity in African contexts*, London and New York: Zed Books, 35–56.

Behrends, Andrea, Sung-Joon Park and Richard Rottenburg (2014) *Travelling Models in African Conflict Management: Translating technologies of social ordering*, Leiden: Brill.

Bjarnesen, Jesper and Henrik Vigh (2016) 'The dialectics of displacement and emplacement', *Conflict and Society*, 2(1): 9–15.

Blumenberg, Hans (1981) 'Lebenswelt und Technisierung unter Aspekten der Phänomenologie', in *Wirklichkeiten in denen wir leben*, Stuttgart: Reclam.

Bolz, Norbert (2012) *Das Gestell*, Munich: Wilhelm Fink Verlag.

Bornstein, Erica and Peter Redfield (2011) *Forces of Compassion: Humanitarianism between ethics and politics*, Santa Fe, NM: School for Advanced Research Press.

Braukämper, Ulrich (1993) 'Notes on the origin of Baggara Arab culture with special reference to the Shuwa', *Sprache und Geschichte in Afrika*, 14: 13–46.

Burr, J. Millard and Robert O. Collins (1999) *Africa's Thirty Years War: Libya, Chad, and the Sudan 1963–1993*, Boulder, CO: Westview Press.

Calkins, Sandra (2013) *Who Knows Tomorrow? Uncertainty in north-eastern Sudan*, Oxford and New York: Berghahn.

de Waal, Alex (1989) *Famine That Kills*, New York: Oxford University Press.

—— (2004) 'Counter-insurgency on the cheap', *London Review of Books*, 26(15): 1–8.

—— (2005) 'Who are the Darfurians? Arab and African identities, violence and external engagement', *African Affairs*, 104(415): 181–205.

El-Battahani, Atta (2002) 'Tribal peace conferences in Sudan: the role of the Joudiyya Institution in Darfur, Western Sudan', in Günther Baechler, Kurt R. Spielmann and Mohamed Suliman (eds), Transformation of Resource Conflicts: Approach and instruments, Bern: Peter Lang, 379–448.

—— (2004) 'Ideologische, expansionistische Bewegungen und historische indigene Rechte in der Region Darfur, Sudan. Vom Massenmord zum Genozid', *Zeitschrift für Genozidforschung*, 5(2): 8–51.

El-Tom, Abdullahi Osman (2006) 'Darfur people: too black for the Arab-Islamic project of Sudan', *Irish Journal of Anthropology*, 9(1): 5–11.
Fassin, Didier and Mariella Pandolfi (2010) *Contemporary States of Emergency: The politics of military and humanitarian interventions*. New York and Cambridge, MA: Zone Books.
Flint, Julie and Alex de Waal (2005) *Darfur: A short history of a long war*, London and New York: Zed Books.
—— (2008) *Darfur: A new history of a long war*, revised and updated edition. London and New York: Zed Books.
Glasman, Joël (2017) 'Seeing like a refugee agency: a short history of UNHCR classifications in Central Africa (1961–2015)', *Journal of Refugee Studies*:1–26.
—— (2019) *Humanitarianism and the Quantification of Human Needs: Minimal humanity*. Oxon and New York: Routledge.
Glick Schiller, Nina and Ayse Çağlar (2015) 'Displacement, emplacement and migrant newcomers: rethinking urban sociabilities within multiscalar power', *Identities*, 23(1): 17–34.
Harir, Sharif (1994) '"Arab Belt" versus "African Belt": ethno-political conflict in Dar Fur and the regional cultural factors', in Sharif Harir and Terje Tvedt (eds), *Short-Cut to Decay: The case of the Sudan*, Uppsala: Nordiska Afrikainstitutet, 144–185.
Jackson, Michael (2013) *Lifeworlds: Essays in existential anthropology*, Chicago, IL: The University of Chicago Press.
—— (2017) *How Lifeworlds Work: Emotionality, sociality, and the ambiguity of being*, Chicago, IL: The University of Chicago Press.
Jánszky, Babett (2014) 'Überleben an Grenzen: Ressourcenkonflikte und Risikomanagement im Sahel', Dissertation, Philosophische Fakultät der Universität Köln.
Johnson, Douglas H. (2003) *The Root Causes of Sudan's Civil Wars*, Oxford: Currey.
Khayar, Issa Hassan (1984) *Tchad: regards sur les élites ouaddaïennes*, Paris: Centre National de la Recherche Scientifique.
Koselleck, Reinhart (2002) 'Some questions regarding the conceptual history of "crisis"', in *The Practice of Conceptual History: Timing history, spacing concepts*, Stanford, CA: Stanford University Press, 236–247.
Lewis, David and David Mosse (2006) *Development Brokers and Translators: The ethnography of aid and agencies*, Bloomfield, CT: Kumarian Press.
Malkki, Liisa H. (1995) *Purity and Exile: Violence, memory, and national cosmology among Hutu refugees in Tanzania*, Chicago, IL: The University of Chicago Press.
Mamdani, Mahmood (2009) *Saviors and Survivors: Darfur, politics, and the war on terror*, New York: Pantheon Books.
Marchal, Roland (2004) 'Le Soudan d'un conflit à l'autre', Les Études du CERI. *Centre d'études et de recherches internationales Sciences Po*, 107–108.
—— (2006) 'Chad/Darfur: how two crises merge', *Review of African Political Economy*, 109: 467–482.
McFalls, Laurence (2010) 'Benevolent dictatorship: the formal logic of humanitarian government', in Didier Fassin and Mariella Pandolfi (eds), *Contemporary States of Emergency: The politics of military and humanitarian interventions*, Cambridge, MA: Zone Books, 317–334.
O'Fahey, Rex Sean (2007) 'UMM KWAKIYYA or the damnation of Darfur. Review article', *African Affairs*, 106(425): 709–717.
Prunier, Gérard (2005) *Darfur: The ambiguous genocide*, Ithaca, NY: Cornell University Press.
Redfield, Peter (2010) 'The verge of crisis: Doctors without Borders in Uganda', in Didier Fassin and Mariella Pandolfi (eds), *Contemporary States of Emergency: The politics of military and humanitarian interventions*, New York: Zone Books, 173–195.
Reyna, Stephen P. (1990) *Wars without End: The political economy of a precolonial*

African state, Hanover, NH: University Press of New England.

—— (2010) 'The mother of damnation returned on helicopters: population displacement and war, Darfur 1950–2004', Humanitarian and Conflict Response Institute, University of Manchester and Max Planck Institute of Social Anthropology.

Roitman, Janet (2011) 'Crisis'. *Retrieved from:* www.politicalconcepts.org/issue1/crisis/.

—— (2014) *Anti-crisis*. Durham, NC: Duke University Press.

Rottenburg, Richard (2000) 'Accountability for development aid', in Herbert Kalthoff, Richard Rottenburg et al. (eds), *Ökonomie und Gesellschaft. Facts and Figures: Economic representations and practices*, Marburg: Metropolis Verlag, 143–173.

—— (2009) *Far-fetched Facts: A parable of development aid*, Cambridge, MA: The MIT Press.

Ruiz, Hiram (1987) 'When refugees won't go home: the dilemma of Chadians in Sudan', Refugees Studies Programme, Documentation Centre, Oxford.

Scott, James C. (1998) *Seeing Like a State: How certain schemes to improve the human condition have failed*, New Haven, CT: Yale University Press.

Spittler, Gerd (1989) *Handeln in einer Hungerkrise: Tuaregnomaden und die grosse Dürre von 1984*, Opladen: Westdeutscher Verlag.

Star, Susan Leigh and James R. Griesemer (1989) 'Institutional ecology, "translations" and boundary objects: amateurs and professionals in Berkeley's Museum of Vertebrate Zoology, 1907–39', *Social Studies of Science*, 19: 387–420.

Suliman, Mohamed (2003) 'Ethnicity from perception to cause of violent conflicts: the case of the Fur and Nuba conflicts in western Sudan' [contribution to workshop] 1997 [cited 26 March 2003]. Retrieved from: www.ifaanet.org/The%20Inversion%20of%20Ethnicity.htm.

Tubiana, Jérôme (2008) 'The Chad–Sudan proxy war and the "Darfurization" of Chad: myths and reality', Small Arms Survey, HSBA for Sudan and South Sudan, Working Paper no. 12.

Tubiana, Jérôme, Victor Tanner and Musa Adam Abdul-Jalil (2012) 'Traditional authorities' peacemaking role in Darfur', *Peaceworks*, no. 83, United States Institute of Peace.

Vigh, Henrik (2008) 'Crisis and chronicity: anthropological perspectives on continuous conflict and decline', *Ethnos*, 73(1): 5–24.

—— (2010) 'Youth mobilisation as social navigation: reflections on the concept of dubriagem', *Cadernos de Estudos Africanos*, 18/19: 140–164.

Wai, Dunston (1981) *The Africa–Arab Conflict in the Sudan*, New York: Africana.

2 | Encamped within a camp: transgender refugees and Kakuma Refugee Camp (Kenya)

B Camminga

Introduction

> You know I don't think that I can go to Kakuma? Probably, I'd rather go back to Uganda and get killed there. Better than running away from one fire and then you go to something worse than that. (Sabri, transgender woman and refugee living in Kenya)

Since 2014, Kenya has emerged as a discernible hub on the African continent for people fleeing violence and persecution on the basis of sexual orientation and/or gender identity. This might seem surprising given that the country upholds colonial-era penal codes, criminalizing 'acts against the order of nature,' that broadly criminalize lesbian, gay, bisexual, transgender and queer (LGBTQ+) people. In combination with widely held religious beliefs, which also condemn homosexuality, this has led to a situation in which, according to Akiniyi Margareta Ocholla (2011)

> people are … very quick to condemn non-conforming elements in society, even those that they don't understand or that don't really pose any harm to society. So a lot of homophobia and transphobia still persists. There have been several reported incidents of physical and sexual assaults meted out on lesbian, gay or transgender individuals … Many have been dismissed from their jobs or been forced out of their rented houses by landlords. (p. 95)

Kenya is, for the most part, an environment like many others across the African continent. One which, at the very least, can be considered unconducive to the existence of LGBTQ+ people let alone their active protection by the state. Yet, LGBTQ+ people from the East African and Great Lakes region have been migrating to Kenya and seeking asylum since at least 2005. This is due to the somewhat peculiar role of the United Nations High Commissioner for Refugees (UNHCR) in the country. Although the Kenyan state does not protect or indeed outrightly acknowledge LGBTQ+ rights, the UNHCR, through its mandate of international protection, does. In some sense, particularly with regard to the protection of LGBTQ+ people, the UNHCR has run what can be understood as a parallel legal regime within the country (Nanima 2017). Concomitantly, Kenya practices a system of encampment requiring all refugees to reside in either the

Dadaab or Kakuma refugee camps. However, this has never been strictly implemented due to the fact that it has never been 'enacted into law or regulation' (Human Rights Watch 2002: 148). In combination with the presence of the UNHCR, this lax implementation has been positive in that it has 'allowed' refugees, particularly those most vulnerable such as the relatively small number of LGBTQ+ refugees, to reside as urban refugees in Nairobi.

This would all shift drastically between 2014 and 2015 in the wake of Uganda's Anti Homosexuality Bill which saw the arrival of over 400 LGBTQ+ Ugandans seeking asylum in Kenya. This coincided with the implementation of Kenya's counter-terrorism project 'Operation Usalama Watch'. Though unrelated, the two events in combination drastically shifted the landscape for LGBTQ+ refugees in Kenya, most crucially through the stern reissuing of the state's encampment policy, making it illegal for refugees to live outside of designated encampment areas. In its targeting of foreign nationals, Usalama Watch heightened LGBTQ+ 'vulnerability to arrest, detention, abuse and deportation' (Zomorodi 2015: 14). In the following months, Kenyans were asked to report refugees or illegal immigrants outside of the camps to the authorities. Police began to roundup refugees and transfer them back to the camps, in particular Kakuma, among these LGBTQ+ refugees, some of whom 'were met with violence' (Kushner 2015). The sudden increase in LGBTQ+ people being sent to the camps, and the sudden injection of Ugandans to Kakuma specifically, was something for which the UNHCR, at the time, was ill-prepared.

Drawing on archival media material about LGBTQ+ refugees alongside interviews done in 2019 with transgender refugees in Kenya, this chapter considers the tensions of visibility, invisibility and hyper-visibility in relation to various forms of displacement for LGBTQ+ refugees in Kenya. In particular, this chapter considers the impact of two UNHCR strategies in addressing the arrival of LGBTQ+ refugees to Kakuma. First, the sectioning off of LGBTQ+ people in a specific protection area within Kakuma – encamping them within the camp – and second, the request that LGBTQ+ people in the camp practise a certain amount of 'discretion', so as not to draw unnecessary attention to themselves. In particular, in this chapter, I focus on the story of Julia, a trans woman from Uganda, enduring forms of both physical and psychological displacement that are, seemingly, bureaucratically invisible and yet violently hyper-visible. I unpack what it might mean to ask transgender refugees, those who have availed themselves of the protection of another country, to practise 'discretion'. Indeed, to attempt to practise a form of imposed, but largely impossible, invisibility of the self.

A hotbed of homosexuals

In 2014, the Constitutional Court's challenge of Uganda's Anti-Homosexuality Bill (AHB), recently signed into law, sent ripples through the continent and garnered international condemnation (Paszat 2017). The bill was extreme in its criminalization of LGBTQ+ people in a country just across the border from Kenya. Not only did it criminalize homosexuality, it also extended punishments available to life imprisonment and added new crimes, such as seven years in jail for anyone convicted of advocating for LGBTQ+ rights. Criminalization was also extended to family and friends of LGBTQ+ people in that the failure to report LGBTQ+ people also became an offence. The signing of the AHB into law achieved several things. Firstly, it brought LGBTQ+ issues into stark visibility in East Africa in a way that had never been experienced before. There was global mass media interest from images, to op-ed pieces, to in-depth documentaries covering 'the world's worst places to be gay.' Real or imagined, the country's reputation as a hotbed of homophobia and by extension a hotbed of homosexuals began to be cemented. Secondly, for many transgender refugees I spoke to in Kenya, the AHB brought them into a new kind of visibility within their families and communities. In some sense, this may have been the very point of extending criminalization to families and friends. Among those most often targeted were those most visible to their communities and families as perceived 'homosexuals': transgender people. As Victor Mukasa, a trans man, activist and Ugandan refugee now living in the United States of America, explains:

> Generally, all gender non-conforming people are 'automatically' branded homosexuals as in most of our communities, a man who looks or has tendencies of a woman is the proper picture of a gay man. In the same way, a woman who looks like or has tendencies of a man is declared a lesbian automatically. (Mukasa and Balzer 2009: 124)

If families and communities did not actively ask questions, local tabloids were more than willing to publish photographs, names and addresses. In some sense, though the AHB was eventually struck down by the Constitutional Court, what it did suggest was that LGBTQ+ people were not perceived as rightful citizens of Uganda and that any retributive action to this end, though it may not have been actively supported by the state, would certainly not be denounced. As one LGBTQ+ Ugandan explained:

> By signing the Bill at a fully televised function and making the comments he made at the event, Museveni made it clear that LGBTI [lesbian, gay, bisexual, transgender and intersex] people are considered an anomaly, suggesting that violence against them would not be frowned upon ... More than ever, LGBTIs are a target. Over the past two days, *Red Pepper*, a popular local tabloid, has taken to publishing the names and photos of LGBTI people, including their places of work and residence ... Two hundred people have been forcefully outed so far, making us easy targets for blood-hungry homophobes. (Kings 2014)

The rise in anti LGBTQ+ sentiment in Uganda did not only affect the country but had particular impact on the region more broadly. Given their limited numbers, the low levels of broader discussion regarding LGBTQ+ rights (pre-AHB) in the East African region and the fact that being LGBTQ+ was not yet linked to being a particular nationality – Ugandan – the first LGBTQ+ refugees to reside in Kenya lived fairly inconspicuous lives. Moreover, they were able to live, as noted, due to the lax implementation of Kenya's encampment policy, in urban areas. Initially, the population was made up of claimants from Ethiopia, Somalia and other countries in the Great Lakes region such as Burundi, the Democratic Republic of Congo, Rwanda and Tanzania – countries which, at the time, experienced specific types of political and social unrest considered worthy of international protection. Pre-AHB, many LGBTQ+ people who crossed the border into Kenya then claimed asylum on grounds other than persecution due to sexual orientation or gender identity, though this persecution was often the real reason for their fleeing. In essence, these refugees in Kenya were a small enough group, coming from countries with other forms of unrest recognized as valid for international protection, so as to remain largely invisible, hiding in plain sight within the larger refugee and urban population.

In the wake of the AHB, Uganda, and by extension Ugandans, became synonymous with two interlinked concepts. First, President Yoweri Museveni and state-sponsored homophobia underpinned by perceived brutality, exclusion and the public permissibility of violence. Second, LGBTQ+ people and vice, underpinned by the perceived destruction of the state, Western influence and the corruption of religious morals. Those most targeted were those most visible and by extension those 'most hated': transgender people (Naluzze 2018). In the aftermath, people began to flee, among them large numbers of transgender-identified people, over the border to a country with a history of refugee provision, the presence of the UNHCR and a reputation for being far more lenient in the implementation of its penal codes – Kenya.

Vice and 'Museveni People'

The first group of twenty-three LGBTQ+ Ugandans arrived at the UNHCR offices on 11 March 2014 seeking protection. As noted, there were LGBTQ+ refugees in Kenya prior to the political upheaval of 2014 in Uganda, but this group had not outrightly claimed protection on the basis of sexual orientation or gender identity and had strategically chosen to use the possibility of other claims, given the unrest in their countries of origin, to remain inconspicuous. The majority of the group of twenty-three were in their early 20s, a mix in terms of socio-economic class and predominantly men or perceived as such. They all claimed asylum on the basis of sexual orientation.[1] Given the moment in which the group arrived, around the passing of the AHB, the fact that they were in a country which criminalizes same-sex activity; and being the first to claim asylum on grounds of sexual orientation, they were treated as exceptional cases by the UNHCR. In essence, while many refugees cross borders to escape the conditions which threaten their lives, this group found themselves in a space similar to that which they had left – criminalized. A similar situation meant similar threats (Kushner 2016). It was decided by the UNHCR to fast-track the group's claims while providing them with special protection, safe housing and financial support. According to the UNHCR, this was an almost unprecedented level of support and attention. In general asylum seekers in Kenya wait for months to be notified of whether they qualify for official refugee status and then several more years for consultations and the possibility of resettlement. The group of twenty-three began their interview and resettlement process almost immediately.

Julia, a trans woman from Uganda, was among the first to flee her country and enter Kenya seeking safety. LGBTQ+ refugees through a UNHCR partner organization were initially provided with a stipend and directed to go live within urban communities while waiting to be resettled. Since the organization had never dealt with such large groups of LGBTQ+ people tensions formed around their visibility firstly as a group of Ugandans, which as noted was slowly becoming linked to perceived vice or their assumed sexual orientation and by extension their reason for being in Kenya. This – being Ugandans outside of Uganda seeking refuge in the wake of AHB and a growing regional discourse regarding vice spurned on by the AHB – impeded their safety within urban areas from the outset. Given their visibility due to their perceived gender nonconformity accessing safety was a particular challenge for transgender refugees. As noted to be Ugandan in Kenya in the wake of a heightened discussion around LGBTQ+ rights in the region meant that one was assumed to be 'homosexual' until proven otherwise. As some LGBTQ+ refugees explained, it also meant, given the widespread media coverage, that communities in both Kenya and Uganda were far more aware of and indeed agitated by visible LGBTQ+ existence. Initially, LGBTQ+ Ugandans lived together in fairly large compounds; spaces with high walls, attempting to recreate community and safety among themselves. When the first resettlements began to be awarded, the group held a party to celebrate. Neighbours called the police, the party was raided, and all party-goers were arrested. Due to the fact that they were at a party which they assumed to be safe within the walls of their compound the trans women at the party, Julia among them, were dressed in the manner in which they identified and by extension they were arrested and placed in prison. They were not given the option to change, and so many of the trans women who were arrested arrived at the jail in their female attire. As Julia explains:

> So the police assaulted us right from our arrest until the jail. Then the police announced it to the other jailers that these guys are homos and they are bringing their vice here … [to Kenya]. They are 'Museveni people' … so when these guys entered they started beating us … [saying]: 'These are Museveni people and they brought their vice to Kenya'.

The UNHCR bailed the group out and spoke with the local community in an attempt to allow the group to remain where they had been living. The community refused, according to Julia, stating that 'these Museveni people' would bring 'their vice, their bad manners to our children, we can't live with them'. Given that they had only just been released from jail, the group was still wearing their party outfits from the previous night. This included the trans women of the group. Julia explained that after they were evicted from their compound and the community, the group had no choice but to walk, dressed as they were in heels and dresses, through suburban Nairobi to the UNHCR offices. A spectacle to be sure. On arrival, the UNHCR told them that they would not be allowed to enter through the main entrance of their offices. As Julia explains, the UNHCR was highly agitated by what they perceived as the group's display: 'because of the way we are and the way we were dressed and the way we were behaving … they told us that we were all behaving badly'.

The UNHCR met with the group and suggested it would be prudent in future to stay in smaller groups and move away from the area they had been evicted from. They were also asked to practice discretion; in particular it was suggested that the trans women among them try to dress and behave less visibly trans. For some in the group this was a turning point. After this incident, it became almost standard practice for trans women in particular to attempt to grow facial hair and wear more masculine clothing. This, though, did not change mannerisms, as Jacob Kushner (2016) explains regarding life as an urban refugee in Nairobi:

> Young Kenyans often dress in modern, American-style clothes – dark jeans, brand-name shirts with logos or designs and flat-brimmed hats. Many gay refugees dress this way too and tend to blend in with the crowd – though others, especially transgender people, stand out markedly and encounter verbal abuse and worse as a result. (Kushner 2016)

Julia was no exception. As someone self-described as 'visibly transgender' she explains that in urban Nairobi she continued to be 'an easy target'. Attempts to hide or be discrete did not make sense to her and in many ways she described them as almost nonsensical and impossible tasks. She could not comprehend how she was not supposed to be a woman. She did move to a new area away from the one where she had been arrested. Given her visible gender nonconformity she was very quickly found by people from her previous area and attacked. Her attackers told her, 'you Ugandans we know you, you're gay and you have a lot of money, you should give us your money and your phone'. They grabbed her neck and when she tried to fight back they hit her across the head with a metal bar. She went to the police to report what had happened. The police told her in no uncertain terms, 'we are fed up of Ugandan cases, we know you're gay, we know you're not supposed to be here, you should go back to your place'.

When she returned to her new safe house she reported the attack to her gay Rwandese neighbour, also a refugee. He responded by telling her 'you're actually bringing us attention now, we've been staying here a bit so you should move … you're just new here but already you are being attacked, you are going to create more attention to us'. Julia was told that as a transgender Ugandan she was too visible and courted insecurity and, by extension, made everyone else around her visible and insecure. In essence, Julia's gender expression, something which she found almost impossible to hide even when she did grow a beard, coupled with her nationality as a Ugandan in Kenya made her a lightning rod for anti LGBTQ+ sentiment. Anyone in her vicinity – neighbours, friends or other LGBTQ+ people trying to be discrete – were immediately read as LGBTQ+ and placed in direct danger by extension. For her Rwandan neighbour, this meant that she needed to leave so he could stay. Over the next year, Julia moved safe house several times. She was consistently told by others that the ways in which she walked and moved brought unwanted attention. She, on the other hand, felt that these were things she could not change. Julia returned to the UNHCR for assistance and given that the interdict requiring all refugees to return to the camps had just been put in place, the UNHCR, seemingly exasperated, placed Julia in a transit facility before sending her along with many other LGBTQ+ refugees to Kakuma.

Compounded in Kakuma

Established in 1992, located in north-western Kenya, Kakuma Refugee Camp, comprising Kakuma 1, 2, 3 and 4, has an estimated population of 180,000 people. Since its establishment, the camp has functioned as a refuge for those fleeing various forms of violence and persecution predominantly in the East African region. Refugee camps are commonly understood as spaces segregated from host populations; tented cities supplied almost entirely from the outside. The conditions inside camps are such that people lack privacy, share overcrowded and limited facilities, while existing in a confined space 'within which the whole compass of daily life is to be conducted' (Schmidt 2003: 5). Indeed, camps, unlike living in urban areas, provide a focal point bringing displaced populations into recognisability as refugees with needs and keep those needs visible (Deardorff 2009: 13). Ashraf Jamal suggests that refugees more generally believe that camps make them more discernible, as refugees, to a global audience and 'keep their plight, and the politics that underpin it, in the world's consciousness' (Jamal 2003: 5). Though not ideal, 'with refugees sequestered, concentrated, visible and presumably out of harm's way, camps represent a convergence of interests among host governments, international agencies and the refugees themselves … they help focus attention and provide a safety net' (Jamal 2003: 5). Refugee camps are, then, often posited as non-spaces; places of displacement, places of exile and enforced local invisibility as a trade-off for global visibility as a population in need. They are spaces which offer the basic necessities for survival as provided for by the international community: accommodation, water, healthcare and food rations. Kakuma is no different. Situated in semi-arid desert, a space many consider to be almost uninhabitable, Kakuma rarely appears on any map. As Dave Eggers' (2006) protagonist, Valentino, repeatedly describes it in *What*

Is the What, Kakuma is 'a camp at the end of the world' (p. 455), placed as it is at the borders of Ethiopia, Sudan and Uganda, 'in a land so dusty and desolate … arid and featureless … a place in which no one, simply no one but the most desperate, would ever consider spending a day' (pp. 362–363). In the wake of project Usalama Watch and the move to enforced encampment many, including the most vulnerable, no longer had the choice.

From their entrance into Kakuma LGBTQ+ refugees garnered a particular kind of visibility. Those among them who were transgender bore the brunt of this. First their nationality, as 'Museveni people', as Ugandans, made them especially visible not only to the broader Kenyan community outside the camp but to other national groups within the camp. Almost every transgender Ugandan reported having heard at some point the question, 'your country is not at war, why are you in Kenya?' LGBTQ+ Ugandans arrived speaking English and little Swahili – this was also something associated with 'Ugandans and "suggas" (a pejorative term for homosexuals)' (Buchanan 2016). Jeffrey Crisp suggests that the very nature of encampment is such that it can only promote heightened tension and eventual violence (2002: 14). Guglielemo Verdirame (1999) points to the ways in which the initial system of camps had been structured under the UNHCR, which seemingly allowed for the distortion of the UNHCR mandate, from protection to, at times, perpetration of refugee rights violations. He suggests that international NGOs, given the reputation and perception of the UNHCR are rarely interested in these violations but are far more focused on the state as perpetrator. Veradirame argues that camps in a certain sense, in that they are run by the UNHCR, as protected spaces, fade into a kind of obscurity within their host countries (1999: 18). Those within them, though they might be diverse internally, become a singular assemblage: refugees. This can make differentiated protection needs extremely difficult to manage. In an effort to protect the LGBTQ+ arrivals from the almost immediate hostility from the camp the UNCHR set the group up with a plot of land and organized with a partner organization to construct a set of small huts for them to reside in. In order to further limit their interactions with other refugees, their enclosed area also had a tap with running water placed nearby. A makeshift border was also created around the compound with thorny shrubs. It is unclear if this was to keep the LGBTQ+ refugees in or the threatening elements of the wider refugee population out. Kakuma custom, in responding to refugees as a singular undifferentiated agglomeration, is to give refugees construction materials to build their own houses (Kushner 2016). All of this was largely unheard of treatment.

According to reports, the perceived privilege LGBTQ+ residents received made other camp residents envious, heightening the group's already precarious position. The intent, on the part of the UNHCR, was to assist the group in acclimating to the camp. At the same time, they wanted to cause the least amount of upheaval for both LGBTQ+ refugees and the camp's already existing population. They hoped that by cordoning the group off, they might be better able to stick to themselves and remain inconspicuous. The perceived special treatment had the opposite effect and provided heightened exposure rather than mitigated it. So much so that some transgender people chose to remain confined to their shelters on a continuous basis for their own safety. Reports were almost immediate of beatings, assaults, shelters set alight and difficulty in accessing the camp's available resources because to do so meant coming into contact with other refugees (Naluzze 2018). So much so that not long after arrival the group began to sleep in shifts 'taking it in turns to guard their compound, at night, after an attempt ... to burn it down' (Igunza 2015). It seems that while living together offered the protection of numbers it also made LGBTQ+ people easy targets and marked those living in the protection area, even if they had not been known as such previously, as LGBTQ+. Due to this, many LGBTQ+ people moved or relocated to the camp after the protection area's establishment chose not to stay in the protection area in an effort to live anonymously within the camp's general community (Zomorodi 2015: 16). As one refugee explained in an interview with Wolfgang Tillmans (2019), 'a "protection area" I wouldn't call it that because anyone wishing to carry out an attack on us could do so whenever they feel like'. This marked and shrub-encircled area also made targeting transgender people far easier as the same refugee explained when asked whether they had ever been attacked, 'it happens every day ... Most especially those people who are transgender, who look so "out". It's very dangerous. Anytime' (Tillmans 2019).

Discretion

When Julia was brought to Kakuma she was asked, like others, to remain discrete. Within asylum, discretion is a controversial practice and request. It has often been used historically as a basis on which to reject asylum claims due to the belief that persecution can be avoided if an applicant hides their sexual orientation in their country of origin (Spijkerboer and Jansen 2011: 13). It is arguable that the request of discretion is, in fact, a request to conceal oneself or at least make a very key part of oneself all but invisible.[2] This becomes somewhat difficult, as Julia will attest to, when considering issues of gender identity. Yet, as people claiming asylum on the basis of persecution due to gender identity have become increasingly visible within the global asylum regime, the same reasoning has often been applied to them. The UNHCR is clear in its guidelines that the requirement for discretion, when claiming asylum, should be rejected (UNHCR 2012). Critically, the guidelines make two key points to this end. Firstly, that discretion 'may result in significant psychological and other harms'. Secondly, as Thomas Spijkerboer and Sabine Jansen (2011: 15) have noted, and this is perhaps most crucial for trans people, that discretion has often implied that

> a person's sexual orientation is confined to a mere sexual act, thereby overlooking a range of behaviours and everyday activities otherwise affected by that person's sexual orientation and gender identity. It would, in fact, amount to requiring the

same submissive and compliant behaviour, the same denial of a fundamental right, which the agent of persecution seeks to achieve by persecutory conduct.

In December 2003, the High Court of Australia suggested that discretion 'to avoid the threat of serious harm itself constituted persecution' (Millbank 2009: 391). Following the request to be discrete Julia explained that she could not help wearing her dresses and makeup, 'because those are my clothes'. Within the first few days of doing so in the camp 'people instructed the camp police to arrest me … they said I was bringing bad vices to their kids'. In Kakuma, Julia had resigned herself to the fact that as a trans woman no matter what she did she would be a target. Her very nature in such a confined and monitored space as both a Ugandan and perceived visible deviance meant almost constant scrutiny. She explained that this was the point at which she made a choice: If she would have to die from visibility then she would do so as authentically as possible. Much like in Nairobi the protection officer told her 'to be in Kakuma you have to tone down for your safety … it can be even worse in Kakuma than Nairobi'. Julia insisted that she could not change herself, could not tone down, could not *not* be a woman, and thus she became an immediate target:

> The Sudanese they told me 'you are not that gender. You're a man. You're supposed to behave like a man'. Then one of them shoved me into barbed wire and it cut me like that. Then automatically I had to fight back. When I fought back the other three beat me very badly … [After the attack,] I called the protection officer to tell her about the wounds … the protection officer told me that I should take one of the ambulances that are close by to bring me to the hospital. When I got to the hospital the doctors told me 'we don't work on gays, we don't work on people like you' … Because I had already plaited my hair they told me, 'you come back after unplaiting your hair. If you come back dressed like a man, we will assist you. If you come back dressed like that, we won't help you'.

Julia refused to undo the plaits in her hair. After the incident a group of Sudanese refugees entered the LGBTQ+ compound:

> One of the Sudanese refugees came into the compound, because I was a target … the Sudanese came and told me, 'you are spoiling our kids, you are a bad influence on our kids, we are going to work on you so that you can stop being like this'.

A decision was taken by the leaders of the expanding LGBTQ+ community in Kakuma to get Julia out of the camp to save her life. Given the impossibility of her concealment, her continued heightened visibility, she was once again understood as not only a danger to herself but to other LGBTQ+ people within the protection area. Julia was snuck out of Kakuma under the auspices of receiving medical treatment not available (that is, refused to her) in the camp. Those still furtively living on the outside assisted her move. Once she was safe and had been placed in a safe house, leaders of the community and supporters wrote to the UNHCR to testify that she was not well because of the ways in which she, as a trans person, had been targeted in the camp, having to endure constant surveillance and hyper-visibility. Julia's story is not an uncommon experience for trans women in the camp, many of whom, as noted, remain cloistered in the protection areas almost all the time if they cannot be smuggled out. The letter informed the UNHCR that the only hope for Julia would be to keep her confined within a safe house. Here she would be with other LGBTQ+ people who would be able to provide specific psycho-social support and access the world beyond the walls of the compound to run errands on her behalf. This, they suggested, would ensure a lesser threat of being attacked by neighbours and other migrants. Indeed, it would, in a sense, keep her visibility hemmed in. Walled in. Compounded.

Encamped

Paradoxically, although LGBTQ+ refugees became hyper-visible in the camp, in part due to language issues, perceived special treatment, nationality, beliefs held by other refugees regarding their inherent 'vice' and the placement of their shelters, they also entered a kind of invisibility. As Julia explained regarding life in the camp 'in the camp they [the UNHCR] … don't see you as LGBTI, they just see you as refugee'. After her experience in the camp Julia believes that in some senses though she became hyper-visible to other refugees, she also became bureaucratically invisible by being in the camp. She believes that this is part of the reason for placing LGBTQ+ people in the camp, to make them the same as other refugees: a group confined to a predetermined space seeking services. As she explains,

> to put you there you are just the same … because if it is LGBTI cases … [outside the camp] … they will give them special treatment, they [the UNHCR] … will be forced to maybe invest some resources … maybe other refugees will see them as if they're entitled.

Another gay refugee corroborated this perception, also noting the tension between experiencing visibility as a refugee while at the same time feeling invisible within the camp. He stressed much like Julia that in being encamped within the camp, LGBTQI+ people entered a kind of invisibility, one which they had to fight back against: 'you know we need the visibility so much because if you're just there [in the camp] … you're just there, no one knows anything that is happening here'. In the camp insecurity and visibility no longer matter. Everyone is waiting for something and as a singular mass of refugees in the camp 'even if you have an insecurity, it doesn't affect your case … here in Nairobi you can go and demonstrate and it can affect your case … but there [in the camp] … you don't do anything, they just place you in refugee housing … Invisible, as if you cease to exist'.

In the examples of attacks and assaults within the camp it is clear that 'homophobia is an ingrained part of life in the camp' (Kushner 2016). The request that those within the camp remain discrete, as noted in Julia's case, places the onus of protection on the individual but also, as Johannes Lukas Gartner notes, subverts

> the entire logic behind the establishment of a system that grants surrogate protection. The assumption present in such reasoning is again a view of queer identity as something sexual and behavioural, as opposed to considering queer identity being a highly complex matter integral to one's personal identity. An assumption, which would hardly be applied to heterosexuals. (Gartner 2015: 117)

The critical point Gartner makes here is that discretion, the request to conceal or make invisible, would not be a request levelled at a heterosexual or cisgender person because to be as such is considered innate. In the case of trans people, as Julia's story attests to, being trans only intensifies one's visibility within the already heightened surveillance space of encampment more generally. To then be encamped within a camp, cordoned off in a 'protection area' while also requesting concealment is to request that LGBTQ+ refugees cooperate in their own protection, subverting 'the entire logic of the system' while effectively being corralled in a highly visible area – a situation of impossibility. In response to this the LGBTQ+ members have mounted protests while accusing both the police and UNHCR of negligence, incompetency and abuse. Signs are periodically erected around the camp threatening LGBTQ+ people with death and violence. In 2016, signs appeared around Kakuma calling for the eradication of homosexual behaviour and in mid-2018, after hosting their first camp Pride, posters were put up on camp notice boards stating:

> You must leave the camp because you have spoiled our religion and our children. If you don't leave the camp, we are going to kill you one by one and we mean it. Enough is enough. (Power 2018)

The police are themselves homophobic and hold prejudice. The fact that LGBTQ+ people are criminalized does nothing to prevent these attitudes and, once one is a refugee, confined to a camp space, this can be even more precarious. In an interview, a representative of the UNHCR noted that after an incident of police brutality involving the LGBTQ+ refugees the UNHCR had to specifically tell the 'police they cannot beat people … I told police that, when it is working with any refugee group, they need it to abide by human rights laws' (Buchanan 2016). Note here that it is not the law of the Kenyan state which, although it does not actively promote violence towards LGBTQ+ people certainly does not protect them, that is brought to bear as something the Kenyan police should follow. Influenced by this 'negative social attitudes and persecution of sexual minorities are common. High levels of violence and a lack of police protection lead to acts of mob justice against sexual minorities' (Millo 2013: 16).

Kakuma, as evident from the ways in which LGBTQ+ people are treated, is seemingly a microcosm of life for LGBTQ+ people outside the camp. The difference critically is that it is one tainted with a sense of tension in relation to their heightened visibility in a space, a refugee camp, marked by its supposed invisibility to the broader Kenyan populace. Their rejection by other refugees forces a situation where they cannot simply fade, to repeat Veradirame, into a kind of obscurity within their host countries and become part of the agglomerate of refugees. Indeed, other refugees actively work, often through violent repudiation, to ensure this does not take place. As one refugee explains:

> When I came to UNHCR I was told that because it's not allowed to be gay in Kenya I should stay in the refugee camp; that's when UNHCR will protect me from all the bad things I had suffered when I was in Uganda. [In the camp] I was attacked by my fellow refugees because of my sexuality, and so I had no protection from the problem that I ran away from and that made me a refugee. At first I reported the threats to UNHCR protection officers who forced me to stay in the camp until I was attacked. They realize it's a bigger problem for gays in the camp but if we get special treatment the other refugees will attack us more and if we don't get a special place then we are still attacked because they hate us gays.

Conclusion

Prior to the arrival of the 'Museveni people' in Kenya, LGBTQ+ refugees living in urban Nairobi practised a form of active invisibilization. They attributed their ability to conceal themselves to the fact that LGBTQ+ issues were not as visible within the public sphere and LGBTQ+ refugees, in particular, were not even thought of as existing within Kenya's broader refugee community. Though the LGBTQ+ Ugandans brought a kind of spotlight to the community at large, which concomitantly increased insecurity for LGBTQ+ refugees more broadly, many have felt that this visibilization has allowed them to actively claim who they are with pride. As Divine, a trans woman from the Great Lakes region explains:

> [Before the Ugandans] we fear everything. We fear even when they are doing the interviews, we are not comfortable to answer all the questions or we are not comfortable to say something related to our sexual orientation … But after the Ugandans come they tried to make us open our eyes to don't feel guilty.

Kakuma, as the main camp in which LGBTQ+ refugees have resided, is a space set at the borders of the country meant to gather the displaced and present them to the international community as people in need. It is in many senses the prototypical non-place of refugees or, as Jamal has described it, a 'forlorn agglomeration' (2003: 4–5). Several studies have suggested that encampment, particularly long-term encampment, fosters conditions that impede the ability of camp residents to realize their human rights. Indeed, that the very nature of the refugee camp model is 'incompatible with the realisation of human rights' (Sytnik 2012: 22). This seems particularly true in this case for LGBTQ+ people. The two methods proposed by the UNHCR for their protection – encampment and discretion – both play on particular types of visibility and vulnerability in displacement. Neither, as shown, have been nor can achieve their intention: freedom from threat. In fact, it is arguable that each has elicited the inverse, creating situations of hyper-visibility which trans people within the camp are most burdened with.

Yiftach Millo (2013: 1) is critical of the UNHCR to this end, noting that though they may have made significant strides at an international level, as is evident for instance in the rejection of the principle of discretion in the guidelines, protection in the field and in some country operations for LGBTQ+ refugees 'remains extremely limited'. Their protection is affected by a general misconception of lack of need and urgency resulting from the 'invisibility of their plight'. This, as has been highlighted through Julia's story, can be particularly harmful for transgender refugees. Sociologist Avery Gordon (1997: 17) notes that the relationship between visibility and invisibility is not always as dialectical as believed. That hypervisibility in certain circumstances can also actually render one invisible. Transgender refugees in their displacement, in a sense, experience being largely bureaucratically invisible as refugees. At the same time, their specificity as people experiencing persecution due to their gender identity makes them, paradoxically, violently hypervisible within the less than welcoming agglomeration of heightened surveillance that is the camp. To then place them in a protection area is effectively to also corral them into a single identifiable zone where neither thorny shrubs nor night vigils will ever truly keep them safe, as Julia's terrifying experiences attest to. Aren Aizura suggests that 'at the root of many trans and gender non conforming people's desire to be mobile is this persistent fantasy: that somewhere else other trans and gender non conforming subjects are more free' (2018: 173). Trans refugees are no different. But perhaps unlike the desire for mobility of trans people more generally, the displacement experienced by trans refugees such as Julia, as she explains, is always inflected with questions and tensions of security and visibility not just for herself but for those around her. For Julia, displacement as a trans person has meant in some sense attempting to perform the impossible:

> We [trans women] are supposed to look out … not to be visible … for the safety of everyone because for people who are visibly transgender they are really at the mercy of the community, the homophobic, the transphobic community more than the gay men. So, for them [trans women] to keep safe, you have to tell them 'change your mannerism'. I know it's bad [but] because you don't want to put people in trouble and you know you'll be that trouble because at the end of the day, and you also need to be yourself … So, it still remains that sad … you know

> that it's not their [gay men's] fault … that we are all visible security threats … You keep asking yourself: 'Okay, when will I ever be myself? Like when will I ever think about being me?'

Perhaps, given the world in which we live and the ongoing murders of trans people and particularly trans women of colour globally,[3] the question is really is this even possible?

Notes

1 It is common practice on the African continent for asylum seekers, even if they are transgender identified, to claim protection on the basis of sexual orientation (see Camminga 2019).

2 See for example *JD (Zimbabwe) v. Secretary of State for the Home Department* [2004] UKIAT 00259 – a lesbian from Zimbabwe, seeking asylum in the UK, claimed that she could not maintain a 'cloak of invisibility' because she had been exposed in Zimbabwe. The UK Asylum and Integration Tribunal held that she could internally relocate and act with discretion in order to 'attain invisibility'.

3 As the recent murder of two trans women in the US (bringing the death toll for 2019 to nineteen) indicates, there is 'an epidemic of violence against the transgender community, an epidemic which disproportionately affects trans women of color' (Martinez and Law 2019).

References

Aizura, A.Z. (2018) *Mobile Subjects: Transnational imaginaries of gender reassignment*, Durham, NC and London: Duke University Press.

Buchanan, E. (2016) 'Meet the LGBTI Ugandan community living in fear in Kenya's Kakuma refugee camp', *IBTimes UK*, 21 June. Retrieved from: www.ibtimes.co.uk/meet-lgbti-ugandan-community-living-fear-kenyas-kakuma-refugee-camp-1566516.

Camminga, B (2019) *Transgender Refugees and the Imagined South Africa: Bodies over borders and borders over bodies*, New York: Palgrave Macmillan.

Crisp, J. (2002) 'No solutions in sight: the problem of protracted refugee situations in Africa', The Center for Comparative Immigration Studies University of California, San Diego, Working Paper no. 68.

Deardorff, S. (2009). 'Questioning the legality of long-term encampment through a human rights lens', Refugee Studies Centre Working Paper Series no. 54.

Eggers, D. (2006) *What Is the What*, New York: Vintage Books.

Gartner, J.L. (2015) '(In)credibly queer: sexuality-based asylum in the European Union', in A. Chase (ed.), *Transatlantic Perspectives on Diplomacy and Diversity*, Germany: Humanity Action Press.

Gordon, A.F. (1997) *Ghostly Matters: Haunting and the sociological imagination*, London: University of Minnesota Press.

Human Rights Watch (ed.) (2002) *Hidden in Plain View: Refugees living without protection in Nairobi and Kampala*. Human Rights Watch. Retrieved from: www.hrw.org/reports/2002/kenyugan/

Igunza, E. (2015) 'Gay Ugandans regret fleeing to Kenya', *BBC News*, 10 November. Retrieved from: www.bbc.com/news/world-africa-34764968.

Jamal, A. (2003) 'Long-term refugee situations in Africa', *Forced Migration Review*, 16(January): 4–6.

JD (Homosexual – MDC Supporter – Internal Relocation) Zimbabwe v. Secretary of State for the Home Department, [2004] UKIAT 00259, United Kingdom: Asylum and Immigration Tribunal / Immigration Appellate Authority, 17 September 2004. Retrieved 18 September 2019 from: www.refworld.org/cases,GBR_AIT,43fc2d6b22.html.

Kings, S. (2014) 'Gay Ugandans send out SOS to the world', *Mail & Guardian*, February 28. Retrieved 30 March 2016 from: http://mg.co.za/article/2014-02-27-gay-ugandans-send-out-sos-to-the-world/.

Kushner, J. (2015) 'Inside the nightmares of Africa's LGBT refugees', *Public Radio International*, 26 June. Retrieved 14 February 2018 from: www.pri.org/stories/2015-06-26/inside-nightmares-africa-s-lgbt-refugees.

—— (2016) 'The brutal consequences of Uganda's infamous Anti-Gay Law', *Vice*, 17 March. Retrieved 16 January 2019 from: www.vice.com/en_us/article/5gqz5x/on-the-run-kenya-lgbt-v23n1.

Martinez, G. and T. Law (2019) 'Two recent murders of Black trans women in Texas reveal a nationwide crisis, advocates say', *Time*, 12 June. Retrieved 18 September 2019 from: https://time.com/5601227/two-black-trans-women-murders-in-dallas-anti-trans-violence/.

Millbank, J. (2009) 'From discretion to disbelief: recent trends in refugee determinations on the basis of sexual orientation in Australia and the United Kingdom', *International Journal of Human Rights*, 13(2/3): 391–414.

Millo, Y. (2013) 'Invisible in the city: protection gaps facing sexual minority refugees and asylum seekers in urban Ecuador, Ghana, Israel, and Kenya'. Retrieved 15 March 2019 from: www.hias.org/sites/default/files/invisible-in-the-city_0.pdf.

Mukasa, V. and C. Balzer (2009) 'People have realized the need for an African trans movement', interview with Victor Mukasa, African trans activist representing IGLHRC (International Gay and Lesbian Human Rights Commission) and TITs Uganda (Transgenders Intersex Transsexuals Uganda), *Liminalis*, (3), 122–127.

Naluzze, S. (2018) 'LGBT+ Ugandan refugees in Kenya face assault and harassment', News.Trust.Org, 31 October. Retrieved from: http://news.trust.org/item/20181031104239-gn3xw/.

Nanima, R.D. (2017) 'An evaluation of Kenya's parallel legal regime on refugees, and the courts' guarantee of their rights', *Law, Democracy & Development*, 21(1): 42–67.

Ocholla, A.M. (2011) 'The Kenyan LGBTI social movement: context, volunteerism, and approaches to campaigning', *Journal of Human Rights Practice*, 3(1): 93–104.

Paszat, E. (2017) 'Why "Uganda's anti-homosexuality bill"? Rethinking the "coherent" state', *Third World Quarterly*, 38(9): 2027–2044.

Power, S. (2018) 'Death threats for LGBTI refugees who threw Pride parade at Kenyan camp', *Gay Star News*, 21 June. Retrieved 29 January 2019 from: www.gaystarnews.com/article/death-threats-for-lgbti-refugees-who-threw-pride-parade-at-kenyan-camp/.

Schmidt, A. (2003) 'FMO thematic guide: camps versus settlements', *Forced Migration Online*. http://repository.forcedmigration.org/pdf/?pid=fmo:5134.

Spijkerboer, T. and S. Jansen (2011) 'Fleeing homophobia asylum claims related to sexual orientation and gender identity in Europe'. Retrieved from: www.refworld.org/docid/4ebba7852.html.

Sytnik, S. (2012) 'Rights displaced: the effects of long-term encampment on the human rights of refugees', Refugee Law Initiative, Working Paper no. 4, 1–32.

Tillmans, W. (2019) 'Fighting for LGBTI rights in Kakuma refugee camp', *I-D*, 4 January. Retrieved from: https://i-d.vice.com/en_uk/article/kzv5gz/fighting-for-lgbti-rights-in-kakuma-refugee-camp.

UN High Commissioner for Refugees (UNHCR) (2012) *Guidelines on International Protection No. 9: Claims to Refugee Status based on Sexual Orientation and/or Gender Identity within the context of Article 1A(2) of the 1951 Convention and/or its 1967 Protocol relating to the Status of Refugees.* Retrieved from: www.refworld.org/docid/50348afc2.html.

Verdirame, G. (1999) 'The rights of refugees in Kenya: a social legal study', Refugees Studies Program. Retrieved from: repository.forcedmigration.org/pdf/?pid=fmo:199.

Zomorodi, G. (2015) *LGBTI Forced Migration in East Africa: Fleeing Uganda after the passage of the Anti-Homosexuality Bill*, New York: Global Philanthropy Project.

3 | An unsettling peace: displacement and strategies of invisibility in post-war Burundi

Andrea Purdeková

Introduction

Taking post-war Burundi as its case study, this chapter explores what and who is made visible and invisible, and how, in the space of post-war return and purported peace. It looks at how the socio-spatial ontology of 'post-war' and 'return' (in)visibilizes certain dislocations, movements and unsettlings. As such, the chapter extends the debates on (in)visibility typically focused on vulnerable populations *in transit* such as irregular migrants (Andersson 2014, 2016; Brachet 2018); or people dislocated from their home contexts such as urban refugees and migrants (Polzer and Hammond 2008; Sommers 2001; McDougall 2015; Balakian 2016), or those invisibly displaced in situ *in crisis* (e.g. involuntary immobilities, see Lubkeman 2008) to those who have returned, or refuse return, to post-war and officially 'post-crisis' state, here Burundi between the years 2005 and 2015.

During this time, Burundi was considered to be largely at peace, with armed factions progressively laying down arms and joining the political process, and an intricate, inter-ethnic consociational power-sharing architecture assuring no less than 'inter-ethnic pacification' (Reyntjens 2015). Burundi's government led by rebellion-turned-dominant party CNDD-FDD also embarked on providing integration and resettlement to the hundreds of thousands of Burundians returning from exile and internal displacement sites (Fransen 2017; Fransen and Kuschminder 2014; Falisse and Niyonkuru 2015; Maniraguha 2011; Vorrath 2008). But amid this narrative of resettlement and peace-building, many of its intended beneficiaries came to question it. People living in lingering IDP (internally displaced persons) sites and resettlement projects across the country spoke to me of conflicts and forces of displacement that remained largely invisible in the broader narrative outlined above (Purdeková 2016, 2017). More than this, they pointed to the invisibility of displacements connected to the peace-building and integrationist project itself.

In this regard, the chapter offers reflections on two dynamics of invisibilization, looking at (i) the ways in which powerful tropes and interventions associated with the post-war space such as integration and resettlement mediate and obscure certain dislocations; and (ii) the strategies people deploy to subvert or embrace invisibilization. Drawing on the experiences of 'coming together' and integration in post-war Burundi, the chapter considers how returnees, IDPs, and stayees have used (in)visibility in strategic ways to negotiate their position and to stake their claims in the emergent socio-spatial order. They have done this by re-interpreting, obscuring and subverting the dominant renderings of their identities and contexts via 'peace order labels' (e.g. 'returnees').

While recent literature has considered (in)visibility in relation to (il)legality or protection/security (wearing a protective cloak), normative and ethical concerns of the academic gaze (Polzer and Hammond 2008), withdrawal or simply lack of attention/visibility (see Gale 2008 on the 'invisible refugee camp'; Fiddian-Qasmiyeh 2012 on 'overlapping refugeedom'), or the political strategies of the displaced themselves when outside of their country of origin, my research considers (in)visibility in *the staking of claims to post-war place*, via strategies in physical and conceptual space (see also Purdeková 2017). With regard to the latter, Burundians not only 'speak' through their actions, they act through their speech and self-presentation. They invoke refugeeness in the space of return, or erase displacement in precarious sites in order to contest powerful notions of integration, settlement and peace that serve as dominant frames. I use the term 'ontopolitics'[1] to look at how different actors from internally displaced to returnees and stayees use (in)visibility in order to construct or contest the post-war socio-spatial order. Are inhabitants of peace villages 'settled' and are inhabitants of former IDP sites 'continuously displaced'? Burundians themselves upend powerful tropes and depictions that visibilize and invisibilize at the same time.

The chapter is structured around two seemingly opposed experiences – those of returnees and those of the internally displaced – to highlight the diversity of 'invisible' displacements in post-war Burundi. The first example considers invisible dislocations within spaces framed as 'resettlement sites' such as the peace villages of Mutambara, Busebwa and Buzimba. The chapter will show the different ways in which resettlement in these places unsettle, and the ways in which people have tried to unwork the dominant frame and the invisibility it imposes, whether through strategies in physical space, through narratives of continued displacement, or in re-defining their predicament. The second portion of the chapter looks at Burundi's lingering IDP sites from Bugendana to Mwaro Ngundu and Ryanonyi, which are relatively invisible in scholarship, even as they are salient and a thorn in the eye of the government, which has been pushing for their disbanding and pressuring inhabitants to disperse from them.

The methodology underpinning this research is qualitative, combining ethnographic observation methods, informal exchanges and interviews. It draws on a broader body of data collected in Burundi in 2013 and 2015, including over 110 semi-structured interviews with rural Burundians, a number of focus groups, debates and observation sourced from visits to peace villages,[2] integrated village projects,[3] former IDP sites[4] as well as scattered settlements in the provinces of Makamba and Bujumbura Rural.

Burundi's peace villages: the invisible dislocations of 'resettlement'

The Mutambara peace village, much like any other resettlement site in Burundi, is composed of straight lanes of about 300 houses, all the same and constructed with geometric precision. Each house has its 'tag' – its number printed on a plate just under the roof, alongside the benefactor's signature – in this case, DANIDA. In the morning, as we walk the lanes, children encircle us and follow us cheerfully all the way to the *nyumbakumi*'s[5] house. The bigger children in the back chastise the smaller ones running in the front, imitating the adults with a playful tone: 'Do not raise the dust! This is bad behaviour, what type of education are they giving you in school!' On the surface, Mutambara is a quiet place, of an eerie physical order, a large expanse of dry earth and dust in the coastal areas of Bururi, so unlike the lush hilly terrains of most of the country. But as anywhere, surfaces, labels and tags can mislead. This 'peace village' was a tangle of complex conflicts and invisible displacements. A quintessential place of settling, a resettlement site, producing powerful unsettling and dislocation for many.

Peace villages (*ibigwati vy'amahoro*) like Mutambara were constructed in the wake of war and mass returns of Hutu Burundians from protracted, multi-generation exile in neighbouring countries, principally Tanzania. They were specifically meant to accommodate returnees 'without address', those who were, for various reasons, unable to locate their ancestral lands. But the pragmatic concerns to resettle the *sans-adresse* were married to a social engineering agenda of peace-building by mixing different ethnicities, and hence returnees with stayees, in the space of the village. Mutambara was composed of 80 percent returnees (Hutu), and 20 percent 'residents' (classed 'vulnerable stayees', mostly Tutsi and Twa). In this, Mutambara was not unique. The four peace villages in the vicinity of Mutambara II (Mutambara I, Buzimba I and II and Busebwa), and in fact peace villages in general, were similarly composed. They also came to share similar challenges, which simply reached an unusually sharp relief in places like Mutambara.

After discussions with those inside and outside of the Mutambara site, it became clear that the 'peace village' designation was an oxymoron. The resettlement site was beset by conflict. But the tensions had precious little to do with inter-ethnic mixing per se – no one spontaneously mentioned this aspect, and when asked, they all brushed it off with 'it is fine' before moving on to more pressing matters. The conflict had to do with land, dispossession and livelihoods, and was tied to the peace village resettlement project *as such* and the layers of displacement it was entangled with. Even if the conflicts pitted returnees and stayees against each other, the protagonists vehemently pointed to the government as the underlying problem.

So what were these layers of invisible displacement, and how exactly were they invisible? How was unsettling produced through settling? Focusing on the single case of Mutambara helps us see the intersections and complexity of settlement post-war, and the different ways in which resettlement can be productive of conflict and displacement. Specifically, Mutambara shows three different invisibilized dynamics, dynamics not acknowledged by the government or tackled explicitly by donors or local agencies, and more broadly dynamics obscured by dominant labels and discourses of peace and resettlement: (1) the ways in which the production of resettlement sites is predicated on displacement; (2) the way in which 'occupation' of the peace village resulting from these forceful clearances generates desires to flee; and (3) broader processes of outmigration from the village (executed, planned or merely aspired to) on account of its unviability in producing sustainable livelihoods.

Mutambara was established on a previously inhabited site, and in this again, it is not unique. Before Mutambara was constructed, 'the government came, took residents who had houses here and expelled them', a young woman living just outside the village explained. A *nyumbakumi* in Mutambara II summed it up thus:

> The problem started with the project to build the village because the core issue is that there was a kind of traditional village here – 300 people were living here for so long that they thought [claimed] this is their land ... So some have been living here for so long. Others bought land here because they heard about the village project and expected more money if they sold back the plot.
>
> AP: Do other villages have the same problems?
>
> This is a problem across the whole country.[6]

Another such story of conflict and displacement was unfolding just as we first arrived. Having had trouble finding Mutambara, we parked in an adjacent area, sparsely inhabited with makeshift structures and simple adobe houses, hoping to find the village on foot. Later, we came to learn that the place where we arrived was known as 'the burned area' where the local government tried to expel the residents by force, offering similar reasons – that the area would be used for establishing Makonde, a new peace village, in the future. The inhabitants of that area followed us to Mutambara and insisted that they, too, needed to be interviewed. 'About 400 people are living in the burned area, but only fifty were given land in Makonde', a woman who had returned since the dispersal explained.[7] 'They [the authorities] came with the military, supervised what was happening ... it was 4am ... They said they had a plan, a programme for this land, but until now, we don't see any plan', said another older woman from the area:

> You are being chased because of a returnee, you are expelled because your land will be given to a returnee, how can relations be good? [But it is] authorities antagonizing us against each other ... The problem before us: the authorities that should advocate for us, they are chasing us.[8]

It soon became clear that the boundaries of the peace village, not only as an official conceptual construct, but as a physical space, were limiting – one had to look outside and beyond the 'peace village' in more than one way – in order to understand it.

Those displaced by resettlement did not just disperse. In the burned area, new simpler structures were visible. 'Are you not afraid the government comes back?', I asked one of my interviewees. 'That is what I was about to tell you, we are still in a war-like situation, during the night we cannot sleep because we are afraid … sometimes our children are not staying in the house [in the night]'.[9] In Mutambara, some of the previous residents occupied the village itself. They had erected small mud houses adjacent to, or even directly attached to the new, inhabited structures in protest. About twenty-five houses were affected.

A young returnee brought us to his house and pointed to the mud house attached to one of the walls of his own house:

> He [the occupier] claims he has paid money and cannot leave. We don't have peace, we don't even talk to each other … The resident [occupier] said: Between us, either you or me, one should die … I have never experienced war, so I am very afraid of this language, even at night I cannot sleep. The authorities know our situation, they say 'wait, we are analysing your situation'. They have been saying this for years … so maybe take us back to Tanzania.[10]

A widow with an 'occupant' pointed to the mud structure just by her DANIDA house:

> As soon as we entered, the residents came, they built houses just in front … We submitted our case to the administration, they did nothing … we started with the local administration, the *chef de colline* … all the way to the Ministry of National Solidarity, we even submitted our case to the UNHCR representative … There is no answer, and now we are even thinking of going back to Tanzania … This issue is the government's fault, the government is not addressing the problem it has caused itself … at some point we will flee … it is the government that is chasing us because our security is not guaranteed.[11]

After the widow showed us around and explained the history of the 'situation', my research assistant and I decided to approach the women visible in the adobe structure. The village was in a tense situation, and we did not want to cause more fear and fuel the conflict by appearing to be siding with a particular group. A woman came out with a large machete and a militant attitude, she listened in silence as we spoke. We said we came with no particular interest into the village, she responded that she assumed the contrary because we came with 'them'. When we saw she was not willing to engage, we said we merely wanted to assure her so she would not be afraid.

'I am not afraid!' she exclaimed angrily, 'did she tell you the full story? Did she tell you why I am here and she is there?'[12] The 'occupants' were neither resident, settled nor resettled, they were displaced; a precarious situation they tenaciously held on to even as they did not choose it themselves. Their ad hoc structures were starkly visible and this was part of the defiant act of staking a claim. They wanted their displacement to be made visible.

Besides land-related conflicts, most of the 'beneficiaries' of peace villages have questioned these sites as viable spaces of resettlement, as places where sustainable livelihoods could be created. They tied this unviability to imagined, planned or already-executed return, this time back to exile in Tanzania. Resettlement villages were thus quite literally sites of active unsettling. Importantly, Mutambara inhabitants were unequivocal in seeing this as 'forced' movement. And even if 'livelihoods' were involved, the creation of unviable settlements was read as a starkly political issue.

Almost everyone touched on this assertion in one way or another. Some had left, others were planning to leave, yet others merely expressed a desire. A young returnee sighed: 'Many things were promised [to entice us to return] but we no longer believe in this … like me, I am living here and always thinking of going somewhere else … not only Tanzania, anywhere'.[13] An older returnee man expressed similar sentiments:

> [In exile] we used to have good life … now we are thinking of returning to Tanzania … for me, to be honest, if I could get a ticket, I could go there immediately, because here we are dying of hunger … Those who could find a ticket, they returned to Tanzania, even my son, he returned there because he was alone, not married yet … all the youth, they are going there.[14]

The widow with an 'occupant' introduced above responded to my question on whether people were going back to Tanzania: 'Beeenshi! (So many!) Men are selling these houses to go back … you cannot live by just looking at the house, you cannot eat the house!'[15]

The residents and returnees in Mutambara were not only *showing* through their struggles how powerful tropes of peace and settlement were misleading, they actively *re-narrated* their experience and openly subverted these terms by pointing to 'war', 'warlike-situation', 'no peace', 'chasing', 'expelling' and 'refugeehood' at home. The intellectual labour here was theirs, not mine. To them these realities of conflict and displacement were not invisible – this was what consumed them on a daily basis.

But through their insistence and elaboration, it became clear that they felt they were nonetheless invisible, to those in power, to the donors and even to the researchers, who like me, came in asking questions that were not dealing with what was most pressing. The 'challenges' I came to explore were people's perceptions of transitional justice and peace-building, and I wanted to set these against their lived experience of conflict, exile and return. While most obliged my questions, it was clear that they wanted to impress different sorts of conflicts on me and that they pushed me to reconsider basic terminology.

The people I spoke to in and around Mutambara resisted assumptions derived so easily from the post-war, transition, peace and peace-building labels that formed the dominant ontology of the political order in which they found themselves, and in which they were 'resettled', 'returnees', moving towards peace through coexistence with ethnic 'others'. Instead, returnees and residents alike inverted official narratives of citizenship, statelessness, exile and home to provide a critical reading of the political status quo.

Interestingly, memories of exile continued to be invoked to highlight the returnee sense of dislocation 'at home'. Speaking about land conflict and harassment by local officials and police when trying to recover his land, the Chef de Village in Buzimba peace village exclaimed: 'It is as if you were introducing a nail to a wound ... that is how we are feeling now. We should not be refugees in our own country'.[16] The widow with an 'occupant' in Mutambara claimed she lived in a 'war-like situation' and her request was that 'these residents should give us peace, and to get titles ... this would prove we are citizens like other citizens, now we are like *abanyamahanga* – foreigners'.[17]

While returnees played with refugeehood to subvert the notion of return and peace, stayees/residents appropriated 'refugeeness' as a narrative resource too. They perceived 'refugeehood' and 'return' as a status that attracted resources and attention of the kind they did not have access to. 'I am a refugee!' lamented a woman in the burned area outside Mutambara village. Another widow from the burned area reflected on her predicament and the reasons for pushing them out:

> Nobody could tell us why ... maybe because we are not Burundians who fled and came back [insinuating a preference/bias for returnees] ... Are we not Burundians like other Burundians? Maybe we could flee, return and be welcomed ... because we realize we are not citizens like other Burundians.[18]

Twisting the tropes in Burundi's IDP sites: staking claims to stay against threats of dislocation

The Bugendana informal settlement is far removed from the village of Mutambara, in more than one way. It is certainly physically distant, located about a one hour drive outside the city of Gitega in central Burundi. Unlike Mutambara, this is not a space of return and resettlement, but rather a lingering IDP site from which its inhabitants stubbornly refuse to leave. It is an unofficial, precarious settlement with 500 houses spreading away from an informal memorial graveyard to 670 victims of a vicious attack on the camp in 1996, allegedly perpetrated by the then CNDD-FDD rebels, now the dominant political party. But quite like Mutambara, Bugendana is a site that challenges dominant narratives and attempts at integration, that unworks any easy notions of 'post-war' or 'peace', and that is itself a site of invisible displacements.

The site of Bugendana is not unique. Almost 120 IDP sites[19] with 80,000 inhabitants (predominantly Tutsi) still lingered on at the time of my fieldwork and the numbers (of both sites and IDPs) has seen only a modest decrease since 2005.[20] These entrenched sites have been relatively ignored in scholarship (see Purdeková 2017), which has focused predominantly on the challenges of return and land-sharing in rural areas.

The lack of academic attention, however, was certainly not matched by political invisibility – the sites were highly salient and a thorn in the side of the government, which has mounted a variety of pressures for their dispersal. In this context, I found two dynamics of 'invisible displacement' at play: first, the threats and pressures of forced displacement of the inhabitants and destruction of the site that so intensely consumed their lives; and second, the inhabitants' simultaneous attempts to invisibilize themselves as internally displaced in order to resist the threatened removal and entrench themselves *in situ*.

When I entered Bugendana, its inhabitants quickly navigated me to what is not readily visible and yet palpably present, 'occupying' the mental space of the settlement – the continuous threats of removal and clearance of the site made by the government. The authorities had announced the plan to develop the site into a second airport, in line with broader plans to develop the centrally located city of Gitega into the capital of Burundi. People in Bugendana thus pointed to a different sort of invisibility – anticipated, threatened, symbolic displacement. The narratives were pouring out and have overwritten my initial core interest of collecting perspectives on dealing with the past.

The story of the airport was confirmed via other sources, including a local authority, but many in the settlement questioned the official reasons given for their dispersal. The young *chef de site* (an informal position) explained:

> It is true; there is a government programme to destroy the sites. It is not only this site, if you heard … Ruhohoro, Mutaho … They are trying to destroy all sites, and then invent unrealistic projects, like here – an international airport – but we realized this was just a way to threaten us, just the way to destabilize us.[21]

There were indeed other narratives and other incentives to dispersal – the narrative on the importance of inter-ethnic 'integration' and the undesirability of mono-ethnic settlements, and of course the incentive to destroy a site that doubled as a reminder of a major atrocity perpetrated by the ruling party.

The displacement might have been 'merely' a threat in the case of Bugendana, but this requires a number of caveats. The threats were always already having a profound effect on the inhabitants in stoking anxiety and fear. They related not only to the inhabitants' physical removal but also to the destruction of the memorial graveyard, and hence to the dislocations of memory. The inhabitants – in a vast majority Tutsi fleeing genocidal violence of the early 1990s – were still deeply concerned about their security back in their hills of origin. In resisting 'return' and 'integration', they invariably pointed to the fear of what such return would entail. Person after person emphasized that they did not feel safe *mu mitumba* – in the hills – where no perpetrator was punished and where they could not trust their neighbours. Relations were good during the day and on the surface, but not in 'the heart'. 'We want to stay here',[22] people in Bugendana said repeatedly. 'No one is returning', said an older woman in Mwaro Ngundu, 'They [some Hutu neighbours] say they would kill us … So I hope that the government will not force us to leave this area. You should deliver this message to the authorities'.[23] 'We cannot go back', a young man with a stern and angry expression emphasized as he and his friends intercepted us in the streets of the Mwaro-Ngundu site: 'if we go back, we will be cut!'[24]

Seeing the government pushing them back to their communities of origin and yet unable to assure their safety there, people in Bugendana concluded that it was the government itself that was vested in persecuting them. To my question as to why they thought the government wanted to remove them, an old woman exclaimed: 'Because they want us to die! It is those with this [ethnic hate] ideology who are planning this'.[25] A number of people proposed similar ulterior, ultimate motives. Their insistence, and what some saw as 'extreme' narratives of the government's purposeful plan at their extermination thus must be read in this light. In sum, the inhabitants of Bugendana were 'fleeing' the predicament of insecurity in the hills, by actively staying put.

At the same time as they pointed to these broader forces of insecurity in their rural homes – forces which in essence maintained their predicament as internally displaced (i.e. the broken link between citizen and state; the sense of being 'chased') – the inhabitants of Bugendana also weaved together strategic narratives that claimed the opposite. They purposefully tried to invisibilize themselves as continuously displaced and instead have laboured to redefine their informal sites as homes and legitimate settlements. 'We rely on this place', a young woman, a supervisor at a local secondary school, explained, 'many children were born here, they think this is their home'.[26] Another man disputed the IDP label directly: 'They should not call us IDPs, we are just a population like the others … It is a way of discriminating you [referring to targeting of the population for dispersal and return]'.[27]

Those in Bugendana and other similar sites were drawing on the state's own dominant rhetoric and practices of integration in order to subvert its pressures for dispersal and return. Some suggested their site could be converted into a 'peace village', referring to the latest villagization drive.[28] 'Since you are building peace villages over there', an old woman in the Mworo Ngundu site suggested, pointing across the road,

> you should just extend it [to here] … since we cannot afford going to the peace village … you could provide us with iron sheets and we can build right here. And then we live in harmony, a Hutu would come and establish a house here … the community is [in fact] mixed, [there are] even Hutu, even Batwa over there.

> Since this land belongs to the government, we said since we are already mixing, should we [not] stay here.

Another elderly woman produced a starkly similar narrative, suggesting this was a broader strategy:

> Here [in the site] it is peace ... Our wish is that the top leaders should give us peace and we should stay in this village. If anyone comes to ask if we would like to return, we tell them – even others [Hutu] are coming to live with us, all ethnic groups are represented here.[29]

Similarly to Mutambara's inhabitants, those in Bugendana and other IDP sites also question the basic terms of the new political order, and Burundi as a space of peace and return. 'There is no peace, only a little bit',[30] an old woman in Bugendana insisted. 'Peace is not there yet',[31] an old man in Mwaro Ngundu emphasized. Others suggested that it was the government's threats themselves that upended their peace: 'Our wish is, let us stay in this village because if they stop disturbing us, we are living in peace',[32] a young boy told us in the Yanonyi IDP site. The push to return and reintegration was perceived as a threat to many and as a form of invisible displacement. In resisting it, the inhabitants of *les sites* were questioning who was displaced, and how, and they deployed different strategies of invisibilization to stake their claims to stay put.

Conclusion

In conclusion, spaces from Mutambara to Bugendana speak of resistance to integration and of its disintegrative effects – the forces that upend return even as they claim to encourage it. The people I visited and spoke to often felt they were left to their own devices to deal with conflicts that were inadvertently or purposefully created from above. To them, the forces of dislocation were painfully visible. They lobbied me to describe them, but they also used strategies in physical and conceptual space to combat them, though not always successfully.

On one level, the (in)visibilities I describe relate to tangible political dynamics of integration. But more broadly, they are also a result of the politics of post-conflict discourse with its dominant tropes, literally organizing concepts that have the power to shape space and relations in it, in part through their (in)visibilizing effects. The way this (in)visibilization manifests itself in the discourse on displacement and refugees is through a clear bias in its focus on 'crisis'. Displacement discourse (comprising both theory and praxis) speaks of distinct 'waves' of refugees, even if they come from the same country, within a relatively short span of time, and in fact, if it is the very same people. Burundi's mass return after the war has been hailed as a major success story by the UNHCR, only to be upended years later in 2015 by a mass wave of displacements, often from the same spaces and by the same people. Part of the problem of properly capturing re-displacement is the lack of attention to the space 'in-between', the post-return status quo and its powerful discontents and dislocations.

For a truly dynamic theory of displacement, we cannot stop with return and resettlement. If refugeehood is at its core about the broken bond between citizen and state, then it is important to continue investigating that link and the breaks in it in spaces of 'return' and 'peace'. This will help us understand why seemingly beneficent drives to integration, resettlement and peace-building become sites of – and even drivers of – displacement.

In the peace and conflict discourse, lacunae remain too. While concepts such as human security bring the focus back on the individual and the local level, there still seems to be a difficulty in connecting the macro and the micro, a difficulty that does not appear to be present in local actors' own frames and narratives. Radically local problems like those in a small villagization site in Mutambara do not have radically local causes. People tie these conflicts to local and national politics and the way in which power and governance operate in Burundi. Their insistence on calling their state a 'war' or 'war-like' situation is not meant to suggest that insurgents are fighting with the government for the capture of power. Their insistent subversion of dominant labels is meant to highlight continuity, to underline just how similar their sense of insecurity and disconnect feels in a purportedly radically different socio-political order.

Notes

1 'Ontopolitics' refers to struggles over the power to posit order, name its constituent parts, their nature and relations.

2 Fieldwork was conducted in three peace villages around Rumonge: Mutambara, Busebwa and Buzimba. Additional data were gathered in two peace villages in Bubanza.

3 These include Makaba, Gishubi and Kagwema.

4 Data were gathered in three IDP sites in Bugendana, Mwaro Ngundu and Ryanonyi.

5 *Nyumbakumi* refers to an informal leadership position in the settlement, a leader responsible for a section of the village.

6 Interview with the *nyumbakumi* (local village leader) in Mutambara II village, April 2015.

7 Interview outside Mutambara II village, 16 July 2013.

8 Interview with a woman in the burnt area outside Mutambara II village, 16 July 2013.

9 Ibid.

10 Interview with a young returnee man, Mutambara II village, 17 July 2013.

11 Interview with a woman living with an 'occupant' in Mutambara II, 17 July 2013.

12 Discussion with a woman 'occupying' a returnee's plot in Mutambara II, 17 July 2013.

13 Interview with a young returnee man in Mutambara II, 17 July 2013.

14 Interview with a returnee from Tanzania, Mutambara II, 16 July 2013.

15 Interview with a woman living with an 'occupant' in Mutambara II, 17 July 2013.

16 Interview in Buzimba peace village, 18 July 2013.

17 Interview with a woman living with an 'occupant' in Mutambara II, 17 July 2013.

18 Interview with a woman from the burnt area, 16 July 2013.

19 Known informally as *les sites*, a shortened version of *les sites de déplacés* (displacement sites).

20 The last comprehensive IDP survey conducted by the UN Office for the Coordination of Humanitarian Affairs in 2005 suggested that 117,000 IDPs lived in settlements at that time (cited in IDMC 2011: 7).

21 Interview with *chef de site*, Bugendana IDP site, 23 July 2013.

22 Interviews with residents of Bugendana site, 23 July 2013.

23 Interview with an older woman in Mwaro Ngundu, 24 July 2013.

24 Interview in Mwaro Ngundu, 24 July 2013.

25 Interview in Bugendana, 23 July 2013.

26 Interview with a young girl, supervisor in a secondary school, Bugendana, 23 July 2013.

27 Interview in Bugendana, 23 July 2013.

28 Since the early phases of post-war villagization geared to accommodate returnees, the government has started a much more widespread project of villagization, encouraging rural populations living dispersed on the hills to opt into a more 'integrated' settlement of a village project (see Purdeková 2017). While the inter-ethnic engineering remained in these new projects, the houses were not free.

29 Interview with an old woman on the Mwaro-Ngundu site, 24 July 2013.

30 Interview in Bugendana, 23 July 2013.

31 Interview with an old man in Mwaro-Ngundu, 24 July 2013.

32 Interview on the Yanonyi site, 26 July 2013.

References

Andersson, R. (2014) *Illegal Inc.: Clandestine migration and the business of bordering Europe*, Berkeley, CA: University of California Press.

Andersson, R. (2016) 'Europe's failed "fight" against irregular migration: ethnographic notes on a counterproductive industry', *Journal of Ethnic and Migration Studies*, 42(7): 1055–1075, DOI: 10.1080/1369183X.2016.1139446.

Balakian, Sophia (2016) '"Money is your government": refugees, mobility, and unstable documents in Kenya's Operation Usalama Watch', *African Studies Review*, 59(2): 87–111.

Brachet, J. (2018) 'Manufacturing smugglers: from irregular to clandestine mobility in the Sahara', *The Annals of the American Academy of Political and Social Science*, https://doi.org/10.1177/0002716217744529.

Falisse, J.-B. and R.C. Niyonkuru (2015) 'Social engineering for reintegration: peace villages for the "uprooted" returnees in Burundi', *Journal of Refugee Studies*, DOI: 10.1093/jrs/fev002.

Fiddian-Qasmiyeh, E. (2012) 'Invisible refugees and/or overlapping refugeedom? Protecting Sahrawis and Palestinians displaced by the 2011 Libyan uprising', *International Journal of Refugee Law*, 24(2): 263–293.

Fransen, S. (2017) 'The socio-economic sustainability of refugee return: insights from Burundi', *Population, Space and Place*, 23(1), https://doi.org/10.1002/psp.1976.

Fransen, S. and K. Kuschminder (2014) 'Lessons learned from refugee return settlement policies: a case study on Burundi's rural integrated villages', *Refugee Survey Quarterly*, 33(1): 59–76.

Gale, Lacey A. (2008) 'The invisible refugee camp: durable solutions for Boreah "residuals" in Guinea', *Journal of Refugee Studies*, 21(4): 537–552.

IDMC (2011) 'Burundi: secure tenure and land access still challenges for long-term IDPs. A profile of the internal displacement situation', Geneva:

Internal Displacement Monitoring Centre. Retrieved from: www.internal-displacement.org/assets/library/Africa/Burundi/pdf/Burundi-August-2011.pdf.

Lubkeman, S.C. (2008) 'Involuntary immobility: on a theoretical invisibility of forced migration studies', *Journal of Refugee Studies*, 21(4): 454–475.

Maniraguha, J.P. (2011) 'Challenges of reintegrating returning refugees: a case study of returnee access to land and to basic services in Burundi', Master's Thesis, University of Tromso.

McDougall, E.A. (2015) 'Hidden in plain sight: Haratine in Nouakchott's "niche-settlements"', *The International Journal of African Historical Studies*, 48(2): 251–279.

Polzer, T. and L. Hammond (2008) 'Invisible displacement', *Journal of Refugee Studies*, 21(4): 417–431.

Purdeková, A. (2016) '"Barahunga Amahoro – they are fleeing peace!" The politics of re-displacement and entrenchment in post-war Burundi', *Journal of Refugee Studies*, 30(1): 1–26.

—— (2017) 'Respacing for peace? Resistance to integration and the ontopolitics of rural planning in post-war Burundi', *Development and Change*, 48(3): 534–566.

Reyntjens, F. (2015) 'Burundi: institutionalizing ethnicity to bridge the ethnic divide', in A. Kuperman (ed.), *Constitutions and Conflict Management in Africa: Preventing civil war through institutional design*, Philadelphia, PA: University of Pennsylvania Press, 27–51.

Sommers, Marc (2001) *Fear in Bongoland: Burundian refugees in urban Tanzania*, New York: Berghahn Books.

Vorrath, J. (2008) 'From refugee crisis to reintegration crisis? the consequences of repatriation to (post-) transition Burundi', *L'Afrique des Grands Lacs annuaire 2007–2008*: 109–127.

4 | Sufficiently visible/invisibly self-sufficient: recognition in displacement agriculture in north-western Tanzania

Clayton Boeyink

Introduction

In *Politics of Innocence*, Simon Turner (2010) analogizes the top-down humanitarian logic to a description of a bird's-eye view of Tanzanian refugee camp, Lukole: 'defying the surrounding countryside with its straight rows of blue and white huts, its equally straight roads, and its evenly distributed water stands' (p. 16). If you flew over Nyarugusu camp, also in Tanzania, you would see that half of the camp has thatched roofs, and the other half has metal roofing. On the thatched side are the Congolese who have resided in Nyarugusu since its inception in 1996, and the tin-roofed half of the camp was constructed in 2015 with newly available funds for the influx of Burundian refugees. This is symbolic of the camp's 'place-making projects' (Novak 2007) and explains the economic inequalities between the Congolese and Burundians. Extending Turner's visual analogy, widening your gaze from the camp you would see acres of surrounding farmland. Unseen to the observer, however, are the refugee and migrant mobilities that make up this agrarian system. These agricultural spaces are illegal because it is forbidden under Tanzanian refugee law to leave the camp without official permission. The humanitarian actors respect the sovereignty of Tanzanian law, so farming is also outside the 'visibility field' of the humanitarian government (Feldman 2008). From the top-down view of Tanzanian national law and humanitarian programming, agriculture outside the camp is unrecognized and thus invisible. This means the actors are 'invisibly self-sufficient' beyond the support of international aid. When the field of vision shifts to the actors on the ground, however, there is a refraction of visibility. Recognition occurs between the interactions and relations involved in the buying and selling of land and labour. Refugees and migrants, therefore, must also ensure they are 'sufficiently visible' to market themselves to participate in the agricultural system, yet 'invisible enough' to the authorities of an increasingly hostile state.

The Kigoma region of north-western Tanzania has hosted hundreds of thousands of refugees since colonial rule, and today hosts around 280,000 Burundian and Congolese refugees in three remaining camps: Nyarugusu, Nduta and Mtendeli. Nyarugusu, the primary site of my research, is roughly split by

Congolese and Burundians, whereas Nduta and Mtendeli camps were reopened for the 2015 caseload of Burundian refugees. Immediately surrounding these camps are extensive 'displacement economies' (Hammar 2014) of agricultural systems that amalgamate land rental and labour between Tanzanian host communities, Burundian and Congolese refugees, and Burundian labour migrants. The three camps and agricultural spaces include many displacement experiences and temporalities, or 'place-making projects' (Novak 2007), which inform stereotypes and prejudices that are central to the process of renting land. This chapter analyses the juxtaposition of visibility and invisibility among refugees and migrants in Tanzania since colonialism with a focus on the current conjuncture under President John Magufuli. The question guiding this research is how has visibility and invisibility been imposed upon or produced among the actors in the agricultural systems surrounding the camps, and how does this differ for Congolese refugees and Burundian migrants and refugees over time?

Methodology

The original point of departure for my doctoral research was to explore the shift by the World Food Programme (WFP) from food aid to cash in Nyarugusu refugee camp. My research in Nyarugusu lasted from May to November 2017. In early August, the Tanzanian government abruptly shut down the WFP cash programme, forcing me to change my focus of research (Boeyink 2019). The primary methodology employed is called 'financial diaries' popularized by the book *Portfolios of the Poor* (Collins et al. 2009). My research assistants[1] are residents of the camp, and we met bi-weekly with more than seventy households in Nyarugusu split between Congolese and Burundian families to record their financial transactions for a year. I conducted more than 200 interviews, primarily with camp residents and also the UN, implementing partner NGOs and Tanzanian government officials. Before fieldwork, I was unaware of the extensive agricultural system surrounding the camps as they were not present or glossed over in the current academic and policy literature (WFP 2016; CHS 2016, 2017).

The financial diaries helped me learn about the agricultural system because it was prevalent among many households we interviewed. One day while interviewing a Congolese woman named Furaha, a Burundian labour migrant she employs stopped by to visit. With his consent, I visited the *shamba*[2] on which he was currently working. On the visit, I interviewed twenty-eight Burundian labour migrant men and boys. Shortly after leaving Tanzania, my research assistants conducted interviews with refugee land renters, refugee paid labourers, Burundian labour migrants and multiple Tanzanian landowners participating in this system. I returned in February and May in 2018 for consultancy research on refugee and host community livelihoods with the UNHCR and another UN body researching smallholder Tanzanian farmers near the camps. These consultancies added forty focus group discussions and nearly 200 interviews that deepened my understanding of agriculture in the region. The voices and perspectives of state actors such as the police and Ministry of Home Affairs (MHA) in Nyarugusu are absent because, like the informants in this chapter, I was also trying to be invisible to them. I decided to avoid them so as to not bring attention to myself and thus not be surveilled, put the informants at risk or be barred from conducting further research in the camp as has been known to happen.

Invisibility and recognition

At first glance, there is a clear cause and effect link between a host state imposing invisibility on displaced populations through encampment. These policies are designed for containment, which results in migrants, asylum seekers and refugees, registered or otherwise, enacting invisibility or 'invisibilization' in order to seek opportunities outside the camp. In addition to discussing ethical dilemmas and raising awareness of blind spots in academic and policy involving these populations, this was a main point in the special issues on invisible displacements in the *Journal of Refugee Studies* (Polzer and Hammond 2008). What is missing from this conceptualization of invisibility is the visibility within the lived experience of these populations. A refugee or migrant must be seen to be able to make a livelihood, which is the primary motivation for those who leave the legally protected space of the camp or their home country. Borrowing from the philosophy of recognition, this chapter proposes a different framing of imposed invisibility to include actors such as agricultural labourers and renters who are seen but not recognized (Honneth 2001a). This section briefly reviews how invisibility has been used in forced migration studies, and how the philosophy of recognition can more completely capture the precarious realities of displacement in Tanzania.

In Liisa Malkki's (1995) groundbreaking work, she introduces the nascent field of forced migration studies to 'town refugees' referring to self-settled Burundian Hutus who employ 'strategies of invisibility' in order to live in Kigoma town of Western Tanzania instead of mandated refugee settlements. She argues that town refugees in Kigoma shed their national Burundian and Hutu identities for 'creolized, rhizomatic' or 'cosmopolitan' identities (Malkki 1995: 36). Malkki's contemporary, Gaim Kibreab, also elucidated the steady rise of urban refugees in Africa such as Ethiopians and Eritreans in Khartoum (Kibreab 1996). He disputed Malkki's theory of deterritorialization by asserting that 'town refugees' in Kigoma were being tactically deceptive: 'the strategy of invisibility was an act of defiance and resistance rather than being a manifestation of submissive behaviour or a lost identity' (Kibreab 1999: 394). He described Eritrean refugees in Khartoum strategically toggling between religious identities to their benefit (Kibreab 1999: 397–398). Burundians in Tanzania are still invisibilizing today by obscuring ethnicities, changing names and intermarriage despite many being given Tanzanian citizenship (Daley et al. 2018). It is not my intent to relitigate the identity and belonging debate between Malkki, Kibreab and others. What is largely missing from this discourse on invisibility, however, are the instances where town refugees are necessarily seen; whether they are recognized or not. Kibreab (1996) alludes to this notion, but makes this point in relation to humanitarian policy actors who are more biased toward rural refugees: 'If rural refugees were, in the 1970s, "what the eye did not see", today refugees in many of the African urban centres are what the eye "refuses to see"' (p. 131). This ocular analogy between what the eye sees or refuses to see follows the logic of recognition of philosopher Axel Honneth.[3]

Honneth uses the Hegelian notion that one's self-awareness and value are relationally or 'intersubjectively' constituted. He distils Hegel's theory to assert, 'our idea of justice is essentially connected with a conception as to how, and in what way, individuals recognize one another reciprocally' (Honneth 2001b: 45). The challenge of theorizing recognition, which is the biggest cause of disagreement among scholars, is how to widen recognition to the level of society. The opposite of recognition is disrespect or humiliation, which can occur at the individual or group level by intentionally causing harm or through a social exclusion of legal rights (pp. 46–52). Drawing from Ralph Ellison's novel, *The Invisible Man*, Honneth (2001a) relates the narrator's humiliating experience of being black in America and feeling invisible because people see through him. Honneth interprets this to mean that the narrator is not physically invisible, he is 'cognized' as having a 'spatio-temporal framework as an object with situationally relevant properties' (p. 113). He is figuratively and socially invisible because he is not recognized or validated. In other words, relating to Kibreab's description of urban refugees, invisibility is what the eye *refuses* to see. Invisibility is fundamentally about recognition. Yet there are two definitions of recognition that Honneth often uses interchangeably. One way is to distinctly notice somebody interpersonally, the second is to acknowledge somebody's validity or rights. This distinction can become blurred. For example, urban refugees may desire recognition from host and humanitarian governments, but unlike Ellison's narrator, they seek to be unrecognized by and anonymous to their neighbours and authorities in the city. It is therefore important to clarify to whom and at what level displaced people seek to be visible and recognized, or invisible for safety and protection. This makes Kelly Oliver's (2015) critique of Honneth especially prescient for refugees and migrants in Tanzania: 'recognition is experienced as conferred by the very groups and institutions responsible for withholding it in the first place. In other words, recognition is distributed according to an axis of power that is part and parcel of systems of dominance and oppression' (p. 474). Tanzania's asylum and migration history demonstrate the inconsistency of the state's recognition for refugee and migrant populations.

City-dwelling refugees described by Malkki, Kibreab and others live a daily *modus operandi* or 'habitus' of invisibility. With the impossibility of legal recognition, they strategically enact invisibility in order to camouflage themselves among diverse, dense and transient urban populations to survive. They are cognized in the city by being a part of its fabric, but intentionally avoid recognition as refugees. The forms of invisibility that take place in agricultural settings around the camps in rural Kigoma do not fit these characterizations. For example, Burundians share many physical, cultural and linguistic features with the Ha ethnic group and impersonate them in places like Dar es Salaam. However, to attempt to do the same in the largely homogenous Ha villages surrounding the camps, Burundians would instantly be outed and exposed (Daley et al. 2018: 30–31). When Honneth's analysis of invisibility is applied to refugees and migrants in and around Nyarugusu we see refractions of recognition depending on the level of analysis. On the ground level of the village and *shamba*, refugees cannot blend in because they will always be identified as 'the other' to the host community. However, they achieve a level of recognition by entering into business agreements over land and labour. When shifting to the level of the state and humanitarian programming, they will remain unrecognized and invisible until asylum law in Tanzania changes. Refugees and migrants must find a balance of what I consider '(in)visibility sufficiency'. Invisibility, in this case, is about hiding *enough* from the state and police while being visible *enough* to network and negotiate for land and wages. Also different from urban refugees, migrant and refugee land-renters and labourers are forced into limited moments of invisibility as they transit the imaginary legal veils of the Burundi–Tanzania border and the camp boundaries.

Recognition is not evenly conferred upon all refugees and migrants in Tanzania. This is the case when comparing Congolese and Burundian refugees, first-time and repeat refugees, or between legal Burundian migrants and refugees. These groups with overlapping geographies and temporalities of displacement and mobility resemble the various 'place-making projects' among Afghan refugees in Pakistan (Novak 2007). Place-making projects encapsulate multiple power relations influenced by refugees' multiple displacement registers, temporalities, ethnicities, religious identities and governance structures. 'It is only by unravelling the different projects simultaneously attributing significance to the same people and territory, and their interactions, that the process of place-making can be captured' (Novak 2007: 255). The various place-making projects and the stereotypes that reify them determine degrees of recognition in these agricultural spaces.

Displacement agriculture

In *Displacement Economies in Africa*, Amanda Hammar (2014) and contributors widen the normative conceptual frame of forced displacement to 'observe the emergence of, and articulation between, a range of new physical, social, economic and political spaces, relations, systems and practices that displacement itself was producing' (p. 3). Despite being the poorest region of Tanzania, Kigoma has produced agricultural surpluses in recent years, even during times of droughts throughout East Africa (WFP 2016). Moreover, unlike in neighbouring Burundi, population density is low, and land is abundant in this area and not difficult to obtain for Tanzanians. From this excess, many Tanzanian landowners decide to rent land to refugees to produce 'displacement agriculture'. The full scale of land rental practices around the camps is unclear as there is limited data on this practice. According to the Community Household and Surveillance (CHS) study, 46 per cent of the households from all three camps had access to land. Of this number, 3.8 per cent reported leaving the camp to lease land (CHS 2017: 3). The population of the three camps at the time was nearly 320,000, which suggests 5,500 people have somebody in their household involved in these agricultural rental networks. This number is almost certainly low as many would be reluctant to report illegal activities outside the camp.

There are two main entrances to the camp guarded by Tanzanian police at its south-east and western edges. The camp has no fencing or walls with countless footpaths leading out of the camp. Those leaving the camp simply walk from the nearest border of the camp to their destination. Prospective labourers or renters must make themselves visible to attain livelihoods. They wait along the main roads in the mornings, go to village centres or directly to peoples' farms to inquire about land or wage availability. When I took these same paths to interview labourers, I did not expect to see the large numbers of people walking in and out of the camp with no cover of darkness or bush. Apart from a few households of Burundian migrants described below, most participants in displacement agriculture barely invisibilize themselves at all, yet the consequences for being caught by the police are dire. These movements are literally and figuratively out in the open. All actors interviewed near the camp – refugees, host community members and aid workers – were aware that these practices existed. The only form of evasion was to simply run and hide at the moment a police officer was heard or sighted. With the ubiquity of these farming practices, I was surprised to learn that the majority of those I spoke with had at one time or more been apprehended by the police, which carries harsh consequences. If a refugee or migrant is caught by the police without a work permit, they are often beaten and if unable to pay a large enough bribe they are sent to the local prison for six months where they face further physical punishment and conscripted farm labour. Migrant labourers at times have lost all of their earnings for the year. Moreover, I heard many reports that Tanzanians often extort refugees and migrants they rent land to or hire as labourers by giving incorrect measurements of land, stealing crops or refusing to pay wages with the threat of reporting them to the police.

There are small pockets of Burundian migrants who invisibilize themselves through tactics of seclusion. For instance, five households of Burundian migrants found Tanzanian landowners willing to let them live and work on their land permanently. Knowing they would be detected and not allowed to live and integrate into nearby villages by Tanzanians, these households were sequestered far away from villages or roads to avoid detection. Like other Burundian migrants and refugees, they were displaced from Burundi through lack of access to land or employment and conflict. What is unique about this group is that they brought their wives and families to live with them, rather than returning circularly like other migrants. One of these informants, Moise, explained this choice: 'I decided to live in Tanzania because

Tanzania made me freer than Burundi'. This group was only visible and recognized by their employer who paid the chairman of the nearest village to maintain their invisibility. Recent events show how precarious this secluded invisibility is, however.

On 1 August 2019, Tanzanian military forces conducted an operation in villages where clashes had taken place between Sukuma cattle herders arriving from northern Tanzania and local Ha landowners. According to my research assistant, the military had shoot-to-kill orders and machine-gun fire was heard in nearby Nyarugusu camp. The Sukuma herders lived close to the settled Burundian migrants introduced above. While not the target of the operations, they fled and stayed in villages hidden by their Tanzanian employers or in Nyarugusu camp. This operation had an intense chilling effect on all participants in the displacement agriculture *shambas* and the camp economy. Refugee land renters and labourers were too afraid to leave the camp immediately afterwards. The price of firewood and charcoal gathered outside the camp more than doubled. This event illustrates the precariousness of displacement agriculture. It also shows the speed with which the Tanzanian state can shut down these practices, but prior to this event had chosen not to. It occurred to me that if the local police wanted to crack down and stop these practices, it would not be difficult to do so. Instead, it seems the police were striking a balance between doing random searches as a source of revenue, but without conducting crackdowns to the point of ending the practices altogether. Those involved in this system understood the risks of participating but endured because they had so few alternative options for livelihoods. People with the least amount of recognition from the state and host communities – Burundians in general, and Burundian migrant labourers in particular – endured greater amounts of exposure and risked being visible to the police.

Host community land owners There are high variances in class, motivations, attitudes, costs and profits among all the participants in displacement agriculture in Kigoma. Without the demand and complicity of the Tanzanian host community, displacement agriculture would not exist. In Kasulu District where Nyarugusu is located, 85 per cent of income is estimated to be generated from agriculture, however, nearly 80 per cent live below the poverty line. The need for cash is a large motivating factor for many to rent land to refugees. Others have decided to rent their surplus land to refugees due to friendships formed through interactions at the Common Market shared by Tanzanians and refugees. Nehemiah, who rents to Congolese, describes this relationship:

> We knew each other for a year. Then he asked me if I have a piece of land to rent. Because we were already friends, I decided to give the land. We met when I was selling bananas at the Common Market in camp, then he invited me to visit his family. They hosted me and treated me well. As a gift, I rented them two acres and gave another for free.

Others, like Yakub, rented or gave away land for free out of a humanitarian impulse: 'I saw that some people suffer a lot. Then I decided to rent but usually, I give for free'. For most who rent land to refugees, however, it is more of a neutral business-like transaction where refugee land seekers show up to Tanzanian farms or villages and a price is negotiated.

Refugee land renters Like Tanzanian landowners, refugee land renters encompass a wide spectrum of motivations and outcomes for their farming practices. It is generally understood that more Congolese rent land than Burundians, although this is changing as Burundians' economies are growing. For Burundians to acquire land, they must pay more or travel greater distances outside the camp. One reason for this is that the Congolese are more established economically in Nyarugusu than the Burundians who arrived in 2015. The other reason, which will be explored further below, is due to the negative stereotypes associated with Burundians in the region. Ranging from a half-acre to four, renters pay anywhere from as low as TZS 20,000 (USD 8.65) to as much as TZS 170,000 (USD 73.54) to rent various acreages of land per year. Land has been more expensive recently due to the increased demand after the arrival of the Burundians in 2015 and the decrease in food rations. Many borrow money or take loans to acquire this land. Some only consume what they grow whereas others eat and sell their produce. One household reported earning more than TZS 1,200,000 (USD 520), which is nearly double the GDP per capita for Kigoma (NBS 2012). This was the only source of income for about half of the households renting land. Motivations for renting land include hunger from reduced food rations, or a desire to diversify their food rations to be more culturally appropriate. The majority use Swahili phrases like *maisha magumu* – the 'difficult life' – to describe what drove them to rent land. For these refugees, other livelihoods or self-reliance strategies such as paid employment or petty trade in the market were difficult to obtain. For Kiza, 'I did farming because it is the only thing that I am used to. Others like selling, but this is tough for me. I needed a place where I could cultivate things and generate some money'. This deeply ingrained desire to cultivate was not only borne out of desperation, however. For others like Isaelo and Laurent, it seemed to be a form of 'habitus': 'I am accustomed to cultivating. I do not like staying anywhere without cultivating'. Laurent added, 'I decided to do this because I had always thought that agriculture is the main thing in the life of a human being'.

Refugee labourers Camp refugees who sell their labour for wages to both refugees and Tanzanian landowners have bleaker livelihood prospects than land renters. Eighteen-year-old Christoph recounts, 'I had no education and failed to continue with my studies due to the difficult life. I lost my parents, so I decided to make a little money'. Another Burundian refugee in Nduta described his predicament: 'I normally go there during the hardest moments – especially following ration cuts. I take the risk of going to work in the village even though I know we are not allowed. But what can

I do if my family has nothing to eat? How can they survive without food?' In the best of cases, they enter farm wage labour for a few days or a week to raise capital to supplement their existing business or temporarily address an economic shock. In more desperate situations they work five to six days a week throughout planting and harvesting seasons. The more these labourers have to work outside the camp, the greater their chances of visibility to Tanzanian police. Refugee labourers can find jobs from within the safety of the camp by leveraging their relationship with fellow refugees, through referrals from previous employers, inquiring in public places such as the market, or asking door to door. Others who are less connected must wait along the footpaths leading to the *shambas* or along the main roads to ask potential employers. In the illegal and unregulated space outside the camp, there are high divergences in wage ranges and how wages are determined. For example, people are paid daily rates by the task such as digging, planting and harvesting, or by the crop that they are cultivating. Informants even said that each village has different ranges of pay. While this category of actors is structurally disadvantaged, Burundian migrant labourers face the most precarious and vulnerable position.

Migrant labourers Burundian labour migrants have travelled to Tanzania as farm labourers for generations. Celestine explains, 'it is our nature. We take from our parents and our grandparents growing and cultivating in Tanzania'. Arriving primarily from the border regions, but also as far north as Kirundo and Ngozi provinces, migrants cross over the porous border by foot or bicycle. Some transit only for a couple of months at a time, but others like Moise, mentioned above, have attempted to live permanently in Tanzania. A few migrants return to the same farms each year where they have positive relationships with Tanzanians and refugee land renters, whereas others, like André, 'do not make a choice, I only go where I heard there is a job. I am like a flag blowing in the wind'. This takes people as far as Rukwa region south of Kigoma or Kagera region to the north. They typically do not venture further as they would be more at risk of arrest.

The key difference between many of the migrants and refugees is that unlike many of the re-displaced Burundian refugees who do not have access to land back in Burundi, the migrants I spoke with still own land, which they can effectively access (Purdeková 2016). They cross into Tanzania because they have little or no means for gaining cash or wages in Burundi. Also, unlike the camp-based renters and labourers where women participate as renters and labourers, usually only men engage in the circular labour migrations while the women stay behind. While camp refugees and migrant labourers receive the same ranges of pay, these wages have been markedly depressed since the labour supply skyrocketed with the arrival of Burundians in 2015. Refugees in the camp have overhead expenses such as food, shelter and other services provided by the humanitarian apparatus, thus affording them to take lower wages. This has further lowered prices labourers receive for work. Migrants are also exposed outside the legal and physical protection of the camp and must create makeshift huts on the *shambas* or live in the forest in an attempt to remain invisible to an increasingly hostile state. Moreover, some say migrants are arrested more often than refugees because they often seek jobs in villages where there were more likely to be police patrols rather than utilizing networks in the camp.

History of migration and asylum in Tanzania

Tanzania shows the oscillating nature of state recognition over time. During colonialism, the goal of the state was to visibilize or make legible mobile populations in order to manipulate their labour and control their movements. President Nyerere continued this policy under a more benevolent guise of self-reliance, while simultaneously glorifying anti-colonial freedom fighter refugees for foreign policy gain. The wholesale change to invisibilization came in the 1990s through strict encampment policies. Under President Magufuli there has been an increase in police vigilance patrolling the sources of livelihood *outside* the camp, as well as a crackdown on livelihood opportunities *within* the camp. As a result, refugees and migrants are forced to be invisibly self-sufficient in the face of dwindling aid.

Colonialism: visibility as manipulation To borrow from James Scott (1998), 'legibility is a condition of manipulation' (p. 183). At the heart of the colonial project was the exploitation of African labour, but to benefit from labour, populations had to be made legible or visible to the colonial state and then controlled. To make the populations visible for manipulation, colonial officials created 'tribal' or 'ethnographic maps' (Miller 2011: 18). The colonial state felt high degrees of anxiety with uncontrolled movements of African subjects across and within borders. The colonialists wanted to limit neighbouring Africans or 'alien natives', from 'detribalizing' their simplistic, yet effective indirect rule (Miller 2011: 18–19).

During German and British rule, refugees arrived in Tanganyika[4] from neighbouring colonies to flee excesses of labour conscription. Tanganyika was ruled as German East Africa from the 1880s until becoming a British Mandate in 1919. In 1899, the Portuguese colonists enacted forced labour decrees in Mozambique and thousands fled to south-eastern Tanganyika. These movements from Mozambique to Tanganyika continued under British control into the 1920s and 1930s. Both colonial regimes in Tanganyika tried to block these flows. The Germans and British discouraged mobility *into* Tanganyika because they feared similar movement *away* from Tanganyika. The colonists were anxious their subjects would flee their own coercive labour tactics, which would lead to a decrease in cash crop production as well as in their pool of taxation. 'In other words, controlling migration had bearings upon the profitability of the colonial project itself' (Chaulia 2003: 149).

From the 1930s onward, Western Tanganyika became a 'labour reserve' for large-scale plantations, especially sisal. Many Burundians fled Belgian colonial conscription while being recruited by British Labour Officers. This was a contradictory policy period for the British. On the one hand, there was a need for workers and migrant recruitment. On the other hand, colonial authorities were worried about detribalization in border regions as well as the spread of disease. In response, the British passed the Defence War Evacuees Regulations Act (1946) and the Refugee Control Ordinance (1949), which granted powers to the state to remove refugees and to control movements, and which still provides the spine of refugee policy in Tanzania today (Daley 1989: 111). Host communities quickly welcomed those from neighbouring countries to ease their conditions. Chiefs would recruit migrants and refugees for cheap, sometimes free, labour, or as a buffer for native subjects from harsh colonial labour conditions (Chaulia 2003: 153). Recognition of migrants and refugees was granted insofar as these populations benefited colonial interests and remained confined to designated areas of the country. President Nyerere, while known for his generosity and openness, also exhibited these tendencies.

Nyerere: visibility as foreign policy and exploitation Tanzania's first president, Julius Nyerere, was a revered pan-African statesman, which was the central platform of his foreign policy. Ruling from Independence in 1962 until 1985, part of this reputation stems from his posture toward refugees and asylum seekers. Tanzania's refugee policies under President Nyerere went beyond bringing visibility to the refugees for the sake of legibility as it was under colonialism. These policies projected a bright enough light on refugees to reflect positively on the Tanzanian state to the region and the world. President Nyerere was praised for supporting anti-colonial 'freedom fighters' from the region and the 'Open Door' policy that granted access to land and self-sufficiency for refugees. While bordering policies fit President Nyerere's pan-African ideals initially, this is contrasted by the Tanzanian state's at times heavy-handed tactics of control of and capitalization from refugee labour from Rwandan and Burundian refugees.

Nyerere was at the forefront of anti-colonial resistance by aiding many dissidents from Zimbabwe, South Africa, Namibia, Angola and Mozambique. Nyerere was influential in drafting the Organisation of African Unity (OAU) and the 1969 Convention expanding the rights of refugees beyond the 1951 Refugee Convention to include those fleeing anti-colonial conflicts. Guerrilla movements housed in Tanzania at the time were given extensive freedom of movement and employment (Chaulia 2003: 155–156). This golden age of asylum in Tanzania brought more than a legal recognition for asylum and residence but evoked positive visibility that exalted fleeing anti-colonial dissidents. They were seen as '*wageni*' or 'guests' instead of the colonial moniker of 'aliens' (Miller 2011: 25–27).

The narrative of framing anti-colonial refugees as *wageni* eventually made way to referring to refugees who fled internal war, such as Rwandans and Burundians, as 'settlers'. The term refers to refugees' 'settlement' or de facto 'integration' into the country (Miller 2011). Settlers were seen more ambivalently than the aforementioned freedom fighter refugees, and their reception followed a less altruistic anti-imperialist logic. Refugee recognition in the country, though not as harsh as the colonialists', was dependent on their contribution to the economic development of the peripheries and acquiescence to state control. Settler refugees faced restrictions to move freely within the country.

Rwandan Tutsi refugees began arriving in 1959 due to a violent Hutu uprising and were given land to cultivate for self-reliance without humanitarian aid. The Rwandans rejected this recognition and visibility and resisted any integration such as planting crops or constructing permanent structures due to a desire to return to Rwanda as soon as possible (Gasarasi 1990: 90). Some even destroyed crops in defiance of integration. The Tanzania government took a heavy-handed response by withdrawing rations, closing schools and dispensaries, prohibiting gatherings and bulldozing protesters' huts (Gasarasi 1990: 90–91). Resistance faded over time and eventually resulted in Tanzanian citizenship for 30,000 Rwandan refugees by the early 1970s. President Nyerere has been largely lauded for the provision of land and livelihoods to Rwandan and later Burundian refugees; however, there is considerable economic self-interest and labour exploitation in these settlements. This included bush clearing and the construction of infrastructure such as roads and buildings. Remuneration by Tanzanian authorities and NGOs was as low as one Tanzanian shilling or provided in-kind as food rations, clothing or as a ride in officials' vehicles (Gasarasi 1984: 41–42).

The 1972 caseload of Burundian Hutu bears many echoes of the Rwandan refugee situation, but on a larger scale. Approximately 150,000 Burundian refugees were placed into three locations now known as the 'old settlements': Mishamo, Katumba and Ulyankulu. The land set aside for the settlements was under-cultivated and sparsely populated due to villagers being cleared out as part of President Nyerere's *ujamaa* policy of villagization. Moreover, this land was largely forested marshland that was difficult to farm and inhabited by disease-carrying tsetse flies (Chaulia 2003: 157). As Daley (1989) describes, Burundian refugees were 'vehicles for the exploitation of peripheral areas' (p. 79). Many of the crops prioritized were exportable crops such as coffee and tobacco and were sold by parastatals to benefit the state (Daley 1992). Both the Rwandan and Burundian settlements were successful in becoming food self-reliant within a few years; this meant settlement no longer necessitated humanitarian aid and settlers were eventually offered citizenship. Under Nyerere, refugees were visible because they were useful and capitalizable for the state. The tragic irony is that the settlement model of agricultural self-reliance – though not perfect – which gave Tanzania and President Nyerere plaudits internationally, has given way to one of the strictest asylum policies in Africa since the 1990s.

1990s encampment policy: codifying invisibility Overwhelmed and under-resourced, asylum policy in the 1990s departed from the settlement model to a strict encampment policy. Immense refugee numbers gave refugees and camps in Tanzania visibility to the international community, which resulted in greater funding to the hands of UNHCR, which became responsible for governing camps. This marked the end of local integration and self-reliance practised since Nyerere. This era, however, pushed labour outside the camp where refugees and migrants had to invisibilize or face violent round-ups. By the 1990s, Tanzania was reeling economically and in a debt crisis, which led to the dismantling of the Tanzanian state's control of the economy, public sector and social spending through structural adjustment policies pushed by the International Monetary Fund (IMF) and World Bank. Tanzania was unable to mobilize the resources to care for refugees, paving the way for Tanzania, the UNHCR and NGOs to construct refugee camps near the western peripheries of the country (Daley 1992: 144). These camps were tightly controlled and did not allow for mobility or livelihood activities.

The massive movement of people in the 1990s far surpassed the displacements of the 1960s and 1970s. First, 300,000 Burundians arrived in 1993 with the assassination of President Ndadaye, although most returned within a year. Additional conflict came in the mid-1990s and by 1999 there were again between 200,000 and 300,000 Burundian refugees and an estimated additional 400,000–500,000 living in the country unregistered. The Rwandan genocide in 1994, however, prompted an estimated 2,000,000 Rwandans to flee the country. Six hundred thousand of these refugees arrived in the Kagera region of Tanzania (Landau 2008: 66). Under President Benjamin Mkapa (1995–2005), control and force were used more frequently with refugee populations. Some key events during his presidency include 483,000 Rwandans being forcibly repatriated in 1996 (Whitaker 2002); operations in 1997 by security forces to round-up Burundians living outside camps; and the passing of the 1998 Refugees Act, which stipulated that refugees could not travel more than 4 kilometres outside camps or seek wage-earning activity outside the camps. In 2005, President Jakaya Kikwete ran on a platform to make Tanzania 'refugee-free' by 2010. This led to two vastly different outcomes for Burundians of the 1972 and 1993 caseloads. For the 1972 caseload, around 200,000 Burundian refugees were given Tanzanian citizenship beginning in 2007, which brought international praise reminiscent of President Nyerere's legacy (Kuch 2016). For the remaining Burundians of the 1993 caseload, their fates were less secure. At the end of 2012, the remaining refugees living in Mtabila refugee camp – nearly 40,000 in total – were violently forced to repatriate to Burundi against their will (Hovil and Mbazumutima 2012).

Not yet mentioned is the locus of this research, Nyarugusu camp, and the emergence of Congolese refugees in Tanzania. The camp was created in 1996 due to the First Congo War and grew throughout the Second Congo War. Nyarugusu was the last remaining camp in the country until the Burundian crisis in 2015. Alexander Betts (2013) attempts to disentangle the 'paradoxical response' to why in the 1990s and 2000s

Rwandans and Burundians faced a series of forced repatriations, while Congolese have not experienced the same fate. In short, he concludes that Congolese face hostility from local and regional political actors such as the Regional Commissioner of Kigoma, but the decision for repatriation is decided in Dar es Salaam by the central state. The UNHCR has been relatively successful in forging a relationship with the MHA in Dar es Salaam and advocating against repatriation for Congolese.

2015–present: entrenching invisibility The year 2015 saw two events that further constricted Tanzanian refugee policy: the third wave of displacement of Burundian refugees, and the election of President John Magufuli, whose nationalist 'Tanzania first' policies have shrunk the space of democracy and asylum even further. Since April 2015, more than 400,000 Burundian refugees have fled to neighbouring countries, primarily Tanzania. This exodus, in an acute sense, was caused by President Pierre Nkurunziza overstaying his mandate and instilling an environment of state-sanctioned repression and intimidation by the youth wing of the ruling party known as the *imbonerakure*. Purdeková (2016) argues that rather than a current crisis, the 2015 displacement should be seen in a broader political sense where Burundians are entrenching displacement due to a profound distrust of the state founded over decades. Nyarugusu doubled from 62,000 mostly Congolese to 132,000 residents and resurrected two former camps: Nduta and Mtendeli.

The Burundian influx in 2015 coincided with the election and swearing-in of President Magufuli who came to fame in a rush of populist moves curtailing corruption and challenging international mining corporations. He has since been criticized for 'authoritarian inclinations' (Cheeseman 2016). These authoritarian tendencies include clamping down on free press and opposition, culminating in jailing, disappearing and even assassination attempts on journalists and opposition leaders (Kabendera 2018). What has largely stayed out of the press has been the regime's assault on asylum in the camps. Some of these actions have included: suddenly shutting down a popular WFP cash transfer programme in Nyarugusu in August 2017 (Boeyink 2019); pulling out of the Comprehensive Refugee Response Framework (CRRF), a pilot programme designed to enact more progressive refugee legislation in exchange for greater international aid; and in July 2018 and again in February 2019 the shutdown of the Common Markets shared by refugees and host communities (Van Laer 2018).

These government actions have exacerbated a protracted refugee situation experiencing 'chronic underfunding', which has resulted in food and non-food item reductions and shortages, and lack of health and education services (UNHCR 2019: 8). With severe livelihood and aid constraints, the situation in the camps has impelled many to repatriate to Burundi, which calls into question how 'voluntary' these voluntary returns are (IRRI 2019). Moreover, many of the re-displaced refugees that were violently expelled from Mtabila in 2012 fear that these actions are precipitating another forced repatriation similar to Mtabila. One Burundian man sums up these fears of déjà vu:

> I do not feel like returning to Burundi. I do not have land; I do not have a job. The same causes are still going on. How could you expect me to leave? In 2012, we were forced to go back to Burundi. We lived there for three years and were forced to come back. The same will probably happen.

The restricted refugee environment today bears many similarities to the regressive asylum policies during the 1990s and 2000s, replete with round-ups and forced returns. Refugees, Burundian labour migrants and Tanzanian hosts who have lived through both eras agree that the key difference between then and now is that participating in agriculture outside the camps has been more policed and dangerous under President Magufuli than before. President Magufuli has increasingly criminalized these agricultural spaces, yet livelihood opportunities are continually being squeezed in the camps and in Burundi. This is causing a pincer movement forcing people into displacement agriculture to be invisibly self-sufficient when self-reliance in the camp is nearly impossible.

Place-making in Kigoma

Nyarugusu is essentially two camps within one. There is the Congolese side or a 'protracted refugee camp' where Congolese have resided since 1996, and the Burundian side, or 'emergency refugee camp', considered a 'blank slate' economy (Betts et al. 2017: 140). By many wellbeing metrics, Congolese refugees are faring better than Burundian refugees in Tanzania. For example, in Nyarugusu in 2016, Congolese refugees only had 19 per cent in 'asset very poor' category and 4 per cent in 'asset rich' compared to 75 per cent of Burundians in 'asset very poor' and none in the 'asset rich' category (CHS 2016: 13). Congolese have better measurements than Burundians in the Coping Strategies Index, food consumption score, Household Dietary Diversity, livelihoods metrics, and per capita expenditures (CHS 2017). The simplest explanation for Congolese prosperity over Burundians is that many have lived in Nyarugusu since 1996 and have had longer to establish networks. Since 2012, nearly 30,000 Congolese have been resettled from Nyarugusu to the US, Canada and other countries (UNHCR 2019: 5). This leads to remittances being sent to friends and family remaining in Nyarugusu, which has strengthened the camp economy.

According to WFP estimations, 60–80 per cent of the most recent 2015 arrivals have been 're-displaced' from the civil war in the 1990s or as far back as the genocide in 1972 (Purdeková 2016: 7). Many of these refugees who returned to Burundi faced extreme economic hardship primarily because they lost access to their land while in exile. Some informants explained that they used the political crisis as a pretext to flee the poverty of Burundi to Tanzania even before they faced intimidation and persecution. People left with the few resources they possessed, and most said they had to spend what they had to pay for transportation or payments to police or *imbonerakure* on the journey to Tanzania. Upon arrival, they faced inadequate housing and a cholera outbreak, and the capital people had was spent on buying food or paying for medical supplies. Most Burundians did not have the capital to start businesses – the main reason Burundians sell their labour on farms outside the camp. Conversely, Congolese rent land from Tanzanians at higher rates, and it is rare for Congolese to work as paid labourers on the farms. Economic stratification is not the only explanation for these outcomes, however, as a Burundian man explained to me: 'There are Burundians who rent land, but not very many. Congolese have been in the region for longer and have relationships with Tanzanians. It is more about relationships to get land than just having money'. In seeking to better understand how these relationships are formed, I found that stereotypes play a critical role.

A Burundian man in Mtendeli camp gives a telling illustration of these stereotypes:

> If a Congolese and a Burundian are on a bus and the police stop them, then a Burundian will be taken off and the Congolese can continue on. Burundi has a bad image in Tanzania. The bad image is attached for a long time. Burundians are highly attached to the war from before. All are labelled as bad or dangerous people.

Two labels attached to Burundians persist, that Burundians are untrustworthy thieves prone to violence, or that they are hardworking and capable farmers. The former stigmatization is forcing Burundian land renters further away from the camp to find landowners willing to rent land to them. For the latter categorization as strong labourers, this is seen both positively and pejoratively from their history of labour in the country. Malkki (1995) analyses 'mythico-histories' of Mishamo that residents use to make sense of protracted exile. Prominent in these cosmologies were the sentiments of having their cultivation exploited. Malkki recounts these sentiments: 'We are the granaries of the Tanzanians … We feed all the poor regions of Tanzania … We have become their slaves. We have been given a pet name here, "the tractors". They benefit by us' (pp. 119–120). Felix da Costa (2017) noted that Burundians are still being called 'our tractors' by Tanzanians (p. 20). This also helps them to find employment as labourers because they are said to finish the work faster than Tanzanians.

In relation to Burundians, Congolese are seen as their opposite – as trustworthy and honest, but lazy. A Tanzanian describes, 'Congolese do not do labour for others. They are not strong like Burundians. Congolese like soft jobs and music. They like to dress smart even if they do not have any money'. This, in turn, has been internalized by Congolese because even among those who live in extreme poverty in the camp, it is rare to find Congolese paid farm labourers. While stereotypes are highly problematic on many levels, they are born from a history of place-making in the region and must not be dismissed too hastily as they form the basis of relationships and livelihood outcomes among the actors in and around the camp.

Conclusion

Invisibility has been conceptualized in forced migration studies with a singular lens that does not capture the entire experience of displaced populations. Scholars have focused on instances where displaced people are invisible to policy-makers and academics or, due to restrictive policies, must enact strategies of invisibility to avoid detection. If people are not recognized or validated by the state at the top, they avoid being recognized or detected from below. What is missing from these accounts is the mirrored edge of visibility in Tanzania. During colonialism and immediately after, visibility was the goal of migration and refugee policy to benefit the state. Strict encampment during the 1990s and increasingly today under President Magufuli created the need for refugees to invisibilize or blend into spaces like towns and cities because refugee life is only recognized in camps.

The same top-down policies that impel invisibilization in urban settings do not produce uniform invisibility in rural Kigoma, however. Local integration for refugees and migrants is more difficult when everybody knows their neighbours and outsiders are recognized and unwanted. The only possibility to invisibilize is to live in seclusion like the Burundian migrants who rely on their Tanzanian employers to keep them hidden. To rent land or sell labour in the *shambas* surrounding the camps, people must have connections or make themselves sufficiently visible out in the open along heavily trafficked roads and footpaths, in villages, or at the farms. People who have no other access to incomes in the camps or in Burundi must spend more time at the farms and are at greater risk of encountering police. This is experienced more by Burundians in general, and Burundian migrants in particular, compared to Congolese refugees due to the costs of re-displacement, chronic poverty and regional prejudices and stereotypes. For those involved in displacement agriculture who are forced to be invisibly self-sufficient beyond humanitarian aid, visibility is less enacted than it is *endured*. As less-than-voluntary repatriations are increasing in this restrictive political and economic environment, it appears that endurance is wearing thin.

Notes

1 My utmost thanks go to Kaskil Ibrahim, Dieudonne Makila, Upendo Upson, Safi Mgeni, Fredy Kaganga, Nibigiri Thamarie and Niyokwizera Levis for their eagerness and insights making this research possible.

2 *Shamba* is Swahili for farm.

3 Thanks to Lotte Pelckmans for this suggested source.

4 Tanganyika was the name of the mainland of modern Tanzania before Zanzibar and Pemba islands unified in 1964.

References

Betts, A. (2013) *Survival Migration, Failed Governance and the Crisis of Displacement*, Ithaca, NY: Cornell University Press.

Betts, A., L. Bloom, J. Kaplan and N. Omata (2017) *Refugee Economies: Forced displacement and development*, Oxford: Oxford University Press.

Boeyink, C. (2019) 'The "worthy" refugee: cash as a diagnostic of "xeno-racism" and "biolegitimacy"', *Refuge*, 35(1): 61–71.

Chaulia, S. (2003) 'The politics of refugee hosting in Tanzania: from open door to unsustainability, insecurity and receding receptivity', *Journal of Refugee Studies*, 16(2): 147–166.

Cheeseman, N. (2016) 'Deconstructing the Magufuli miracle in Tanzania', *Democracy in Africa*, 16 October. Retrieved 15 April 2019 from: http://democracyinafrica.org/deconstructing-the-magufuli-miracle-in-tanzania/.

Collins, D., J. Morduch, S. Rutherford and O. Ruthven (2009) *Portfolios of the Poor*. Princeton, NJ: Princeton University Press.

Community Household and Surveillance (CHS) (2016) *Refugee Camps in North Western Tanzania Community Household and Surveillance (CHS)*. Protracted Relief and Recovery Operation (PRRO). United Nations Development Assistance Plan (UNDAP).

—— (2017) *Community Household and Surveillance (CHS) in North Western Tanzania*. Protracted Relief and Recovery Operation (PRRO). United Nations Development Assistance Plan (UNDAP).

Daley, P. (1989) 'Refugees and underdevelopment in Africa: the case of Barundi refugees in Tanzania', PhD Thesis, University of Oxford.

—— (1992) 'The politics of the refugee crisis in Tanzania', in H. Campbell and H. Stein (eds), *Tanzania and the IMF: The dynamics of liberalization*, Boulder, CO: Westview Press.

Daley, P., N. Kamata and L. Singo (2018) 'Undoing traceable beginnings', *Migration and Society*, 1(1): 22–35.

Feldman, I. (2008) 'Refusing invisibility: documentation and memorialization in Palestinian refugee claims', *Journal of Refugee Studies*, 21(4): 498–516.

Felix da Costa, D. (2017) '"You may think he is not a human being": refugee and host community relations in and around Nduta and Mtendeli refugee camps, Western Tanzania', Danish Refugee Council.

Gasarasi, C.P. (1984) *Tripartite Approach to the Resettlement and Integration of Rural Refugees in Tanzania*. Uppsala: Scandinavian Institute of African Studies.

—— (1990) 'The mass naturalization and further integration of Rwandese refugees in Tanzania: process, problems and prospects', *Journal of Refugee Studies*, 3(2): 88–109.

Hammar, A. (2014) *Displacement Economies in Africa: Paradoxes of crisis and creativity*, London: Zed Books.

Honneth, A. (2001a) 'Recognition: invisibility: on the epistemology of "recognition": Axel Honneth', *Aristotelian Society Supplementary Volume*, 75(1): 111–126.

—— (2001b) 'Recognition or redistribution?', *Theory, Culture & Society*, 18(2–3): 43–55.

Hovil, L. and T. Mbazumutima (2012) 'Tanzania's Mtabila Camp finally closed', *Pambazuka News*. Retrieved 14 March 2017 from: www.pambazuka.org/governance/tanzania's-mtabila-camp-finally-closed.

International Refugee Rights Initiative (IRRI) (2019) '"They don't even understand why we fled": the difficult path to reintegration in Burundi'.

Kabendera, E. (2018) 'Tanzania: the tentative but rising resistance to Magufuli's repression', *African Arguments*, 14 August. Retrieved 15 April 2019 from: https://africanarguments.org/2018/08/14/tanzania-tentative-rising-resistance-magufuli-repression/.

Kibreab, G. (1996) 'Eritrean and Ethiopian refugees in Khartoum: what the eye refuses to see', *African Studies Review*, 39(3): 131–178.

—— (1999) 'Revisiting the debate on people, place, identity and displacement', *Journal of Refugee Studies*, 12(4): 384–410.

Kuch, A. (2016) 'Naturalization of Burundian refugees in Tanzania: the debates on local integration and the meaning of citizenship revisited', *Journal of Refugee Studies*, 30(3): 468–487.

Landau, L. (2008) *The Humanitarian Hangover: Displacement, aid, and transformation in Western Tanzania*, Johannesburg: Wits University Press.

Malkki, L. (1995) *Purity and Exile: Violence, memory and national cosmology among Hutu refugees in Tanzania*, Chicago, IL: University of Chicago Press.

Miller, C. (2011) 'Who are the "permanent inhabitants" of the state? Citizenship policies and border controls in Tanzania, 1920–1980', PhD Thesis, University of Iowa.

National Bureau of Statistics (NBS), Tanzania (2012) Retrieved from: http://tanzania.opendataforafrica.org/TZSOCECD2016/social-economics-of-tanzania-2016?region=1000170-kigoma&indicator=1002980-gdp-per-capita-at-current-prices-tshs.

Novak, P. (2007) 'Place and Afghan refugees: a contribution to Turton', *Journal of Refugee Studies*, 20(4): 551–578.

Oliver, K. (2015) 'Witnessing, recognition, and response ethics', *Philosophy and Rhetoric*, 48(4): 473–493.

Polzer, T. and L. Hammond (2008) 'Invisible displacement', *Journal of Refugee Studies*, 21(4): 417–431.

Purdeková, A. (2016) '"Barahunga Amahoro – they are fleeing peace!" The politics of re-displacement and entrenchment in post-war Burundi', *Journal of Refugee Studies*, 30(1): 1–26.

Scott, J. (1998) *Seeing Like a State: How certain schemes to improve the human condition have failed*, New Haven, CT and London: Yale University Press.

Turner, S. (2010) *Politics of Innocence: Hutu identity, conflict and camp life*. Oxford and New York: Berghahn.

UNHCR (2019) *Tanzania Country Refugee Response Plan*, Regional Refugee Coordination Office, Nairobi.

Van Laer, T. (2018) '"There is pressure on us": Burundian refugees in Tanzania pushed to return', *African Arguments*, 21 August. Retrieved 15 April 2019 from: https://africanarguments.org/2018/08/21/pressure-burundi-refugees-tanzania-pushed-return/.

Whitaker, B.E. (2002) 'Changing priorities in refugee protection: the Rwandan repatriation from Tanzania', *Refugee Survey Quarterly*, 21(1–2): 328–344.

World Food Programme (2016) *Market Assessment: Nyarugusu Refugee Camp, United Republic of Tanzania*. Cash Based Transfer Market Assessment: May 2016. World Food Programme.

Section 2

State in/visibilities

5 | War refugees in Northern Cameroon: visibility and invisibility in adapting to the informal economy and the 'tolerant' state

Trond Waage

Introduction

In 2013, the Central African Republic (CAR) was ravaged by a coup, the fifth since the country's independence. The country has since then experienced waves of violent attacks on villages and hamlets by various rebel groups. The population has adapted to the continuous violence by hiding in the surrounding bush or fleeing. Those who flee to Cameroon use migratory routes that in former times were used for seasonal migration. There are many challenges for poor refugees in Cameroon without identity documents and difficult access to income. The incoming refugees depend on each other to find housing and find their way around the city. They are building networks that support each other, coming from the same region and ethnic group in north-west CAR. In these settings, mother tongue and regional belonging are important. Migrants have to deal with the many corrupt civil servants, and they have to adapt to the informal economy in the city through establishing relations to possible employers. In Ngaoundéré there are rumours saying that Centrafricains cannot be trusted, that they are violent thieves and do not do proper jobs. To get income through day-jobs they have to hide their ethnic and national identity. Formal authorities are a constant threat demanding money, and even imprisoning people without identification documents. Those who have come (*les venants*) have to find the balance between visibility and invisibility to adapt to the complex social and cultural swirl on the Adamaoua plateau.

I have been collaborating with researchers and universities in northern Cameroon since the 1990s and have seen the region change and the cities grow. In 2015, I returned to Ngaoundéré to screen my new film *Les Mairuuwas* (Waage 2015b), depicting young men who for various reasons had come to town trying to find a way of living, using the water transportation in a Muslim Fulani neighbourhood as a starting point for income activity. I then observed two major changes since my last fieldwork: first, the open landscape behind where I lived with my family five years earlier, which then was a combination of farmland and 'wilderness', was now turned into a neighbourhood with thousands of inhabitants. And in the down-town neighbourhood I have known for twenty years, and the arena for the film, the atmosphere had changed.

There were many newcomers around the neighbourhood. The 'Mairuuwas' that I had known for years, and who had taken years to manoeuvre into social relations where they could obtain day-jobs or more or less stable employment connected to nearby households, were now being contacted several times a day by refugees in need of work. The water post, a place for looking up information and possible contacts, was constantly visited by newly arrived boys and men from CAR. The 'Mairuuwas' had to protect their scarce work possibilities. The neighbourhood had changed. I could sense the scepticism towards the newcomers; rumours said they were violent, lazy and not trustworthy. The results of civil war in CAR, which started two years earlier, could be seen and felt in Ngaoundéré some 330 km from the border.

I started empirically following some of these newcomers, like Jean, to the households on the outskirts of the city where he lived with other Centrafricains. There was a combination of friends and family members who lived in a house belonging to an acquaintance who spent the rainy season in a village where he cultivated crops. After cultivation he would return and reclaim his house. Jean spent much time trying to get updated news from his countrymen in and around Ngaoundéré, finding a new place to stay, learning about news from home and job possibilities. I followed him to the village where other family members were living, and in the various work situations he and other men in the network engaged in. Using what Gobo and Molle (2017: 110) call a snowball sample I followed him into this growing network of people, first for some months in 2015, then again in 2016 and 2019. I have been filming these many situations, to get people in the network to understand my position and to encourage them to collaborate in this project. Visual tools were also used to achieve a reflexive discovery process (Grimshaw and Ravetz 2009). The presence of a camera(man) would be a catalyst for discussions, and images would be 'sites of meaning potential' (MacDougall 1998) where discussions on the meaning of things and situations would develop. Gradually I realized that Jean's network mostly consisted of family members and neighbours from Pagoua and the Ngondai Subdivision in CAR who had come to Cameroon forced by the violence back home, and who lived by day-jobs (bricklaying, brickmaking, renovation, transportation and other services) in the dry season and cultivation in surrounding villages in the rainy season.

This chapter empirically describes this network of Centrafricains of Mboum Panna origin in which Jean and his cousin Clara are the centre of attention. The next section introduces the reader to the internationally neglected conflict in CAR. It recounts some of the stories I have been told by migrants about their dramatic flight, escaping and hiding from various rebel groups in CAR and their travel over the border to the Adamaoua province in Cameroon, hiding from roadblocks and police officers. Tens of thousands of refugees have come to Ngaoundéré since 2013. The UNCHR reports state that there are 22,000 urban refugees from CAR in Cameroon (2020). I would claim that in Ngaoundéré alone the number of urban refugees of Centrafricain origin is more than double the UN's official numbers for urban refugees in the country as a whole.

The following section describes how these war refugees adapt to their new lives. Their coping strategies and identity management will be understood in relation to what I see as two important organizing aspects of this society: the ethnic organization of the informal economy and the persistent corruption among civil servants. These refugees have to adapt to the labour market. Women try to start some kind of sale–resale activity, men are mostly involved in seasonal manual work. The informal economy depends on job provider–job taker relations, which function in a hierarchical, trust-based patron–client system (Waage 2015a). This is a system with long historical lines, which symbolically is constructed around ethnic and religious markers. The war in CAR and the resulting degradation of its people's reputation as violent and distrustful has led to complicated access to jobs. Refugees are forced to maintain a low profile, make their Centrafricaine identity invisible and perform as a certain category of Cameroonians. This is done by mastering a series of cultural codes, speaking Fulani and French, and claiming origins from villages on the Cameroonian side of the border.

Secondly, there are two logics which characterize the Cameroonian state important for this study. The first is the locally named 'l'administration tolérante' (French: the tolerant administration) with a logic that can be summarized as 'as long as there is no problem there is no problem-attitude', and second the same administration is known to 'makes a fetish of the rule of law' (Comaroff and Comaroff 2006: vii). It is a public secret in Ngaoundéré that the outskirts of the city and their more rural surroundings are populated by clandestine migrants, people without papers. It is a partial and wilful blindness that creates invisibility. For civil servants, such as the gendarmes, police, customs and immigration personnel, these clandestine migrants represent a continuous flow of opportunities for possible income, because if someone does not have their papers, they have to meet the consequences.

This chapter will analyse war refugees as conscious actors that have to adapt within an ethnically organized informal economy where they meet corrupt state representatives.

These refugees are part of lively neighbourhoods dominated by Centrafricains, where they speak their mother tongues Mboum-Panna and Songo (the official language in CAR) and share news about issues such as the situation back home, work possibilities in town (in the dry season) and access to land in surrounding villages (in the rainy season). A solidarity has developed among refugees coming from these territories as they have undergone much violence and they help each other confront the various challenges in this new situation. In their relations with Cameroonians in both the informal economy and the formal state, invisibility is an asset. Evasion and the under-communication of ethnic and national identity are situational and can be seen as an innovative transformation of identity markers (language, behaviour codes, place of birth, etc.) that permits access to the informal economy, both in town and in the nearby villages. To succeed in the informal economy, they have to be mobile, both in Ngaoundéré and in travelling to the various villages where they cultivate fields in the rainy season. The many roadblocks in and around the town make them develop strategies not to be seen as they travel. Processes of in/visibility can be understood as products of social contingency. Life is uncertain, and invisibilization, laying low, is productive as it is used 'when negotiating uncertainty and act[s] as [a] source for imagining the future and hope' (Cooper and Pratten 2015: 2). Depending on the situation they either under- or over-communicate markers linked to their ethnic identity. Processes of invisibility and visibility are key drivers in refugees' situated adaptions. It is the claim of this chapter that the processes of situational invisibilization are an important reason for the reproduction of ethnic hierarchies within the informal economy and the stronghold that corruption has in this city and region. These refugees have many uprooting experiences. But with their socio-economic adaptations to the informal economy in Cameroon they continue to live according to traditional ways of living.

'The crisis in Central African Republic is the worst conflict that people don't know anything about'[1]

To understand how clandestine refugees adapt when coming to Cameroon, we need to know some of the recent violent history in the Central African Republic. Far too little has been written about the ongoing war in CAR, and even less has been told about how its population copes with the extreme violence, poverty and displacement. The ongoing crisis is invisibilized as it has been given low priority by the international community. Even in the Cameroonian newspaper *L'oeil de Sahel*, covering northern Cameroon, the CAR conflict is given little attention. A recent UNICEF report (2018) states that the war in CAR is a 'neglected, dangerous and deteriorating crisis … where 2 of 3 children require humanitarian assistance'.

I often find that information given through media and research reports deviates from the statements refugees give. Names of rebel groups and where they are in control can have three different versions depending on whether I speak with refugees, CAR officials or read media reports. A trustworthy and complete overview of CAR's recent history is hard to obtain; violence is spread over a vast territory with low population density and low state presence in addition to a continuous diversifying of conflict dynamics and rebel groups.

In late 2012, a rebel group called Seleka (the Songo word for freedom) invaded the country from Sudan and Chad. They were predominantly Sudanese and Chadian ex-combatants,with some Central Africans, gathered by Michel Djotodia and other Central African elites to overthrow the sitting president, Bozize, who himself came to power through a military coup in 2003–2004 (Lombard 2016). The Seleka first invaded the north-west region, with its diamond and gold fields, then they took one town and one village after the other on their way to Bangui, the capital. The Seleka soldiers attacked homesteads, villages and towns, where they robbed, raped and burned villages. In the first period they robbed the rich, later everyone. Many trucks with their loot were loaded and taken to Chad. Seleka members were predominantly Muslims, but it is not a sect or dogmatic organization such as Boko Haram in Nigeria/Niger/Cameroon.

Bangui fell into the hands of Seleka in March 2013. The Christian president Bozize escaped in a helicopter only minutes before the city was taken (Carayannis and Lombard 2015). As Seleka approached the capital, the weak CAR army disappeared. People where angry over being dispossessed, yet again, by Muslim foreigners. In 2003 CAR had been loitered by Muslim militia from Chad (Lombard 2016). Leading officers from the resigned army joined the building of a counter movement, the Anti-Bellaka (Bissakonou 2015).[2] Poorly equipped in modern Western weapons, armed with machetes, traditional black powder guns (*'fuciles artisanales'*) and powerful witchcraft, making them invulnerable to bullets, their response was extremely violent. Coming from Chad and Sudan, Seleka soldiers were slim, dark and tall. Most of them spoke neither Songo nor French (official languages in CAR). The Anti-Bellaka were predominately from native groups in the forest, animists, wearing protective amulets. Being less uniformed, they could easily mingle with the general population.

The two fighting groups were not unified entities: at various points in this, by now, more than seven-year-long war, each divided into several sub-groups. Rebel groups are now many and their ideologies are, at the best, blurred. In 2013 France launched a military operation, 'Sangari', in CAR (lasting to 2016) in which they disarmed the Selekas. Without weapons they became helpless when confronted with the rage of the Anti-Bellaka, ending in a mass slaughter of Selekas.

Since then the landscape of violent groups has diversified and become even more complex. In the Khartoum peace negotiations on the CAR conflict in January 2019, fourteen rebel groups were represented.

MINUSCA (United Nations Multidimensional Integrated Stabilization Mission in the Central African Republic), the UN intervention force, had more than 14,000 troops on the ground but it failed to disarm all militia groups and there were fresh clashes in different parts of the country (*Le Monde Afrique* 2018). Currently, MINUSCA consists of a contingent of Bangladeshi soldiers operating in the north-western part of the country. These troops are now said, by the refugees in Cameroon, to be the only stabilizing factor in the north-west, contributing to security and stability where they operate. What most reports seem to agree upon is that to understand the conflict as one along Muslim–Christian divide is far too simplistic. The main reason cited for taking up arms was fear of attacks[3] and ensuring one's own security. In 2017, the violence reached new heights, and the UN warned of genocide.[4] In 2018 it calmed the conflicts down but 2019 has seen new groups and new brutal violence, frequently between cattle herders and farmers over land issues. More than 1 million Central Africans are displaced, which is 20 per cent of the population. Several reports claim that the complicity of European and Chinese logging and mining companies is funding the CAR conflict (Global Witness 2015).

Many are those who can tell dramatic stories about how their village or homestead was attacked by rebels. When asked who the attackers were their answers would be: 'It was the rebels, right!' They do not know whether they were Seleka, Anti-Bellaka or any other groups. Many do not know the reason for the war, and do not know the difference between the groups. They simply know that they are all involved in looting, robbing and raping, controlling gold and diamond mines, and setting up roadblocks along main roads in the areas they control.

Leaving CAR: forced migration in historical routes

Although these refugees react to violent chaotic incertitude in the Central African Republic, their routes of flight follow incorporated patterns of seasonal mobility. Throughout the Chad basin and the Adamaoua region, there is a long history of circular migration (Issa 2012; Domo 2010). In the dry season, after the harvest, in times of hardship, or at certain periods of their lives, young people would move towards urban centres to earn some money, often to prepare for marriage or, more recently, in order to pay school fees and buy agricultural implements, bicycles and other necessities. When the work period was over, the migrant would go back home to his/her village. However, in recent years circular migration has increasingly become one-way migration (Solé et al. 2016; Waage, 2015a). In Ngaoundéré today there are many Centrafricains that settled after the violent coup in CAR back in 2003, just as there are many Chadians in Ngaoundéré who came during periods of violence in the 1990s.

De Bruijn (2007), in her article on the 'culture of migration' in Chad, underlines the relationship between mobility, resources (of various kinds) and society for studies of mobile populations. The decision to leave is understood on the basis of a combination of personal histories, interpretation of circumstances and of the moment. Most Central Africans who have come to the Adamaoua region since 2013 have done so due to the armed attacks by rebel groups on their home villages and the difficult living conditions they have caused. However, their choices of when to leave, what routes to take, how to orient themselves, depend on a whole series of variables such as former migration experience, access to information, relational repertoire along the migration route and economy. Knowledge and relations through past experiences inform migration routes.

The many stories about why people are fleeing from CAR are similar: the village is attacked by 'rebels', arriving during daytime on pick-ups (when the men and most women are in the fields), armed with automatic rifles, stealing everything of value (house belongings, cars, motorcycles and animals) and setting thatched roofs on fire – causing of panicked villagers to flee. In the following section I will present some different migration trajectories on this backdrop.

Sam was out hunting when his village was attacked. Coming back, he found his house in ruins. He searched for his wife and other family members for several days. Unable to trace his wife, and after sincere consideration, he left for Cameroon and the city where he used to work before marrying. Clara, Sam's wife, was in the village when the rebels attacked. She grasped her little daughter in panic and fled into the forest. Arriving at her uncle's homestead the next morning, she found him and his wife dead. In tears and profound despair, she didn't know where to hide and what to do. After a few days, afraid of returning to their home, she found herself with two women she knew, deciding to walk towards the Cameroonian border. With no functioning mobile phone network, she could not know, but only hope that her husband might be there. On their six-day walk to the border, they survived by eating wild fruit and green leaves. In Toboro, the border town, she found some temporary work, until she had enough to pay for the bus ticket to Ngaoundéré.

Asta was a young teenager when she had to flee. There were shootings everywhere. The village was on fire. She left in a panic. Her mother was in hospital giving birth, and Asta had responsibility for her five younger siblings. Scared to death she fled with a friend and they found their way together. Years later, Asta would talk about how bad she felt about leaving her siblings behind, without knowing what happened to them.

Jean's father was kidnapped by the Seleka. His family had to sell all their belongings (the livestock, the motorcycle and most of the kitchen utensils) to ransom him. The Seleka later killed Jean's elder sister and her husband. When violence escalated, Jean, who was working in Cameroon at the time, went back to CAR and brought his parents and his two nephews over the border along with eight other family members.

Many of the attacked villagers hid in the forest, returning to their homesteads after a while, under the condition of accepting the taxes imposed by the rebels. Monthly taxes (a goat, a cow or chickens) and other burdens where imposed on the villagers. Jean's brother Abel endured in his village for five years under these conditions, till 2018, trying to save his remaining cattle. When a new rebel group took control over his home area they increased taxes. Abel told them that he had lost all his animals due to years of heavy taxes. Spies where sent by rebels and they found his herd. His first wife was shot dead when she tried to prevent them from taking the animals. Abel sent for Jean and another brother, both settled in Cameroon, to come and help them flee. Getting small children through the wooded savannah, outside the rebel-controlled main roads, required knowledge about the routes. With eleven young children, below fifteen years of age (from a polygamous marriage), there are few opportunities in the city. After a three-week walk they came to the UN refugee camp.

Families with elderly members and many small children in particular do not have the capacity to flee. The long walk through the forest is demanding. They would hide in the bush. Clara's older brother with eighteen family members spent more than three years in the bush, in constant fear of snakes and predators, with hardly any accessible clean water, scarce food and frequent malaria. They would once in a while search for the undercover weekly market in certain villages to get salt and soap.

Sam's brother had been moving back and forth between the forest and the village, depending on where the rebels are and the level of violence, over a period of five years. Finally, when he gave in, he came with his family to Ngaoundéré, searching to meet the Alhaji (the businessman) that he had worked with in his youth.

All the people I present in this chapter are from the Pagoua and the Ngondai Subdivision in the north-west of CAR; both prefectures are closer to the Chadian border than to the Cameroonian. They have not fled in panic, to the nearest secure area.[5] Rather, these migrants' mobility is informed by interpreting the options of staying behind and calculating the possibilities seen by fleeing. Mobility, even in extremely violent circumstances, is embedded in cultural and social patterns that have historical links. In these links they see opportunities.

The urban hub of Ngaoundéré: ethnic organization of the informal economy

Ngaoundéré, the fast-growing city, where most of these refugees seem to be heading, is situated on the Adamaoua plateau in northern Cameroon. It became the capital of the Adamaoua region during the Fulani-organized jihad at the turn of the nineteenth century. Within a few decades, Ngaoundéré became one of the most important centres in northern Cameroon (Burnham 1996). The wealth and power of Ngaoundéré was largely built through the practice of slavery. In the name of a holy war, the Fulani sought to convert people through violent raids. In reality, the raids were carried out to capture slaves (Roitman 2006; Schilder 1994). Slaves did most of the manual and domestic work in Ngaoundéré. In 1950, three out of five inhabitants were slaves, vassals or servants (Froelich 1954: 25). The city was created by and is still developed by immigrants.

Through the nineteenth and twentieth centuries, a hierarchical system with clearly defined social positions and notions of personhood was established in Ngaoundéré and throughout the Adamaoua plateau. The basic division was between slaves and free men. Typically, the latter were Muslims, cattle owners and merchants; they were Fulani, Kanuri or Hausa and lived in town. They claimed to be guided by the values of *pulaaku*[6] and Islam, to be pure, proud and independent. Some were elected to be members of the sultan's court. The slaves taken by the sultan's men came from the different agricultural populations around the Adamaoua plateau,[7] stretching into the area which is now the Central African Republic. They came from the 'un-civilized bush' (*ladde* in Fulani) and served as herders, cultivators, guards and household servants. Their masters considered them non-believers, dirty, rude and unworthy of personhood, and without *pulaaku*, due to their shameful behaviour.

When Cameroon became independent, the sultan lost his economic and military power, public taxes were introduced and slavery forbidden, and gradually, the Muslim populations lost their privileged positions. The once large cattle herds diminished, as their owners had to pay taxes and salaries for the work that slaves previously had done. The state economy went into crisis in the mid-1990s, when the CFA currency was devaluated by 50 per cent, due to IMF requisitions. The economic crisis had at least two consequences. It forced Fulani men to do work that had formerly been perceived as degrading and violating the norms of *pulaaku*. Secondly, civil servants lost up to 75 per cent of their salaries and had to find new ways of earning money. The new uncertainty was productive (Cooper and Pratten, 2015) in the sense of forcing people to be creative. The civil servants' reaction to the loss of income is one of several explanations for the corruption in the country (Oliver de Sardan 2015). A kind of creative fending (*débrouillardise*) was developed and widely spread (Waage 2006); people had to actively search for positions and relations where they could make a living.

As one of the many fast-growing medium-sized cities in Africa south of the Sahara, Ngaoundéré[3] attracted immigrants from all directions: in addition to the situation in CAR, the Boko Haram insurgency in the north and the Anglophone crisis in the south-west contributed to this blend. The city has developed from a social space with a more or less well-known ethnic blend to a super-diverse city, with a multidimensionality that has expanded 'above and beyond' what was previously there (Meissner and Vertovec 2015). As in many other urban settings around the world ethnic boundaries have become fuzzy, but the distinction between the Muslim Fulani and the Christian Animist 'others' persists. The distinction between those with and without *pulaaku*.

Ngaoundéré has shown an impressive ability to host many new urban citizens. This capacity is due neither to industrialization nor to extensive growth in the administrative sector, but to the steadily expanding informal economy. As Ferguson (2010) has shown, the majority of the population in African cities are not likely to become wage labourers. They will need social assistance or find ways to fend for themselves. This is done within the informal economy. It is the only legitimate way to earn money. In former work I have shown how the successful among the rural children and youth coming to Ngaoundéré are those who have managed to adapt to the former slave role and establish trust-based work relations to Muslim women (Waage 2015a). Trust in patron–client relations are founded on the silent acceptance of the work conditions and often based on the ethnic divide that defined owner–slave relations back in the nineteenth century, where work was distributed according to ethnic markers, language, clothing, dirt/purity and religion.

Increased migration has changed the atmosphere in Ngaoundéré. The centre of the city appears crowded with an intense pulse. Native city dwellers express a high degree of suspicion towards the recently arrived Centrafricains. There are many examples of people wanting to have their house repaired, a toilet to be dug, or a wall to be constructed, who need workers, and who would usually employ seasonal migrants, being reluctant to trust Centrafricains. They are said to be lazy, dishonest and capable of stealing your belongings. In this fast-growing city there is a high demand for a labour force, but many of those willing to take these jobs are not considered, because of suspicions and lack of mutual trust. Mallki (1995) studied a similar situation with Hutu refugees from Burundi in a Tanzanian city. The Hutus were statistically significant but difficult to find in the town. They were afraid when she confronts them with their past and their background. They made themselves invisible. This is to some degree similar to the situation observed in Ngaoundéré. Centrafricains are under-communicating their ethnic and national identity when engaging with job-providers and in relation to state representatives, but in the residential areas on the outskirts of Ngaoundéré it is their ethnic identity and languages that are the foundation of their social organization.

Clandestine refugees and the state: '*l'administration tolérante*' Shadow counterfeit activity happens in various forms throughout Central and West African countries. Despite Cameroon being a country obsessed with lawfulness (Comaroff and Comaroff 2006), there are many reports of policemen turning checkpoints into private enterprises, tax-collectors collecting for personal ends and other civil servants exploiting their position. This phenomenon is often contextualized in the manner that 'police and customs personnel, especially where their pay is low or unreliable, frequently take part in modest extraction in which insignias of public position are deployed to raise rents' (Blundo and Oliver de Sardan 2006; Roitman 2005: 186). Due to this discrepancy between public norms and laws on the one hand and effective, concrete practices on the other, there is a space where alternative norms are in use. Oliver de Sardan (2015) recommends that this gap is where ethnographers should study governance. These practices are not a symptom of anomie, chaos or chance: they are recurrent, tolerated and regulated, albeit in an 'informal register'. As Arntsen (2018) has shown from his studies in the far north region in Cameroon, public servants do not just decide autonomously how to act within such a system. These corrupt practices are not anarchic, they are regulated within a system: 'the administrators form part of solidarity networks. On the one hand, streams of money run upwards through the bureaucratic system, outside formal channels. On the other hand, money is distributed locally through administrators' networks of close social relations' (Arntsen 2018: 86).

Oliver de Sardan (2015) uses Goffman's famous concept of 'frontstage and backstage' to explain the difference between official (frontstage) and practical (backstage) norms in such systems. Many problems are resolved backstage, according practical norms. Anyone stopped by the police at roadblocks without identification documents has to pay the amount the police ask for. If they can't pay, they will be held back, until someone comes and pays their fee. Knowing the thoroughness of the system, people prepare themselves. For example, if you are travelling in long distance buses between larger cities in Cameroon you should find out which bus company has negotiated with the traffic police so that its buses are not stopped at the many technical and identity paper controls.

It might appear somehow paradoxical that there does not exist a public structure that reacts over the fact that there is a large unregistered, clandestine population settled on the outskirts of Ngaoundéré. The state representatives (gendarmes, police, customs officers) stress a legal approach to all these arrivals by forcing them to pay for their 'tolérance' of the violation of the law. This is a practice that is often named '*l'administration tolérante*'.[9] This is a tolerance with its own logic. As one bureaucrat in the Ministry of Immigration explains: 'In the Cameroonian law it's said that there can only be one bar every 500 meter in a city centre. But if you go downtown in any Cameroonian city, this law is not followed, because there is no problem with having bars close to each other'. The law can be interpreted with tolerance. '*L'administration tolérante*' is immensely creative in crafting practical norms besides public ones, finding space for negotiation, manoeuvring and corruption. Someone with a bar could, at an appropriate moment, be made aware of that law. Any bar owner knows this and prepares himself accordingly. Someone without identification documents also knows that she/he has to be prepared.

A frequent discussion in Ngaoundéré concerns what the authorities or the police could do with all the Centrafricains who are illegally gathered in the suburbs. In these debates the principle of 'l'administration tolérante' is often mentioned. As long as they are not causing any problems, there is not a problem. But if they cause problems, they will be punished.[10]

Another explanation for why they are left in peace is that to send all these 'clandestine' migrants out of the country would take a large police manoeuvre, with lots of police officers and cars. Moreover they would have to imprison many, and would then have to provide the captured with food and transport. It would be a very costly operation. These migrants do not have much money. If they are put in custody as a group no one will be there to pay for their release. Their poverty protects them, makes them invisible and ignored by the authorities.

'*La tracasserie*' (the harassment) by public officials is increasingly experienced by the Cameroonian population in general, but by refugees in particular (Waage 2018). As Cameroon is practically at war on three fronts (against Boko Haram in the north, the Ambazonians in the south and north-west and highway robbers on the Adamaoua plateau), more and more roadblocks have been set up to control and extort the suffering population. There is clear evidence that these control mechanisms are strategies for corrupt policemen to improve their livelihoods. One example comes from Toboro, the border town, where refugees pass to get into Cameroon. Toboro is situated in the dangerous red zone[11] with much highway robbery and other violence. A gendarme working there was posted to another, less violent area near the capital. The gendarme refused to leave. He paid his boss several times his monthly salaries to let him stay. The reason is obvious; it is easier to earn extra money in the red zone, as there are much more irregular activities than elsewhere. Cameroonian media has revealed several examples of police collaborating with highway robbers in the Adamaoua region (Canal 2, 15 February 2019). Sarcastic comments were heard in Ngaoundéré when a policeman was killed by a suicide bomber in the Far North Province of Cameroon (late 2015), during the Boko Haram insurgency. Instead of doing his job, the policeman asked for 'his' 100 CFA. The policeman had chosen to stop the poor-looking young boy, who he understood did not have identification documents. The boy pulled the trigger device and both of them died.

Blending into historical relations

Crossing the border from CAR the refugees arrive at Toboro, at the Chad–CAR–Cameroon border. As many arrive penniless they have to earn some money for further transportation. The journey will then continue, either to one of the many villages on the Adamaoua plateau where they can find work as cultivators, or they follow the main road to Ngaoundéré. Arriving in Ngaoundéré, they blend into this city, where their possibilities to a large extent are defined by having family members there, previous relations and from avoiding having to show identity papers.

Construction work and then farming: men's strategies Jean first came to Cameroon as a seasonal worker. After harvesting of his family's fields, he would migrate to Cameroon to look for work, just as his father and brothers had done before him. In Ngaoundéré, he worked with a cousin doing construction work with mud bricks. When rebels became a menace in his home village, Jean went back to CAR and got his parents, the two children of his deceased sister and eight other family members over the border. In Ngang-ha they were arrested by the police, having neither papers nor money, and were not allowed to move on. As life is cheaper in the village, and farming is what they know, they stayed in the village. Jean later went to town to earn money, hoping to be able to pay school fees and medicine for family members. Two years later, when violence diminished in the region they come from, his parents, worried about the children they had left behind, returned to their home village. Jean is still responsible for his two nephews, who he now has placed in CAR families in different villages where they can cultivate in the rainy season.

Jean is now established as a bricklayer/housebuilder in a Muslim Fulani quarter in Ngaoundéré, and is frequently offered new jobs. He always speaks Fulani or French there (never his two native languages: Songo and Mboum Panna) and I have seen him trying to defuse possible tensions, either with work colleagues or towards patrons. While filming Jean making bricks, in a neighbourhood I know well, the man Jean worked for approached me. We chatted and he explained that 'Jean is always doing a good job; that's why I give him new tasks over and over again. He is a good guy. He accepts not being paid immediately', and then: 'He is from Toboro; he is a Cameroonian'. Jean himself confirms that even after three years working in the neighbourhood people there do not know he is Central African. When he is working, surrounded by strangers, he claims to be a Mboum from Cameroon. He is also someone who never quarrels with his patrons, is always patient and obedient, and always accepts that the salary might be lower than agreed upon; not objecting when his boss says that the well he has been digging is a metre shallower than he knows it is. By holding a trusted position he has been able to recruit his family members and other acquaintances to work with him. One day he brought Severine with him to help him doing a brick-making job. They had an open quarrel over the softness of the dirt used for the bricks. Jean was later called by the employer saying that he didn't want to see Severine again. He had misbehaved.

In every other social setting where I met Jean, he is Central African and Mboum Panna. Then he is outspoken, a lively man making a lot of jokes, often searching for new information about CAR or talking about people back home. He spends time getting information about the home-region from people he knows. He maps where people are and what they are doing. He collects information about which village has suitable and affordable land for cultivation in the rainy season. He uses this kind of information in his daily practices. He sent his two nephews to a village where he had networked so they could cultivate. He sends soap to his family when he hears someone is passing by, and so on.

Sam spent several years in Cameroon in his teens. He first came to Adamaoua when he was fourteen years old. His father could not afford to pay for his school fees anymore, so Sam came to earn money for his future education. This was in 2003, the same year Bozize effected a coup in CAR, and violence spread throughout the country. In Ngaoundéré he started to offer his labour at building sites. Fluent in Fulani, obeying, never quarrelling with his employer he gradually got a reputation for being a hard-working person that could be trusted. His younger sister married a Cameroonian and moved to a village three hours by train to the south of Ngaoundéré. Sam worked with house construction in Ngaoundéré in the dry season and cultivated land in the village of his brother-in-law in the rainy season.

Sam never continued school. Returning to CAR after six years, he married Clara, and they settled in his village. Jasmine, their first daughter, was only one year old in 2014 when their village was attacked by rebels, and Clara and Sam lost track of each other for months. Coming back to Ngaoundéré he sought people he had been working with on his last stay in Cameroon. Sam maintains a good reputation as a construction worker. He is now leading a team of bricklayers, building a small shopping centre in the commercial centre in Ngaoundéré for an entrepreneur from Douala, in southern Cameroon. He got the job due to being recommended and his fluency in French. Sam has recruited some of his acquaintances from CAR to work with him. Afraid of losing the job Sam and his team accepts to work with irregular payment. In the rainy season he leaves his little family and moves to his sister's where he cultivates maize and soya. This has enabled him to build a small house in Ngaoundéré.

Jean, Sam and others like them never tell anyone they are working for that they are from CAR. They present themselves as being from a nearby village (from the Cameroonian side of the border); they speak Fulani – the local lingua franca – and some French. And they always behave well, never quarrel, never meet the eyes of their patrons etc. They do so because they 'don't want problems'. They do not want to be insulted as coming from the poor and badly governed CAR; they do not want to be harassed and they want to earn decent pay.

To sell on the market: women's dreams Asta is from Jean's village and came to Ngaoundéré with no close relatives or network. She stayed a few months in different households in Ngaoundéré without finding a more permanent place to stay or a way to earn money. Asta and a friend decided to leave for Ngang-ha, a village on the CAR–Ngaoundéré axis, where they knew someone and where they could get access to land they could cultivate. Asta didn't have family in Ngaoundéré, she didn't have money to start trading with vegetables and she understood that she could not just stay without contributing to the rent. She moved away from the city. In Ngang-ha, Asta met Momin, moved in with him and 'gave him three children'. Asta has learned the local language so she can communicate with the locals in their mother tongue. But she is frustrated, as she is always tending to her young children, which prevents her from creating any income. She can't farm as the fields are far away. In addition another obvious form of income closed as the Muslim villagers won't buy food made in the casserole of a Christian woman from Centrafrique, as they prepare and eat animals that have died a natural death. The local Muslim population says that food coming from their casseroles is *haram* (prohibited in Arabic).

Clara, Sam's wife, started to sell potatoes for a local farmer at the market. One day, Clara was robbed while selling. Not being able to pay for the potatoes, she was summoned by the farmer to see the police. Since she did not have identification papers, the whole affair became very expensive: her husband had to pay a convocation fee and make a deal with the farmer. He spent all his savings and borrowed money from his network to release his wife. Clara now envisages starting a 'table' (selling oil, sugar, salt, cubes of spices and soap from a table) just outside the house where she lives, where everyone is a migrant and where there are never any police.

Every woman I have talked with dreams of having their own small retail set-up at the stall-market, where they can sell fruit, vegetables or other goods. These markets are regulated and controlled. To work there they would need identification documents.

Without valid identification documents Patience, a cute baby girl, got her name from her father, the mother told me: 'he wanted to say that his girl must wait for him'. Her father is in jail because he could not pay the fee demanded at the roadblock, not having identification documents.

Jean carries with him a photocopy of identification documents that expired several years ago, hoping that he will be able to talk himself out of situations if he has a problem. Sam carries his marriage certificate from CAR. Asta doesn't have papers but has learned to speak the local language in the village. Clara stays in the neighbourhood, only going downtown when needed, and during the day. None of them have valid identification documents. But there are ways around. It depends on the officer you meet, your ability to negotiate and what you are willing to pay.

Many respond to my questions about identification documents by explaining their plans for what to do when they meet a problem. Sam has worked for El Bashir, a rich trader and member of parliament, so he will call him when in trouble. Jean has the phone number of the wife of a general that he has worked for that he hopes can be useful in case of need.

Clara's children are registered in school through her aunt who came to Ngaoundéré during the 2003 violence, and who has obtained Cameroonian identification documents. When Clara was hospitalized and in need of an urgent operation, Sam was afraid, first for his wife's life and secondly for being asked for identification documents. Neither of them can identify themselves by documents. Due to the seriousness of her illness, he had to take the chance and went to a doctor. Luckily the doctor was a reasonable man, says Sam, he accepted to operate without documentation and did not cause any problems.

A general and shared coping strategy is '*Il faut pas chercher des problèmes*' (stay out of trouble). To do so, one must be alert, informed, obedient and service-minded. Most of all, one must keep a low profile. One must be informed, on a daily basis, about police movements and checkpoints, so as to avoid them if possible. Travelling out of the city, for example to cultivate in the rainy season, takes calculation. They prefer to travel by car rather than by bus, because they can ask the car driver to stop before they reach a checkpoint. The passenger will then switch to a motorcycle-taxi to pass the checkpoint. A motorcycle is rarely checked on national routes. Women travelling will bring small children. Clara tells me how her little son was screaming at checkpoints with armed soldiers, which made them let her pass without paying. But whatever the strategy, there is always a risk of being stopped, when travelling and when moving around in the city, and of having to pay more than what can be afforded.

Getting valid identification documents There are several ways to obtain legitimate, valid identification documents for a refugee in Cameroon. The first possibility is to get a temporary Central African identification card at the CAR consulate in Ngaoundéré. But many migrants do not know that there exists such an institution. In addition, the consulate is not very involved. The consul himself was unaware of the presence of the many unregistered Centrafricains on the outskirts of the city before the anthropologist showed him the new neighbourhoods. Indeed, the identification cards he can provide are not in demand in refugee circles, first because they are expensive and second because they do not prevent the police from asking for money at roadblocks, especially as the cards make them visible as Centrafricains.

The other seemingly obvious way is to get a refugee card from the UN Refugee Agency (UNHCR). This card gives the rights to shelter in a camp, and to food and clothing. With a travel permission, the card can be used for travel. These cards are issued where the UN has refugee camps, near Maiganga and Garoua-Bolai. However, the migrants with which this study is concerned have all crossed the border further north, near the Chad–CAR–Cameroonian border. The migrants have to pass the long way through Ngaoundéré before continuing to the UN camps. This is both costly and time consuming. Formally, new arrivals from CAR can register at the sous-prefet's or mayor's offices, and then get a UNHCR refugee card issued. Those I have met who have tried this solution have been waiting for months without getting any response. Jean got a UNHCR identification document (refugee card) in 2016, three years after he came to Cameroon. He seized the opportunity, which presented itself when he brought his brother's eleven children to the refugee camp south of Maiganga; he got identification documents, issued for two years. When stopped by a police officer thirteen months later, he was told that the card had expired, and Jean had to pay a large sum of money to get it back. Jean's conclusion was that you have to pay whatever you do.

Massek lives with his mother, wife, their two children and aunt in a shabby shack made of bricks that have seen several rainy seasons. He came to Cameroon two years ago with no experience with seasonal migration and has only been able to get hold of paid day-jobs through Jean. Massek replies with tears in his eyes when asked why he still does not have a UNHCR identification card; 'Traveling to Maiganga is 2,500 CFA. First you need that money. Furthermore, between Ngaoundéré and Maiganga you don't know how many checkpoints you meet. And if you don't have the money they ask for, you don't know where they'll take you. And then what?'

The third and most sought-after strategy is to hide, while waiting for opportunities to get a Cameroonian identity card (*carte nationale*). To get such a card, a person keeps a low profile, hides their national identity and performs submissively in public spaces. They settle gradually, earning money offering cheap labour for small jobs in the neighbourhood. Through the process of establishing a social and economic network, they eventually apply for Cameroonian citizenship. It is recognized in the Cameroonian administration system that not all the citizens of the country have a birth certificate. A person without a birth certificate may still be granted a *carte nationale* if warranted by two witnesses and the head of the town district or village chief where the person lives. In practice, it is a matter of the money you have to spend to pass the different 'barriers' when getting the card. The card itself costs 2,800 CFA. Sam once paid 18,000 CFA for his now expired *carte nationale*. It was made possible by his Cameroonian brother in law. In Ngaoundéré, it costs 23,000 CFA. He now has a long-lasting work relation at a construction site, and has an agreement that his patron will cut part of his weekly salary to provide him with a Carte Nationale in six months. Jean and others will not let their patron know that they are of Central African origin before they feel that he can be trusted. For Jean this means that the patron himself proposes new work for him. In the meantime you have to endure, you have to work well, and sometimes you have to accept not being paid. They hope that such obedience will make him a trusted person. When they feel that they can trust their patron, they will ask for his assistance in getting a Cameroonian identity document.

By staying invisible to the native Cameroonians on the outskirts of the city, and being part of a strong CAR network, Central African refugees can get useful information and find ways to cope in the heterogeneous social landscape in which they find themselves. Participating in the informal economy, they have to under-communicate all signs that link them with CAR – language, behaviour codes, etc. Gradually building trust with patrons, they position themselves to obtain identification documents, so they can avoid the recurrent problems that come from meeting civil servants.

Conclusion: clandestine migrants between the tolerant administration and the informal economy

The brutalization of CAR society over the last decade(s) has created a situation of extreme uncertainty for its people. This violence is the concrete reason for a massive migration from the western part of CAR to Cameroon. Others are hiding in the surrounding savannah and many go back and forth between the two countries, depending on the varying level of violence and the season. Among Centrafricains in CAR and in Cameroon, suffering is massive, poverty and hunger more than common, frustrations and despair widespread.

The war in CAR is neglected by the international community. The UN has gravely underestimated the total number of refugees in its statistics. The war is ignored in the media in neighbouring Cameroon, and refugees must adapt to lifestyles that make their CAR identity invisible. Invisibility is omnipresent when it comes to the CAR war.

For these war refugees, authorities in both CAR and in Cameroon spread fear and anxiety. In CAR the authorities are rebel groups, in Cameroon they are state representatives. When refugees such as Clara, Asta, Sam and Jean discuss their plight, they make no distinction between legal and illegal authorities. Along the highway in north-west CAR, the migrants meet roadblocks manned by rebel groups such as RJ, 3R, Seleka and Anti-Bellaka. Crossing the border to Cameroon, they meet the police, gendarmes and customs. In all cases they have to pay money which ends up in the pockets of either rebels or civil servants. The formal functioning state in CAR is almost non-existent (Lombard 2016), whereas Cameroon has a democracy with a state serving its population throughout the country. But seen from below, from the perspective of these impoverished, clandestine refugees, roadblocks are roadblocks.

Both in CAR and in Cameroon, the best solution is to keep a low profile. The migrants and the displaced use similar strategies on both sides of the border. To be invisible is not to be seen by the rebels in CAR, nor by state representatives in Cameroon. In CAR they hide in the forest, near their fields, in Cameroon they hide on the outskirts of the city. Being seen spells trouble: being robbed, raped or killed in CAR, paying more money than they can afford in Cameroon.

Through several years of fieldwork in Ngaoundéré, I have met many refugees who have made the difficult decision to flee their homes, leaving family and loved ones behind. Coming to Cameroon, they have to adapt and find a way of living in line with work relations defined by an ethnic divide. 'Native' Cameroonians have tended to be sceptical and suspicious of Centrafricains since the war started and spread, and since recent highway robberies and kidnappings on the Adamaoua plateau are connected to groups from CAR. Centrafricains have a bad reputation of not being trustworthy. Job possibilities are relatively scarce. These are reasons why migrants from CAR have to under-communicate their origin. In addition, they face problems as refugees without papers or as illegal migrants, with the Cameroonian bureaucracy, with roadblocks, at the hospital and in their small retail stalls at the market.

These clandestine migrants settle on the outskirts of Ngaoundéré where they enter a network of Central Africans coming from a cluster of nearby villages. They share information about jobs, housing, land accessibility for cultivation and the ongoing war. Their vulnerability is known and exploited. Many are those who have experienced not being paid as promised. But they cannot file complaints because they do not have recognized identification documents. They have no rights. It is through getting jobs on a more permanent basis, which takes persistent under-communication of ethnic and national identity, that they can develop a sense of trust with a Cameroonian employer, which they hope will help them obtain valid identification documents, as Cameroonians.

The historical backdrop is relevant to understand why these refugees come to Ngaoundéré and how this city has been able to receive and house so many immigrants. The first Mboum Panna who came to Ngaoundéré from what is now the north-western region of the Central African Republic came as slaves. Later, from the 1970s, they came by free will as seasonal labour migrants; from the early 2000s they have been pushed by armed violence. In Ngaoundéré they adapt to cultural rules established when slavery was legitimate. The dynamics between '*l'administration tolérante*' and the same administration's obsession with rules have created a space to hide. It is the administration's tolerance that lets them install themselves in the suburbs, while the same administration's obsession with rules is the very reason to keep hiding. Gaining access to day-jobs requires under-communicating Centrafricain identity, and over-communicating identity markers locally interpreted as belonging to ethnic groups living on the Cameroonian side of the border, primarily Mboum and Gbaya.

Ngaoundéré can now be described as a super-diverse city (Meissner and Vertovec 2015) with an enormous growth in population and ethnicities. But somehow paradoxically it can be argued that despite this development, social complexity has not increased. This is due to the role that clandestine refugees play in the informal economy in Ngaoundéré. They are constantly under pressure from civil servants trying to compensate for their low wages. These refugees are performing local submissive positions. Their workforce enables the Muslim elite in Ngaoundéré to solve a series of work tasks without paying much and maintaining their social status. Despite the fuzzy boundaries of modern-day ethnic groups in northern Cameroon, the distinction between the Fulani Muslims and the large category of non-Muslims persists. Clandestine migrants thus contribute to the reproduction of Fulani Muslim dominance within the informal economy, by speaking Fulani, behaving with humility, accepting not being paid properly, etc. This dynamic has as one of its consequences the reproduction of the ethnic organization of the city. In addition to being forced to hide, their invisibility strategies are giving civil servants a constant flow of income, which again reinforces corrupt practices within the Cameroonian administration. There are strong economic reasons for keeping these refugees from war invisible.

CAR refugees to Ngaoundéré come in many variants and have many different trajectories. Those with no former experience of seasonal migration to Cameroon and without local networks that can help them into work relations are weakly positioned. They mostly stay on the outskirts of the city, where they try to connect to other Centrafricains to be informed about home and work possibilities. Those who have a background in earlier labour migration or have family members established in the region, have more opportunities. Work relations are based on unequal patron–client relations that involve acceptance of certain cultural codes and certain skills. They must show that they are eager to work and to not make any complaints. Access to work in the informal economy depends on under-communicating CAR belonging.

As before the war started, many men from war-ridden border areas in CAR migrate between jobs in the city in the dry season and rural farming in the rainy season. The difference is that nowadays they have their house in Ngaoundéré and cultivate available land in nearby villages. They can cultivate for somebody (who owns the land) or they can rent land and cultivate it for themselves. The latter is the most beneficial. To cultivate for themselves, they have to have enough money to pay the rent. Those are the 'successful ones' among the migrants. They would typically be persons with large networks of visible Centrafricains living in the outskirt neighbourhoods of Ngaoundéré, where they collect information about the situation back home, job possibilities and available land to cultivate. They have also succeeded in making their Central African background invisible to their Muslim patrons. They have been successful in being invisible to the public servants of various kinds and clever in negotiating with them when needed. If they are able to maintain relations to the patron long enough to feel they can trust him or her, they will use that link to obtain a national identity card. Only then can they relax and travel without being afraid of being seen.

What is surprising in these processes of mass forced migration to the Adamaoua plateau, where clandestine refugees have to perform a delicate balancing act between visibility and invisibility to succeed, is the degree of cultural and social continuity that can be observed among all involved parties. Despite moving from rural CAR to urban Cameroon, the refugees experience a high degree of continuity in ways of earning and living their lives. The same can be said about Fulani Muslim job providers and those in charge of the roadblocks on both sides of the border.

Notes

1 The US ambassador to the United Nations in 2014.

2 'Anti-Bellaka is from the language of the illiterates, who formed Seleka's armed opposition, and who chased the Muslim "anti-balles à ti laka" (anti ti laka bullets). The term "laka" in the street language of the Central African Republic means an AK-47. The anti-bellakas are therefore the bearers of grigris meant to stop Kalashnikov bullets' (Niewiadowski 2014).

3 *African Arguments*. (https://africanarguments.org/2018/04/16/i-just-want-to-live-like-a-normal-man-whats-stopping-central-african-republic-car-disarming/).

4 www.dw.com/en/un-warns-of-genocide-in-central-african-republic/a-40002377.

5 I'm aware of the fact that it can be discussed if southern Chad is secure for refugees from CAR.

6 Chivalry, a kind of respectable behaviour known as a cultural trait among the Fulani.

7 The slaves were from the Pere (from the southwest towards Nigeria), Dii and Mboum (from the region north of Ngaoundéré), Gbaya (from the east towards CAR), Mbomabal/Mboum Panna/Mboum Kari (northwest CAR).

8 In 1950 it had a population of 55,000 (Froelich 1954: 25); in 2019 the population had reached 1,460 million (according the leading regional newspaper: *l'Oeil du Sahel*, 16 January 2019).

9 It is also called flexible, adaptive etc. The point is that the administration might be flexible when it comes to at what point it put its authority into practice, and how it interprets the law.

10 Examples of treatments of thieves that are identified as Centrafricains are awful.

11 Zones defined by the UN and by the Cameroonian government as less secure than other areas. In early 2019 there were three such red zones: Mandara Mountains in the Far North Region (on the border to Nigeria), along the CAR border (to the East), and the Western Region ('Amazona').

References

Arntsen, B. (2018) 'Aggravated uncertainty. the dubious influence of a modern management regime on Lake Chad fisheries', in H. Fyhn, H. Aspen and A.K. Larsen (eds), *Edges of Global Transformation: Ethnographies of uncertainty*, London: Lexington Books.

Bissakonou, J. (2015) *L'autre version de la crise centrafricaine*, Paris: L'Harmattan.

Blundo, G. and J. Oliver de Sardan (2006) 'Everyday corruption in West Africa', in G. Blundo and J. Oliver de Sardan (eds), *Everyday Corruption in the State: Citizens and public officials in Africa*, London: Zed Books.

Burnham, P. (1996). *The Politics of Cultural Difference in Northern Cameroon*, Edinburgh: Edinburgh University Press.

Canal 2 International (TV) (2019) News, 15 February.

Carayannis, T. and L. Lombard (2015) *Making Sense of the Central African Republic*, London: Zed Books.

Comaroff, J. and J.L. Comaroff (2006) *Law and Disorder in the Postcolony*, Chicago, IL: The University of Chicago Press.

Cooper, E. and D. Pratten (2015) *Ethnographies of Uncertainty in Africa*, London: Palgrave.

De Bruijn, M. (2007) 'Mobility and society in the Sahel: an exploration of mobile margins and global governance', in H.P. Hahn and G. Klute (eds), *Culture of Migration: African perspectives*, Berlin: LIT.

Domo, J. (2010) *Le nord du Cameroun. Mythe et réalité*, Paris: L'Harmattan.

Ferguson, J. (2010) 'The uses of neoliberalism', *Antipode*, 41(1): 166–184.

Froelich, J.-P. (1954) 'Ngaoundéré, la vie économique d'une cité peule', Etudes Camerounaise.

Gobo, G. and A. Molle (2017) *Doing Ethnography*, 2nd edition, London: Sage.

Global Witness (2015) Retrieved 5 May 2020 from: www.globalwitness.org/en/campaigns/forets/bloodtimer/.

Grimshaw, A. and A. Ravetz (2009) 'Rethinking observational cinema', *The Journal of the Royal Anthropological Institute*, 15(3): 538–556.

Issa, S. (2012) *Ethnicité, forntiéres et stabilité aux confins du Cameroun, du Nigeria et du Tchad*, Paris: L'Harmattan.

Le Monde Afrique (2018) 'La Minusca et le gouvernement centrafricain se défendent de toute bavure à Bangui', 13 April. Retrieved 5 May 2020 from: www.lemonde.fr/afrique/article/2018/04/13/a-bangui-une-operation-militaire-ravive-les-tensions_5284931_3212.html.

Lombard, L. (2016) *State of Rebellion: Violence and intervention in the Central African Republic*, London: Zed Books.

MacDougal, D. (1998) *Transcultural Cinema*, Princeton, NJ: Princeton University Press.

Mallki, L.H. (1995) *Purity and Exile: Violence, memory, and national cosmology among Hutu refugees in Tanzania*, Chicago, IL: The University of Chicago Press.

Meissner, F. and S. Vertovec (2015) 'Comparing super-diversity', *Ethnic and Racial Studies*, 38(4): 541–555.

Niewiadowski, D. (2014) La République centrafricaine: Le naufrage d'un Etat, l'agonie d'une nation. Unpublished manuscript.

Oliver de Sardan, J.P. (2015) 'Practical norms: informal regulation within public bureaucracies (in Africa and beyond)', in T. De Herdt and J.P. Oliver de Sardan (eds), *Real Governance and Practical Norms in Sub-Saharan Africa: The game of the rules*, London: Routledge.

Roitman, J. (2005) *Fiscal Disobedience: An anthropology of economic regulation in Central Africa*, Princeton, NJ: Princeton University Press.

—— (2006) 'The ethics of illegality in the Chad Basin', in J. Comaroff and J.L. Comaroff (eds), *Law and Disorder in the Postcolony*, Chicago, IL: The University of Chicago Press.

Schilder, K. (1994) *Quest for Self Esteem: State, Islam and Mundang ethnicity in northern Cameroon*, Leiden: African Studies Centre.

Solé, C., S. Parella, T. Martí and S. Nita (2016) 'Introduction: theoretical aspects of circular migration', in C. Solé, S. Parella, T.S. Martí and S. Nita (eds), *Impact of Circular Migration on Human, Political and Human Rights*, United Nations University Series on Regionalism vol. 12, Cham: Springer.

UNHCR (2020) 'Cameroon: Locations of UNHCR persons of concern', April. Retrieved 5 May 2020 from: https://data2.unhcr.org/en/documents/dowload/76097.

UNICEF (2018) *Central African Republic: Humanitarian situation report*. Retrieved 5 May 2020 from: www.unicef.org/appeals/files/UNICEF_Central_African_Republic_Humanitarian_Situation_Report_June_2018.pdf.

Waage, T. (2006) 'Coping with unpredictability: "preparing for life" in Ngaoundéré, Cameroon', in C. Christainsen, M. Utas and H. Vigh (eds), *Navigating Youth, Generating Adulthood: Social becoming in an African context*, Uppsala: Nordiska Afrikainstiutet.

—— (2015a) 'Mutual dependency: young male migrants from the Central African Republic in urban Cameroon', *Zeitschrift fur Ethnologie*, 140: 111–130.

—— (2015b) *Les Mairuuwas – Master of Water*, film, 60 min, Visual Cultural Studies, UiT / Arctic University of Norway.

—— (2018) 'Vulnerability and trust: migrants in search of a better position in urban northern Cameroon', in H. Fyhn, H. Aspen and A.K. Larsen (eds), *Edges of Global Transformation: Ethnographies of uncertainty*, London: Lexington Books.

6 | Entangled hypervisibility: Senegalese migrants' everyday struggles for a place in the city

Ida Marie Savio Vammen

Introduction

This chapter explores the relationship between hypervisibility and overlapping processes of invisibilization and displacement that in different ways shaped the everyday lives of a small group of Senegalese street hawkers at the Retiro Station in Buenos Aires. Like in many other cities around the world, especially since the mid-2000s West African traders have carved out different nodes throughout Buenos Aires from where they use the public space for trading their goods. Restrictive European and North American migration governance, in combination with the global economic recession in the late 2000s, has reconfigured their mobility from 'traditional' migration destinations in Europe and the US towards new destinations and emerging economies, like Argentina (Flahaux and de Haas 2016; Haugen 2012; Pelican and Tatah 2009).

One of these nodes, and the focus of this chapter, was the bustling informal street market surrounding the Retiro Station located along Dr José María Ramos Mejía Avenue, north of the city centre of Buenos Aires. It is one of Argentina's main transit hubs and the location of one of the country's largest bus terminals. Thousands of daily passengers arrive every day in rhythmic flows from the three large train terminals, Mitre, Belgrano and San Martín, each with their railroad line. The station demarcates the limit between the wealthy Retiro neighbourhood, with its posh cafes, luxurious commercial zones and green residential and recreational areas, and Villa 31, one of the city's oldest informal settlements that stretches out next to the highway towards the city's harbour. At the end of 2012, there were around fifteen to twenty African migrants from Senegal, Nigeria and Angola working along the station's wide sidewalk, together with other migrants from the neighbouring countries and with Argentinians earning a living from street vending. The hawkers had turned the space in front of the Belgrano and further down towards San Martín into a bustling informal commercial zone that catered for the needs of thousands of the passengers in transit as well as those of the inhabitants of Villa 31. From their improvised stalls along the sidewalk the hawkers sold a wide variety of goods like electronic gadgets, office supplies, clothing, underwear, socks, pens and fast food. The African migrants had found a niche for themselves in the highly competitive labour market that was already filled with versatile Spanish-speaking migrants from Argentina's neighbouring countries (especially Bolivia and Paraguay) and Peru. Most of the African migrants were selling a wide variety of inexpensive reproductions of designer goods made in China, such as watches, sunglasses and jewellery, and other goods such as leather purses and belts, some with shiny emblems of the city's most popular soccer teams (Boca Juniors and River Plate).

Building on a situational analysis of two emblematic moments at the station, I point to the Senegalese street hawkers' spatial struggle in the city, with the aim to outline the city's racialized topography and displacement logics. Unlike in many European and American contexts, at the time of my fieldwork the migrants' struggle was not so much linked with the borders created by strict migration governance and the fear of being deported. Rather, I show how the migrants were confronting urban borders linked to the country's particular history of invisibilization and displacement of black bodies that keeps shaping contemporary urban policies and police interventions. It was these borders, I argue, that made the Senegalese migrants together with other marginalized people categorized as '*negros*' ('blacks') hypervisible; produced illegality and justified the multiple displacement and invisibilization processes to which they were exposed. The chapter is based on eight months of ethnographic fieldwork carried out between 2012 and 2015 among Senegalese migrants in Buenos Aires who worked in the large informal economy of street hawking. I followed my interlocutors' everyday lives in two neighbourhoods of the city, Once and Retiro. By following my close interlocutors over a period of more than six years, during fieldwork and, later, on Facebook and Skype, it has become possible to make a more nuanced reading of their everyday struggles for a space in the city.

Theoretical departures: centring the analysis on hypervisibility

Beyond the broader literature on irregular migration that often emphasizes how migrants live in the shadows of society (i.e. Lucht 2012; Khosravi 2010; Vigh 2009), invisibility and hypervisibility have also explicitly been an analytical thread in some of the seminal ethnographic literature on Senegalese migration from which this chapter will draw inspiration. Most noticeably, in his book *Navigating the African Diaspora: The Anthropology of Invisibility*, based on ethnographic fieldwork among Senegalese migrants in Turin, Italy, Donald Martin Carter uses the concept of invisibility to explore 'the power to establish or manifest a state of invisibility for specific categories of persons in a given space, location, time, or position' (2010: 5). The notion of invisibility, he argues, helps us to understand the migrants' diasporic experience but also how nation-states operate and everyday discrimination and violence work. Invisibility is 'a corrosive social erasure, insinuated into living memory, that shapes the contours of social imagination and relegates the newcomer to the margin' (2010: 5). It is integrally connected to long periods of nonbelonging to the nation-state, second-class citizenship and dehumanization. He emphasizes that invisibility is an ongoing process that not only marginalizes people but also renders them hypervisible as they come to mark the boundaries of the known world (2010: 6). The Senegalese migrants in Italy were often excluded from public space and censuses, while at the same time being staged as hypervisible 'problems' and 'outsiders' in debates about immigration in Europe. Furthermore, the Senegalese migrants he worked with were confronted with the othering of being black migrants within a largely white space, which, as I will show, resembles the everyday struggles endured by my interlocutors. This was somewhat different for the West African street merchants in New York in Paul Stoller's work that entered a space with a large presence of African Americans, making it easier for them to fall into the background. However, Stoller also emphasizes how the African migrant, like Ralph Ellison's *Invisible Man*, is an unknown and unseen person living in the shadows of society although working every day in plain sight along the streets of New York (Stoller 2002).

These studies demonstrate the dual nature of being at once invisible and hypervisible. In order to understand this apparent paradox, we need to go beyond (in) visibility as a general state of being, and instead unpack the particular moments and situations where particular bodies are rendered in/visible. Inspired by Polzer and Hammond (2008) we must ask who invisibilizes, in what ways and why. As the introductory chapter to this book claims, certain aspects of a person may be visible in certain situations to certain audiences and not to others. By asking the who and why questions, the relational nature of invisibility comes to the fore because the impact of invisibility depends on the power relations and interests connecting those who see and those who are to be seen (or not)' (Polzer and Hammond 2008: 417). During my fieldwork, it became relevant to understand the ways in which and why the migrants time and time again were rendered hypervisible. What were the effects of these moments of intensified imposed visibility and how did they play together with displacement and invisibility both spatially and existentially?

To answer these questions and explore the intertwined processes of power that create hypervisibility, exclusion, displacement and invisibility, I will place these moments in relation to the colonial and post-colonial history of Argentina. The analysis begins with a brief historical contextualization that forms the background for the racialized topography that meets the migrants when they enter the city and makes them visible. The ethnography that follows is structured in three sections all centring the analysis on the migrants' struggle at the station. In the first part, I explore the everyday moment when the migrant goes from being visible to hypervisible at the station. I draw inspiration from Franz Fanon (1952/2008) and Sarah Ahmed's (2006) emphasis on the spatial turbulence that occurs when black bodies enter a space where whiteness is the background for social life. In the second part, I analyse the clearing of the Retiro Station and focus on how structural processes of urban restructuring produced illegality, hypervisibility and displacement. I here draw more explicitly on De Genova's (2013) work by laying out how urban spatial governance and policing produce illegality and legitimize the naturalness of displacement and invisibility.

In the final section, I look more closely at how the migrants navigate their (in)visibility and displacement over time and creatively renegotiate their place at the station.

Black invisibility within a white nation

Arriving with the long-distance bus that had taken them overland from Argentina's northern frontier with Bolivia or Brazil to embark on a new life in the city,[1] the Retiro station was for many of the Senegalese migrants I worked with, their first physical encounter with the city. When they stepped out of the busses close to the riverbed of Río de la Plata and the industrial harbour, they were treading the same grounds that enslaved African people in the eighteenth century had stepped when they arrived to be sold at the Retiro slave market during Spanish colonial rule (see Borucki 2011; Schavelzon 2014). During the seventeenth century, Buenos Aires both absorbed slaves and was a transit space for the trade of African slaves who were moved to the hinterlands of central and northern Argentina, Paraguay, Chile and Alto Peru (present-day Bolivia), where there was a higher demand for labour (Andrews 1980: 24; Borucki et al. 2015). Between 1777 and 1812, at least 70,000 slaves arrived in Río de la Plata from the African continent and Brazil (Borucki 2011: 85).

However, during the formation of the post-colonial Argentinian nation from the 1880s onwards Afro-descendants and the indigenous population were written out of the national history and thereby made invisible. This process of 'blanqueamiento' or whitening of the population and the veiling of non-white racial alterity was part of a complex process of state formation. In a census from 1895, it was announced that the black population had almost vanished and that 'very soon the population will be completely unified, forming a new and beautiful race which is the product of all the European nations made fruitful on American soil' (Andrews 1980: 106). Although it was publicly stated that the black population had disappeared, Buenos Aires had a lively community of Afro-Argentinians with their own newspapers, social clubs and mutual aid societies (Andrews 1980). However, they did not fit with the new national identity that built on the assumption that Argentina was a European enclave in the Americas with a population that descended from the large inflow of European migrants, and as such a country with no blacks or Indians (Grimson 2005). The 'white ideal' of a modern, civilized, Catholic, European nation left little room for diversity and pluralism. The result was a political agenda and a range of policies, laws and regulations that promoted homogeneity while eliminating any non-European ethnic features, pressing Afro-Argentinians and indigenous populations to distance themselves from their origins (Maffia and Zubrzycki 2014).

Throughout this process, links to the country's colonial history with Africa, the African presence in Argentina and the way in which African soldiers had played a crucial role during the Independence war, were downplayed. Instead of creating and consolidating the nation from within by incorporating the existing plurality, the political elites excluded what they saw as 'semi-barbaric' and morally unfit groups (Courtis et al. 2009: 14; Frigerio and Lamborghini 2009; Segato 2007). They trusted that changing the countries' demographic composition through a large-scale eugenic engineering project could make a difference and have a civilizing and economic effect. The result was that the country opened its borders for an increase in European migrants from the 1870s onwards so they could colonize rural areas and support the nation's growing agro-business. Over the next half-century the population grew with the influx of European migrants from 1.8 million in 1870 to 12 million in 1920 (Novick 2010).

Despite the structural invisibility of former enslaved Africans and their descendants, blackness continued to be associated with 'the uncivilized deviant other'. However, over time the term became somewhat detached from its racial connotations with which it was explicitly associated at the beginning of the twentieth century. During the industrialization period of the 1930s, poor working-class men and women who came from the rural areas of Argentina to the urban centres were described by the privileged in Buenos Aires as 'cabecitas negras', little black heads, and seen as an 'aluvión zoológico' – a zoological flood (Sutton 2008). During the first period of Peronism (1943–1955), class, race and politics merged when anti-Peronist movements used racially charged terms such as 'cabecitas negras' and 'negros' to mock the working-class segment within the Peronist movement. To be 'negro' was seen by many observers as synonymous with being Peronist (Eduardo 2016: 195). By stigmatizing the large, popular sectors of society, the elite tried to delegitimize this group's power by treating them as less deserving of full citizenship 'due to their perceived poverty, uncouth behavior, lack of education, or place of residence' (Alberto and Elena 2016: 9).

This particular history shows how marginalization and exclusion of people perceived as '*negros*' has been an oft-unquestioned background in Argentina. The difference between citizens and non-citizens has mutated over time. Today it does not exclusively run along racial lines, but has been extended to include poor, working-class citizens who, in different ways, are seen as less deserving because of their blackness. They distort the image of a white, civilized, modern Argentina – a space that, especially in Buenos Aires, is seen as non-racial and without racism (cf. Geler 2016; Sutton 2008), but which, nonetheless, presents whiteness as the more civilized background. Within the recent decade of neoliberal reforms in Argentina, the gap between the rich and the poor segments of the population has widened, producing further spatial segregation and social marginalization (Eduardo 2016). The middle and upper classes have increasingly become anxious about 'the spatial-bodily proliferation of non-whiteness, especially when the subalterns demanded rights, jobs and assistance from the state or are seen as a part of a "silent invasion" of immigrants who take jobs from Argentinian workers' (Gordillo 2016: 254) or are blamed for the country's social and economic ills (Grimson 2005). In sum, blackness within this particular context draws the borders of the nation's particular racialized topography that has been reworked to also include class and cultural difference (Frigerio 2006; Alberto and Elena 2016). This particular spatial design, as I will argue in the following, continues to affect the Senegalese migrants' struggle over their right to a space in the city, adding layers that in different ways overdetermine them from without.

Hypervisible yet invisible

On a summer day in early 2013, while I was sitting and talking to Abdou, one of my close interlocutors at the station, we suddenly heard agitated voices coming from Fallou's stand, 15 metres further down the sidewalk towards Belgrano Station. Fallou was arguing with a frantic, skinny, young Argentinian teenager. In an instant the situation escalated – the young man caught Fallou off guard and forced him to the ground. The two men tumbled down the sidewalk in front of Fallou's table but quickly got back on their feet. Vigilantly they both tried to seize the right moment to get in another punch. This time Fallou had the upper hand and gave the young, skinny man a heavy push that made him fall over. For a moment, they fixed each other in a tight grip. Fallou got one hand loose and sent his right arm forward, straight to his opponent's head. The blow hit hard and left the young man somewhat dazed. Passers-by stopped to see the fight and a crowd quickly gathered around the two men. The usual police presence at the station was nowhere to be seen. I immediately asked Abdou to go and help Fallou but, like me, he was reluctant to do so. In front of us the fight moved along in silent, dreamlike, slow motion. For what seemed a long time, we passively watched the scene from a distance. Abdou had a serious frown on his forehead while he observed Fallou and the other man roll around on the dusty sidewalk, frighteningly close to the city buses going by. After Fallou's hard punch, the fight was over; both men got back on their feet and the young man handed Fallou some pesos. He tried to play innocent for the crowd, pretending that he did not intend to steal one of Fallou's wallets. Fallou, clearly furious, ripped the money out of his hand. Abdou quickly moved to Fallou's stand and formed a half circle around it, together with two other Senegalese hawkers who also worked at the station. The young man had no choice but to retreat. Almost running, he quickly disappeared, moving towards San Martín and Villa 31, and the crowd started circulating again.

Having made sure that Fallou was not too severely hurt, Abdou walked slowly back to his table and sat down on the stool next to it. An Argentinian woman in her fifties, in a sleek red jacket and matching skirt, followed him and stopped at his table. In a high-pitched voice, she started to insult him with racist remarks. '*Negros de mierda. Tu gente nunca deben pegar a un Porteño, vayanse a su pais!*' Shitty blacks! You people should never hit a Porteño, go back to your country! Abdou's face hardened and he gave her a stern stare and calmly told her to mind her own business. Yet he also felt the urge to explain himself and Fallou's actions: 'I was not part of the fight', he told her. 'It was the young man who tried to steal a wallet from my friend; he was a thief'. The woman turned around and walked away but, after a few metres, she turned her head and twice shouted '*Negros de mierda*', Shitty blacks. Abdou shook his head: 'People here can be very racist, especially when they see us fighting with a white man; they become frightened', he told me. At first, he seemed surprisingly unaffected by the incident and took up our conversation from where it had been interrupted by the fight. Yet, when his close friend Issa came by to chat, it was clear that he felt the need to share what had happened in detail. It was obvious that, more than the violent encounter between Fallou and the young man, it was the racist remarks that had built up a lot of tension and anger in him: 'They are so racist in this country', he told Issa, who agreed.

While the friends talked about the fight, I suddenly out of the corner of my eye saw the young Argentinian guy from the fight moving with greater speed towards Fallou's stand. A few metres away he slowed down and finally stopped in front of the table. He demanded reparation as he claimed he had lost a diamond-like earring during the fight. His voice was high and agitated. Fallou's body became tense. He walked around the table and bluntly told him to f--- off. The two men stared at each other and almost started to fight again but this time Abdou and Issa quickly got up to assist Fallou. Abdou stepped in between them and tried to calm them both down. He resolutely took the young man by the shoulder and started walking towards his own table, covered with goods. 'Hey I will find you a similar earring for free, don't worry', he said in a calm yet firm voice. The young man glowered back at Fallou but followed Abdou without resistance. From the red velvet tray full of earrings and other jewelry, Abdou carefully selected another sparkling 15 pesos 'diamond' similar to the one the young man had in his left ear. Instead of appreciating Abdou's gesture, he hissed 'You guys should be really careful, I have friends, you know, and we will come back – *negro de mierda*!' He pulled out his white T-shirt, slipped his hand underneath, and pointed his index finger towards Abdou like a pistol, suggesting that next time he and his friends would come back armed. Abdou kept calm and, in a soothing voice, told him 'Easy, my friend, easy, I don't want to fight; I am not him, I am not him'. Abdou's pacifist behaviour worked and the young man walked away with the earring. Fallou carefully followed him with his eyes as he moved away once more in the direction of San Martín Station and Villa 31. As he stood there, next to his table, in his light blue polo shirt with a torn collar and his dusty denim jeans, Fallou looked disillusioned and alone. The event only confirmed his general negative perception of Argentina, and he told me that it made him despise the country even more. 'I just came here to work, I do not want to make trouble, but this guy doesn't want to work, he thinks it is okay to steal. It is not right'.

In the weeks that followed, Fallou's disillusionment with life in Argentina increased. It was as if the incident pushed him out of place existentially and confirmed his bewilderment about what he was doing in Argentina. In our conversations, he would return to the way the crowd had naturally seen him as the perpetrator, when all he had done was to catch a thief. 'In Senegal such a crowd would immediately have taken my side and have taken justice into their own hands and punished the thief; in Senegal we know right from wrong', he told me. Furthermore, it disturbed him that some of the other Senegalese migrants had told him that he should have just let the thief go. They knew their position at the station was uncertain and marginal.

A few episodes like this would endanger the livelihoods of all of them, as there was no distinction between the individual migrant and the collective of black migrants. Their presence was precarious and only tolerated by the police because most of the hawkers slipped them weekly bribes, but if there was too much trouble bribes would not be enough.

The Senegalese migrants' livelihood depended on the right kind of visibility in order to catch their customers' attention and mobilize their desires for consumption. Yet their visibility within this particular space also had another layer of visibility, as it was impossible for them to blend in because whiteness was the tacit background for the general social landscape. In such a space, non-white bodies do not automatically pass but involuntarily stand out as they are out of place (cf. Ahmed 2007; Said 1978). As Frantz Fanon has emphasized, the colonial subject's body becomes determined from without when fixated by the white man's gaze and imagination, which objectifies him and restricts his room for action to the extent that his body is no longer his but becomes deconstructed by weaving him 'out of thousands of details, anecdotes and stories' (Fanon 1952/2008: 84). This kind of fixed visibility became especially predominant in instances of racist assault. In these intensified moments, migrants became hypervisible and the borders of the racial topography of the city were fully exposed. Both Abdou and Fallou would have preferred to go about their business as peacefully as possible, but in an instant, they went from being visible black Africans to hypervisible '*negros de mierda*'. Yet, in that instant of hypervisibility during the racist assault, their invisibility also became intensified. It was a moment where both men wanted their own personal experience to matter, not a twisted truth that automatically took the thief's party. They wanted to detach themselves from the categorization that displaced them and made them part of an unwanted black collective unfit for to be part of the imaginary of the white nation. They needed to defend themselves and correct the wrong assumptions about what was going on during the fight, yet nobody really seemed to care or listen to their side of the story.

The clearing of Retiro Station

A few months after the incident, Issa wrote me a short message on Facebook: 'The police have cleared Retiro. We were lucky that they only took our tables and not our goods. We haven't been able to work for two days, it is difficult'. I quickly replied that I would call him. When he picked up the phone, he told me that it was the municipality, together with the Metropolitan Police force, that had cleared the streets and public space surrounding the station. Issa had heard that the Peruvian traders who mostly worked closer to San Martín Station were now negotiating a solution with the municipality. Issa did not sound too worried: 'Hopefully everything will go back to normal soon', he told me. I called a few of the other Senegalese migrants from Retiro who similarly told me that, hopefully, things would go back to normal the next day. However, their abrupt removal turned out to be long-term.

The following days I kept in contact with the people I knew to see how things were developing but none of them were able to go back to their old posts at the station. I decided to go to the station to see the situation with my own eyes. Only the dark green newspaper stands had survived. The normal flow of passengers in transit was still moving through the station but the lively everyday commerce of the many hawkers and the smell from the small food stalls were completely erased without a trace. I walked the long route from the corner of Avenida Libertador all the way to San Martín without seeing a single pitch. Halfway down, I met two of the young Senegalese hawkers who usually traded a bit further down the street; they were without their goods and both expressed disillusionment with the new situation. One of them told me that he just wanted to go back to Senegal. I also met Maria, a middle-aged woman from the province of Buenos Aires who worked at the station just a few stands from Issa's. She was sipping coffee at a small kiosk while carefully observing the new municipal task force that had deprived her of her livelihood. She said:

> We are only exercising our right to work. People assume we are criminals, but we are not, we are just workers providing for our families. All we are doing is creating a better future for our children. We are not asking for resources from the state and we do not want to ruin established businesses; we are just working; there needs to be room for us in the city.

To keep the hawkers from returning, a special taskforce with bright yellow waistcoats printed with the inscription *Espacio Público* was clearly present. I used the opportunity to talk to some of the new inspectors – mostly young students. The eradication of the hawkers and their stands was done to open up the station premises for a large renovation and modernization project, I was told. Their operation was to keep hawkers from coming back and informed them that it was illegal to sell at the station or in any of the more occupied zones of the city.

Over the following weeks, the conflict escalated. Street hawkers like Maria took to the streets not only to try to reclaim their right to work but also to voice their anger towards the police and the government of Buenos Aires which, in their opinion, had robbed them of their goods. Unlike the Senegalese migrants, they had not managed to run away before the police stopped them. They were now left with nothing and wanted their confiscated goods back. The ministry responded that they needed to investigate whether the goods had been obtained legally.[2] For many days, the events at the station attracted national media attention and the 'problem with the hawkers' became hypervisible. The already challenged pedestrian infrastructure of the city was blocked by small groups of people, mothers with their baby prams and small fires. However, none of the Senegalese migrants I knew participated in the demonstrations. I talked to Issa who told me that he had called other migrants from the station who advised him not to participate because it was not right to reclaim something that, in national law, was illegal, and since many did not have legal papers it was, in such intensified situations, better to stay invisible.

In many ways, the clearing of Retiro was a warning of how the city was increasingly closing up. The Senegalese migrants had entered the city during a period where unwanted segments of the population were not particularly welcome. Together with other people categorized as black; the inhabitants of the so-called *Villas miseria*; people who lived on the street; street peddlers; and sex workers, they were among the undesirables that the city tried to disperse to the urban periphery (Marcús 2014; Pita 2012a). In the aftermath of the country's economic crisis in 2001 and the way the urban space of Buenos Aires became associated with both unrest and increasing insecurity, the government of Buenos Aires took action to secure the urban space (Rocca and Motta 2013). When Mauricio Macri, Argentina's current president, and the conservative centre-right political party, *Propuesta Republicana* (colloquially referred to as PRO), took power in 2007, the Autonomous City of Buenos Aires initiated a range of regulatory measures to create urban order and control. One of them was the creation of a new Ministry of the Environment and Public Space in 2008 with the mission to enhance the quality, beauty and renewed order and security in public spaces (Rocca and Motta 2013). It was a special unit under the ministry, *Unidad de Control del Espacio Público* (UCEP), that had cleared the station not only to modernize but also to protect and recover public space from illegal street trading. The idea behind the unit was that the city space should be given back to *los vecinos*, the neighbours (Redondo 2014) who, unlike the Senegalese migrants and other marginalized '*negros*', seemed to be included in the modernization and gentrification process taking place at the time. This new control unit governed urban space with strength and brutality, in close cooperation with the *Policía Metropolitana*, with which the migrants, unlike the *Policía Federal Argentina* or la *Brigada Polica* (PFA), did not have informal agreements. Beyond the clearing of the station, they forced the displacement and exclusion of many poor urban dwellers whose lives, like the Senegalese migrants, depended on their access to the public space. Between the spring of 2011 and the summer of 2012, the unit carried out an ongoing operation to evict street traders with an unusual level of physical violence, drawing unfortunate, disturbing parallels with the above described history but also Argentina's past military dictatorship from 1976 to 1983 (Pita 2012b; Marcús 2014). Despite the strong critique from Argentinian Human Rights organizations that reported that the police's actions in a range of cases were illegal, the unit continued its work and aimed to 'liberate' new areas of Buenos Aires.

Nicholas De Genova has highlighted how border policing and immigration law enforcement produce a border spectacle – a scene of exclusion – where the laws that illegalize migrants remain invisible while the migrants' transgressions of borders through the lens of mass media become hypervisible (De Genova 2013). In many ways the municipality's heightened attention to street hawking and the increasing police raids created similar hypervisible scenes of exclusion. Yet at this moment in time it was not migration laws that shaped the spectacle. Instead, it was the intensification of the urban topography and its borders of race and class that produced hypervisibility and justified the multiple displacement processes. The clearing of the station displaced the migrants and forced them away from their relatively sedentary location at the station, which they knew well. Although there were daily rumours about new police raids, the hawkers depended on being visible and could not afford to stay off the streets. Now displaced to other areas, they had to be on their feet all day trying to find a new spot, using the information their network could provide as a compass. Some moved further away from the city to find a tranquil spot in the provinces of Buenos Aires, as that which is considered a nuisance, dangerous or illegal in the capital is often pushed to the urban periphery or tolerated in the provinces (Grimson 2017b; Marcús 2014; Pita 2012a).

Navigating (in)visibility and displacement over time

Before the clearing of the station I would often find Abdou with a distant look in his eyes while listening to religious Wolof chanting or *mbalax* songs from his favourite musicians Youssou N'Dour and Thione Seck on a small set of loudspeakers he connected to his phone. Abdou especially connected to songs like N'Dour's 'Tukki', which described the migrant's journey and the invisible existential displacement that takes place when the migrant's body is thousands of kilometres away from home, yet his head is in Senegal. He often felt exactly like that. 'I just can't help thinking of the people and the life I have left behind and wondering if it is really worth it', he told me.

After Abdou could no longer work at the station, his trajectory took a different route. While we ate a last meal together in his small room just before I left Argentina in 2013, he told me that if he had 20,000 pesos/1,160 US$, he would return to Senegal immediately, and that maybe even 10,000 pesos/580 US$ would be enough. It was clear from our conversation that the clearing of the station had been a big blow for him but that going home empty-handed was not an option. He told me,

> I would feel so bad, I would not feel worthy after having missed out on so many things. People would also not show me any respect; they expect you to come home with at least something. I would rather stay away ten years suffering than go home without anything.

The event at the station had further fuelled his sense of displacement not only from his family but also from the hope of being a worthy and respected man in Senegal. His dream at that moment was simply to return with a little something to show and start up his business as a shoe merchant again 'from zero'. However, when we parted, this dream was not within reach as he had not found a new place in the city and his pockets were empty. Although Abdou kept in touch with his family, he had not been able to be economically visible in their lives and be the caring head of the household he aspired to be. Abdou was clearly disheartened, yet he kept calm. I trust God, he told me just like he had when he survived drifting eleven days on the high seas of the Atlantic Ocean on a malfunctioning boat on the way to the Canary Islands during his first failed attempt to migrate to Europe.

When I returned to Argentina in 2015, two years later, I could not help but notice how some of my close interlocutors were somewhat more at ease while others seemed to have been further sidetracked. It was impossible for me to see a clear pattern in why some had made it while others had not, although the individual migrant's links to the social infrastructure of Senegalese and other hawkers seemed key. The migrants themselves, though, understood it as luck. Although the police and the municipality had tried to displace them, many had managed to fight back. Despite their ongoing struggles for a space on the sidewalk, it was clear that they felt somewhat more comfortable. They knew the city and its rhythms much better, but most of all they seemed to be more in tune with what they could expect as well as having routinized their everyday life to the whims of the city. As Vigh has pointed out, 'Routinisation is a fundamental act in the construction of social terrains; even an everyday life of perpetuating crisis and warfare can become the routine with its own *modus operandi*' (Vigh 2006: 151).

Most of the hawkers who had formed part of the large bustling informal street market, had not managed to get their old spots back after the station had been cleared. Yet in the far end of the station towards the bus junction and Villa 31 in front of San Martín Station, Abdou and Fallou had found a few small spots on the sidewalk. After the construction work had finished, they had slowly tried to return to the station and had, in a way, succeeded, yet their selection of goods displayed only filled up a fraction of their former large stands with an abundant variation of goods. The police only tolerated their presence when they did not spread their wares too widely, Abdou told me. Fallou was selling from *la maletín*, a small black suitcase and Abdou sold sunglasses, two pairs for 30 pesos. When I saw them again, I initially considered their marginalized position as a further derout, yet my assumptions were contested by their relaxed, laid-back attitude.

While the station had been under construction, they had for months tried to do business in a different part of town without much success. For Abdou and Fallou, their shift to San Martín had meant that they had, yet again, had a semi-fixed place in the city. Although they were at the margin of the station space and still had to play a cat-and-mouse game with the police and pay them off, they did not have to wander all day or to cover the cost of renting a space in a small-scale shopping mall, as other migrants felt compelled to when they had had enough of the constant uncertainty of potential police raids. The eight to ten Senegalese traders who were now working at the station were selling their goods much closer to each other than before, which meant that, while one or two of them watched their stands, the others could, with great amusement, follow the different soccer matches on a television in one of the small permanent food stalls selling fast food at the station. While a friend watched their stall, they had the freedom to go to Once[3] and buy more goods or seek out new opportunities without having to pack up and lose their potential income. Most of the migrants now had smart phones and could hook up to the local Wi-Fi, which meant that they could browse for local news from Senegal and connect to family and friends throughout the day. In short, the migrants at the station now had a more tightly knit social infrastructure that made them more visible as a collective yet also facilitated trade, as well as the social needs and a sense of safety in a potentially hostile environment.

When asking Abdou how he had been, he told me proudly and enthusiastically how he had made a lot of money during the 2014 FIFA World Cup in Brazil. I asked if he, like some of my other interlocutors, had tried to go to Brazil, but he shook his head and, with a smile, explained:

> I was right here at the station. When the World Cup started, we decided to start selling the Argentinian national soccer jersey. We all had them on. In the beginning, there was not too much interest but then Argentina started to play really well, and we started to sell a lot. At least once a day I went to Once to buy more until the town was completely sold out. Also, people at home all of a sudden became aware of Argentina.

Abdou and the other hawkers had seized the day. They had made the bold move of retaking the contested station space dressed in the white and blue Argentinian jersey. Although Abdou's success had not generated enough capital to return permanently to the wife he had married while away, he had finally been able to help his family and he had saved almost all the money for a flight ticket to Senegal so he could visit the family and relax a bit before returning to Argentina.

By creatively seeing an opening in the market and finding an acceptable way to be visible within the urban racial topography Abdou had been able to live up to what was expected of him. By being economically visible in his family's life some of the existential friction he initially had to live with when I first meet him had been eased. In short, he had restored a sense of directionality in his life and felt less displaced. Abdou's stories highlight how some of the migrants navigated visibility and displacement adjusting their everyday lives although they still contained a high degree of uncertainty. They had found their own ways of tactically trying to position themselves favourably in a city they now had come to know for both its brutality and displacing forces, but also for its potential for regaining the life to which they aspired.

Yet soon after Mauricio Macri changed the municipal office with the presidential office in Casa Rosada in 2015, I started to notice various changes in Argentina that in many ways can be seen as an escalation of the struggle over space described in this chapter. The new government's rhetoric increasingly links migration, crime and security and has made legal changes to the progressive migration legislation to accelerate deportation and to enhance border control measures to halt immigration (Grimson 2017a).[4] A direction that potentially would create new forms of illegality and accompanying border spectacles, which the migrants know all too well from the European and American context. The tensions over the urban space of Buenos Aires also intensified after I left the field, culminating in January 2017 when the Senegalese hawkers took to the streets and blocked one of the city's main arterial roads in protest after the area of Once yet again was swept clean of hawkers by the police and the municipality. This time Abdou and many of the other hawkers had had enough and decided to join forces. Unlike when the station was cleared, they actively participated and chose to be deliberately hypervisible in the efforts to have their story heard and open up for negotiations with the city's government. A window was opened when the displaced hawkers were offered a two-month fixed salary if they kept off the streets and registered to become part of the formal economy, and were given the opportunity to rent stalls within a large warehouse to get them off the streets. Yet none of my close interlocutors took this offer as they told me that a shop in a warehouse or in a gallery with many other shops was simply too costly. If they wanted to earn enough to be able to remit money back and stay economically visible in their families' lives in Senegal, they had to take up the fight and creatively find new places for hawking not only within the increasingly constrained urban space in Buenos Aires but this time also by exploring new localities throughout the country.

Conclusion

To illuminate the entangled processes of (in)visibilization and displacement that affect the everyday lives of Senegalese street hawkers in Buenos Aires, this chapter explored, what I see as emblematic moments of hypervisibility. Inspired by Polzer and Hammond's (2008) key analytical questions of who invisibilizes, in what ways and why, I have found it useful not only to look at invisibility but to highlight the intensified exclusionary everyday moments where migrants are rendered hypervisible. These moments show us the dual nature of being at once invisible and hypervisible. As I show ethnographically, the migrants' hypervisibility simultaneously overdetermines the person from without and erases personal traits and histories, by castigating him/her as part of a larger unwanted collective of *negros*. The intensified hypervisibility not only exposes the migrant, but as bordering moments also analytically exposes the exclusionary force of the particular racialized topography of the city and its borders. I argue that this ongoing process of exclusion is closely linked to the historical logics of whitening the nation and the displacement of black bodies. As such, they are part of the unfinished and ongoing history of whiteness (cf. Ahmed 2007) that continues to draw the lines of the racialized topography of the capital city. In an Argentinian context, the Senegalese hawkers not only become hypervisible as they stand out as black African migrants in a white city. The historical context adds another layer of friction to their bodies as they are also perceived as part of the large popular mass of unwanted '*negros*'. I show how the migrant hawkers' black bodies become hypervisible through everyday racist assault. But also how, on a more structural level, urban governance targets the larger unwanted population of '*negros*' in the informal economy and later national migration governance links them to different forms of disorder and illegality rendering them visible to legitimize their expulsion and displacement. In addition to addressing when, how and why the migrants become hypervisible and invisible, I also dwelled on how the migrants' hypervisibility, invisibility and displacement were often accompanied by a sense of existential dislocation and othering. I would therefore argue that asking how the dual nature of being at once invisible and hypervisible is felt by the people that experience it, and in what ways they try to navigate this subject position, is fruitful for a more nuanced understanding of these processes. In the chapter I have therefore drawn attention to how the migrants experience and navigate their positionality over time. Here we see how the consequences of the migrants' physical displacement and invisibility seem to amplify in transnational space, as they struggle to stay economically visible in their families' lives in Senegal. But we have also seen how they, through everyday contestations of the given order, try to resist attempts to displace them from the advances and trajectory that they had hoped to achieve when migrating to Argentina.

Notes

1 See Vammen (2019) for a detailed description of their journey to Argentina.

2 www.clarin.com/ciudades/retiro-puesteros-desalojados-dejaron-micros_0_BJaIfIdjDmx.html.

3 The large commercial zone where most of the Senegalese hawkers bought their goods.

4 www.migraciones.gov.ar/accesible/indexA.php?mostrar_novedad=3384.

References

Ahmed, S. (2006) *Queer Phenomenology: Orientations, objects, others*, Durham, NC and London: Duke University Press.

—— (2007) 'A phenomenology of whiteness', *Feminist Theory*, 8(2): 149–167.

Alberto, P.L. and E. Elena (2016) 'Introduction: the shades of the nation', in P. Alberto and E. Elena (eds), *Rethinking Race in Modern Argentina*, Cambridge: Cambridge University Press, 1–22.

Andrews, G.R. (1980) *The Afro-Argentines of Buenos Aires, 1800–1900*, Madison, WI: The University of Wisconsin Press.

Borucki, A. (2011) 'The slave trade to the Río de la Plata, 1777–1812: trans-imperial networks and Atlantic warfare', *Colonial Latin American Review*, 20(1): 81–107.

Borucki, A., D. Eltis and D. Wheat (2015) 'Atlantic history and the slave trade to Spanish America', *The American Historical Review*, 120(2): 433–461.

Carter, D.M. (2010) *Navigating the African Diaspora: The anthropology of invisibility*, Minneapolis, MN: University of Minnesota Press.

Courtis, V., M.I. Pacecca, D. Lenton, C. Belvedere, S. Caggiano, D. Casaravilla and G. Helpern (2009) 'Racism and discourse: a portrait of the Argentine situation', in T. A. van Dijk (ed.), *Racism and Discourse in Latin America*, Lanham, MD: Lexington Books, 13–56.

De Genova, N. (2013) 'Spectacles of migrant "illegality": the scene of exclusion, the

obscene of inclusion', *Ethnic and Racial Studies*, 36(7): 1180–1198.
Eduardo, E. (2016) 'Argentina in black and white: race, Peronism, and the color of politics, 1940s to the present', in P. Alberto and E. Elena (eds), *Rethinking Race in Modern Argentina* Cambridge: Cambridge University Press, 184–212.
Fanon, F. (1952/2008) *Black Skin White Masks*, Paris: Editions du Seuil.
Flahaux, M. and H. Haas (2016) 'African migration: trends, patterns, drivers', *Comparative Migration Studies*, 4(1): 1–25.
Frigerio, A. (2006) '"Negros" y "blancos" en Buenos Aires: repensando nuestras categorías raciales', *Temas de Patrimonio Cultural*, 16: 77–98.
Frigerio, A. and E. Lamborghini (2009) 'Criando um movimento negro em um país "branco": ativismo político e cultural afro na Argentina', *Afro-Ásia*, 39: 153–181.
Geler, L. (2016) 'African descent and whiteness in Buenos Aires: impossible *mestizajes* in the white capital city', in P. Alberto and E. Elena (eds), *Rethinking Race in Modern Argentina*, Cambridge: Cambridge University Press, 213–240.
Gordillo, G. (2016) 'The savage outside of white Argentina', in P. Alberto and E. Elena (eds), *Rethinking Race in Modern Argentina*, Cambridge: Cambridge University Press, 241–267.
Grimson, A. (2005) 'Ethnic (in)visibility in neoliberal Argentina', *NACLA Report on the Americas*, 38(4): 24–29.
—— (2017a) 'Argentina's anti-immigrant about face', *NACLA Report on the Americas*, 49(2): 123–126.
—— (2017b) 'Spatial politics and urban borders: a study of Buenos Aires', in Miriam Greenberg and Penny Lewis (eds), *The City Is the Factory: New solidarities and spatial strategies in an urban age*, Ithaca, NY and London: Cornell University Press, 178–196.
Haugen, H. (2012) 'Nigerians in China: a second state of immobility', *International Migration*, 50(2): 65–80.
Khosravi, S. (2010) *'Illegal' Traveller: An auto-ethnography of borders*, New York: Palgrave Macmillan.
Lucht, H. (2012) *Darkness before Daybreak: African migrants living on the margins in southern Italy today*, Berkeley, CA: University of California Press.
Maffia, M. and B. Zubrzycki (2014) 'Relationships, significations, and orientations toward a collective acting of the Afro descendants and Africans in Argentina', *African and Black Diaspora*, 7(2): 177–187.
Marcús, J. (2014) '"Vos (no) sos bienvenido": el control y la regulación del espacio urbano en la ciudad de Buenos Aires', *Scripta Nova*, 18, 498(15): 1–17.
Novick, S. (2010) 'Políticas migratorias en la Argentina: experiencias del pasado, reformas actuales y expectativas futuras', in *Estado actual y perspectivas de las políticas migratorias en el MERCOSUR*, Montevideo: Flacso–UNESCO.
Pelican, M. and P. Tatah (2009) 'Migration to the Gulf States and China: from Cameroon', *African Diaspora*, 2(2): 229–245.
Pita, M.V. (2012a) 'Mitologías porteñas en torno al poder policial. Policía, contravenciones y gestión de ilegalismos en la Ciudad de Buenos Aires', *Revista la biblioteca*, 12: 182–209.
—— (2012b) 'Poder de polícia e administração de grupos sociais: o caso dos vendedores ambulantes senegaleses na Cidade Autônoma de Buenos Aires', in Christian Azaïs, Gabriel Kessler and Vera da Silva Telles (eds), *Ilegalismos, cidade e política*, Brazil: Belo Horizonte, 109–141.
Polzer, P. and L. Hammond (2008) 'Invisible displacement', *Journal of Refugee Studies*, 21(4): 417–431.
Redondo, C.G. (2014) 'La expulsión de lo indeseable. La unidad de control del espacio público como parte de la racionalidad política de la gestión del espacio urbano bajo el macrismo', *Avatares de la communicacíon y la cultura*, 7.
Rocca, M.E. and J.M. Motta (2013) '¿Quién tiene derecho al espacio público en la

Ciudad Autónoma de Buenos Aires? Miradas disciplinares y el rol de la arquitectura', *X Jornadas de sociología*, Buenos Aires: Facultad de Ciencias Sociales, Universidad de Buenos Aires, 1–6 July.

Said, E.W. (1978) *Orientalism*, New York: Pantheon.

Schavelzon, D. (2014) 'On slaves and beer: the first images of the South Sea Company slave market in Buenos Aires', *African and Black Diaspora*, 7(2): 119–128.

Segato, R. (2007) *La nación y sus otros. Raza, etnicidad y diversidad religiosa en tiempos de políticas de la identidad*, Buenos Aires: Prometeo.

Stoller, P. (2002) *Money Has No Smell: The Africanization of New York City*, Chicago, IL: The University of Chicago Press.

Sutton, B. (2008) 'Contesting racism: democratic citizenship, human rights, and antiracist politics in Argentina', *Latin American Perspectives*, 35(6): 106–121.

Vammen, I.M. (2019) 'New contested borderlands: Senegalese migrants en route to Argentina', *Comparative Migration Studies*, 7(8): 1–17.

Vigh, H. (2006) *Navigating Terrains of War: Youth and soldiering in Guinea-Bissau*, New York: Berghahn.

—— (2009) 'Wayward migration: on imagined futures and technological voids', *Ethnos*, 74(1): 91–109.

7 | Paths to Paris: hodological space and invisibility among Malian migrants without papers in the French capital

Line Richter

Introduction

At the end of 2014, Adama finally reached Paris. His journey had started more than a decade earlier in the Mopti region of Mali. At first, he had travelled around the region working odd jobs in Senegal and in Côte d'Ivoire. After a short stop back in Mali, he travelled across the Sahara Desert to Algeria where he found work. There he became fixated on reaching Paris. He would spend seven years peddling between Algeria and Morocco, try numerous times in various ways to cross the border into Spain before finally, in the summer of 2014, on a small inflatable boat, avoiding both the Moroccan and Spanish guards who enforce the border, reaching the Spanish enclave Ceuta.

As part of a larger project on migrants' experiences along the Western migratory corridor from West Africa through the Maghreb and into Southern Europe, I had first met Adama in Algeria, then Morocco, then Ceuta and finally in Paris, where his arrival coincided with a longer fieldwork I was undertaking there.[1] We met up at the metro station close to his brother's house in the periphery of the 16th *arrondissement*. The 16th is one of the more bourgeois neighbourhoods in Paris and most of the buildings bear clear marks of the prosperity of its residents. Tall white buildings surrounding the Place de Maréchal Juin and large Hausmannian boulevards meet you as you exit the train station. From the station, we walked towards the outskirts of the *arrondissement* and the large freeway encircling all of Paris, when the architecture started to change. Large high rises appeared and the large roaring freeway and open areas seemingly without purpose sidestepped the neat and ordered chicness of the rest of the *arrondissement*. Not long had passed since I saw him in Ceuta, but Adama looked happier here. In Ceuta we had sat on the beach glaring at the rock of Gibraltar across the strait. As long as I had known him, Adama had always kept in good spirits, but at the beach a gloominess had descended upon him. To lighten the mood, I said 'you have made it to Europe after all this time'. 'This is not Europe, it is Africa', he retorted. This underscores how even though Ceuta is Spanish, its geographical placement on the African continent confines those migrants who illegally cross the borders as they are unable to leave without the assistance in one way or the other of the Spanish authorities; making Ceuta into what many have referred to as a 'large open prison' or 'sweet prison' (cf. Andersson 2014: 215). In Paris, the smile was back on Adama's face. He was wearing a big hat that covered his hair and a leather jacket yet still he was rubbing his hands together to fend off the cold. But he laughed as we both rejoiced in this (somewhat unexpected) reunion in a Parisian neighbourhood emblematic of success and prosperity. Walking towards the house I said, 'we are here, you are in Paris' as both a question and a statement. To my surprise he answered, 'This is Paris. If it isn't I will keep on going'.

Adama's long and perilous journey to Paris, and his assertion that Paris may not be Paris underscores how the migratory journey is not merely a journey in geographical space, but certainly also a journey in social and existential terms. The Paris for which Adama was searching was invoked by a long tradition of migratory narratives and imaginaries that circulate in Mali. However, the images and popular portrayals of the French capital only tell part of the story, because as Adama so poetically expressed, Paris was not synonymous with the evident wealth of the 16th arrondissement, the Eiffel tower or Notre Dame. Paris was a place where he could fulfil his goals and succeed. His phrasing allows us to think of Paris and the migrants' journeys to and in the city as journeys in existential space as well as in physical space. It invites us to move from a geometric and geographical understanding of the space in which the migrants move and live to a social and existential point of departure. Even after Adama reached the French capital – his original goal when I first met him in Algeria – his journey continued.

In this chapter, I will explore how Malian migrants who live in Paris 'without papers', carve out individual paths in their efforts to try to 'make it' (*reussir*). Or in Adama's terminology as they try to 'reach Paris'. The paths of irregular migrants go through landscapes filled with obstacles, where their existence in many ways is confined to the shadows; they are often there to be seen but stay unrecognized, living in the margins of society. Evoking the concept of 'hodological space' I investigate how migrants actively work with processes of invisibility and visibility through their paths in (and to) the city. A hodological approach, I argue, can guide our attention to the way people move in the world, in ways that are simultaneously geographical, social and existential. By using the lens of hodology we can capture the way processes of invisibilization and visibilization ranging from individual concerns to large-scale social forces affect the migrants' lives as they try to make it to and in Paris.

Paths of invisibility and visibility

In the last couple of decades, migration literature has shown how migrants, especially 'irregular migrants' (as well as refugees) in a range of ways and places are structurally 'invisible' or 'invisibilized'. Dealing with large-scale power configurations and their effects, invisibility has become a trope through which we understand the (socio-)political status and exclusion of irregular migrants and refugees within contemporary nation-states. This literature has powerfully shown how 'illegality' is produced and sustained in the everyday lives of migrants in the face of a (more or less) antagonistic political and legal apparatus and how these processes invisibilize the people in question. As is stressed by de Genova, citing Coutin: 'The social space of "illegality" is an erasure of legal personhood – a space of *forced invisibility*, exclusion, subjugation, and repression that "materializes around [the undocumented] wherever they go"' (de Genova 2002: 427, my emphasis).

Zooming in on France, where this chapter is situated, processes of structural exclusion and marginalization of (irregular) migrants (and asylum seekers) have been examined in various ways by using analytical lenses and approaches such as 'moral economy' (Fassin 2005), 'regimes of care' (Ticktin 2011) and labour market organization (Timera 1997) just to mention a few. Focusing on Malian migrants in Paris, Sargent and Larchanché-Kim (2006) show how ideological and institutional constraints shape the identities of migrants whose everyday lives are permanently unstable, leaving them in a type of liminality. While these latter works do not use a lens of invisibility, they point to the extremely precarious situation of irregular migrant workers in France, and the perils of my interlocutors in France echo these analyses. Structural invisibility and invisibilization is very much an issue in the everyday lives of my interlocutors. As I understand it, the goal of this edited volume as it is presented in the introduction invites us to reconsider how processes of invisibilization and visibilization work in the lives of people displaced. It invites us to move beyond analysing in what ways those who are displaced are invisibilized, towards how different processes of invisibilization and visibilization affect and shape the lives of people who are displaced. I welcome the opportunity to focus on the 'productive' aspects of invisibilization, and not least the dialectics between invisibilization and visibilization. In order to understand the paths that migrants like Adama carve out as they journey, not only geographically, but also socially and existentially, I turn to hodology.

Hodology is etymologically derived from the Greek *hodos* meaning path or a way, and thus pertains to the study and knowledge of paths. The concept has surfaced in different places in different ways. In this chapter I follow two strains of thought: one existentialist and one ethnographic. I take my initial cue from Jean-Paul Sartre, who more or less in passing claims, 'the space which is originally revealed to me is hodological space: it is furrowed with paths and highways' (Sartre 2013[1956]: 345). Central to Sartre is the immense power embedded in the sensory capacity of seeing, of 'the look', to which we also should turn in order to understand the hodological space which is revealed to the subject. Introduced into social psychology by Kurt Lewin (1938), from whom Sartre presumably also borrowed the term (Mirvish 1984), the concept of hodological space was meant to challenge the idea of geometrical space as the key to understanding the way people relate to their environment. Lewin's main idea is that 'paths are traced out in the act of going towards a positive valence or for that matter away from a negative one' (Mirvish 1984: 155). The vectors and valences which Lewin is occupied with create a dynamic field of power, integral to the interaction between a subject and its environment (Mirvish 1984: 156). From his large existentialist opus *Being and Nothingness*, the point of departure for Sartre here is the relation between the subject and the Other. The look of the Other installs a sense of being-looked-upon in the subject, upon which the subject becomes objectified by the Other, while the Other comes to appear as subject. As pointed out by Angelina Vaz:

> [F]or Sartre, when I am by myself, I am at the *center* of my 'look-space'. When I am seen by another person my 'look-space' is intruded upon: another 'freedom' has entered my look-space and objectified me in the power of his/her gaze. (1995: 34)

Thus, we must consider the intersubjective relation between seeing and being-seen. One is visible to someone or something. However, as also underscored by Mirvish (1984), there need not be one distinct Other whose gaze rests upon the subject. 'The fact of being-looked-at can not … depend on the object which manifests the look' (Sartre 2013[1956]: 300). The gaze can be 'embodied' by an ephemeral presence of the Other – reminding us of Michel Foucault's notion of panopticon (1979), as also pointed out by Vaz (1995). In terms of the lives of the men which this chapter is about, it reminds us that the whole of the circumstances which the migrants find themselves in relate to a global order of those who are 'desirable', and those who are not (cf. Agier 2011). Hodological space is that space which is revealed to the men through their particular possibilities for being, moving and 'succeeding' in the city.

Michael Barrett's (2009) point of departure is ethnographic. He uses the notion of hodological space to contest universalist ideas of borders and surrounding identity categories (especially the category 'refugee'), and draws from Egenter (2002) and Lubkemann (2001), arguing that the hodological space is a 'path-space' which renders 'migrants as actors in their own life trajectories in time and space' (Barrett 2009: 101). Ethnographically he shows how Mbunda families and men experience the Angolan–Zambian borderland. His intent is to destabilize common assumptions about refugees and the border as a geographical site and instead focus on experiential and existential mobility across the border. This mobility, he argues, depends on the landscape people inhabit, people's social positions, and not least contingencies such as violence or poverty. He thus invites us to move from a geographically bound conception of how human beings move through space to an experientially configured matter.

In what follows, I will combine the two approaches to hodological space outlined above. Sartre's emphasis on being-for-other as it comes into being with the look of the Other (i.e. in a visibility/invisibility duality) can guide us in understanding how hodological space is that space in which one experiences and comes into being, through processes of visibilization. And in understanding that this visibilization is primarily a relation between self and Other – while recognizing that this Other can be ephemeral. In other words, that there is always someone or something to whom one is visible (however intangible this is). Barrett prompts us to consider the specific landscapes in which people live and move, not just as particular sites such as borders – or in this case the metropolis – but as social spaces.

Displacement continued

> Petit-Sékou mon frère, ça fait dix ans que je suis ici. Pour toi, je suis là-bas. Tes rêves n'ont pas changé. Mais les miens oui. Ou peut-être pas. Car je rêve encore de là-bas. Je ne jure que là-bas … où tu es. Mon ici d'hier est devenu mon là-bas d'aujourd'hui. (Gauz 2014)[2]

Ivorian writer Gauz[3] has written a powerful poem, *ici là-bas* ('here there') about life for a West African man without papers in Paris, which I have quoted above. Constructed as a letter from an Ivorian man to his younger brother (Sékou) in his natal village, the poem, published in the French newspaper *Liberation*'s monthly culture magazine *Next* in October 2014, tells beautifully and tragically of the unnamed narrator's experiences in the city in which he longed to be as a boy and where he is now struggling. At home in Côte d'Ivoire, the little brother dreams of the 'there' where his brother is. In return, the narrator in Paris dreams of the 'there' of his little brother's Côte d'Ivoire. His life in Paris is lived '*à côté*' – beside a 'regular' Parisian life in a West African microcosm of menial jobs, seclusion and the constant fear of controls, where his existence is reduced to avoidance. As the poem continues: '*Vie? Je ne vis pas, j'évite*'.[4] Gauz' narrator 'avoids life' in Paris, as he dreams of his native home. His original displacement, away from the village, continues in the city he used to dream of, where he now lives and dreams of elsewhere. The poem resonates powerfully with the experiences of Malian migrants in Paris who, like the narrator, long for their West African villages, towns and cities. The reversal of the 'here' and 'there' that the narrator experiences, where the 'there' so longed-after becomes the 'here' from where another 'there' is longed for, is a classical theme in tales of dislocation and also among my interlocutors. In Paris, the men I talked to longed for their mothers' cooking, for chatting (*causer*) with their friends in the *grins* (friendship groups), for the warm weather, for the starry nights and much more in Mali. But unlike Gauz' narrator, they also dreamed of other things, mainly of 'making it' (*réussir*) in Paris, like Adama did. But 'that's difficult (*a ka gɛlɛn* in Bamanankan or *c'est pas facile* in French), as they would say over and over again, followed by 'we don't have a choice' (*on n'as pas le choix*). Unable to return to Mali 'without anything in the pockets', as they said, the men had to try to find their bearings in Paris. The social pressure to succeed was overwhelming, and the lack of success widened the gap between the migrant and his family.

From the outset their paths were shaped by processes of marginalization and exclusion. The central location of this chapter is Paris, but let me briefly touch upon the journey that precedes the migrants' arrival in the French capital. In Mali, one of the poorest countries in the world, they had very limited possibilities for finding a steady source of income, for founding a family, and for supporting their families. The predicament for youth across the African continent has already been investigated through different lenses, for example that youths are stuck in 'waithood' (Honwana 2014), that they are stuck in a 'social moratorium' (Vigh 2006) or that they are searching for 'emplacement', defined as 'a social positioning that enables the pursuit of existentially meaningful life-making, but as an ongoing struggle for access, rather than as a fixed position or status' (Bjarnesen 2016: 54).

Many of the young men I talked to in Mali, who all expressed desires to leave, told stories of how they 'did not count' and 'were not respected' in their families. This, they said, installed a sense of shame in them – *c'est la honte*. Shame, Sartre argues, 'is shame of self; it is the recognition of the fact that I am indeed that object which the Other is looking at and judging' (2013[1956]: 285). Their original exit, one could say, was thus based on an over-visibility in existential terms, premised upon the inability to escape the sense of being looked at and judged by others.

This burden compelled many to leave. As the tangibility of being-looked-at by their families faded, other processes of invisibilization and visibilization shaped their paths from West Africa to Europe. On these journeys the men did their utmost to stay out of sight of authorities, 'moving under the radar'. In the Maghreb, migrants, in the words of Bensaad, 'adopt a strategy of imposed invisibilization' (2009: 20, my translation, see also Pian 2009) because of fear of authorities and racially motivated assaults. Upon arriving in Europe, they are pushed into the shadows of society (cf. Lucht 2012) as they fall into a particular political category of being 'undocumented'.

Sans-papiers

In many ways, papers (or rather the absence of papers) define the men from the moment they arrive in France. As Gauz further wrote in the poem quoted above: '*je ne suis rien, rien d'autre qu'une absence, une absence de papier*'.[5] The absence of papers has, in its hyphenated form *sans-papiers*, given name to a political status of a person without the legal rights to be (and work) in France (*un sans-papier*) and the political movements of such persons (*mouvements des sans-papiers*). The papers so sought after are residence and work permits that would enable my interlocutors to work and live without fearing controls, to be protected by French workers' and citizens' rights and, perhaps most importantly, to travel back to Mali to see their families. Even before arriving and just talking and dreaming of going to Europe, papers are seen as an essential component of success.

According to Lochak (1997), during the economic boom of the 1960s when manual labour was short in France, workers who arrived irregularly could easily obtain resident and work permits and there was little policing of workers. However, after labour market tensions in the late 1960s, a bill was passed in 1972 forbidding anyone who entered France without a work contract to be regularized (Lochak 1997: 32). This change, according to Lochak, instigated the *mouvement des sans-papiers*. In the 1970s, a range of strikes in France led to new public discourses which was the starting point for constructing illegal migration as a problem. As several observers have noted, 1974 marked a defining turn in French immigration policies from rather open to rather closed. The French government announced a stop to immigration following the increasingly heated debates on immigration, a policy that would later be softened (Lochak 1997; Rygiel 2014). Following this curbing of legal migration, the French state also increasingly sought to control illegal migration. France had opened its borders to (post)colonial subjects willing to do unskilled work in the 'hexagon' (continental France as it is often referred to in overseas and former colonial territories) during the post-war period and immediately after independence but gradually closed them to the point of the contemporary context where they are almost hermetically sealed. Nonetheless, since the defining moment of 1974 two mass regularization periods occurred, first in 1981–1982, when approximately 130,000 migrants 'in an irregular situation' where given residence permits if they could show proof of employment (Lochak 1997), and subsequently in 1997–1998 when approximately 80,000 received papers, this time on the basis of humanitarian and family situations (Martineau 2012). Since then, regularization has been given on a case-to-case basis based on the following criteria: steady work, children enrolled in French schools, marriage to a French citizen or holder of '*titre de séjour*' or if one was a minor when one arrived in France.[6] The collective memory of the regularizations kept many hoping for new sudden mass-regularizations, but few were optimistic about this. The absence of papers which so defined their possibilities lasted for several years, if not decades, for the vast majority of irregular migrants. If the migrants have not been able to recuperate papers, they live in a 'space of forced invisibilization' (cf. de Genova 2002) where their legal status defines not only their relation to the state (and the ensuing rights and obligations), but also, evidently, their possibilities for movements in the city, as they have to stay clear of run-ins with authorities. Thus their 'illegality' 'descends into the ordinary' (cf. Das 2007) and becomes embodied (cf. Willen 2007) as the men try to 'make it' in the city. Their paths in Paris reflected this predicament.

Migrants' paths

Paris hosts a large West African community. While some West Africans left their native countries in the wake of colonial liberation, at a point in time where legal entry into France for workers was possible, others, like Adama, have risked their lives to reach Paris. Each migrant has their own story of leaving their countries of origin, and of arriving in and inhabiting the city. Nonetheless in the city and its suburbs there are certain places, areas and neighbourhoods where West African migrants live or are drawn to for other reasons. These include but are certainly not limited to: the

Gare du Nord train station, the Goutte d'Or[7] neighbourhood in north-western Paris, the Chatelet train station and shopping mall, the Montreuil suburb (jokingly known as Bamako-sur-Seine) and the *foyers de travailleurs étrangers* (migrant dormitories) spread out across the suburbs and within the city. The *foyers* are nodal points in Malian transnational networks. For many, the *foyers* are the first entry points into the city and into a larger network of other Malians who they may be able to rely on to get by. To officially reside in the *foyers*, one needs to be regularized. However, the majority of the *foyers* are immensely overpopulated and host many migrants 'without papers'. The *foyers* function as social nexuses for the migrants when they arrive and as they find their bearings (see also Mbodj-Poye 2016a). Some pass briefly through the *foyers*, while others stay for long periods of time or end up residing in them more or less permanently. The dormitories are visible points in the Parisian architecture and in the social infrastructure available to migrants. While they visibilize the presence of migrant workers (many of whom are West African) across the city, they also conceal many migrants, who are able to live life *à côté* – in the closed off social worlds of the Parisian *foyers* (cf. Gauz' poem), and to be safeguarded from an everyday that in its extreme form could be lived on the street.

Camara Camara lived in a *foyer* in the 13th arrondissement, but when he arrived in Paris in 2014 finding a place to stay was difficult. We met on a cold winter afternoon outside the BULAC University library in the 13th *arrondissement*, and walked the short distance to the Boulevard de France. Lined with modernistic high rises in steel and glass, the large road is a central artery to this old working-class *arrondissement* that now also has a large business district. Shopping centres and large cafés have been built to accommodate the needs of the community of mainly white-collar workers and students in this neighbourhood. In one of these large cafés we found a quiet place to talk. Camara said that most people know someone who can help them out when they arrive, but that he hadn't known anyone. It was really difficult. We talked about his journey; about how he left his home in the region of Mopti; and about how he got by in the *bizness* (of facilitating migration journeys) in the Maghreb before entering Ceuta in a small zodiac in March or April 2014. After many months in the *campo* (Red Cross reception centre) in Ceuta he was sent to Spain, and spent some time in a small town close to Seville, where a lot of Malians live and work in the agricultural sector. He didn't have any family and very few acquaintances in France, but he was set on going there. In Spain he had made contact with a man from Cameroon who was involved in getting people to France and Germany (at this moment the internal European borders were heavily enforced, and many I talked to told me stories of difficult crossings at the Spanish–French border as well as the Italian–French border for those who had crossed from Libya to Italy). The fixer got him to the Spanish–French border where he waited a few days until he got on another bus. They were three people travelling together, brought together by the Cameroonian fixer, but the others were going to Berlin so he was the only one to get off the bus in Paris. As he said:

> So here I am, I am with my bag. If people approach me I talk to them. From morning to night. Someone there told me 'Camara – you go there, there is *foyer* …' because he himself couldn't bring me there. Because if he did, he would have problems. In the *foyers*, if you bring someone you have to take responsibility for him. It is not easy.

I asked if this 'someone' was anyone he knew already, but it was not, it was someone he had just met at the station. Such stories of more or less random encounters that lead to a helping hand are widespread. The migrants I talked to would often explain this with a generalized notion of 'solidarity' between 'blacks' or 'Africans'. That the new friend could not bring Camara to the *foyer*, but merely gave him an address also points to the complex system of the *foyers* and the sometimes subtle limits to the solidarity hailed by my interlocutors. Camara's new friend who could help him but only to a certain extent directs our attention to the specific circumstances of the French *foyers* and the conditions for foreigners (without papers) in France. It also shows how the tables can turn quite fast: while Camara was doing alright for himself in the Maghreb and qua his involvement in the *bizness* of facilitating migrant journeys had been a host of other migrants previously (see Richter 2019 for more on *bizness*), he was an unwanted guest in France trying to find a patron to help him. This aspect of Camara's story highlights how the particular places that migrants move through and dwell in greatly affect the way they are able to act and the social relations they are able to forge and maintain. The more well-structured solidarity of the *foyers* (see Manchuelle 1997) seems to have yielded for a negotiable and unstable type of solidarity in Paris. Mbodj-Pouye (2016b) shows how the transfer of the residents from old to new *foyers* (or *résidences sociales*) becomes a battleground for the meaning and extent of solidarity. New *foyers* are constructed to replace the old and often very run-down *foyers*. Where the old *foyers* have large rooms, shared by between two and eight people (plus the unregistered residents, or *suroccupants*), communal kitchens and halls, the new *foyers* have small studio apartments designed to make it impossible to add more beds/mattresses into the room, and there are no communal facilities. In fact, Adama moved with his brother to one such studio, which increased their expenses significantly. This design makes it difficult for many of the inhabitants who live unregistered to move from the *foyer* as they are often residing in France illegally and therefore do not have the possibility of official residence in public housing; like Adama, who slept on the floor of his brother's room, without being officially registered as a resident. Even if the migrants do have papers, the rent often exceeds what they can afford – even with an extra 'undocumented' in the room.

As outlined above, the *foyer* system is structured partly by public authorities and legal parameters and partly by the social structures which rest on generational agreements (the *noria* system, cf. Manchuelle 1997) and a generalized idea of 'solidarity' between Africans. The social relations become embedded in the actual sites – the *foyers* – that many migrants, like Camara and Adama, pass through on their paths.

As Camara and I walked from the café to the tramway, he pointed to a street below the bridge we crossed and explained that he used to look for work on that street, standing by the side of the road in the early morning hoping an employer would drive by and offer him a day's work. He had been working as a day labourer in the informal sector, struggling to make ends meet without any formal rights or protections (job security, unemployment benefits, sick pay, safety measures, etc.). This really surprised me. Naïvely, I thought that the French labour market was regulated in a way that precarious day labour was something that existed only by creative bookkeeping or the forging of documents, and that the 'illegal' workers were stashed away in dark back rooms, not that they were standing by the road visible to all.

While Camara did what he could to stay out of sight of authorities, his survival in the city hinged here on two modes of visibility. The first was the recognition of a migrant 'brotherhood' – the person he asked about directions was seen by Camara as a migrant right away, and most importantly the person saw Camara as such as well. The second was the purposeful display of himself as manual labour by the side of the road. Finding work relied upon him shaping himself into a day labourer and being visible to potential employers. For the uninitiated observer (such as myself) he might not have stood out as part of the black-market economy. This brings us back to the question of the relational character of visibility and invisibility. While Camara wanted to conceal himself from authorities, he wanted to be visible to employers at the same time. The street under the bridge, concretely and metaphorically, was a place where he was trying to stay out of sight, while in plain sight.

Touré Touré was another young Malian man who, when we met, had recently risked his life crossing first the Sahara then the barbed-wire fences between Melilla and Morocco, and made his way to France. One day when we sat on a bench and talked above the Nation train station, a tall young man approached us. He heard us talking about Bamako and exchanging a few words in Bamanankan and he got curious – he was also from Mali, and the random encounter underlined not only the large number of Malians in Paris but also the way Malians connect with each other in foreign lands, demonstrating the particular type of solidarity mentioned above. The man asked for a cigarette and sat down. He seemed really keen on getting to know us and sharing his experiences with us. His name was Sakho, and he told us that he had recently gained his papers, but work was still not steady and with the papers came a lot more expenses. I asked the two men how much rent they paid where they were staying and Touré said he was living on the mercy of his relative who paid the rent where he stayed. To this Sakho added, 'Yeah, when you are new, you don't pay', underscoring the importance of 'generational agreements' between migrants (cf. Timera 1997) and the solidarity which Camara also invoked to find a place to stay. Touré had been in Paris for around a year at that time, while Sakho told us he had already been there for several years. However, even with papers Sakho's situation was problematic; he no longer counted as '*nouveau*', lived in a place of his own in a distant suburb where the rent was high and he had, with the regularization of his status, lost an essential benefit: the discounted railway pass. At that moment in time, foreigners who did not have legal permission to be in France could by way of the medical aid card (*aide médicale de l'Etat*) get a 75 per cent reduction on their monthly railway pass (*carte Navigo*). The medical aid card permitted foreigners without papers to receive medical attention, and in the Paris region the card also granted the sizable discount on public transportation.[8] At that point in time, it meant that the Navigo pass valid from Touré's house in St Denis and within the city limits of Paris would cost approximately 22€ per month, a cost that would be shared among the housemates so that whenever someone worked or was looking for work and had to use public transportation to get there they would have priority over the pass, as the itinerary of the worker would be less flexible than that of someone whose time was not conditioned by the labour market and who could avoid known points of control. The Navigo pass is personal and carries the photo of the cardholder. When I asked if that did not present a problem when sharing a Navigo, Touré laughed and explained that the controllers can't tell the difference between 'blacks'.

It could, however, prove to be a problem if one was caught without a pass in the Métro and unable to immediately pay the fine. The worst-case scenario, for someone 'without papers', was to be taken to a police station and from there to a *centre de retention*. Staying under the radar when travelling the Métro was therefore of great importance. As Touré pointed out, the evisceration of individual identities of 'blacks' under the gaze of 'whites', made this easier. The constant awareness of the gaze of the other did, however, affect the way the men were able to move, and thus their paths in the city. One of the keys was to look as 'generic' as possible. To shape yourself into a version of a 'black' that did not stand out. Being made invisible by way of blending in with the crowd. A kind of camouflage. Amar, another young Malian man, how he changed his hairdo from a big 'rasta' to tightly braided cornrows in order to avoid being controlled.

Travelling in the train system was not just about making oneself invisible. In specific spots, such as the central stations of Gare du Nord and Châtelet, the men would often want to be visible. At the Gare du Nord they could connect or reconnect with friends they ran into in the large arrival hall, which also functioned as a meeting point. But, as pointed out by Kleinman, the Gare du Nord can also function as a 'hub of creating encounters across difference' (2014: 288) where West African men can connect with people outside the closed off social circuits of migrant living. For my interlocutors they, in particular, were interested in meeting women. Women were often considered a 'fast-track' to papers, given that if you married a woman with French citizenship or a *carte de séjour*, you had a fairly good chance of gaining regularization yourself. But the men's desire to connect with women should of course not be seen in a purely functionalist manner. Like other youths they were also interested in romance, love and flirting. To this avail they had to be visible and shape themselves into desirable men. This would entail dressing in fashionable clothes and standing in places where they could see the flow of people passing through the stations and not least where they could be seen by women.

On a sunny day in the spring of 2016, I met up with Touré near the St Paul metro in the well-off Paris neighbourhood le Marais. I saw him from across the road. He was wearing new clothes and was looking more and more like a young French man from the suburbs.[9] His French also sounded more Parisian. We walked through the narrow and quaint streets in the old Marais and ended up by the Seine. On our way, we talked about life here. Touré had worked the day before yesterday, but it was so rare that the agency called him that he could not support himself with the small pay he gained from the infrequent work. He was, as so many times before, quite distressed and marked by the uncertainty of the situation. Overlooking the river with the reflection of the glistening sun and the blue sky, and its cruise boats filled with happy tourists, Touré once again said, 'what can I do?' as an almost rhetorical question about his situation. As usual I didn't have a good answer, but tried my best to listen to his concerns and prompt him about his options in Paris which for him, 'without papers', were slim. Touré's brother, also in the Paris area, had recently undertaken training to become a security guard, and Touré hoped that when the brother would get a diploma he could also use that and become a security guard. But Touré did not seem too convinced that this would actually happen; he didn't talk about this as a real possibility as such, but rather as one path that might open in a distant future. Maybe he was marred by the many failed attempts he had had at securing a job. Even with his brother's CV and work permit, Touré had been unable to find anything but the occasional day's work in construction that he would get through an agency that mediates temporary jobs.

We walked further into the heart of Paris, and crossed into the area around *les halles*, a large newly-renovated shopping mall in the 1st *arrondissement*. During our walk, we stopped at different places along the river, admiring the view, and agreeing that it was pretty impressive. From time to time we stopped to take pictures in front of the river, in front of the shopping mall, on the picturesque bridges next to tourists speaking languages from all over the world. At one point we sat down on the riverbank, and I asked Touré what his options were. He told me that there were no options, 'if there were you would take them. You have to wait and all of the sudden possibilities may arise. You cannot do anything', he said. While Touré was not usually prone to talking a lot about God or religion, this day was different. He said that he just wanted a good life, just to be well, and to be rich; 'One can do what one can, but in the end, it is God who decides. You have to look for it yourself but it is not certain you will find it. Fifty per cent will fail, and the other 50 per cent will maybe win'.

Not quite grasping the relation between God's almightiness and free will, I asked Touré what he could do himself to 'win'. How could one 'look for it' when it is God who decides? He explained, 'you have to look for your luck. Look for what you want', 'the only way to do that fast is to find a woman'. So far, Touré had far from found his luck in this regard, and that day he told me that he was actually done with women. He had told me this several times before but so far, he had been unsuccessful in his endeavours to find a potential wife.

Sitting on the concrete bank of the river along with small groups of people talking, eating and laughing under the clear spring sun, our conversation turned to Mali. Touré told me that it would be impossible to return there without 'something', even though he would like to. 'They don't understand that there is nothing here', he said, referring to his family. But no matter what, he didn't blame his family, because, as he said, he didn't understand before he left either. I had heard this many times before. The distance between the person who has left and those who are at home only widens as the hardships increase. Images and symbols of Paris and other places abroad, or people there, are everywhere in Mali and many households have a member abroad (often in Europe) who supports the family and sends tokens of his (or her) success, for example in the shape of appliances, money for construction or vehicles. But many Malians abroad are like Touré, far from 'succeeding'. Some people have told me that they do not pick up the phone when their kin call, some even change their numbers to avoid confronting the expectations on the other end of the line. Touré sometimes avoided the calls from his mother to whom he could rarely send money. His father had always told him it is okay to come back – even if he didn't have anything, he could always return. But no one else in the family understood this, so he couldn't return, he said. That would be too shameful. The path that Touré was on led him through Paris in constant search of opportunities, as he tried his best to shape himself into a desirable young man who would stand out to women, while at the same time into someone who did not stand out in the eyes of authorities.

After our pause by the river, we got up and walked back again. Along the riverbank on the small island Île St Louis in the middle of the Seine, our conversation circled back around the difficulty of living in Paris, of finding work, of the family back home who didn't understand. A large river freight boat came into view, and as it approached us its name revealed itself in tall letters: FREEDOM. At the same time, subtly underlining the contrast between the free-flowing riverboat and Touré's struggles in the city, Touré started to sing the refrain from a popular Ivorian song 'Paris is hard, hard like a rock' ('*Paris est dur, dur comme cailloux*').[10]

Indeed, Paris was a tough rock to crack open. In constant search of opportunities, the migrants' paths through the city was wrought with difficulties. As they moved through the geographical and social landscapes their existential paths were shaped concurrently.

Conclusion

There is no doubt that irregular migrants are structurally marginalized, confined to the shadows and invisibilized in various ways across the globe. In France, West African migrants 'without papers' struggle to find their bearings in a difficult environment. Adama, Camara and Touré are but a few examples of West African migrants who in various ways and with various strategies try to 'make it' in Paris. Their struggles are akin, but their stories and journeys are individual. They carve out their own geographical, social and existential paths in Paris. In this chapter I have discussed how processes of invisibilization and visibilization were integral to these paths.

The notion of hodology, as I have used it here, invites us to think of the landscapes migrants move through and live in as primarily social landscapes. It also, if we pause on Sartre's initial usage of the notion, invites us to turn our attention to the power embedded in the sensory capacity of sight, and to how we see and are seen as we (try to) move through these landscapes.

The Malian migrants' paths through the city depended on a range of factors. First, it is important to note that their original displacement from Mali was primarily based on a lack of possibilities and lack of social mobility. Marred by poverty, unemployment and without steady sources of income, the men were impelled to move. The displacement follows the migrant as they move through the world. 'Without papers' in France their pursuits of success are shaped by the lack of papers and the 'forced invisibilization' under which they live. Second, their paths are shaped by the social relations they are able to rely on in the city. Some of them were established long before their arrival, while others are made in the city. Some are tight, like Adama's relation to his brother who he lodged with, while others are fragile, like Camara's relation to the person who initially helped him. Still others exist mainly in a potential future such as Touré's idea of connecting with a woman. Third, these paths through Paris are existential. Adama's assertion that he might not have reached Paris tells a tale of a pursuit of happiness that transcends geographical and social landscapes. It tells a tale of a longing for a future where he could realize his dreams.

Adama did find a version of Paris. A few years after he arrived, he married a French woman, who shortly after gave birth to their first child. He gained a *carte de séjour*, formal employment in a kitchen and is now dutifully taking classes with a local NGO in order to get his elementary school exam (he had very little formal education in Mali). However, he tells me, life is not always easy. Like Sakho, he talks about how expensive life with papers is, how low his salary is compared to the expenses he and his wife have: rent for their small flat in a suburb, the daycare for their child, the remittances that must be sent to Mali and all of the everyday expenses that come with life in a European metropolis. Finding one's Paris, is thus not about reaching a particular geographical point – it is an ongoing journey towards 'making it'.

Notes

1 For more see Richter (2018).

2 'Little-Sékou my brother, it's been ten years that I have been here. For you I am there. Your dreams haven't changed. But mine have. Or maybe not. Because I still dream of there. I swear only of there … where you are. My here of yesterday has become my there of today'. My translation, here and henceforth.

3 *Nom de plume* for Armand Patrick Gbaka-Brédé.

4 'Live? I don't live, I avoid'.

5 'I am nothing, nothing but an absence of paper'.

6 www.jurifiable.com/conseil-juridique/droit-des-etrangers/regularisation-des-sans-papiers.

7 A neighbourhood in north-western Paris known for its large migrant population and not least the dramatic events of the l'église Saint-Bernard de la Chappelle where mainly West African migrants 'without papers' were forcefully evicted after seeking refuge in 1996.

8 'L'aide médicale de l'État (AME) est un dispositif permettant aux étrangers en situation irrégulière de bénéficier d'un accès aux soins'. www.service-public.fr/particuliers/vosdroits/F3079. The rules have been changed as per January 2016, so that the discount on the Navigo no longer applies to foreigners in an 'irregular situation'.

9 It is the small things (how your jeans are fitted, the way you wear your hat, your hair, etc.) that distinguish one group (newly arrived Malians) from the other (French youth), and often it is very blurred.

10 'Paris', by Petit Yode & L'enfant Siro.

References

Agier, Michel (2011) *Managing the Undesirables: Refugee camps and humanitarian government*, Cambridge: Polity.

Andersson, Ruben (2014) *Illegality Inc.: Clandestine migration and the business of bordering Europe*, Oakland, CA: University of California Press.

Barrett, Michael (2009) 'The social significance of crossing state borders: home, mobility and life paths in the Angolan–Zambian Borderland', in Stef Jansen and Staffan Löfving (eds), *Struggles for Home: Violence, hope and the movement of people*, New York: Berghahn Books, 85–107.

Bensaad, Ali (2009) 'L'immigration en Algèrie. Une réalité prégnante et son occultation officielle', in Ali Bensaad (ed.), *Le Maghreb à l'épreuve des migrations subsahariennes: immigration sur émigration*. Paris: Karthala.

Bjarnesen, J. (2016) 'Between labor migration and forced displacement: Wartime mobilities in the Burkina Faso–Côte d'Ivoire transnational space', *Conflict and Society*, 2(1): 52–67. doi:http://dx.doi.org/10.3167/arcs.2016.020107.

Das, Veena (2007) *Life and Words: Violence and the descent into the ordinary*, Berkeley, CA: University of California Press.

de Genova, Nicholas P. (2002) 'Migrant "illegality" and deportability in everyday life', *Annual Review of Anthropology*, 31: 419–447. doi: 10.2307/4132887.

Egenter, Nold (2002) 'Otto Friedrich Bollnow's anthropological concept of space: a revolutionary new paradigm is under way', *The Internet Journal of Architecture*, December.

Fassin, Didier (2005) 'Compassion and repression: the moral economy of immigration policies in France', *Cultural Anthropology*, 20(3): 362–387. doi: 10.1525/can.2005.20.3.362.

Foucault, Michel (1979) *Discipline and Punish: The birth of the prison*, New York: Vintage Books.

Gauz (2014) 'Ici là-bas', *Libération Next*, vol. 65.

Honwana, Alcinda (2014) '"Waithood": youth transitions and social change', in T. Dietz, D. Foeken, L. de Haan and L. Johnson (eds), *Development and Equity: An interdisciplinary exploration by ten scholars from Africa, Asia and Latin America*, Leiden: Brill, 28–40.

Kleinman, Julie (2014) 'Adventures in infrastructure: making an African hub in Paris', *City & Society*, 26(3): 286–307.

Lochak, Daniel (1997) 'Les politiques de l'immigration au prisme de la législation sur les étrangers' in Didier Fassin, Alain Morice and Catherine Quiminal (eds), *Les lois de l'inhospitalité. Les politiques de l'immigration à l'épreuve des sans papiers*, Paris: La Découverte.

Lubkemann, Stephen (2001) 'Embedded time and dispersed place: displacement and gendered differences in Mozambican

"lifespace"', *XXIV IUSSP Congress*, Salvador, Brazil.
Lucht, Hans (2012) *Darkness before daybreak: African migrants living on the margins in southern Italy today*, Berkeley and Los Angeles, CA: University of California Press.
Manchuelle, François (1997) *Willing Migrants: Soninke labor diasporas, 1848–1960*, Athens, OH: Ohio University Press.
Martineau, Pauline (2012) 'Régularisations: comment le cas par cas est devenu la norme', *liberation.fr*, 29 June. Retrieved from: www.liberation.fr/societe/2012/06/29/regularisations-comment-le-cas-par-cas-est-devenu-la-norme_829821.
Mbodj-Pouye, Aïssatou (2016a) 'Fixed abodes: urban emplacement, bureaucratic requirements, and the politics of belonging among West African migrants in Paris', *American Ethnologist*, 43(2): 295–310. doi: 10.1111/amet.12306.
—— (2016b) 'On n'ignore pas la solidarité', *Genèses*, (3): 51–72.
Mirvish, Adrian (1984) 'Sartre, hodological space, and the existence of others', *Research in Phenomenology*, 14: 149–173.
Pian, Anaik (2009) 'Entre "visibilisation" et "invisibilsation", les migrations subsahariennes au Maroc', in Ali Bensaad (ed.), *Le Maghreb à l'épreuve des migrations subsahariennes: immigration sur émigration*, Paris: Karthala.
Richter, Line (2018) 'Gaps in a bordered world: Malian men trying to make it to and in Europe', PhD dissertation, Department of Anthropology, University of Copenhagen.
—— (2019) 'Doing bizness: migrant smuggling and everyday life in the Maghreb', *Focaal. Journal of Global and Historical Anthropology*, (85): 26–36.
Rygiel, Philippe (2014) 'Les migrations étrangères en France: une histoire européenne', in Marie Poinsot and Serge Weber (eds), *Migrations et mutations de la société française*, Paris: La Découverte, 19–28.
Sargent, Carolyn F. and Stéphanie Larchanché-Kim (2006) 'Liminal lives immigration status, gender, and the construction of identities among Malian migrants in Paris', *American Behavioral Scientist*, 50(1): 9–26.
Sartre, Jean-Paul (2013[1956]) *Being and Nothingness: An essay on phenomenological ontology*, translated by Hazel E. Barnes, London: Routledge. (French edition 1943).
Ticktin, Miriam Iris (2011) *Casualties of Care, Immigration and the Politics of Humanitarianism in France*, Berkeley, CA: University of California Press.
Timera, Mahamet (1997) 'L'immigration africaine en France: regards des autres et repli sur soi: La France et les migrants africains', *Politique africaine*, 67: 41–47.
Vaz, Angelina (1995) 'Who's got the look? Sartre's gaze and Foucault's panopticism', *Dalhousie French Studies*, 32: 33–45.
Vigh, Henrik (2006) 'Social death and violent life chances', in Catrine Christiansen, Mats Utas and Henrik E. Vigh (eds), *Navigating Youth, Generating Adulthood: Social becoming in an African context*, Uppsala: Nordic Africa Institute.
Willen, Sarah S (2007) 'Toward a critical phenomenology of "illegality": state power, criminalization, and abjectivity among undocumented migrant workers in Tel Aviv, Israel', *International Migration*, 45(3): 8–38.

8 | Invisibility as a livelihood strategy: Zimbabwean migrant domestic workers in Botswana

Joyce Takaindisa and Ingrid Palmary

Introduction

> When you are a passenger in public transport, you should greet them in their language by saying 'dumela' because if you speak your own language, they don't like it at all, they want to hear their own language all the time. You must try by all means to be like them. (Kuda interview, 2017)

Migrant domestic workers from Zimbabwe carry an ambivalent status in Botswana as unwelcome immigrants, yet their labour as domestic workers is desired by employers. This chapter draws on research conducted by the first author as part of her doctoral studies programme from 2017 to 2019 on the everyday experiences of mothers who migrated from Zimbabwe to Botswana for informal care work in order to highlight how their invisibility is produced, challenged and maintained in this specific context. Based on their accounts, transnational mothers fluctuate between extremes of visibility, invisibility and hypervisibility as a result of immigration policies and state practices.

At individual level, we focus on strategies that they employ to render themselves invisible from the state gaze. We also focus on structural invisibilities produced as a direct result of state actions against irregular migrants. By focusing on the strategies of invisibility employed by transnational mothers, findings revealed that invisibility is used of a livelihood strategy to fulfil familial obligations back in Zimbabwe. On the other hand, hypervisibility is imposed by dominant groups and usually supported by social structures (Buchanan and Settles 2018). As such, the presence of migrant domestic workers in Botswana is famously known as the 'Zimbabwean illegal problem'. Consequently, it regularly appears in the media, portrayed as a constant menace but in contrast to the notion of invisibility addressed here, media representation renders them hypervisible to the public gaze, albeit negatively. Moreover, frequent mass deportations, done in full public view are carried out as a way of 'cleaning' out the problem and it renders them highly visible. Through processes of hypervisibilization by the state, media or the public, these actions confirm the widely circulated negative stereotypes which perceive them as criminals, job grabbers or public nuisances.

In this view, the work they do as domestic and care workers is not acknowledged therefore making their labour invisible in public discourse. Instead, what continues to dominate is the state and media rhetoric that depicts them as 'Zimbabwean illegals' causing a crisis in Botswana. Based on the foregoing, we unpack the processes of strategic invisibility by drawing on the concept of 'transitory dwelling places' (Lollar 2015) to show that invisibility and living in liminality is not always disadvantageous. We aim to show that invisibility is not always a negative position but can be used as a tool to sustain one's livelihood. We also illustrate the interrelatedness of visibility, invisibility and hypervisibility of undocumented migrants as categories that are not mutually exclusive. Instead, findings suggest that one can be (in)visible in one context and hypervisible in the next context or simultaneously experience both aspects of (in)visibility and hypervisibility (Lollar 2015; Buchanan and Settles 2018; Settles et al. 2019).

Although Botswana is an inhospitable dwelling place when one is undocumented, migrant women's endurance primarily stems from their perceptions of domestic work in Botswana as the only viable livelihood strategy for their family's survival, meagre as the earnings may be. Through sharing their narratives of strategic invisibility, this chapter contributes to the understanding of the invisibilization of undocumented migrants and the manner in which they respond to and manage surveillance. This study thereby contributes to the literature on global care chains, migrant domestic work and the growing body of literature on invisibility, migrant strategies and agency.

Global care chain theory and the (in)visibility bargain

Within the field of transnational migration studies, care chain literature (Hochschild 2000; Ehrenreich and Hochschild 2003; Parreñas 2001, 2005a, 2005b; Yeates 2004, 2009, 2012) has tended to focus on the commodification of care through the labour of migrant women from the Global South who migrate to the Global North as care workers. A typical global care chain is one where migrant domestic workers play an enabling role for their employers by allowing them to move into and stay on in the workforce, pursuing their professional occupations. Lutz and Palenga-Möllenbeck (2012: 17) have defined the 'global care chain' concept as 'a process in which several phenomena such as capitalism, globalisation and the feminisation of migration interact with gender relations, care and emotional work'. Global care chains have been created as a result of importing care and love from poor to rich countries, a process which facilitates the transfer of those services normally associated with the traditional roles of wife or mother.

In the process of doing so, migrants often leave behind their children in the care of other female kin. While much of the transnational literature (Glick Schiller et al. 1992) has been characterized by a South–North bias, little attention has been paid to commodified care that circulates within the boundaries of the Global South. With much of the scholarship focusing on migration streams from Asian and Latin American to Global North countries, this research fills a theoretical as well as empirical lacuna in the study of migrant domestic work by focusing on strategies of invisibilization used by undocumented migrant domestic workers in Botswana. The study illustrates this particular care chain as one that consists of a precarious care work-force in pursuit of sustaining livelihoods amid a harsh mobility regime that actively curtails their activities every single day.

In this study, we focus on a care chain that originates from Zimbabwe to seek care work in Botswana. There is an apparent link between migrant care work, which in the context of Botswana is highly criminalized, migration status and the ensuing conditions of either visibility, invisibility or hypervisibility. The conditions of invisibility and hypervisibility in this study serve to illuminate how migrant domestic work is inherently tied to power relations as it reflects on social hierarchies of power and how these conditions are also socially constructed based on difference/otherness. Although migrant domestic workers from Zimbabwe contribute immensely to care work in Botswana, their presence is met with anti-immigrant sentiments (Nyamnjoh 2002; Morapedi 2007). They therefore resort to strategies of staying under the radar or acts of shifting their identities in order to avoid detection by police and immigration officials.

Transnational migration involves elements of both choice and constraints (Carling 2002) making its experiences heterogeneous as it is mediated by one's class positioning, gender, legal status and location among many other factors (Salih 2001). In this study, transnational mothers' legal status play a key role in shaping their experiences in Botswana. Marked as illegal migrants in both media and public discourse, they are highly deportable subjects (De Genova 2002; Galvin 2015) but often resort to their own counter-strategies that work to obscure their presence in Botswana. Given that undocumented migration is often conflated with crime and threats to national security, women are forced to employ strategies that make them invisible in order to ensure their well-being (Rojas-Wiesner and DeVargas 2013).

Mainly, they choose to employ strategic anonymity and invest in hiding their status to avoid being detected despite the fact that care work in Botswana relies on an invisible pool of undocumented migrant domestic workers from Zimbabwe. Pugh (2018: 979) has reasoned that in order to reconcile competing host society requirements for social exclusion and economic gain, in relation to immigration policy, migrants and citizens live with a 'de facto invisibility bargain' – an unwritten set of expectations in which the host state/society implicitly accepts the presence of foreign migrants as long as they are seen to bring economic benefits to the country as well as maintain political and social invisibility.

Ironically, they are hidden yet their presence is an open secret. Accordingly, these women often find themselves manoeuvring between visibility and invisibility precisely because the invisibility bargain, premised on a set of informal expectations, demands that undocumented migrants should minimize some aspects of their identities, such as language, accent or cultural practice, especially in public, yet at the same time, exploiting their economic capacities (Pugh 2018) in order for their presence to be tolerated.

Fundamentally tied to power relations, invisibility represents a lack of power where an individual may not be fully recognized or appreciated (Brighenti 2007). Invisibility is thereby imposed on migrant domestic workers who lack a legal migration status, forcing them to negotiate their presence in Botswana with law enforcement agents and their employers who have the power to exploit their labour without facing any sanctions. For example, when confronted by the police, they can negotiate their release if they pay a sufficient bribe. Resorting to the use of various forms of agency with the aim of either resisting abuse or challenging power is perceived by undocumented women to be a viable survival strategy, especially when faced with no other opportunities back in their home country. Although invisibility may allow their mobility, it is usually not enough to guarantee a good quality of life as the gains of invisibility are usually short-term.

Significantly, in examining the conditions of invisibility and hypervisibility, what is key is to analyse the structural conditions that lead women to resort to invisibility. In this article, our main focus is on social invisibility which is defined as the everyday practices of seeing and being seen (Baird 2014: 3). Polzer and Hammond (2008) point to the necessity of questioning who or what is invisible, to whom it is invisible, why it is invisible and in what way it is invisible. Essentially, invisibility is relational and dependent on power relations and interests of those who are either to be seen or not to be seen (Polzer and Hammond 2008). In this way, invisibility and hypervisibility are forms of identity-based mistreatment of marginalized others (Buchanan and Settles 2018).

Scott (1985) conceptualizes invisibility as one of the weapons used by the weak in which the vulnerable work hard towards staying invisible to the 'powers that be'. Invisibility in this instance is therefore a resource. Leinonen (2012) further argues that invisibility should be studied intersectionally in order to highlight how certain groups are made either more visible or invisible through factors such as nationality, language skills or public behaviour (Toivanen 2014). Intersectionality further brings attention to the fluctuating nature of (in)visibility (Leinonen 2012). Moreover, (in)visibility is a form of agency and can also be characterized by performative dimensions (Juul 2014; Lollar 2015).

In the present study, performative dimensions of (in)visibility arise against a background of restrictive immigration laws, public discourses and labour policies in Botswana that essentially render migrant domestic workers invisible in the labour markets, with a bias towards negative reporting of their presence. Borrowing from the theory of performativity, people learn to act or behave in certain ways in order to fit into society. As such, people deliberately engage in repetitive acts that seek to portray certain identities (Butler 1990). For the mothers in this study, their embodied enactments through deliberate actions to dress, speak and walk in a similar fashion to the local Batswana translates into the domain of their everyday survival strategies.

Strategic invisibility towards the police, immigration officials and local Batswana citizens is a choice to either stay under the radar and therefore out of sight or, alternatively, to hide in plain sight or camouflage/blend in, which consequently becomes a means of protection in the absence of any other formalized social protection. Following this, we use the concept of strategic invisibility to unpack acts of agency or resistance by migrant domestic workers in Botswana as a means through which they may remain hidden as undocumented care workers. Visibility is central to human experience because it is through visibility that emotions, thoughts and passions are expressed (Arendt cited in Lollar 2015: 303–304). Nevertheless, visibility also involves an element of choice about what to either show to or hide from to others. The politics of self-representation gives each person control over what they may see fit to reveal about themselves (Lollar 2015).

In addition, the powers that be, in this case immigration officials and police officers, can also decide who to make visible or invisible; hence one may oscillate between being invisible in one context and hypervisible in another context, suggesting that neither conditions are static to human experiences. There are rules and expectations of engagement, which can make places either hospitable or inhospitable (Lollar 2015). Strategic invisibility is thus a response to an inhospitable dwelling place for illegal Zimbabwean migrant domestic workers in Botswana which they use as a form of resistance to their vulnerable situations as undocumented and unwelcome guests. Through the Botswana immigration law, which essentially denies them a regular status, these women's continued presence in Botswana is dependent on what actions they take to mitigate their visibilities in social spaces in Botswana.

Data and methods

In this chapter, we draw on empirical findings from the first author's unpublished doctoral research in order to analyse the everyday strategies of invisibility employed by Zimbabwean migrant domestic workers in Botswana. The data came from a larger study on the re-configurations of motherhood in transnational families as well as the experiences of maternal separation and perceptions of motherhood by left-behind children in Zimbabwe. It also incorporated the views and perceptions of the children's caregivers. Participants for the study were from Botswana and Zimbabwe through a matched sampling approach. A qualitative methodology was employed through the use of narrative story-telling, semi-structured interviews and solicited diaries. Ethical clearance for this study was sought from the Witwatersrand University Ethics Committee.

In Botswana, the target population was mothers who had left children back in Zimbabwe and migrated for domestic work to Botswana, while in Zimbabwe the children of transnational migrant domestic workers and their care-givers were the primary targets. The original research therefore consisted of ten migrant mothers, nine left-behind children and seven caregivers, all sampled through a combination of snowball and purposive sampling techniques. We focus on key findings that relate to the nature of invisibility as both an assigned status and adopted strategy of migrant domestic workers. We illustrate how Zimbabwean women working in Botswana as domestic workers employ strategic invisibility in order to remain undetected by authorities in Botswana.

In the first instance, the first author asked a single narrative question as a starting point for story-telling. Borrowing from Wengraf's (2004) biographical method, a single question aimed at inducing narrative was posed to the respondents in order to capture their in-depth experiences and patterns of care-giving as distant mothers. The question posed asked them to tell their story, without any parameters and in their own way and this allowed them to tell their stories freely without any interruption and interjections. All stories were audio-recorded with the participants' consent. The second stage involved listening and re-listening to their stories, after which questions were jotted down for follow-up interviews.

This involved coming up with a semi-structured interview schedule for each participant. By virtue of their stories being different, each interview schedule was different as it had to be customized to the specific story told by each woman. Respondents were asked if they would be willing to diarize their stories for at least six months and each participant who consented to keeping a diary was given a diary in which to record their stories in whatever way they preferred. Participants were, however, given an orientation, which involved explaining and giving examples of the nature of information they could include such as communication with their children, remittances, feelings or any aspect of their experiences as physically separated mothers from their children. All interviews were transcribed from the audio-recordings verbatim and transcripts were coded in order to identify recurring themes.

For this chapter, the emphasis is on notions of invisibility and hypervisibility characteristics that shape their experiences as an undocumented and unacknowledged labour force. All the names used in the findings are pseudonyms adopted to protect the privacy and confidentiality of participants. What is key in understanding the experiences of (in)visibility for migrant domestic workers is how they regulate themselves in the social sphere and how they engage in relationships in public. In response to such threats, these women employ a number of invisibility strategies to remain under the radar. In the next section, we expand on how the notion of strategic invisibility is tied to their livelihoods, family survival and emerging family structures.

'We have many ways of playing hide and seek with them': everyday strategies of invisibility

Police and immigration officials pose the most significant threats to migrant domestic worker livelihoods in Botswana. Through constant surveillance, undocumented migrants live with the threat of deportation hanging over them. Indeed, deportability is part of their everyday life (Galvin 2015). For these women, being undocumented means that they are entangled with different layers of power relations from various actors, mainly the police, human smugglers, their employers and citizens. Consequently, they have to navigate these power dynamics through invisibility strategies in order to protect their livelihoods. These processes therefore involve transnational mothers negotiating in/visibility with the aforementioned actors.

Alice, a mother of one teenage son who migrated to Botswana in 2005, has never had a legal migration status in Botswana, yet she has persisted as a domestic worker for fourteen years, albeit with some arrests and deportations in between. Below, she explains her strategies of remaining invisible:

> We hide our names because you will end up spoiling your name when you always get arrested. Though we are aware of the risks of using fake names, we don't care even though this can work against you. Like this one year, a deportation truck on its way to the Zimbabwean border was involved in a fatal accident and some Zimbabweans died. But always when we get arrested, we register using fake names, we don't keep any identity documents with us anyway. We know that what we are doing is risky but we tell ourselves whatever happens, it's okay, death is death anyway.

Alice's narrative brings to the fore the ongoing cycle of migrant deportations but significantly, also exposes the institutional weaknesses inherent in its deportation policies. With no means to verify the deportees' identities, such a loophole works in favour of deportees as they resort to using fake names. Even though Alice recognizes the risk of using a fake name in case of her untimely death and the ensuing need for body identification, that is not a concern to her and she reasons that identity does not matter in death.

Upon probing why she hid her name, she explained:

> I would rather lie about my true identity. So, for me, once I am in detention, I don't care, I use different names all the time and even if I die in detention, at that point it does not matter to me. Besides, think about it this way, when we are smuggled through the forest, where or with whom do we register our names anyway? Yet you can die in transit in the forest and no one will even know your name. So, for me, even with the police, any name I think of is what I tell them, they can't prove my identity anyway without a passport or anything.

She reasons that when they engage smugglers, they are not officially registered hence her identity is unknown by the smugglers. She therefore does not see the reason why the police should know her real identity when she is arrested. In this instance, we see that she is using strategic invisibility through hiding her real name from the police so that she does not have her arrests on official record. For Kuda, a mother of four who has been in Botswana for the past fifteen years illegally, her strategic invisibility involves avoiding public places by confining herself to her employer's premises. She therefore uses the strategy of staying under the radar through disengagement from public spaces. However, in instances where she may have to leave her employer's premises, her strategic invisibility calls for constant awareness of how she is seen in public spaces and constantly watching out for police officers.

> When we are out there, our eyes look everywhere, we look here and there so that we identify police. Once you spot a police officer, you quickly change direction. But if it's too late and you find yourself face to face with police, then pray to God silently; don't show panic on your face; look directly into the eyes of the officer and be very confident. Don't let your eyes wander around and make sure your body is relaxed and walk confidently past him or her, don't look back. As soon as you pass this stage, then sprint for your life, they will not catch you.

Another rule, in relation to public spaces, involves managing one's voice and language. For Mary, Sundays are the days she looks forward to as she gets to meet up with her older sister who also works as a domestic worker in Botswana. Both are undocumented but on Sundays they always meet to catch up and do some activities such as shopping together. However, when they go out, they use the strategy of hiding in plain sight through managing of how they walk and speak in public spaces.

> When we are out there with my sister, we rarely converse in public spaces. Instead, we walk a few metres apart, with one ahead of the other so that if one gets arrested, the other has the chance to run away. Besides, if we walk side by side, our language will sell us out and they will easily identify us as Zimbabweans. You know that you cannot speak your language in public when you are an illegal, this country does not want that at all.

Anne also expressed similar views on public spaces in relation to how they are forced to avoid some places because police, seemingly aware that Zimbabweans patronize such places on Sundays, take the opportunity to go and arrest them there.

> Nowadays, we avoid spending too much time in Chinese shops. These are the cheapest shops in Gaborone and the police know that by virtue of our low wages, that is where we shop. So, they come and arrest there. You will go inside a shop and when you are exiting, you will find them waiting by the door and asking for your passport, just like that. So, we now know which shops to avoid.

For Anne, her strategic invisibility involved withdrawal from public spaces, in particular the Chinese shops that most undocumented migrant workers regularly patronize during weekends. Yet another undocumented migrant prides herself for essentially winning the battle against surveillance. She boasts that the authorities have essentially failed to get rid of them in Botswana no matter how much they have tried. In her narrative, she exposes the powerlessness of the state against extra-legal actors whom she credits for helping them to be in Botswana. Secondly, she also exposes the corruption of some state actors who are willing to look the other way for the right fee.

> They have failed to get rid of us even though they try, simply because we have many people that we work with; we work with human smugglers; bus transporters; police officials; immigration officials; some villagers living near the border etc. The human smugglers help by creating alternative routes we use to come to this country, they clear the bushes if need be, they cut trees or cut fences where there is need to and the good thing about them is once they create a new route, they never forget a route they have created.

Alice added that being invisible means you have to blend in with the local ways of dressing, walking and even language. She related the following:

> A long time ago, when we were still naive, police knew that if they saw a person whose dressing was not properly matched or a woman who was wearing a long loose dress or skirt, that would definitely be a Zimbabwean. Now that we have opened our eyes, we have learnt that 'when you are in Rome, do as the Romans also do'. So, we also copy the way they dress. Of course, we may have different skin colours but still, others are really trying to match the Batswana complexions through skin bleaching and lightening. We are definitely ahead of them in our thinking.

From Alice's narrative, camouflaging or blending in works as her strategic invisibility plan because she is able to blend in with the local citizens by imitating the way they dress. In order to survive, she discards her true identity as a Zimbabwean and adopts another identity which is in sync with local norms of dressing. Mary echoes the same sentiments although she admits that the kind of dress-code she copies makes her very uncomfortable as it contradicts her own culture, yet she has to do it for survival and protection of her livelihood.

> Where we come from, our dressing is so different but here we try to dress like them. You are forced to wear mini dresses even though you may not like it but you do it because of your situation. Short dresses and skirts can actually rescue you from the gaze of the police. It doesn't mean that we will take those dresses to Zimbabwe, they are just for wearing this side because once you get home, you cannot wear such things. I cannot wear short dresses in front of my family or children. I cannot walk around displaying my bare thighs, that shows a lack of respect and if I do that, it means I am now taking Batswana culture back to my children, imagine what my children will think of me when they see me like that.

Another transnational mother, Grace admits she dresses like the locals and even attempts to walk like them as a way of blending in but like Mary, she is also adamant that the dress-code they copy is indecent and unacceptable back home as it would invite all sorts of ridicule and shame not only from her immediate family but also from the home community. However, while in Botswana, it is a necessary strategy if she is to avoid arrest and subsequent deportation.

> Besides our children, the communities where we come from, when they see us dressed in short revealing clothes, they will just conclude that we are prostituting in Botswana. That's because where we come from, such kind of dressing is often associated with ladies of the night [prostitutes].

From the foregoing, it is clear that strategic invisibility is all about survival in an inhospitable dwelling place (Lollar 2015), hence undocumented migrants adopt strategies that may not be in tandem with their culture. Significantly, this demonstrates the linkage between migration status and livelihoods and ultimately the necessity of strategic invisibility. Another key finding in this study also illustrates the importance of communicative technologies in engendering strategic invisibility. As such, social media applications such as WhatsApp have been effective tools in aiding strategic invisibility.

As a group strategy, most participants confirmed their memberships to Zimbabwean virtual groups which specifically served to send out alerts of police locations, raids and roadblocks. Essentially, participants expressed that physical distance did not hinder exchange of information and ideas among undocumented migrants in Botswana. Through the WhatsApp platform, they could easily exchange information without the privilege of physical proximity.

> When we go out there, we easily identify each other through language, body structure or the way we dress so we automatically become friends or family. So, if you meet another Zimbabwean, male or female, you request their number and then go on the WhatsApp group administrator and request the new person be added.

This participant further explained that they used their own unique coded language. For example, if they wanted to request for someone to be added to the group, they simply wrote 'Admin, please may you add this new eye to the group'. The reference to a new member being called a new eye is premised on the assumption that you are adding another pair of eyes to surveil the police for every member's benefit. Once a new eye is added, that eye also identifies other eyes to be added and through this group strategy, they create a form of social capital that is helpful for effective invisibility.

Netsai emphasized the necessity of always moving around with two essential items if ever she were to go out and these were a phone and at least BWP200 (approximately 15 euros) as these can help one escape the police:

> Firstly, the money is needed to bribe the police in exchange for your release. If that fails, the money will assist one to return to Botswana from the border after being deported. Secondly, you need a phone with some data loaded in order to

> be able to communicate to WhatsApp group members alerting them of where you have spotted police raids or roadblocks. If arrested, you need to make a quick call before getting into the cells and communicate to the group about your arrest. You are likely to get help through other members who have police friends or your friends who can bring you some decent food.

Rudo's narrative illustrated the ways through which undocumented migrants could negotiate in/visibility with the police through bribery. When confronted by the police, the officers could choose to act officially for the state by arresting them. Alternatively, subject to a bribe, they could also choose either to look away or to release the undocumented migrants.

> I really appreciate the police, especially on the highway to the border. You should just not be stingy with your money and at least wherever you are, keep some money with you to give to the police officers for them to buy drinks or lunch; they can make your illegal journey much easier.

In the preceding narrative, the participant exposes how police officers can either act for or against state policies suggesting that even law enforcers are complicit in assisting migrant women to remain illegal in Botswana. Chipo expressed similar sentiments and shared her recent encounter with the police in Gaborone.

> I was recently arrested together with another friend on our way to church at the bus rank. The two police officers asked us to walk with them back to the station. One was walking beside me whilst the other was walking behind us with my friend. At some point, I looked back and realized my friend had disappeared and it was only the police officer behind us. Immediately, I knew she had paid the officer a bribe for her release. Suddenly, the officer who was walking with me asked how much I had. He demanded BWP200 and I told him I did not have that much on me. I only had P50 so I opened my purse and showed him the BWP50. He took it and signalled for me to disappear and I went straight back home. Oh my God, I was so lucky that day.

Although the police are susceptible to bribes and actively participate in invisibilizing undocumented migrants, there is, however, a limitation to this complicity. As Ruth's narrative will show, even though she moves around with bribe money, it is still essential for her to conceal her identity and her address. She explained that it was essential to always carry at least between BWP200 and BWP250 (approximately 15–19 euros) with you in case you encountered the police, but you still need to hide your true identity:

> Sometimes when police catch you, they will drive you in their car for hours, without going to the police station until you pay them a 'little something', then

> they can release you. Again, if you get arrested and want to pay a bribe, rather call someone to bring you the money. Don't show them where you live or disclose your true identity because you will have invited permanent trouble. Every time that officer needs some money, he will come and knock on your door because you are illegal and powerless.

As the findings revealed, it was not only the police that participated in invisibilizing migrants. Findings also suggested that employers who employed them as domestic workers were also complicit in invisibilizing their presence in Botswana. In need of their services for care and domestic household work, employers willingly participated in invisibilizing their workers.

> Our employers also help us to be invisible. When I get paid, I ask my employer to send my money back to my family in Zimbabwe so she goes to send through Western Union on my behalf so that I do not have to be out there exposing myself.

Another role played by employers is in relation to the acquisition of fake residence and work permits for their domestic workers. Nyarai's permit shows that she is employed as a herd-girl at a farm outside Gaborone, yet she is a domestic worker. Her employer managed to get this permit with the help of a consultant and a farm owner for a fee. Although obtained through false representation, the documents were genuine permits that allowed her flexible mobility without being arrested as she was legally a resident of Botswana.

For most participants, their employer's premises were strategic sources of upholding their invisibility. For example, Matipa reasoned that it was better to live on the premises with her employer instead of commuting to work because her employer's home offered a safe place to hide. Although there was a trade-off as staying on the premises meant she would work longer hours without compensation for overtime, this strategy was still necessary in order to protect her from surveilling officers and risk being arrested. As it emerged, employers were willing to assist in invisibilizing their employees as they also stood to benefit from their labour.

Moreover, with an undocumented migration status, their labour was cheap and exploitable. Similarly, for Debra, being invisible meant she had to be grounded in one place by staying under the radar. The threat to her livelihood posed by constant police surveillance led her to completely disengage from the social and public spheres:

> You have to look out for yourself, don't just go out for the sake of it or just because you want to get some fresh air outside, fresh air for what? Rather stay indoors and be safe. I only go out if I am sick and need to visit a doctor. Usually, my boss drives me to the doctor so I can remain hidden, otherwise what will happen to my family if I am arrested, what will they eat?

The preceding narratives have illustrated the vulnerabilities faced by migrant domestic workers in Botswana but most importantly how they navigate the spaces they inhabit in order to protect their livelihoods in what is an inhospitable dwelling space (Lollar 2015). Although deportability is part and parcel of their everyday lives (Galvin 2015), through the strategic invisibility, they embark on a series of actions to avoid being arrested and deported. In navigating their challenges, they get assistance from and through other actors such as police, human smugglers and their employers among other others.

Although there are unequal power relations between migrant domestic workers and their employers or police officials, their strategy of remaining invisible requires constant negotiations with the main aim of avoiding deportation. There is an established link between migration status and livelihoods which leads migrant domestic workers to employ various strategies at individual or group level through social media platforms in order to safeguard their livelihoods. Through strategies of staying under the radar or camouflaging, they use their agency to navigate spaces that are governed by unequal power relations.

Structural invisibilities in transnational care chains

Necessarily, it is equally important to acknowledge the complicities of the origin state in understanding why women in this study left their children behind to pursue livelihoods in another nation-state. Seemingly, economic failures in their country of origin is key in understanding their precarity and subsequent invisibilities in Botswana. Consequently, invisibility is not merely achieved from their own individual agency but imposed from a broader structural context of their country of origin as well as the reception context of their identities as undocumented migrants and their nationality and class positioning intersect with state and immigration policies in Botswana to create conditions of (in)visibility for migrant domestic workers.

The role played by extra-legal actors in perpetuating their invisibility in Botswana also begs further interrogation. Without the assistance of parallel structures, these women would have long ceased to work informally in Botswana; specifically, the roles played by human smugglers, transport and bus operators, immigration officials and soldiers at both the Zimbabwean and Botswana borders cannot be excluded in the analysis of strategic invisibilities of migrant domestic workers. Likewise, the role of that privileged woman who sits at the top of the care chain as an employer of a migrant woman is equally fundamental to our understanding of how and why strategies of invisibility persist and are sustained for women in the present study.

Significantly, given the link between being undocumented and the need for social/public invisibility (Baird 2014), the privacy and security guaranteed by the employer's home in exchange for unregulated labour is crucial to the processes of invisibilization undertaken by migrant women as part of their daily lives. While it partially helps us to account for the persistence of undocumented migration in Botswana, our aim here is to further illustrate why strategic invisibility is necessary for migrant women and why they continue to pursue it in inhospitable dwelling places where they live in the shadows of society.

Shortt's (2015) concept of transitory dwelling places was relevant in order to advance our argument that Botswana ceases to be a liminal space for undocumented migrants because 'when liminal spaces are constructed by workers as vital and meaningful to their everyday lives, they cease to be liminal spaces and instead, become "transitory dwelling places"' (p. 633). Although Shortt (2015) used this concept in relation to formal organizational spaces, we have borrowed it in order to understand the strategies of invisibility employed by migrant domestic workers and to expand the reasons why invisibility is an essential component of their experiences.

In this instance, spaces of migrant domestic workers may widely refer to spaces such as informal border routes, employers' places, private homes, etc. Essentially, for migrant domestic workers, such spaces can be anywhere and everywhere they inhabit in pursuit of their transnational livelihoods in Botswana. As such, transitory dwelling spaces were meaningful to participants as they directly linked to their livelihoods and the survival of their families back in Zimbabwe.

Without necessarily discounting their negative everyday experiences in liminal spaces in Botswana, we take the standpoint that liminal spaces have multiple meanings as they are subjectively lived. Based on Turner's (1979) assertion that anything can happen in liminal spaces, we connect this to participants' experiences of spaces in Botswana where anything happens i.e. from being smuggled into the country, to being exposed to violence and danger, yet at the same time, to being the spaces in which they can earn their living.

The issue is that in their liminal spaces (which we take to be Botswana and in particular, encompassing the private, social and public realms), their experiences are constantly shifting and exude both positives and negatives that they have endured as undocumented migrants because of the meaningfulness of the spaces in Botswana as 'transitory dwelling spaces' (Shortt 2015). This is so because in spite of the negative experiences of the spaces, they are still meaningful to them as domestic workers because they are significantly attached to their families' livelihoods.

Accordingly, the meaningfulness they attach to such spaces where they are irregular and where spatial dimensions of space include but are not limited to border zones, bounded work spaces and detention centres to name but a few, require conceptualizing such spaces beyond their liminality in order to understand strategic invisibility as a key weapon for survival that the weak (cf. Scott 1985) use in defence of their livelihoods. Moreover, when people temporarily inhabit specific dwelling places, it allows for creation of acts of resistance because the spaces where 'resistance' work is done are those spaces that are meaningful to the migrant domestic workers in question.

Accordingly, they resist conformity to immigration laws because of the significance they attach to Botswana – as a place of survival and livelihood, especially given the lack of opportunities back home. In doing so, they resist and mitigate inhospitable dwelling places (Shortt 2015) and significantly, these acts of resistance are productive for the sustenance of their livelihoods. Although they are criminalized, we conceptualize their actions beyond criminality as steps that reflect economic activities for livelihood purposes. Botswana is thus a meaningful location for them, regardless of the ambiguities it conveys to them. This we argue is crucial in understanding why mothers continue to pursue transnational livelihoods through strategic invisibilities in the face of a harsh mobility regime (Glick Schiller and Salazar 2013).

Due to constant raids, the police act as tools of visibilization in Botswana because through constant surveillance, hidden identities of migrant domestic workers are rendered hypervisible. For instance, when Zimbabwean irregular migrants are arrested, they are detained for some days or weeks before being deported. The process of deportation mimics what De Genova (2002) has termed the border spectacle where huge and uniquely designed trucks are seen driving 'illegal migrants' back to the Zimbabwean border. Subsequently, migrant domestic workers' strategies to remain invisible are partly overturned when they are arrested.

Through public displays of deportations, undocumented domestic workers in Botswana are made hypervisible to the public with their presence problematized, thereby justifying their evictions from Botswana. Consequently, their daily experiences include oscillating between conditions of visibility and invisibility. The findings have also suggested the necessity of analysing their (in)visibilities through an intersectional analysis (Crenshaw 1989; Yuval-Davis 2006). Migrant domestic workers' in/visibilities should thus be analysed at the intersections of their migration status, class positionalities, nationality and gender.

For example, the use of their chiShona language makes them audibly detectable and may be met with hostility or ridicule by local Batswana. Inevitably, migrant workers respond to such a threat by avoiding their local languages in public spaces. However, should this strategy fail and they are arrested by police officials, their invisibility cover is in essence lifted, leading to them being publicly arrested, detained and subsequently deported back the Zimbabwean border in uniquely designed deportation trucks. This then produces an opposite effect by rendering them hypervisible and portraying their presence as criminal and therefore problematic for Botswana yet simultaneously rendering their labour invisible.

Therefore, when Zimbabwean migrant domestic workers are visible in Batswana public space and discourse, it is often in a negative light, as criminals who ought to be arrested and deported back to their country. Meanwhile, the contributions they make as labourers and carers in private homes remains publicly unacknowledged.

Instead, what is made visible to the public is the spectacle of their arrests and subsequent deportations. Ultimately, they gravitate between states of invisibility and hypervisibility in their interactions with the state, media and the public in Botswana.

Conclusion

The research on Zimbabwean migrant domestic workers in Botswana illuminates the significance of invisibility as a protective measure against disadvantage and also as a form of agency which the undocumented use to protect their livelihoods. Accordingly, findings demonstrate that invisibility is not necessarily a disadvantage though the conditions that lead to it stem from being a disadvantaged identity. Invisibility therefore works as an effective strategy of camouflaging their nationality through certain aspects of their identities such as their dress, public behaviour or language. As such, by framing strategic invisibility within the notion of meaningful dwelling places (Shortt 2015) in the context of illegality and precarious labour conditions, we have offered a concrete perspective on how and why migrant domestic workers consciously resort to the status of being irregular and making themselves invisible.

By illustrating the various ways through which strategic invisibility manifests in the everyday lives of our participants, we have shown how these strategies are significant in fulfilling familial care and financial obligations. Accordingly, our analysis moves beyond the popular notion that casts migrant women as mere passive victims of globalization by demonstrating how they use their agency by deciding which aspects of their lives should be observed or hidden and by or from whom (Brighenti 2007). The study has also demonstrated that illegality and the ensuing strategic invisibility are co-produced by undocumented migrant domestic workers, the state and non-state actors in Botswana.

In essence, the findings have also highlighted the ambiguity of migration governance in Botswana as an institutional weakness which allows for loopholes that migrant women can use to their advantage in order to remain working in Botswana, albeit illegally. By casting attention on the multiple ways through which undocumented women interact with formal state officials and extra-legal actors to make strategic decisions for their livelihoods, we have shown how migrant domestic workers negotiate or circumvent legal barriers through their everyday practices of seeing and being seen (Baird 2014). They thus oscillate between invisibility, where they are a form of hidden and exploitable labour in the private homes of their employers, and hypervisibility, when they are arrested and subsequently deported.

Furthermore, we have demonstrated that invisibility practices are not only located within individual agency but may also be collective in nature. The story of adding eyes to migrant WhatsApp groups exemplifies this notion, where cooperation is underscored by group vulnerabilities vis-à-vis threats to their livelihoods. Additionally, by locating the present study within global care chain theory

(Hochschild 2000) we have further shown how individual class positionalities intersect with local, national and global forces to produce subordinated relations which render migrant domestic workers an unrecognized workforce in Botswana. Furthermore, the study has shown how undocumented transnational domestic work engenders strategic invisibility as counter-strategies against restrictive mobility regimes and non-recognition.

This chapter therefore underscores the necessity to study invisibility hierarchically in relation to the intersections of class, nationality, geography, legal status and gender (Leinonen and Toivanen 2014) of the migrants. Overall, the study has illustrated different layers in/visibilization firstly by considering hypervisibility as a by-product of subordinated power relations between various structures in the receiving country and migrant domestic workers. The study has also shown that strategic invisibility is undertaken as a response to a system that does not allow domestic workers mobility through regular channels. As a consequence, strategic invisibility is used as a plan to circumvent expulsion from Botswana, which is their space for sustaining livelihoods.

Lastly, although the study focused on Botswana, its significance is broader in scope in so far as it relates to undocumented migrant experiences in various geographical contexts. Even though both visibility and invisibility in this context expose vulnerabilities of migrant domestic workers, their stories demonstrate resilience and resistance, illustrating how humans, no matter how constricted, always find ways to exercise their agency, albeit under very difficult circumstances, as shown through their attempts to turn inhospitable dwelling places into hospitable places because of their meaningfulness to their livelihoods. Theoretically, we conclude that invisibility and hypervisibility are impermanent and constantly shifting to produce both advantage and disadvantage to the migrants concerned.

References

Baird, T. (2014) 'The more you look the less you see', *Nordic Journal of Migration Research*, 4(1): 3–10. https://doi.org/10.2478/njmr-2013-0008.

Brighenti, A. (2007) 'Visibility: a category for the social sciences', *Current Sociology*, 55(3) 323–342.

Buchanan, N.T. and I.H. Settles (2018) 'Managing (in) visibility and hypervisibility in the workplace', *Journal of Vocational Behavior*, 113: 1–5.

Butler, J. (1990) *Gender Trouble: Feminism and the subversion of identity*, New York: Routledge.

Carling, J.R. (2002) 'Migration in the age of involuntary immobility: theoretical reflections and Cape Verdean experiences', *Journal of ethnic and migration studies*, 28(1) 5–42.

Crenshaw, K.W. (1989) 'Mapping the margins: intersectionality, identity politics, and violence against women of color', in M.A. Fineman and R. Mykitiuk (eds), *The Public Nature of Violence: The discovery of domestic abused*, New York: Routledge, 93–117.

De Genova, N.P. (2002) 'Migrant "illegality" and deportability in everyday life', *Annual Review of Anthropology*, 31(1): 419–447.

Ehrenreich, B. and A.R. Hochschild (eds) (2003) *Global Woman: Nannies, maids,*

and sex workers in the new economy, New York: Metropolitan Books.
Galvin, T.M. (2015) '"We deport them but they keep coming back": the normalcy of deportation in the daily life of "undocumented" Zimbabwean migrant workers in Botswana', *Journal of Ethnic and Migration Studies*, 41(4): 617–634.
Glick Schiller, N.G., L. Basch and C. Blanc-Szanton (1992) 'Transnationalism: a new analytic framework for understanding migration', *Annals of the New York Academy of Sciences*, 645(1): 1–24.
Glick Schiller, N. and N.B. Salazar (2013) 'Regimes of mobility across the globe', *Journal of Ethnic and Migration Studies*, 39(2): 183–200.
Hochschild, A.R. (2000) *Global Care Chains and Emotional Surplus Value. On the Edge: Living with global capitalism*, 3(4): 130–146.
Juul, K. (2014) 'Performing belonging, celebrating invisibility?', *Nordic Journal of Migration Research*, 4(4): 184–191. https://doi.org/10.2478/njmr-2014-0030.
Leinonen, J. (2012) 'Invisible immigrants, visible expats? Americans in Finnish discourses on immigration and internationalization', *Nordic Journal of Migration Research*, 2(3): 213–223. https://doi.org/10/2478/v10202-011-0043-8.
Leinonen, J. and M. Toivanen (2014) 'Researching in/visibility in the Nordic context: theoretical and empirical views', *Nordic Journal of Migration Research*, 4(4): 161–167. https://doi.org/10/2478/njmr-2014-0025.
Lollar, K. (2015) 'Strategic invisibility: resisting the inhospitable dwelling place', *Review of Communication*, 15(4): 298–315.
Lutz, H. and E. Palenga-Möllenbeck (2012) 'Care workers, care drain, and care chains: reflections on care, migration, and citizenship', *Social Politics*, 19(1): 15–37.
Morapedi, W.G. (2007) 'Post-liberation xenophobia in Southern Africa: the case of the influx of undocumented Zimbabwean immigrants into Botswana, c. 1995–2004', *Journal of Contemporary African Studies*, 25(2): 229–250.
Nyamnjoh, F.B. (2002) 'Local attitudes towards citizenship and foreigners in Botswana: an appraisal of recent press stories', *Journal of Southern African Studies*, 28(4): 755–775.
Parreñas, R.S. (2001) 'Mothering from a distance: emotions, gender, and intergenerational relations in Filipino transnational families', *Feminist Studies*, 27(2): 361–390.
—— (2005a) *Children of Global Migration: Transnational families and gendered woes*, Stanford, CA: Stanford University Press.
—— (2005b) 'The gender paradox in the transnational families of Filipino migrant women', *Asian and Pacific Migration Journal*, 14(3): 243–268.
Polzer, T. and L. Hammond (2008) 'Invisible displacement', *Journal of Refugee Studies*, 21(4): 417–431.
Pugh, J.D. (2018) 'Negotiating identity and belonging through the invisibility bargain: Colombian forced migrants in Ecuador', *International Migration Review*, 52(4): 978–1010.
Rojas-Wiesner, M. and M. DeVargas (2013) 'Strategic invisibility as everyday politics for a life with dignity: Guatemalan women migrant's experiences of insecurity at Mexico's southern border', in T.-D. Truong, D. Gasper, J. Handmaker and S.I. Bergh (eds), *Migration, Gender and Social Justice: Perspectives on human insecurity*, Heidelberg: Springer, 193–211. Retrieved 15 March 2019 from: https://link.springer.com/chapter/10.1007/978-3-642-28012-2_10.
Salih, R. (2001) 'Moroccan migrant women: transnationalism, nation-states and gender', *Journal of Ethnic and Migration Studies*, 27(4): 655–671.
Scott, J.C. (1985) *Weapons of the Weak: Everyday forms of peasant resistance*, New Haven, CT: Yale Press University.
Settles, I.H., N.T. Buchanan and K. Dotson (2019) 'Scrutinized but not recognized: (in) visibility and hypervisibility experiences of faculty of color', *Journal of Vocational Behavior*, 113: 62–74.

Shortt, H. (2015) 'Liminality, space and the importance of "transitory dwelling places" at work', *Human Relations*, 68(4): 633–658.

Toivanen, M. (2014) 'The visual lexica of (national) belonging and nonbelonging in the accounts of young Kurds in Finland', *Nordic Journal of Migration Research*, 4(4): 192–200. https://doi.org/10/2478/njmr-2014-0027.

Turner, V. (1979) 'Frame, flow and reflection: ritual and drama as public liminality', *Japanese Journal of Religious Studies*, 6(4): 465–499.

Wengraf, T. (2004) 'The biographic-narrative interpretive method - shortguide', NCRM Working Paper. Unpublished. eprints.ncrm.ac.uk/30.

Yeates, N. (2004) 'Global care chains', *International Feminist Journal of Politics*, 6(3): 369–391.

—— (2009) *Globalizing Care Economies and Migrant Workers: Explorations in global care chains*, Basingstoke: Palgrave Macmillan.

—— (2012) 'Global care chains: a state-of-the-art review and future directions in care transnationalisation research', *Global Networks*, 12(2): 135–154.

Yuval-Davis, N. (2006) 'Intersectionality and feminist politics', *European Journal of Women's Studies*, 13(3): 193–209.

9 | The Nigerien migrants in Kaddafi's Libya: between visibility and invisibility

Oriol Puig Cepero

For me, Libya was like a paradise. (Nigerien returnee migrant)

Introduction

For decades, Kaddafi's Libya was an appealing country for thousands of people from regions south of the Sahara, attracted by economic opportunities and the pan-African ideas of the Libyan leader. Citizens from neighbouring countries such as Niger travelled to Libya to work, earn money and go back home, enacting circular and temporary mobilities within the Sahara–Sahel space (Mounkaila and Boyer 2010; Boesen and Marfaing 2007). It is what Nigerien migrants call the *Libya Kaman Turaï* – 'Libya like Europe' in Hausa – comparing Libya to Europe in terms of 'equality, modernity and social justice' (see Puig 2017). This positive vision of the Libyan state contrasts with the racism, xenophobia and violence of the Libyan society against Black African people during Kaddafi's regime (Bensaâd 2012). The leader used migration as a 'diplomatic tool' in international affairs and he shifted from opening Libya's borders to sub-Saharan migrants in the late 1990s to shortly after, in 2003, signing agreements with Europe to become its protector against irregular migration (Rodier 2009; Paoletti 2011). This outsourcing of European border control to Libya affected the journeys and sojourns of all sub-Saharan citizens in the country, including Nigerien nationals, obligating them to renegotiate their (in)visibility throughout their migratory process.

This chapter analyses the process of invisibilization of migrants as the interaction between institutional non-recognition and persecution, on the one hand, and the creation of resistance mechanisms and solidarities 'from below', on the other. The chapter thereby explores the structural dynamics that reproduce migrant clandestinity, vulnerability and persecution (Carter 2010), as well as the capacities of migrants to adapt, negotiate and manipulate their own roles in various contexts. To avoid the victimization of migrants, which international organizations, NGOs and policy makers tend to reinforce, the text explores the relational processes of (in)visibilization (Polzer and Hammond 2008).

The chapter describes four different stages in the migration process of Nigerien migrants to Libya, namely the journey across the Sahara Desert; the sojourn in Libya;

the war of 2011; and the ensuing return, respectively. The study examines the variety of actors involved in every phase, emphasizing how the impacts of migrant (in)visibilization 'depend on the power relations and interests connecting those who see and those who are to be seen (or not)', following Polzer and Hammond (2008: 417). I approach the concept of (in)visibility, not just as social exclusion and marginalization (Carleheden et al. 2012), but also as a strategy of displacement, ultimately determined by policies and structural factors but with certain room for manoeuvre for people on the move. In this sense, I focus specifically on avoidance and cloaking tactics as well as conscious visibilization to seek particular objectives. Consequently, the text highlights the process of migrant invisibilization in the journeys from Niger to Libya, focusing on the so-called *Gidan Bachi* – which means 'exchange bureau' in Hausa – a sort of prison located in Sebha where clandestine migrants are forced to live and work in order to earn enough money for their onward journeys. The emergence of the *Gidan Bachi* serves to illustrate the transformation from traditional smuggling to human trafficking, in large part caused by the externalization of European border control to Libya in the early 2000s (Puig 2017).

Moreover, the chapter seeks to analyse the dynamics of migrant in/visibility in Kaddafi's Libya, which include both strategies of avoidance in public spaces in some contexts and intentional exposure or visibility in other contexts, for example in the search for work in the city. Through the analysis of these in/visibilization strategies, the chapter contributes to our understanding of the racialization and persecution of sub-Saharan African nationals in the Maghreb (Collyer et al. 2012), which were aggravated during the Libyan conflict, when these migrants were increasingly targeted as 'suspicious people', leading many to return home (De Haas 2011). Finally, the chapter also points out the will of returnees to recover their visibility upon their return to Niger, for example in an effort to become visible towards the international community in an appeal for assistance (Olivier de Sardan 1995; Turner 2016).

The chapter is based on ethnographic research between 2011 and 2016 in Niamey, the capital of Niger, with different groups of returnees, mainly men, who lived in Libya during the 2000s and returned because of the conflict around 2011. The text is structured around the four different time periods chronologically, preceded by a brief introduction to trans-Saharan mobility from Niger to Libya as well as an elaboration on Libya as a destination territory, beyond its better-known role as a 'transit' state on the journey towards Europe (Collyer et al. 2012; Elbreki 2018). In this regard, the chapter emphasizes inter-regional mobility within West Africa, which represents the vast majority of the movements of African migrants,[1] as a counterpoint to the tendency to over-emphasize the role of African migration towards Europe in public and policy debates across Europe (De Haas 2007; Andersson 2016). In this sense, the study provides a challenge to the dominant political discourses in much of the global North by emphasizing the dynamics and complexities of South–South mobilities.

The Libyan dream

Niger is a Sahelian state and among the poorest countries in the world (UNDP 2018), located in the middle of the Sahara Desert with three-quarters of its territory composed of sand. The former French colony has the lowest rates in terms of literacy and education and the highest fertility and fecundity rates in the world, with 7.2 children born to every woman.[2] In recent years, Niger has become a corridor for migration towards Europe and, for this reason, plays an important role in the control of migration to the Old Continent, as Kaddafi's regime did in the past (Hamadou 2018; Prestianni 2018). Agadez, the doorway to the Sahara, is an historically crucial junction of African routes to the Maghreb zone and to Europe (Bredeloup 2012). The Sahel–Sahara space worked historically as a circulation area, a zone of passage between Africa south of the Sahara and the Arab world, a 'moving space' according to Boesen and Marfaing (2007), but also a 'symbolic frontier' between these two areas (Temlali 2011; Retaillé and Walther 2008). At present, international organizations and the European Union (EU) define Niger as a 'transit country' (Collyer et al. 2012) because 90 per cent of people arriving in Europe pass through this country, according to the figures of the International Organization for Migration (IOM).

Niger, however, is also a departure country, not primarily to Europe, but also to neighbouring states, traditionally to Ivory Coast, Nigeria and Ghana (Alpha Gado 2000; Boyer 2003) and since the second half of the twentieth century towards the Maghreb, particularly to Algeria and Libya (Bensaâd 2012). Nomadic pastoralist groups such as Tuareg and Tubu were moving around the Sahara Desert long before the consolidation of nations-states in the region in the 1960s, and also after the acceleration of drought cycles in the following decades (Bourgeot 1995; Claudot-Hawad 2002). Other Nigerien migrants, mainly from the Hausa and Kanuri regions, travelled to Libya in the 1980s through temporary and circular displacements during the dry season (Grégoire 2004). Finally, at the end of the 1990s and the beginning of the 2000s, migrants from urban areas[3] like Niamey, self-designated as 'adventurers' (Bredeloup 2013) or 'exodants' (Boyer 2015), joined these itineraries towards the north as a consequence of economic and political crises.[4]

For its part, Libya has been a destination country for several decades, and not just a 'transit space', as often implied in European political and media discourse (Lessault and Beauchemin 2009; Crawley et al. 2016). It was an attractive country for thousands of sub-Saharan African nationals to achieve their aspirations of finding livelihood options elsewhere. *Libya Kaman Turaï* – 'Libya like Europe' in Hausa – became a popular expression used by Nigerien migrants to express the qualities of Libya as a destination country, valued for its 'equality, modernity and social justice' during Kaddafi's regime. As a Nigerien returnee explained in Niamey, 'Libya was different from other countries. It was like a European country close to our home. In Europe, however, the life was so expensive while in Libya it was very cheap. Accommodation, electricity, water … All services were financed by the state' (Interview with Mamane, Niamey, April 2015).

The majority of Nigerien return migrants appreciated the economic opportunities in Libya, praising the good salaries, the possibility to send remittances to the family (*Libya noro*, Libya's money in Hausa), as well as the chance to live their own life far from their community (Oumarou 2008, Kleist 2017).[5] They refer to this as the *belle vie* (or beautiful life) in French, whereby they are able to work, make steady incomes and even acquire technical training thanks to their jobs in international companies (Haimzadeh 2011).[6] Despite these encouraging perceptions of Libya, a large number of Nigerien migrants – the majority of sub-Saharan African nationals – were undocumented in Kaddafi's era. The requirements for official papers were strict, and expulsions based on labour demands according to internal and international political standards were frequent. In some cases, migrants could obtain residence permits but they were rarely able to regularize their status in Libya (Staub 2006).

The clandestine journey: the *Gidan Bachi*

During his forty-year regime, Kaddafi used migration for his own interests and experimented with different strategies, going from pan-Arabism in the 1970s and 1980s to pan-Africanism and pan-Sahelism in the 1990s, on account of the international embargo which isolated him from the global North (Haddad 2004).[7] He mainly sought to import cheap labour to work in his companies linked to the gas and oil economy, initially orienting his interests towards Arab countries, before turning to the sub-Saharan region. He combined recruitment programmes with mass deportations depending on his needs.[8] During the embargo, he promoted the African Union (AU) or regional institutions for the Sahel zone like the Community of Sahel-Saharan States (CEN-SAD). In this way, he advocated an open borders policy for sub-Saharan African nationals, with speeches like this: 'Africa is not 50 States. It is a nation, a town, a culture, an economy, a defence and no border', delivered in 1999 (Pliez 2006). However, a few years later, in 2003, seeking international vindication and the lifting of the embargo, he presented himself as the gatekeeper of sub-Saharan migration flows towards Europe and he accused 'Black Africans' in Libya of being 'carriers of diseases, crime and drug trafficking' (Haddad 2009). He signed different agreements with the EU and some individual member states, such as a $5 billion deal with Italy which included the training of its coastguard through Frontex and the reinforcement of land borders, as well as donations of control technologies and the setting up of detention centres for repatriation.[9] This shift in Kaddafi's strategies led to the criminalization of so-called irregular migration in Libya with direct consequences for the daily lives of migrants as well as for the journey across the Sahara before arriving to shoreline cities (Figure 9.1).

A very clear example was the *Gidan Bachi*, a sort of jail in Sebha, in the south of Libya, where migrants were locked in residences and forced to work and call their families, friends and relatives in Libya to pay to regain their freedom and

Figure 9.1 Trans-Saharan routes: migration and transport paths from Niger to Algeria and Libya

continue the journey. Resembling other detention centres created by Kaddafi around the country, these specific places were the first process of the *ghetto's*[10] clandestinization led by militias, smugglers and traffickers, especially Tuareg and Tubu elites who managed the historical cross-border area trade (McDougall and Scheele 2012).[11] The emergence of the *Gidan Bachi*, Ines Kohl (2015) illustrated the transformation of *migrant smuggling* to *human trafficking* as a result of the criminalization of migration and the externalization of European border control in Libya during the Kaddafi era. This shift implied an invisibilization of smuggling with evidence of threats, coercion and extortion towards migrants (Pierce 2014).[12]

> It's some kind of trafficking they do. They tell you that if you want to get to Sebha from Gatron you have to give them money, maybe 25,000 FCFA, but they bring you to Sebha and then they redo its price. It is villas with separate rooms where they will put people to lock them up. They will tell you that you must pay 300,000 FCFA[13] to leave. How do you do it? They will give you the phone and if you have someone in Tripoli,[14] they should send you the money. If you do not have anyone, you will stay there one or two months before leaving. It is the slavery. They beat people. The work that they force you to do is the hardest, a work for dogs. *Wallahi*,[15] the person suffers and if you do not have luck, they probably kill you. There are people missing. Those who try to run away, they shoot them and they kill them. (Interview with Daouda, Niamey, May 2012)

The *Gidan Bachi* was created around 2004, just after the implementation of Kaddafi's containment policies. At the beginning of the 2000s, smuggling was more visible and worked directly between drivers from one side of the border to the other. However, the subsequent application of restrictive measures and the gradual criminalization of migration forced the smugglers and migrants to become more invisible towards the authorities, so the persecution increased as well as the corruption around the transport business. Consequently, this hardening of migration policies made people on the move more vulnerable and pushed them to more dangerous routes, reinforcing the smuggling networks and exposing them to all the actors involved – such as *coxeurs* (or recruiters), drivers, mediators, the military, police officers, bandits, politicians, etc. As Brachet summarizes,

> '[the] criminalization of travel to and through the Sahara has led to the development of specialized passenger transport as a clandestine activity … Thus, smugglers, as a particular category of actors, appear as directly manufactured by the migration policies that were drafted to control them. (2018: 16)

In the same vein, Andersson blames 'the closure of legal pathways into Europe, along with the border security response, that has strongly contributed to the development of irregular land and sea entry routes in the past two and a half decades' (2016: 1059).

During the first decade of the twenty-first century, hence, an unknown number of migrants passed through the *Gidan Bachi*, especially those who travelled in a more vulnerable situation, without enough resources to continue their onward journey. Our informants in Niamey called it '*voyage à credit*' or 'travel on credit', referring to those who travel the route in a precarious way, especially in Niger where the situation deteriorated since 2005.[16] In this context, the *Gidan Bachi* provided migrants with the possibility of continuing the journey by using their ability to work, or their transnational and translocal networks to pay the expenses for reaching their final destination (Wimmer and Glick Schiller 2003). The majority of migrants knew about this traffic and despite its negative aspects, they often decided to take the risk instead of remaining in their country of origin (Puig 2017).

> *Gidan Bachi*, we created it ourselves. Why do I say that? Because I tell my friends that I want to go to Libya, but I do not have money, so I travel on credit. Once I arrive to Libya I refund the money to my friend, we made an agreement. If you take me to a place, you give me a quantity. Certain migrants do not have anyone in Libya and if they do not know anyone, I ask myself who will pay for you? Sometimes, they lie to go in and because of that Libyans create all this stuff, the torture and mistreatments and so on … all that started after [my journey]. (Interview with Hari, Niamey, March 2015)

As the explanation above shows, not all migrants chose to stay in the *Gidan Bachi* and not all smugglers worked in it. Actually, some smugglers distinguished themselves from traffickers and described the activity as a sin – *haram* in Arabic. 'With a single trip to the *Gidan Bachi* you can finance a new vehicle. They give you a lot of money, but I would never do that. It is not good; it is the traffic of human beings. It is not good', a smuggler in Agadez argued. It is important, thus, to clarify the concepts even if 'the UN, international agencies, and government agencies continue to blur the boundaries between smuggling and trafficking, referring indistinctly to the people involved in migrant housing and transportation', as Brachet (2018) suggests. So, the *Gidan Bachi* could be considered the precedent of the recent practices of slavery in Libya reported by the international media in 2017[17] and the confirmation that more repression does not reduce mobility but rather renders it more vulnerable and invisible.

(In)Visibility strategies in the final years of Kaddafi's Libya

The clandestinity of Nigerien migrants in the final years of Kaddafi's Libya, from 2005 to 2011, continued along the route from Sebha to Tripoli – around 700 kilometres. The journey was undertaken in 4×4 vehicles, the same vehicles used to cross the desert. Migrants without documents were forced to hide from Libyan authorities. For some of them, this passage was even more difficult than crossing the Sahara Desert. Once they arrived at their destination in Libya, their relatives, parents and friends, acting as 'drop points' (Timera 2001), welcomed them in the *ghettos* – also called *foyers* – providing useful information about job networks or daily life in the country. It was a kind of solidarity emerging from a 'sensation of being part of the same common destiny of African Black people in the Arab world',[18] as Bredeloup and Pliez explain (2005: 17). It was a response to their racialized condition (Sáenz and Manges Douglas 2014) in a country where racism against Black African people dates back to the Trans-Atlantic trade in which Arabs were the captors and the people from sub-Saharan Africa the slaves (Lecocq 2010; Altaleb 2015). Because of this, all sub-Saharan migrants in the country were called 'slaves' through different tags: *abdel, abdou, kahala* or *Afriqiya* – derogatory terms for someone coming from 'Africa' – which designates a 'social position as a servant, certifying the violence of exclusion',[19] according to Bensaâd (2012: 100). A large part of Libyan society rejected their own Africanness, even when Kaddafi was advocating for it. 'They usually said Libya is not Africa, they felt more as Europeans. The Europeans, by contrast, said that Libya was Africa, and actually it is, but they refused it', a Nigerien returnee explained. Kaddafi exploited these racialized hierarchies and marginalizations and contributed to aggravating them, establishing a 'state xenophobia', according to Bensaâd (2012), with daily racist attacks and humiliations.

> A child could insult you by saying 'black skin' but you had to accept it. They insulted you and you should not answer, you should let them pass. Also in taxis, you were attacked. There were young bandits who had taxis and when you saw one or two people and a black person entered, they came to bother you, to make fun of you. They took out their knife and said: 'give me everything you have'. If you did not give it to them, they stabbed you and they threw you out of the car. (Interview with Hassan, Niamey, May 2012)

Sub-Saharan people occupied the lowest position in the hierarchy of Libyan society, below other Arab nationalities such as Egyptian, Moroccan or Tunisian (Drodz and Pliez 2005). Race, nationality, class and ethnic affiliation stratified the workforce in relation to Libyan 'autochthonous' people. Like in other contexts, the native population rejected some kinds of low-skilled jobs, because leaving them to foreigners 'has a symbolic value that causes a *déclassement* of the autochthonous', according to Bredeloup and Zongo (2005: 142). In this stratification, Black Nigerien migrants had a submissive image linked to their roles in the trans-Saharan slave trade and they were perceived as honest, hardworking and obedient. The only exception is the Tuareg and Tubu groups from the same state that generally occupied better jobs thanks to their lineage, clan and tribal connections with Berber and even Arab groups.[20] The racialization of Black Africans thus associated them to domestic servants and cheap labour in public or private companies as well as in part-time jobs, referring to them with the English expression *fucking jobs*.

At the beginning of their stay in Libya they did casual labour called *yaumia* acquired in *mahatas* – meaning bus stations, in Arabic – or looked for other work opportunities by hanging out around different roundabouts in Tripoli or other cities. In these places, they became visible to offer their services for construction, carpentry, plumbing or other craftwork. 'If an Arab wants someone to work for one or two hours, he goes to the crossroads to find people. They discuss the price and if they understand each other, they go together. The person did it and the other paid it', a Nigerien returnee described. Without underestimating the structural racism, we can observe here how migrants strategically used their abilities and their visibility due to their skin colour to present themselves as potential workers for Arab people.

On the other hand, they also employed invisibility strategies to avoid xenophobic attacks. One example was the prioritization of jobs like *bladia*, the municipal garbage collection services, where they worked during the night, evading the public eye under the cover of night. The reasonable salary, combined with the possibility of combining it with other daytime jobs, made this job the most common among Nigerien urban migrants in Libya.[21] That choice illustrates how migrants generally sought to avoid public spaces; they preferred not to walk the streets alone and they spent most of their time in the *ghettos*. Their lives were as hidden as possible, because they were afraid of being attacked.

> The foreigners were more numerous than Libyan people, but we were not visible, because Kaddafi made us neither too free, nor too helpless, nor locked up. We were there and we went to work, to eat and we ended up there. We did not have the right to earn a lot of money or marry Libyan women. That makes foreigners not very visible. They did not allow us to have a walk, to go to restaurants, to nightclubs or to public places. They managed all that and we did not care so much about it, because if we went there they looked at us badly. We were bound, therefore, not to go. In Libya, we were invisible, even if we were more than them. (Interview with Ali, Niamey, March 2016)

During this period, Libya was characterized by a hardening of exclusionary conditions, enforced by legal norms[22] as well as by social representations (Danish Refugee Council 2013).[23] It was not a spatial separation because there were no specific neighbourhoods for Arabs and for Black migrants; segregation was shaped rather by experiences in public or private spaces. Nigerien migrants were required to change their common social practices as well as their way of relating to each other, due to their confinement to the *ghettos*. They had minimal interactions with Libyan people and they socialized among themselves by nationality, ethnic affiliation, urban/rural belonging or kinship. They reproduced a common site of interaction from their country of origin, what they call *fadas*, the most important masculine Nigerien social space. *Fadas* are groups of male friends and relatives, drinking tea and talking, discussing diverse topics in any corner of Nigerien streets (Masquelier 2019) and they are considered a prolongation of the family and an appropriation of public space (Boyer 2014).

Whereas meeting in *fadas* in Niger is a daily and spontaneous activity, in Libya these meetings became concealed and limited to a single day, normally on Fridays, the holy day off in Muslim countries. Migrants usually met each other in *ghettos* to drink tea and talk about news from Niger as well as collect information about families and relatives and to go to pray in the mosque, because the rest of the week they did it at home (Puig 2017). This mandatory concealment made some Nigerien migrants seek work in companies (Haimzadeh 2011)[24] to be placed in quarries, with all expenses paid. As a way to escape daily harassment and to feel safe, they preferred to live in isolated and prefabricated modules creating a delimited environment. It was a tactical avoidance to not be exposed to racist attacks. 'Life in the quarry was better than in the city. You did not see Libyans and they did not bother you. We were free, we were calm, we worked and we had a rest: we watched television, and we played football with all African people. Everything was fine', a returnee explained. The Nigerien migrants valued the comforts included in these places, such as common spaces – kitchen, gymnasium or basketball and soccer grounds – where they could have more communal life than in the cities. They emphasized the possibility to socialize with people from all over the world, from sub-Saharan Africa but also from the Maghreb region and Asia (Peraldi 2012) as a kind of 'cosmopolitanism from below' (Tarrius 2002).

> We were not just Nigerien; there were Filipinos, English, French, Egyptians, Moroccans, Koreans. We were the world in miniature; we got along with everybody. There were rules and there were no fights. Everyone should be united; there was no discrimination or racism. There were Libyan leaders, but in Vinci [the name of the company] there was no racism. If you were Libyan and I was Nigerien, we were friends anyway. We came to the city only twice a month to do the shopping and then returned to the countryside. We felt comfortable, we had an Internet connection, we had everything. (Interview with Ibrahim, Niamey, March 2015)

These artificially created spaces with physical boundaries promoted a kind of multicultural community subdivided by ethnic and national affiliation, but also blurring some identity categories. They consolidate the 'common destiny of African Black people in the Arab world' (Bredeloup and Pliez 2005) and contribute to create a more general category as 'irregular migrants' linked to the illegal status of people from around the world in Libya.

The 2011 war and the return: from imposed invisibility to persecution

In 2011, at the beginning of the war in Libya, the structural and social racism intensified and the racialization of Black African migrants was aggravated. Kaddafi, still in power, evoked the threat of an African invasion of Europe to avoid the international NATO sanctions, with no luck, and his opponents from the National Transitional Council (NTC) also manipulated the racism to accuse Black African migrants of being accomplices of the Libyan leader. These accusations, based on Kaddafi's recruitment policies and the creation of special militias (Vallée 2012),[25] stigmatized sub-Saharan African migrants as 'mercenaries' of the regime (De Haas 2011; DeVargas and Donzellia 2014). There were indeed migrants enlisted in militias for financial gain, but this enrolment was 'marginal', according to Moisseron and Belalimat (2012). However, 'arbitrary detentions became the norm, along with widespread human rights abuses' (Andersson 2016: 1064). During this period, Amnesty International (2015) denounced various acts of mistreatment, torture and violence against migrants in Libya, similar to during the violent riots of 2000.[26] The situation in 2011, however, was even worse and entailed the 'involuntary return' of thousands of people (Kleist 2017) after the ultimatums in Benghazi and Tripoli to force them to leave the country.

> The Arabs began to attack the Black people. If they saw a black man passing by, they would attack you, stab you. I did not go out during the day I stayed at home. They have started to attack the Black people. It was so dangerous. For Arabs, a Black person is a Black person and no matter how many times you will tell him that you are not a mercenary, for him you are. (Interview with Yssiaka, Niamey, May 2012)

The sub-Saharan African workers were used as scapegoats against the regime, 'invoking the worst racist anti-black stereotypes', according to Pierre (2013: 548). Therefore, the strategies of (in)visibility during Kaddafi's regime changed because of the war and hiding in the *ghettos* became the only option. The few contexts in which to be seen were restricted even further and seclusion was imposed.

> At that time, we did not work, we just waited. Our boss told us not to leave. We were always there; we had showers inside, there was everything. We slept there. We were three months like this and then we started to have troubles to drink water. Our water ran out and we called the boss, but his phone did not work. Thanks to Allah, one day the water began to fall. It was raining and we put a big cup to drink … There was no water, we had nothing to eat, we would have died. (Interview with Yssiaka, Niamey, March 2015)

In this context of persecution, a minority of Nigerien migrants decided to remain in the country, but a large number of them went back through the repatriation programmes of international organizations, especially the IOM or the United Nations High Commissioner for Refugees (UNCHR), or by their own resources, what Italian and French leaders called a 'biblical exodus' (Bensaâd 2012: 84). Around 300,000 people returned to Niger without anything, leaving all their belongings in Libya, according to our fieldwork. The Nigerien migrants generally planned to return home, but not under these precarious circumstances, due to the war and without money. This involuntary return implied collective and individual aspects 'embedded in local expectations, family reciprocities and ideals of masculinity', as Kleist shows (2017: 322). Their empty-handed arrival provoked frustration, culpability and feelings of failure towards their community and relatives, but also the recovering of their social visibility denied in Libya. 'There [in Libya] you ate well, they paid you well, but they did not respect you. Here, you are calm, you are free, you can circulate everywhere at any time' (Interview with Mamadou, Niamey, March 2015), one returnee explains.

This unpredicted return offered two main options for migrants to rebuild their disrupted life projects (Puig 2017): re-migration to other destinations or even going back to Libya; or remaining in Niger trying to regain their status in the community. Those who stayed used their condition as 'forced returnee' or 'repatriate' to access UN agencies', humanitarian organizations' and NGOs' donations, what Olivier de Sardan (1995) calls 'development rent seeking'.[27] The forced return rendered them visible to the international community, benefitting from the heightened international attention towards migration in this context (Agier 2011). IOM, for example, promised reintegration subventions of around 200,000 FCFA (300 euros) to start up a business project. A large number of returnees applied for that in Niamey but only a few benefitted. The majority, however, worked hard for several years to get funding to regain their position as a provider and as a man, to reclaim their social status. Because of that, they continued maintaining their visibility as 'returnees' and 'victims' with some setting up an NGO and looking for financing from this 'development rent'. In short, my Nigerien interlocutors had travelled clandestinely in vulnerable conditions; they were treated as 'slaves' in Libya and also during the journey, using conjunctural strategies of visibility and invisibility; and on their return, they tried to take advantage of their migration experience, both of their suffering and capabilities, to contribute to their families and communities.

Conclusion

The chapter has shown the importance of intra-African mobility and the relevance of Libya as a destination country, beyond its better-known role as a 'transit' territory on the journey towards Europe (Collyer et al. 2012; Andersson 2016). I examined four different temporalities of Nigerien migration projects in Kaddafi's Libya, paying attention to different (in)visibility strategies in response to restrictive policies. The analysis demonstrated how the externalization of European border control in Libya since 2003 (Rodier 2009) had consequences for the journeys of Black African migrants in getting to the country as well as during their sojourn and work in Libya.

One significant feature of these changes was the *Gidan Bachi*, the transformation of this form of migration from smuggling to human trafficking in the south of Libya, in Sebha, where migrants were tortured, mistreated and forced to work using their transnational networks to continue their journey (Puig 2017). This criminalization process due to restrictive migration policies demonstrates that 'the fight against illegal migration (as it is commonly known) is counterproductive' and 'produces what it is supposedly meant to curtail – more distressing forms of "illegal migration"' (Andersson 2016; see also Brachet 2018). In this way, the *Gidan Bachi* could be considered the predecessor of the current consequences of the externalization of European borders in the Maghreb and Sahel regions, the most important ones being the displacement of routes and the invisibilization of migrants, directly related to more violations of human rights.

In the same way, the restrictive migration mechanisms in Kaddafi's Libya intensified the rooted xenophobia of that society (Lecocq 2010; Altaleb 2015) and provoked the further invisibilization of sub-Saharan migrants, who were consistently diminished and racialized by the Arab population. Stigmatized by race and class, their daily activities were usually invisibilized, with the exception of their intentional visibility to search for work in public spaces at the beginning of their sojourn. Migrants spent most of their everyday life in Libya in the *ghettos* where they managed to create solidarity networks by nationality, ethnic affiliation and urban or rural belonging. Likewise, they developed strategies to avoid structural racism through jobs in isolated quarries of international companies where they could avoid xenophobia and interact with people from around the world, consolidating different forms of solidarity 'from below' (Bredeloup and Pliez 2005).

The 2011 conflict entailed an intensified, racialized persecution of Nigerien migrants in Libya. Black African workers were persecuted and accused of being Kaddafi's 'mercenaries'. Thousands of people were forced to return home, empty-handed and without planning. Among them, around 300,000 Nigerien migrants went back to a precarious situation and where they faced different social and community tensions, because of their disrupted migration projects. As Kleist observes, this involuntary return migration had consequences 'embedded in local expectations, family reciprocities and ideals of masculinity' (2017: 322). Returnee groups in Niamey highlighted the recovery of their social visibility, their sense of belonging and their freedom of movement in their country of origin. However, they also emphasized the loss of social status as a man and as a provider and they created different strategies to regain their sense of social worth. One such strategy was to benefit from international aid and donations by UN agencies and humanitarian NGOs, what Olivier de Sardan (1995) has called 'development rent seeking'. By making themselves visible to the international community, returnees sought to render their migration experience useful to their community and family, even if ultimately, they also take part in the European externalization of border control by trying to benefit from the funds dedicated to it.

Notes

1 According to UN estimations, 75 per cent of African migration takes place within the continent, and 90 per cent of West African migrants remain within the sub-region (United Nations 2017).

2 These rates represent the vulnerability of this country, with more than half of the population below the poverty line and exposed to several challenges such as climate change, terrorism – different jihadist groups operate in this territory, especially Boko Haram and Al Qaida in the Islamic Maghreb (AQIM) and some other factions – and structural food crisis.

3 Our ethnography is focused on this mobility, characterized by original particularities based on ethnic aspects and urban practices and experiences.

4 According to our research, these mobilities started due to the Nigerien economic crisis as a result of structural adjustment plans, the impoverishment of the urban middle class and after the political instability created by several putsch in 1996 and 1999.

5 In different parts of Africa and also in Niger, mobility is conceived as a rite of passage and adventure according to some ideals of masculinity of adulthood, responsibility and accumulation (Bredeloup 2013; Wong 2013).

6 Many migrants learnt several manual trades such as carpentry, painting or plumbing, as well as qualified jobs like mechanic, electrician or industrial technician during their work for international enterprises. All of them value the acquisition of these skills upon return, which can be understood as 'social capital' or 'social remittance' (Levitt 1998).

7 Kaddafi's regime was accused of financing terrorism in several attacks in the Scottish locality of Lockerbie and in the Tenere desert that caused hundreds of deaths because of the explosion of two planes during mid-flight.

8 For example, in the 1980s, he drastically reduced the number of foreign workers limiting their entry and he ordered mass expulsions after becoming aware of his dependence on the foreign labour, according to Grégoire (2004).

9 According to Human Rights Watch (2006), between 2003 and 2005, Kaddafi expelled 145,000 sub-Saharan citizens, some of whom were taken to retention camps, such as Katib Rashia's. There, the food, sanitary and hygiene conditions were deplorable and some people had to work to pay for their freedom, while others were robed of everything they had before being jailed (Hamood 2006).

10 The *ghettos* are the host houses along the desert, owned by the smugglers, where migrants are divided by 'nationality, ethnicity or language' (Brachet 2009) before following the next step of their journey (Schapendonk 2017). In the past, the *ghettos* were more visible but they started to be hidden due to the implementation of the European strategy to control migration (Hamadou 2018).

11 Historically, the zone was characterized by transferring all sort of merchandise, products and goods and recently, also illicit goods like weapons, drugs, tobacco, as well as people (Lecocq 2010).

12 Pierce (2014) highlights the differences between *migrant smuggling* and *human trafficking* that are frequently overlooked. According to the author, *migrant smuggling* is 'legally moving people across border, usually at their request', while *human trafficking* includes 'exploiting another human being'.

13 Approximately 457 euros. Euros have an equivalent exchange with CFA Franc, so 1 euro is 655.957 FCFA.

14 The majority of migrants stayed in the capital of Libya, even if there were others spread out around the country, in places like Misrata, Benghazi or Sirte, among others cities and villages.

15 *Wallahi* is a common expression in Niger, taken from the Arab language, meaning 'I swear to you'.

16 In 2005, a food crisis or 'famine' took place in Niger (Olivier de Sardan 2007) as a result not only of the structural factors already known from deficit agro pastoral campaigns, but also for the disproportionate increase in the price of staple foods at the regional level.

17 Nowadays, the *Gidan Bachi* continues in different forms and cities around Libya led by militias and armed groups, creating 'a captive market where migrants may be warehoused, and harmed or tortured with impunity since smugglers know that authorities offer no protection to their charges' (Andersson 2016: 1061).

18 'Le sentiment d'appartenir à une même communauté de destins des Noirs Africains dans le monde arabe' (Bredeloup and Pliez 2005: 17).

19 'Désignant également une position sociale de serviteur, atteste la violence de l'exclusion' (Bensaâd 2012: 100).

20 Tuareg and Tubu groups were historically linked with populations from

the north, especially with Berber people to whom they are related, but also with Arabs due to commercial relations. During his entire regime, Kaddafi also developed customer relations with elite Tuaregs and Tubus (Pellerin 2012).

21 Commonly, they do not explain this to their families and relatives in Niger, because they consider the work shameful and they do not want to lose the 'prestige, authority and status' frequently granted to them as migrants (Åkesson and Baaz 2015).

22 Since 1998 and until the beginning of 2007, entry into Libya for African nationals was not subject to the requirement to hold a visa. However, in August 2005, 'the conditions of entry into Libya are reinforced with the addition of the obligation to hold, in default of a Libyan invitation, the sum of five hundred dinars (about three hundred euros)' (Perrin 2008: 3).

23 There are different legal classifications in Libya, which vary according to the requirements of the time and conjuncture. Broadly speaking, it can be categorized by 'nationals, residents, workers with permits and tourist visa holders'. According to a report of the Danish Council (2013), Filipinos and Bangladeshis hold the majority of the work permit category, which a priori certifies their legal entry into the country.

24 After the lifting of the embargo, Libya's economy became more open to foreign companies. The liberalization of public enterprises increased the job opportunities for migrants, even if some of them already worked for Kaddafi's big projects such as the Great Man-Made River, a pioneering network of pipelines, which provides water to the main Libyan cities by channelling from the desert.

25 Kaddafi's distrust of the regular army could turn against him as it did in the past when he took power from King Ydriss in 1969. For this reason, he surrounded himself with foreign groups with a large number of Tuareg members that were naturalized prior to the war.

26 During the summer of 2000 a series of pogroms in different Libyan cities ended with hundreds of deaths, mass expulsions and thousands of returns. Bensaâd (2012) attributes them to the political use of migration by Kaddafi.

27 Olivier de Sardan (1995) understands the 'development rent' as the foreign aid that makes the state dependent and assisted from external rent. According to him 'the 'development rent' transits essentially through national intermediaries, who are separate and distinct from the classic public administrators and political systems. The growing importance of NGOs as development agents, as well as that of the 'project' system, in both bilateral and multilateral co-operation, provides ample evidence' (1995: 173).

References

Agier, Michel (2011) *Managing the Undesirables: Refugee camps and humanitarian government*, Cambridge, UK and Malden, MA: Polity.

Åkesson, Lisa and Maria Eriksson Baaz (2015) *Africa's Return Migrants: The new developers?*, London: Zed Books.

Alpha Gado, Boureima (2000) 'Migration anciennes et contemporaines: contribution bibliographique', *Peuplement et Migrations*, Niamey: CELTHO, 189–215.

Altaleb, Amal (2015) 'The social and economic history of slavery in Libya (1800–1950)', PhD Thesis, Department of School of Arts, Languages and Cultures, University of Manchester.

Amnesty International (2015) *Libya Is Full of Cruelty: Stories of abduction, sexual violence and abuse from migrants and refugees*, London: Amnesty International.

Andersson, Ruben (2016) 'Europe's failed fight against irregular migration: ethnographic notes on a counterproductive industry', *Journal of Ethnic and Migration Studies*, 42(7): 1055–1075.

Bensaâd, Ali (2012) 'La Libye révolutionnaire', *Politique Africaine*, 125, March.

Boesen, Elisabeth and Laurence Marfaing (2007) *Les nouveaux urbains dans l'espace Sahara–Sahel. Un cosmopolitisme par le bas*, Paris: Karthala.

Bourgeot, André (1995) *Les sociétés touarègues. Nomadisme, identité, résistance*, Paris: Karthala.

Boyer, Florence (2003) 'L'enfermement du voyage: construire des frontières pour passer la frontière: Exemple des migrations temporaires de la zone de Bankilaré vers Abidjan', *Les Cahiers d'Outre Mer*, (222): 229–254.

—— (2014) '"Faire fada" à Niamey (Niger): un espace de transgression silencieuse?', *Carnets de géographes*, (7), June, 1–17.

—— (2015) 'La figure de l'exodant: la culture de la mobilité au regard des enjeux migratoires contemporains au Niger', *Acte colloques Agadez.*

Brachet, Julien (2009) *Migrations transsahariennes: vers un désert cosmopolite et morcelé (Niger)*, Bellecombe-en-Bauges: Croquant.

—— (2018) 'Manufacturing smugglers: from irregular to clandestine mobility in the Sahara', *Annals*, 676: 16–35.

Bredeloup, Sylvie (2012) 'Sahara transit: times, spaces, people', *Population Space and Place*, 18(4): 457–467.

—— (2013) 'The figure of the adventurer as an African migrant', *Journal of African Cultural Studies*, 25(2): 170–182.

Bredeloup, Sylvie and Olivier Pliez (2005) *Migrations entre les deux rives du Sahara*, Paris: IRD Editions.

Bredeloup, Sylvie and Mahamadou Zongo (2005) 'Quand les frères burkinabè de la petite Jamahiriya s'arrêtent à Tripoli', in S. Bredeloup and O. Pliez (eds), *Migrations entre les deux rives du Sahara*, Paris: IRD Editions.

Carleheden, Mikael, Carl-Göran Heidegren and Rasmus Willig (2012) 'Editorial: recognition, social invisibility, and disrespect', Distinktion, 13(1): 1–3.

Carter, Donald Martin (2010) *Navigating the African Diaspora: The anthropology of invisibility*, Minneapolis, MN and London: University of Minnesota Press.

Claudot-Hawad, Hélène (2002) *Touaregs. Apprivoiser le désert*, Paris: Gallimard.

Collyer, Michel, Frank Düvell and Hein de Haas (2012) 'Critical approaches to transit migration', *Population, Space and Place*, 18(4): 407–414.

Crawley, Heaven, Franck Düvell, Katharine Jones, Simon McMahon and Nando Sigona (2016) *Destination Europe? Understanding the dynamics and drivers of Mediterranean migration in 2015*, MEDMIG Final Report.

Danish Refugee Council (2013) *We Risk Our Lives for Our Daily Bread*, December.

De Haas, Hein (2007) *The Myth of Invasion: Irregular migration from West Africa to the Maghreb and the European Union*, Oxford: International Migration Institute. IMI research report, October.

—— (2011) 'African migrants become easy target for racist violence in Libya', 21 February. Retrieved from: http://heindehaas.blogspot.com.es/2011/02/gaddafi-regime-fuels-racist-violence-in.html.

DeVargas, Maria and Stefania Donzelli (2014) 'Sub-Saharan migrants' masculinities: an intersectional analysis of media representations during the Libyan war 2011', in T.-D. Truong, D. Gasper, J. Handmaker and S.I Bergh (eds) *Masculinities and Intersectionality in Migration: Transnational Wolof migrants negotiating manhood and gendered family roles*, Heidelberg and Berlin: Springer.

Drodz, Martine and Olivier Pliez (2005) 'Entre Libye et Soudan: la fermeture d'une piste transaharienne', in S. Bredeloup and O. Pliez (eds) *Migrations entre les deux rives du Sahara*, Paris: IRD Editions, 63–80.

Elbreki, Reem (2018) 'The case of Libya: from a destination country to a transit one', *International Journal of Humanities and Cultural Studies*, 5(2): 66–75.

Grégoire, Emmanuel (2004) 'Les migrations ouest-africains en Libye', in L. Marfaing and S. Wippel (eds), *Les relations*

transsahariennes à l'époque contemporaine. Un espace en constante mutation, Paris: Karthala.
Haddad, Saïd (2004) 'Fruits et défis de la normalisation libyenne', *L'Année du Maghreb*, 1: 221–235.
—— (2009) 'Enfermer pour s'insérer: contraintes et paradoxes de la questions', in A. Bensâad (ed.), *Le Maghreb à l'épreuve des migrations subsahariennes. Immigration sur émigration*, Paris: Karthala, 395–411.
Haimzadeh, Patrick (2011) *Au coeur de la Libye de Kadhafi*, Paris: JC Lattès.
Hamadou, Abdoulaye (2018) 'La gestion des flux migratoires au Niger entre engagements et contraintes', *La Revue des droits de l'homme*, 14: 1–24.
Hamood, Sara (2006) *African Transit Migration through Libya to Europe: The human cost*, Cairo: The American University in Cairo.
Human Rights Watch (2006) 'Stemming the flow: abuses against migrants, asylum seekers and refugees', *Human Rights Watch*, vol. 18, no. 5, September.
Kleist, Nauja (2017) 'Disrupted migration projects: the moral economy of involuntary return to Ghana from Libya', *Africa*, 87: 322–342.
Kohl, Ines (2015) 'Tuareg trans-border business: Afrod will never end, afrod is our work!' In: *The Broker. Collecting Worlds of Knowledge*. Sahel Watch Programm, Expert Opinion, October 16.
Lecocq, Baz (2010) *Disputed Desert: Decolonisation, competing nationalisms and Tuareg rebellions in Northern Mali*, Boston, MA: Brill.
Lessault, David and Cris Beauchemin (2009) 'Ni invasion, ni exode. Regards statistiques sur les migrations d'Afrique subsaharienne', *Revue Européenne des Migrations Internationales*, 25(1): 163–194.
Levitt, Peggy (1998) 'Social remittances: migration driven local-level forms of cultural diffusion', *International Migration Review*, 32(4): 926–948.
Lucht, Hans (2012) *Darkness before Daybreak: African migrants living on the margins in southern Italy*, Berkeley, CA: University of California Press.
Masquelier, Adeline (2019) *Fada: Boredom and belonging in Niger*, Chicago, IL: The University of Chicago Press.
McDougall, James and Judith Scheele (eds) (2012) *Saharan Frontiers*, Bloomington, IN: Indiana University Press.
Moisseron, Jean Yves and Nadia Belalimat (2012) 'L'après-Kadhafi: noveaux défis en Libye et au Sahel', in M. Mokhefi and A. Antil (eds), *Le Maghreb et son Sud: vers des liens renouvelés*, Paris: CNRS Éditions, 73–90.
Mounkaila, Harouna and Florence Boyer (2010) 'Partir pour aider ceux qui restent ou la dépendance face aux migrations. L'exemple des paysans sahéliens', *Hommes et Migrations*, 1286–1287: 214–221.
Olivier de Sardan, Jean-Pierre (1995) *Anthropology and Development: Understanding contemporary social change*, London and New York: Zed Books.
—— (2007) 'Crise alimentaire et malnutrition infantile au Niger: le bilan de la "famine" de 2005', *Critique internationale*, 4(37): 37–49.
Oumarou, Hamani (2008) 'Le rôle des ressortissants et des migrants à Bambey face à la crise', *Afrique contemporaine*, 1(225): 199–216.
Paoletti, Emanuela (2011) 'Migration and foreign policy: the case of Libya', *Journal of North African Studies*, 16(2): 215–231.
Pellerin, Mathieu (2012) 'Le Sahel et la contagion libyenne', *Politique étrangère*, 4: 835–847.
Peraldi, Michel (2012) 'Le Maghreb, laboratoire des nouvelles migrations', in M. Mokhefi and A. Antil (eds), *Le Maghreb et son Sud: vers des liens renouvelés*, Paris: CNRS Éditions.
Perrin, Delphine (2008) 'Aspects juridiques de la migration circulaire dans l'espace euro-méditerranéen. Le cas de la Libye', *CARIM*, Florence: Robert Schuman Centre for Advanced Studies, no. 23.
Pierce, Sarah (2014) 'The vital difference between human trafficking and migrant smuggling', *Open Democracy*, 12 November.

Pierre, Jemima (2013) 'Race in Africa today: a commentary', *Cultural Anthropology*, 28(3): 547–551.

Pliez, Olivier (2006) 'Tripoli: vers l'effacement de l'africanité de la capitale libyenne?', *Migrations-société*, 18(107): 199–211.

Polzer, Tara and Laura Hammond (2008) 'Invisible displacement', *Journal of Refugee Studies*, 21(4): 417–431.

Prestianni, Sara (2018) *The Dangerous Link between Migration, Development and Security for the Externalisation of Borders in Africa: Case studies on Sudan, Niger and Tunisia*, Roma: ARCI.

Puig, Oriol (2017) 'Libya Kaman Turaï. El Dorado libio: los retornados nigerinos en Niamey', PhD Thesis, Department of Social Anthropology, University of Barcelona.

Retaillé, Denis and Olivier Walther (2008) *Affaires de patrons: villes et commerce transfrontalier au Sahel*, Bern, Berlin and Brussels: P. Lang.

Rodier, Claire (2009) 'Externalisation des frontières au sud de l'Europe. L'alliance Union européenne-Libye', in A. Bensâad (ed.), *Le Maghreb à l'épreuve des migrations subsahariennes. Immigration sur émigration*, Paris: Karthala.

Sáenz, Rogelio and Karen Manges Douglas (2014) 'A call for the racialization of migration studies: on the transition of ethnic immigrants to racialized immigrants', *Race, Ethnicity and Immigration*, 1(1): 166–180.

Schapendonk, Joris (2017) 'Navigating the migration industry: migrants moving through an African–European web of facilitation/control', *Journal of Ethnic and Migration Studies*, 44: 663–679.

Staub, Vincent (2006) *La Libye et les migrations subsahariennes*, Paris: L'Harmattan.

Tarrius, Alain (2002) *La mondialisation par le bas. Les nouveaux nomades de l'économie souterraine*, Paris: Balland.

Temlali, Yassin (2011) 'Las migraciones subsaharianas en la prensa diaria argelina', in R. Bustos, O. Orozco and L. Witte, (eds) *El Magreb y las migraciones subsaharianas: el papel de asociaciones y sindicatos*, Madrid: Casa Árabe-IEAM, 85–100.

Timera, Mahamet (2001) 'Les migrations des jeunes Sahéliens: affirmation de soi et émancipation', *Autrepart*, 18: 37–49.

Turner, Simon (2016) 'What is a refugee camp? Explorations of the limits and effects of the camp', *Journal of Refugee Studies*, 29(2): 139–148.

United Nations (2017) *International Migration Report: Highlights*, New York: United Nations.

UNDP (2018) *Human Development Indices and Indicators: 2018 Statistical Update*, New York: UNDP.

Vallée, Olivier (2012) 'Kadhafi: le dernier roi d'Afrique, La Libye révolutionnaire', *Politique africaine*, 125: 147–169.

Wimmer, Andreas and Nina Glick Schiller (2003) 'Methodological nationalism: the social sciences and the study of migration. An essay in the historical epistemology', *International Migration Review*, 37(3): 576–610.

Wong, Madeleine (2013). 'Navigating return: the gendered geographies of skilled return migration to Ghana', *Global Networks*, 14(4): 438–457.

10 | Violence, displacement and the in/visibility of bodies, papers and images in Burundi

Simon Turner

Introduction

When the Burundian president declared his intention to run for a third term in April 2015, the youth of the capital city, Bujumbura, took to the streets to mark their dissatisfaction with what they saw as an unlawful '*troisième mandat*' (third term). The young men and women in certain areas of the city chanted, danced, shouted, burned car tyres and built barricades of branches to cut off the streets and prevent the police from entering. The colourful crowds had a performative air – they were covered intensely by the independent media in the country and their images were distributed rapidly on various social media platforms.

The violence committed by the police during the demonstrations was equally visible and dramatic, as teargas was thrown and youth carried away by officers in uniforms. When I talked to Burundians who had fled the violence in 2015, however, they claimed that the real violence took place in more sinister and invisible ways: at night, youth militia and the secret police would allegedly drive into the neighbourhoods where the demonstrations took place (*les quartiers contestataires*). They would enter the neighbourhoods in cars without number plates and without headlights and take individuals, known to the authorities, away to secret detention centres, where they would be tortured and killed, their mutilated bodies re-appearing in ditches and rivers in other parts of the city. The real fear of state violence – and where it had the strongest effects – lies in the fact that it is perceived to be secret, hidden and dark. This chapter explores the multiple ways in which violence and in/visibility intersect in the Burundian crisis, and how those displaced by violence strategically deploy invisibility and visibility as a response to this violence.

People in the neighbourhoods would take turns to do rounds at night, and they would use whistles to alert the inhabitants, if anyone or anything unusual entered the area. An alternative to this collective measure of uncovering the secret intrusions of the state was a more individual strategy of making oneself invisible to the eyes of the state. Individuals who believed that they were particularly targeted by the regime would stay the night with friends in other parts of the city. Later, they might decide to leave the country. However, the move itself caused unwanted exposure and they would go to great lengths so as not to be seen or recognized along the way. The need to hide depended on the position of the person involved. Those who were believed to be most exposed to state violence – such as politicians and journalists – would hide in the boots of cars. Young people travelling alone on public transport were also at risk and would have to hide their intentions of going abroad by avoiding the direct bus from Bujumbura to Kigali – a trip of only four hours. They would instead take several buses, sometimes via Congo, in order to cover their tracks. Finally, families going by private car were free to drive straight to Rwanda.

In other words, both the state and civilians were actively using various kinds of visibility and invisibility strategically in the context of violence. There was, however, no simple relationship between visibility and power. While the demonstrations against the third term were powerful in their visibility, they also rendered the participants vulnerable to the vindictive power of the state. Similarly, the state used open violence as a performative assertion of its power; it also maintained its sovereign power by installing a fear of invisible violence in the population.

Identity papers played a role in these strategies of visibility and invisibility. While documents could ease the movement of bodies, in particular across borders, identity papers could also expose the identity of the holder to the punitive measures of the authorities. In this case, having a paper with an address from the *quartiers contestataires* was a problem, as police officers, immigration officers and militiamen would suspect the holder of being part of the demonstrations and of having connections with rebel groups in Rwanda. Therefore, people deployed various strategies in relation to obtaining papers, on the one hand, while hiding certain papers in certain contexts, on the other hand. The routes, means of transport and use of papers depended on their position and the given context – making themselves visible in particular ways to specific audiences. In other words, the strategies of invisibility were relational, as they made themselves invisible to specific others. Likewise, they made only specific aspects of their identities invisible while remaining visible in other ways. This might be related to their profession, where they lived and their ethnicity. So, while their bodies may have been visible, the identity markers that went with them were rendered invisible, and identity papers played a role in reifying such identities. Passports, ID cards and photos would leave 'traces' that could 'fix' them to places and events. Finally, activity on social media also left traces, and authorities did their best to follow these traces by asking for the mobile phones of those who were trying to escape the state. People fleeing violence would do their utmost to remove these traces by removing WhatsApp accounts, suspicious messages and phone numbers of controversial individuals. On the other hand, social media were also used to expose and unveil the secret violence of the state.

In this chapter, I explore the ways in which Burundians strategically deploy visibility and invisibility in the context of violence and displacement. I argue that violence always targets bodies, either in highly performative manners or through hidden means of making bodies disappear. These bodies are located in place and marked by gender, age, class and ethnicity. As these markers determine whether the individual body is liable to be exposed to violence, people deploy a number of strategies to render them invisible and hence avoid violence. I argue that ID papers and images are means that the authorities use to reveal the true identity of a body, and that those who risk being subject to state violence deploy a number of strategies to avoid such visibilization and identification. However, while the state does its best to render its subjects visible and hence susceptible to violence, and people do their best to become invisible to state violence, an opposite process is also taking place: state violence seeks to be hidden, secret and partly invisible while the objects of this violence are doing their best to unveil and make visible the horrors of the state – in this way making its violence impotent.

The paper follows the process in four sections. First, I explore the violence, briefly outlined above, and how it shaped visible and invisible bodies. Then, I explore the different strategies of escaping the violence and fleeing to Rwanda as a means of invisibilization. Third, I explore the role of identity papers in becoming visible in the right way to the right audience. Fourth, I explore how ICT and social media visibilized and invisibilized bodies and violence before, during and after flight and how both authorities and refugees would manoeuvre these sites.

Kigali as field-site

The chapter is based on my long-term engagement with Burundi and more specifically on fieldwork conducted in August 2015 and July 2016 among Burundian refugees in Kigali. Around 20,000 Burundians fled to Kigali in neighbouring Rwanda in relation to the violence in 2015.[1] Some fled even before the president declared that he would run for a third term, in anticipation of the violence that might come. The Burundians whom I encountered in Kigali, were almost exclusively Tutsi, the majority came from the capital city, Bujumbura, and were predominantly middle-class. Often, their decision to relocate to Kigali had been made as a family decision and made in steps, as the conflict developed. In some cases, young men and women had fled to Kigali on their own, because they were believed to be most at risk of being arrested by the secret police or attacked by the *imbonerakure*, the youth wing of the ruling party which has effectively functioned as a militia since 2010. Furthermore, they often had no income, and therefore the families could afford to send them off, while other members of the family had to remain and keep the family's income flowing. In other situations, families with young children chose to bring their children out of harm's way until the unrest blew over. Fathers and mothers would tell me that they had gone to Kigali, believing that it would be over within weeks and they would be able to return to work and school after the summer break. After a while, they were met with the tough decisions of whether to return to their homes and jobs in Bujumbura or remain in Kigali without income. Furthermore, the hospitality of friends and relatives with whom they had initially stayed, was wearing thin. In these situations, one of the parents might return to Bujumbura and their job, commuting to Kigali regularly to be with the family and bring cheap foodstuffs from Burundi, as life in Kigali is expensive. Some families would leave the children in Kigali in the care of a young relative who did not have an income. While many of my interlocutors expressed anxiety, they also expressed hope when I met them for the first time in August 2015, just a few months after the violence had broken out. They had hopes that a solution would be found, and they would be able to return. When I met them again almost a year later, their hopes had dwindled and despair was taking over (Turner 2020). This also meant less mobility between Bujumbura and Kigali. While parents could cross the border to Rwanda by car relatively easily in 2015, this was becoming close to impossible and parents gave up their employment in Burundi to join their families in Rwanda. Similarly, it was increasingly unrealistic for young people to return from Rwanda, as they would be accused of being rebels.

My access to the Burundian refugees in Kigali was mainly through a research assistant who was a Burundian refugee herself. Many of the Burundians were sceptical of each other and of talking to me, as they feared spies from the Burundian secret service in their midst. The fact that I returned after a year helped me gain their confidence. The interviews on the other hand, were frank and open, as people were willing to share their experiences and their fears and hopes.[2]

I shape my argument around the flight narratives of three interlocutors. I explore how they narrate the strategies of 'the system' in terms of violence and (in)visibility and how they narrate their own flight in terms of hiding from the system. All three narratives are relatively dramatic compared to the majority of Burundians whom I met in Kigali, and I make references to these other – more mundane – flight narratives along the way to put them into perspective. However, in their drama they illustrate the complexities of state violence, sovereignty and visibility in a manner that other narratives do not convey. The three flight narratives serve the purpose of bearing witness to state violence and the exercise of sovereign power. However, they also illustrate broader tropes in narratives on state violence, secrecy and flight in Burundi. They are therefore to be treated as narratives as such.

Violence and in/visibility

State violence following the 2015 crisis played on the fine line between the visible and the invisible. On the one hand, the visibility of the victims was central to the violence committed against the population, as it demonstrated the sovereign power of the state in a 'state spectacle' (Hansen and Stepputat 2005). At the same time, however, the violence committed by the militia, the police and the secret service remained obscure – albeit known. The sovereignty of the perpetrator lies in exactly this fine line between obscurity and visibility (Turner 2007). Sovereign power relies on being unpredictable and imponderable. My research assistant explained to me how cars would enter the neighbourhoods at night – and that these cars had no number plates, thus making themselves known to the population but difficult to identify and hence hold accountable. State violence was a public secret (Taussig 1999).

Pacifique's story[3] During my second visit to Kigali, my research assistant was working hard on establishing an interview with a young man, whom she did not know personally but who, according to her, had experienced some serious police violence. She was quite excited about the fact that he had agreed to talk to us, although I had assured her that I was equally happy to talk to people who had witnessed no violence at all and had left the country by plane or car. When we met him in a bar in downtown Kigali, he was very open about his experience and very quickly volunteered to pull up his shirt and show us his scars. His openness actually made my assistant comment afterwards that she found his behaviour abnormal, and she was unsure whether to attribute it to the traumatic experiences he had endured or whether he had always been like that.

After showing us his wounds and some initial confusion about the drinks he wanted, Pacifique began – without further ado – to recount his story chronologically from beginning to end. He was very precise with dates, names and places. Apparently, he had been to the bank in central Bujumbura on 23 June 2015, when he was accosted by a young man, whom Pacifique recognized as Jérôme a former student whom he had taught a course on 'religious morale' in 10th grade. The young man was with a group of policemen, led by a certain Kazungu, an officer who was well-known for his brutality. In his narrative about the incident, Pacifique managed to mention that Kazungu had the rank of major, although he never passed 5th grade primary school, just as he mentioned several times how the police officer and several of the militias spoke in Swahili, a language that indicates that they probably belonged to a rebel movement in the 1990s based in Tanzania or Congo and that they were from 'the bush', while Pacifique is educated, urban and speaks fluent French. The heavily armed group beat him and stabbed him with their bayonets. He mentioned how Kazungu commanded Jérôme to stab him and that Jérôme hesitated and only stabbed him lightly, which might be the reason he survived. He lost consciousness and woke up in a pit in Kamenge, a relatively poor neighbourhood, known to be a pro-government Hutu stronghold, where twenty to twenty-five other bodies had also been dumped. He was saved by a woman (*une maman*) who had seen him blink. I will return to his escape in the section below, as it relied strongly on issues of invisibility and assistance from the enemy. Meanwhile, let us explore the kind of violence, how it targeted specific persons and how this relates to invisibility, keeping in mind the way Pacifique recounted and dramatized it to me, the audience. Pacifique was attacked in the middle of the city in broad daylight. At this point in time, four months after the initial demonstrations had taken place, the conflict had escalated to a degree that there were very few people out in the streets – even during the day – which meant that police violence could be quite open. Furthermore, the media had been shut down and most journalists had fled the country. This meant that police violence could routinely take place without having to hide. Towards the end of our conversation I asked why they had chosen him. He answered that 'the power' (*le pouvoir*) had decided to kill all the men and boys in a bad way – especially those who had participated in the demonstrations. 'I had only participated twice and for two reasons. First, I lived in the neighbourhoods where the demonstrations took place, and second, if you don't take part, you are seen to be on the side of "the power"' (Pacifique, Kigali, 2016). And while the demonstrations took place, the *imbonerakure* took photos, he explained. It was such photos that made people like himself visible and vulnerable to 'the power'. The photos would haunt him later, as he tried to cross the border to Rwanda.

The violence of '*le pouvoir*' or '*la système*' was, in other words, directed towards certain individuals who belonged to certain groups: journalists, human rights activists and members of the opposition were clear targets. They were known figures and had to go into hiding in order to avoid violence. I talked to a journalist who hid in a friend's house for weeks until he was smuggled out of the country in the back of a car. He knew that he was specifically targetted due to his profession, and that he would be recognized on the street. I also talked to Jean-Pierre, who was the leader of the youth wing of an opposition movement in a small town. He was a known face in his home town and had to flee to Bujumbura in order to 'hide in the crowd'. Unfortunately for him, he was recognized by a police officer who had been sent from his hometown to Bujumbura to assist in controlling the demonstrations in the city. And he was almost shot.

Others were targeted in a less clear manner, as Pacifique's story shows. The secrecy of the violence and disappearances and the denial of such violence by the authorities added to the uncertainty and anxiety about who could be targeted, when and why. It was not even clear who was committing the violence. Was it the secret police or was it the *imbonerakure*? This led, of course, to rumours and speculations, as people tried to understand the violence and act accordingly. It was generally believed among the Burundians with whom I talked in Kigali, that the youth from the '*quartiers contestataires*' were targeted, as were those who were believed to have taken part in the demonstrations. These categories were sufficiently vague to be able to hit anybody who was not a staunch supporter of the regime. Later, anyone who had been to Rwanda was also at risk of being accused of being a rebel.

While everyone knew about the violence, the system also made it invisible, creating a public secret (Taussig 1999) with immense powers. While Pacifique was attacked in broad daylight in the city centre, others would mention being taken from their homes at night and taken to hidden houses where people were interrogated, tortured and sometimes killed.

Disappearing dead bodies When talking about the violence, the issue of where the bodies were dumped featured strongly in people's accounts. Even people who had not had a close shave with death, as Pacifique had, would mention the bodies. It was commonly held that the bodies of those who had disappeared would turn up again in ditches, often in neighbourhoods that were far from where they had disappeared. A friend explained to me how the secret police dumped the bodies in Musaga, where he lived. They would even shoot the dead body in the head in Musaga, he explained.

In that way, they could blame the inhabitants of that neighbourhood for the death and use it as an excuse to raid their houses (David, Kigali, 24 August 2015).

Talking to my research assistant, Jeanette, the following year, she explained how the secret service had changed its modus operandi. In the months following my first visit in August 2015, the situation 'calmed down' and became 'normal' – or so the government claimed. There were no riots in the streets and no riot police either. This was, however, just a surface phenomenon and government propaganda, she claimed. The conflict was what we might call 'closed' – a term Burundians use to describe historical periods of apparent calm and which are perceived to be particularly toxic (Turner 2007, 2009). Jeanette explained that the secret police was still abducting and torturing people, but now the bodies of the missing people never turned up. There were speculations that they were using acid to dissolve the bodies, she claimed. I suggested to her that there might be mass graves. However, she responded by reference to an incident in December 2015 where mass graves north of Bujumbura were discovered by satellite images, bringing international attention to the state violence. After December 2015, the regime had stopped this practice, according to Jeanette; people simply disappeared and no bodies were found.

While we might see her narrative as a typical conspiracy about covert operations, taking place at night and in secret locations, it did turn out that there were indeed mass graves. In December 2015, Amnesty International was able to reveal that mass graves existed – using a combination of eye-witness accounts, a video clip that a local had taken on his cell phone and satellite imagery (Amnesty International 2016). On 11 December, rebels attacked military bases outside Bujumbura and the army had responded. However, eyewitness accounts claimed to Amnesty International that the regular army, various special forces and the *imbonerakure* also pulled young men from their homes in the *quartiers contestataires*, in particular Musaga and Nyakabiga, and shot them at close range. The bodies were left in the street until the following day when police and local officials arrived in pickup trucks and drove the bodies away (Amnesty International 2015). It is believed that at least twenty-five of these bodies had been buried in the mass graves north of the capital. According to Jeanette, the secret police had therefore used other methods in recent months to make bodies disappear completely. They put them into some kind of acid bath that dissolved the flesh and bones. In this way, the regime could continue to cover its tracks.

In sum, state violence was at once a visible spectacle – leaving dead bodies in the street, beating people in full daylight – and hidden and concealed – abducting individuals at night and making the bodies disappear. At one level, this in/visibilization was about the state covering up its own excesses in order to avoid being condemned too harshly by the international community. At another level, it was communicating to those it sees as its enemies that it was able to use excessive violence while also signalling that this violence was covert and impossible to pinpoint, making it all the more dangerous. The targets of this violence, on the other hand, applied a number of strategies to become invisible to the state and thus avoid its violence. I explore the strategies of escape in more detail in the next section. Meanwhile, it is important to note that while violence might be symbolic and the struggles might be linked to political identities, the violence is inflicted on real, corporal bodies (Hansen and Stepputat 2005: 12–13). This is to say that the body remains, whatever is done to make it disappear. Ultimately, even dead bodies may seep back into the domain of the living and bear witness to the violence that the regime is trying to hide (Fontein 2014; Stepputat 2014).

Escape

During this period of heightened violence and anticipation of more violence to come, it was important not to fall into the category of those who might be targeted by the state. Some were more at risk than others by fact of their ethnicity, political activism, profession (especially journalists were in danger), place of residence, age and gender. Young men from the '*quartiers contestataires*' were more at risk than others. They rarely mentioned ethnicity, but these neighbourhoods were predominantly Tutsi, which meant that young men who had Tutsi traits were more at risk. They would use various means to blend in and avoid the state. However, if they feared that they could no longer avoid being targeted by the secret police or the *imbonerakure* due to being a known face, looking Tutsi or coming from a certain area, they would choose to leave. Leaving the country was, however, not an easy endeavour, as Pacifique's story illustrates.

Pacifique's escape Pacifique, who was left for dead in a pit, was discovered by a woman who recognized him as the catechist who had helped baptize her children. When recounting his story to me, he consistently called her a mother, confirming her identity as the mother of the baptized children rather than a member of the ruling party, the CNDD-FDD.[4] The fact of being saved by someone within 'the system' features prominently in most flight narratives. People like Pacifique were visible to these helpers as individuals who had other identities than the ones attributed to them by the system. To these helpers they were also visible as school friends, colleagues, and teachers or catechists. I would argue, however, that there is also a certain magical quality to the helpers in these flight narratives, as they play a central role in the plot. In a sense, they mark a split in the 'other', drawing attention to the fact that the system is not perfect, and that it was this imperfection that saved their lives. By doing so, the system also reveals that it is unnatural – and evil – and bound to break down some time in an unknown future. The 'mother' took Pacifique to a military hospital in Kamenge. At this point in time the loyalty of the army was not yet entirely with the president. He spent two weeks at the hospital, until Kazungu got news that he was still alive and started searching for him. The 'mother' knew about this, due to her connections to the ruling party, and got her brother, who was a doctor 'and a major in the army', to drive him to his house in Kigobe – an affluent area with many cadres in the ruling party – where Pacifique stayed for another two weeks. He was then transferred once more because the doctor feared that his servants might expose to the authorities where Pacifique was hiding. There is an ethnic/class twist to this dynamic, as we may assume that the servants are Hutu and hence support the regime. Furthermore, there were lots of rumours about bounties being promised for exposing people like Pacifique, which would tempt a poor houseboy more than a doctor. After hiding in another house, he was taken to the border in the back of the doctor's car on 16 September. 'The mother who found me and her brother who helped me flee were both in this system of killing (*ce système de tuerie*) because they had a paper that gave them access to pass through the checkpoints without being checked'. Here again we see the inside–outside position of the mother and her brother which turned out to be helpful for Pacifique in flying below the radar. Thanks to 'the paper', they were able to transgress the boundaries of being inside and outside the system, which made them able to access information and manoeuvre in manners that others could not. It was, however, also a highly risky position where they constantly needed to hide their intentions.

After a few close shaves with truckloads of *Interahamwe*,[5] they made it to the border. At the border, they remained at a distance in the car, while he walked to the immigration officers. According to Pacifique, there were photos of him at all border posts. These photos had been taken when he was lying in the street 'in my white T-shirt, covered with blood'. Apparently Kazungu and his men had taken it as proof of killing him, 'to get the salary that they had been promised by the president'. It is not quite clear why they should also choose to distribute the photos to all border posts, if he had been left for dead. In any case, Pacifique explains that the border guard seemed to have recognized him and asked him to sit outside and wait. 'There were two boys sitting next to me and they were the ones who were supposed to finish me off … without me knowing'. The boys greeted him in Swahili. 'My phone rang, and it was the officer who had accompanied me. He said, "You know. They know that it is you, and these boys are waiting for the signal to kill you". He spoke to me in French because the boys didn't understand French'. Now things became dramatic, as Pacifique simply ran towards the border post, was hit by a police baton but was saved by a Rwandan police officer who had offered him her baton, that he grabbed, and she dragged him onto Rwandan soil. This made the wounds on his stomach break open again. Pacifique's dramatic flight narrative reveals the dangers of being exposed to the regime, the various ways the regime attempts to find and identify him (photos and checkpoints) and the central role of the doctor and the mother as insiders/outsiders who were able to skillfully navigate the system and assist his escape.

Jean-Pierre I first met Jean-Pierre at the catholic school in Kigali, which the Burundian community borrowed in the afternoons in order to keep their children up to date with the Burundian curriculum. Jean-Pierre volunteered as a teacher. He was a young, unmarried man, who was struggling to make ends meet in Kigali. When I met him the following year, he looked distinctly thinner and more disheveled – although his good spirit was intact. Jean-Pierre kept telling me, 'There are two reasons for running. There are some who flee because of fear and others who flee because they are wanted. There is a list of people to be killed in all the communes. I am number one on it'. He belonged to the latter group, being the leader of the MSD (Movement for Solidarity and Democracy) opposition party in his hometown. He explained how a friend who was a member of the ruling party, CNDD-FDD, had warned him that 'they' would come to his home to kill him. When they saw that he was not at home, they killed his dogs and his pigs. Apparently, he had exercised with the person who helped him escape. 'Not all are bad: just some of them', he added, showing that even members of the system have other – more humane – identities. After hiding for three days in the forest, his friend took him on the back of his motorbike by night to Gitega. They could not drive directly to Bujumbura because of all the police checks. In Bujumbura he joined the demonstrations against the third term. However, by this time, the government was calling police in from all over the country to assist the police in Bujumbura that had been overburdened by the month-long demonstrations in the city. This meant that Jean-Pierre was recognized by one of the police officers from his home town who had been seconded to Bujumbura. The police officer shot at him but missed and shot one of his friends instead. It was generally held by my interlocutors that the police or the secret service took photos of the demonstrators, just as it was held that photos of certain targeted persons were posted to all border crossings. How much this is a verifiable fact and how much it is part of their narratives about the all-seeing powers of '*la système*' I do not know. In any case, it had the effect that he felt he was under surveillance.

After being recognized by the police officer in Bujumbura, he decided to leave the country. He had no money and hitched a ride as far as Kirundo, after which he walked across the border, avoiding the checkpoints that were manned by *imbonerakure*. Jean-Pierre could not hide in anonymity and keep his head down, as many others did, because he was a known face in the community, and apparently on a government list.[6] His strategy of escape took several steps. First, he hid in the forest while the *imbonerakure* went to his home and killed his animals. Next, he decided to go to Bujumbura by night where he could camouflage his identity in the crowds. Finally, when this did not work out, he had to leave the country, crossing the border by foot.

Others who were not known to the system explained how they could take minibuses directly from Bujumbura to Kigali in the beginning, but as the conflict grew, this became unviable. Faustin, a journalist who used to work for the independent radio station RPA (*Radio Publique Africaine*), spent three days getting from Bujumbura to Kigali. Other high-profile journalists had even harder times leaving. The director of Radio Bonesha hid in his friend's house for a week, frantically phoning his contacts at the European Union and various embassies to drive him out of the country in a diplomatic car. He found this week of hiding extremely stressful, as his phone was constantly ringing with people wanting interviews while he had no idea how he was going to get out of there. In the end, he left by plane – timing his escape with the day that Innocent Mohozi (from an independent TV station) was summoned to court, diverting the attention of the authorities. He did, however, admit that it was probably luck that saw him through the migration control (Head of Radio Bonesha, Kigali, 21 August 2015).

In sum, escaping the violence of the system was about physically removing your body from the territory of Burundi. However, in the process of moving, people fleeing would have to negotiate their own visibility and hence their position as targets of the violence. The testimonies of escape often involved the help not just of friends but also of representatives of '*la système*' as if it were these gaps in the system that made the difference between life and death. Once they were on their own, without the protection of helpers, they were vulnerable. This was often at specific junctions that would interrupt the flow of bodies, such as checkpoints, airports and border crossings. Photos and dossiers helped the authorities manning these posts to recognize them, and it seems that it was almost by chance that they were able to cross unnoticed.

The paper trail

Moving in violent situations is, as we saw above, very much about bodies that can be beaten, shot, saved, cured, hidden in cars, rushed through airports, tortured, and then can walk, crawl and even be pulled across a border. These bodies are material objects that may be hidden from or exposed to violence. But they also link to other material objects – most notably photos and identity cards of one sort or the other – both of which are means to pin down the identity of these particular bodies. On the one hand, they allow governments, militias and other public authorities to govern and punish the bodies. On the other hand, they may provide the kind of visibility that enables recognition from authorities such as governments, the United Nations High Commissioner for Refugees (UNHCR) and NGOs, and therefore also provide some kind of protection against violence.

A recurring theme among many of my interlocutors was the fact that a Burundian ID card states where you live, and having an ID card that shows you live in one of the '*quartiers contestataires*' made travelling very difficult, especially if you were young, and in particular if you were male. Some tried to obtain driving licences from other parts of the country. Others were fortunate to hold a passport where the place of residence is not stated. However, passports reveal how many times you have been abroad and where you have been. Many stamps from Rwanda were a liability to the holder. Finally, some were protected by having contracts with international NGOs or UN missions.

Photos were also often mentioned as having a detrimental effect on those who attempted to flee. People like Jean-Pierre and Pacifique mentioned that their photos had been distributed to all border posts, linking their images to the demonstrations in Bujumbura or to specific political parties and civil society organizations. The fear of having their photos taken followed them to Kigali, where Burundians claimed that the Burundian government sent spies who took photos of them – even when they were gathered at church.

Others felt stuck in Kigali without certain papers. Richard had passed his exams in psychology shortly before leaving the country in 2015. However, his bachelor's degree was at the university and he had to collect it in person. When I visited him in August 2015, he was fretting between risking his life by making a short return trip to Bujumbura, so that he could find a job in Kigali, and letting it go and continuing to live off alms in Kigali without the diploma. After a year in Kigali, Josephine got a job as a school teacher, but could not open a bank account without a passport. Neither could she receive money from a relative in Canada via Western Union. So, she returned to Burundi to collect her passport. On the way back to Burundi, she hid her Rwandan refugee documents and claimed that she had only been in Rwanda to seek work. Burundians living in Rwanda were suspected by the authorities manning the roadblocks of being rebels. While back in Burundi, she was approached by a man from the neighbourhood who was now working for the government. 'He was like a spy. I know him and he knows me very well. He comes to our home and he says "Eeeh, Josephine, they say you live in Rwanda now. Is that true? Why did you flee the peaceful country?"' She told him that she was working in Kigali. He continued to ask her questions and asked for her phone number, which she gave him. She had to be friendly and appear to be honest in order not to raise his suspicion. She was using all her social skills in this meeting. She explained how she didn't want a conflict with him and knew that she had to be humble with him, 'but my heart was beating'. (Josephine, 10 July 2016).

Josephine's story is one of needing documents in order to prove her identity and become visible to the Rwandan state as an employable school teacher and visible to Western Union as a receiver of money. Meanwhile, she had to hide her true intentions while in Burundi. This was not limited to hiding documents at roadblocks but also involved using all her social skills to hide her true identity from her childhood friend while remaining friendly and open towards him in order not to arouse any suspicion.

In sum, documents were coveted items that helped mobility and recognition. They could, however, also have the consequence of 'fixing' a body and a face to a specific identity, limiting the room for manoeuvre and the ability to go below the radar and become invisible. Burundian refugees were negotiating these double tensions of the paper trail.

Out of site/sight but still online

Mobile bodies did not just leave a paper trail – they also left tracks in cyberspace. At checkpoints, manned by police, soldiers or militias, phones were checked in order to verify the pathways of the holder, thus exposing not only their routes but also their possible connections. Anyone passing the border and other checkpoints would make sure to remove WhatsApp and Facebook apps from their phones and delete any compromising pictures, names or text messages. One young man in Kigali explained that it was a good idea to buy a LIMITEL sim card, as they were controlled by the regime. In that sense, the regime would believe that it had you under its surveillance.

The trick, he explained, was not to use the account for anything that could compromise your safety (Pascal, 22 August 2015). In other words, the simple way to become invisible was to remove WhatsApp and other compromising material from one's phone. However, this could raise suspicion that one was hiding something. The more sophisticated strategy, Pascal suggested, was to appear to be visible to the system, in this manner shifting the spotlight away from what must remain invisible. This resembles Josephine's strategy of seeming open and forthcoming towards the inquisitions of her neighbour.

While social media could make individuals visible to the regime and hence vulnerable to its violence, a counter-strategy would be to visibilize the violence of the regime on social media. Burundians in Kigali would often receive images of dead and mutilated bodies would circulate on social media. Burundians in Kigali would receive these images from WhatsApp groups and would share them further.[7] Twitter activists – such as Teddy Mazina – put an effort into documenting the atrocities of the government by sharing images of missing persons (Paviotti 2019; Falisse and Nkengurutse 2019; Turner and Berckmoes 2020). The goal of these groups and individuals was to unveil the secret violence of the regime. In particular, the Twitter activists had an explicit audience; they would tag heads of state in the region, the president's office and various UN agencies, hoping to make the violence visible to them and to make them act accordingly.

Reverien: exposing the other in order to survive Reverien provides the third, larger flight narrative of this chapter. His story teaches us that people fleeing violence do not always try to hide their identities and intentions on social media; they may strategically use social media to make themselves visible and make the violence of the system visible and hence vulnerable. His story obviously also speaks to themes from Pacifique's and Jean-Pierre's flight narratives.

I met Reverien in a café in a modern high-rise in central Kigali the night before I was scheduled to return home from fieldwork. I was tired and had no prior knowledge of his story. He was a polite man who clearly was well-educated and at ease speaking French. As opposed to Pacifique, who put much drama and bravura into his story from the beginning, Reverien's story started out slowly, explaining where he lived, what he used to work with and how many children he had. It was only well into the interview that I began to realize the horrors he had experienced.

'My story is a bit complicated', he began, when I asked him to tell his story of leaving Burundi. Reverien lived in Mutakura, one of the '*quartiers contestataires*'. He was not targeted by the regime but felt unsafe because of stones being thrown by demonstrators and bullets shot by the police. He decided to drive his wife and three children to Rwanda, while he returned to Bujumbura in order to keep his job, and he would visit his family at least once a month. Going back and forth every month was difficult. 'You are considered an enemy', he explained, and told me about an incident that had occurred on a bus on one occasion when he was returning from Rwanda to

Burundi. The *imbonerakure* had stopped the bus and asked his brother-in-law, with whom he was travelling, to disembark, but Reverien had intervened and asked what he was accused of. Then they asked Reverien to show his documents. 'I gave them my passport … They realized that I had often travelled from Rwanda since the crisis'. They claimed that the brother-in-law was not the rebel, and that Reverien was the rebel, and took the passport with them to their superior. Fortunately, their boss could see that he had travelled to Rwanda before the crisis as well. He asked where Reverien worked, which was at the airport; who his boss was and who was the chief of police at the airport, and eventually let him go. In this sense, his ability to verify his identity saved him – although it hid the fact that his family were indeed refugees, just as he concealed the fact that he no longer worked at the airport.

All this happened in August 2015, he explained. On 11 December that year, he returned to his home in Musaga from a month's travel to Uganda, Rwanda and the countryside. This was the day of the attacks on the military camps and the reprisals by the army (see also Amnesty International 2015). 'The twelfth we stayed sheltered in our houses, and the thirteenth I went to the office because I realized that staying one more day in our neighbourhood would be difficult for me'. A neighbour called him and told him to leave the office fast because the police and *imbonerakure* had demolished his house. Reverien hid at a friend's place and started planning how to leave the country.

He explained in great detail how he called a friend working at Rwandair and asked him to get him on a plane as soon as possible. This took some negotiation and persuasion, but finally the friend sent him a ticket for the following day via WhatsApp. Having experience and contacts from the time he used to work at the airport, he planned his trip so that he did not need to spend more than five minutes in transit. He had enquired from the emigration desk, and they had no dossier on his name. The police had not reckoned that he would escape via plane and so fast. However, when he was on board the plane 'a friend called me and asked; "what's happening? People from 'la documentation' (the secret service) are here and are asking which flight you are on"'. It was too late; he was on his way to Kigali.

After some months in Rwanda, working with the same employer but in the Kigali office, his employer demanded that he return to Burundi if he was to keep his job. 'How can I return when I am wanted and I don't know what I am wanted for?' he lamented. On the other hand, he could not live in Kigali without a job. 'After weighing the pros and cons, I decided to go back and die like a man'. On 9 April 2016, Reverien travelled by bus back to Burundi. Although he made it across the border, the bus was stopped shortly afterwards by four armed men, of which only one was wearing a police uniform. Reverien explained in great detail how they entered the bus, asked for his papers, demanded he get out of the bus, told the rest of the passengers never to tell anyone what they had witnessed, 'or we will find you and kill you', and told the bus driver to drive off. They told Reverien that they would kill him and started beating him. At one point they gave him two injections and he lost consciousness. He awoke many hours later in a dark house. 'It was in a forest, I guess, because there were many animal noises. And in an almost uninhabited house'. Although it was pitch black, he sensed that there were other people in the house. After a few minutes, he realized that he still had his phone and wrote a message to two people on WhatsApp, which he quickly erased afterwards.

His captors interrogated him, asking about his alleged rebel training in Rwanda, which he denied, insisting that he had been working in Kigali. They claimed that they knew everything and that they would kill him. However, he heard them discussing outside the house, and one of them saying he did not want to kill him. They could see his employment contract and his service badge from Kigali. So why kill him? The others responded that they had to kill him because he knew too much now. They took his phone and went outside again.

Some hours later, they received a phone call and started arguing. His message had gotten out on Facebook and numerous other social media. The person who had received his WhatsApp message had used Reverien's Facebook account to send out an alert. They had also sent it to a civil society activist who had published it on all social media platforms – WhatsApp, Facebook, Twitter – '*et l'alerte est devenue chaud*' (and the message went hot). The result was a lot of squabbling among his abductors and a lot of phone calls being made. They suspected each other of unveiling their secret. They realized that if they killed him, the whole world would know that they had killed him, so they decided once more to sedate him and dump him on a street in Bujumbura.

Space does not allow me to do justice to the rest of Reverien's ordeal. In short, he decided to leave the country by car the very next day. At the border, the guard recognized him immediately and called the local head of the secret service who started scolding Reverien on the phone. Meanwhile, Reverien called a friend who had become chief commander of the military in the district. When the latter arrived to pick him up, the local border guard was embarrassed and had no choice but to let them take Reverien, minutes before the chief of the secret service arrived to pick him up.

As opposed to Pacifique and Jean-Pierre who simply tried to be invisible, Reverien did not just hide. He also used the connections he had to make the system give in. First, he sent the WhatsApp message – making the crimes of '*La système*' visible and hence forcing them to release him. At the border he then used his connections in the army to embarrass the border guard – even when the border guard gave him the head of secret service on the phone. By making the violence of '*la système*' visible to a broader audience, he managed to survive. The actions of '*la système*' could not stand the light of day, and by shedding light on them, he managed to deflate their power. The secret of the public secret was exposed.

Conclusion

In this chapter, I have tried to explore the relationships between violence, displacement and in/visibility in the context of the Burundian crisis. Bodies are central to violence, displacement and in/visibility. It is, after all, bodies that are subjected to violence, that move across space and that are rendered either visible or invisible in the process. The Burundian refugees with whom I have spoken have all to varying degrees had to make themselves – and their intentions – invisible to the authorities in order to flee. They could either hide their bodies (in the boot of a car, in the forests) or make themselves unrecognizable by camouflaging their intentions (by catching numerous buses, by sweet-talking the neighbour) or hide their identity (by manipulating identity cards).

Their bodies are rendered identifiable by their connection to certain documents that connect them to specific places (*les quartiers contestataires*, Rwanda), specific events (demonstrations, political parties) or even professions (journalists). ID papers and photos 'fix' their identities in the eyes of the authorities, and they do what is in their might to shed themselves of these markers – that mark their bodies and make them targets of violence.

Meanwhile, they also seek visibility in various ways. First, ID papers may provide them with recognition and degrees of protection. Richard and Josephine could be recognized as degree holders and apply for jobs that fit their level of education, and without their documents, they could not be recognized for whom they are. While Richard and Josephine seek recognition through documents, others seek visibility at a more general level in order to uncover the invisible wrongdoings of '*la système*' and seek justice. They are not seeking to render themselves visible but rather to render the violence towards them visible. This was the case when Reverien sent a WhatsApp message from captivity. The widespread sharing of images and testimonies of police beatings and abductions, missing persons and mass graves, are also a means to render visible the hidden sides of 'le pouvoir'. In other words, while trying to become invisible in order to survive, the Burundians in exile are also trying to visibilize the violence to which they are exposed.

This chapter suggests that if we are to understand how power works in situations of violent crisis, it is useful to explore how violence and violent displacement are imbricated in processes of visibilization and invisibilization. These processes are productive both in terms of supporting sovereign power and in its unravelling. Likewise, strategies of avoiding violence – through, for instance, migration – rely on visibility and invisibility. There are, however, no one-to-one relations between these processes. We cannot, for instance, assume that sovereign power relies on visibility and that those who are subject to it rely solely on invisibility. Rather, they are entangled in multiple ways; challenged and reversed in these struggles.

When sovereign power is challenged, it needs to reassert its sovereignty through violence. This violence, we saw, balances between performative spectacles on the one hand and public secrets on the other. The protagonists in this chapter have demonstrated how people may react to such violent manifestations of sovereign power, as they have either tried to avoid the gaze of the state, or they have attempted to uncover its intentions, thus rendering the sovereign impotent. Burundians would tell me that the conflict has always existed, but sometimes it is closed and other times it is open, and while open conflict is painful, at least it is legible, they would say. At least your enemy reveals their true intentions.

Notes

1 According to UNHCR figures there are around 350,000 Burundian refugees in the region (UNCHR figures, 31 January 2019), the majority of whom live in camps in Tanzania (200,000). Roughly 35,000 are registered in Uganda, 43,000 in DRC and 70,000 in Rwanda (UNHCR figures, 31 January 2019). UNHCR has registered an estimated 20,000 Burundian refugees in Kigali while the rest live in camps (UNHCR figures, December 2016).

2 What turned out to be most difficult to find any certain information on was their present incomes. On the one hand, many were embarrassed by the social decline that they had experienced and tried to cover it up. On the other hand, they were not comfortable telling me how they, as refugees, could afford to drive cars and send their children to private schools.

3 All names are pseudonyms.

4 Jérôme is another actor with a double identity: soldier and former student. Within the constraints of the situation, Jérôme was not able or willing to save Pacifique – except, perhaps, when he failed to jab him hard enough with his bayonet. Was this by chance, or was he unsure whether to be the soldier or the student?

5 Interestingly, Pacifique uses this term which denotes the Hutu militia that were responsible for much of the genocide in Rwanda in 1994.

6 The issue of 'lists' has a long genealogy in Burundi and Rwanda. It is widely held that the government had lists of Hutu to be killed in 1972, that the Hutu president had a list of Tutsi to be killed in 1993, that the army had lists of Hutu to be killed in 1993 and that Hutu extremists had lists of prominent Tutsi and Hutu to be killed in Rwanda in 1994.

7 The circulation of disturbing images on social media resulted in a lot of emotion work among Burundians in the diaspora who had to filter the information in order to minimize the emotional strain on themselves and their kin (Turner and Berckmoes 2020).

References

Amnesty International (2015) '"My children are scared": Burundi's deepening human rights crisis'.

—— (2016) 'Burundi: suspected mass graves of victims of 11 December violence'.

Falisse, J.-B. and H. Nkengurutse (2019) 'From FM radio stations to Internet 2.0 overnight: information, participation and social media in post-failed coup Burundi', in M. Dwyer and T. Molony (eds), *Social Media and Politics in Africa*, London: Zed Books, 173–195.

Fontein, J. (2014) 'Remaking the dead, uncertainty and the torque of human materials in northern Zimbabwe', in F. Stepputat (ed.), *Governing the Dead: Sovereignty and the politics of dead bodies*, Manchester and New York: Manchester University Press, 114–143.

Hansen, T. and F. Stepputat (2005) *Sovereign Bodies: Citizens, migrants and states in the postcolonial world*, Durham, NC: Duke University Press.

Paviotti, A. (2019) 'Ethnic memory and interactions in periods of crisis: an analysis of Burundi's Twittersphere', in S.E.A. Geenen (ed.), *Conjonctures de l'Afrique Centrale*, Paris: L'Harmattan, 351–375.

Stepputat, F. (2014) *Governing the Dead: Sovereignty and the politics of dead bodies*,

Manchester and New York: Manchester University Press.
Taussig, M. T. (1999) *Defacement: Public secrecy and the labor of the negative*, Stanford, CA: Stanford University Press.
Turner, S. (2007) 'Corruption, conspiracy and the power of concealment in Burundi's political landscape', in M. Nuijtens and G. Anders (eds), *Corruption and the Secret of Law: A legal anthropological perspective*, London: Ashgate.
—— (2009) 'Betraying trust and the elusive nature of ethnicity in Burundi', in T. Kelly and S. Thiranagama (eds), *Traitors: Suspicion, intimacy and the ethics of state-building*, Philadelphia, PA: University of Pennsylvania Press.
—— (2020) 'Hope against hope: changing emotions in the Burundian crisis', *Journal of the Royal Anthropological Institute*, 26(4).
Turner, S. and L. Berckmoes (2020) 'Reticent digital diasporas in times of crisis: the shifting emotion work of the Burundian Diaspora', *African Diaspora*, 1–26.

Section 3

Social in/visibilities

11 | (Dis)Connectivity and the invisibility of mobile Fulani in West Africa

Roos Keja, Adamou Amadou and Mirjam de Bruijn

Introduction

The droughts and ecological crises of the 1980s and 1990s have been a driver of mobility for many Fulani pastoralists. It can be said that their mobility changed from pastoral nomadism to poverty-driven nomadism. These mobile people, young families or individuals, mostly men, largely fell outside of all categorizations the international world provided for at the time; environmental refugee was not yet a recognized status. They left no traces back home, so they were 'lost' to (local) administrative bodies. This vanishing has to do with the fact that leaving out of poverty is shameful to a Fulani; in this sense, breaking all social and familial ties is a strategy to survive in a decent way (De Bruijn and van Dijk 2003). They generally ended up living in the fringes of sedentary societies in the South, sometimes as Muslim scholars or marabouts, or as herders for the wealthy urban elites, but certainly as invisible mobile people. In the present-day situation of increasing insecurity, drought and famine in the Sahel, we are observing similar patterns. Recent research on Fulani 'mobiles' who flee the Central African Republic (CAR) and central Mali indicate that many Fulani become invisible, living on the fringes of urban and rural economies (Loftsdóttir 2004; Boesen 2007; Amadou 2018; see also www.nomadesahel.org). The empirical material in this chapter is based on intensive research with Fulani pastoralists and former pastoralists in Chad, Cameroon, Mali and Niger.

The concept of (dis)connectivity to which we refer in the title is not limited to technology, but is about literally (dis)connecting the social. In the unfolding of this story, we will explore in which ways technology of connectivity becomes more important. In the past, invisibility for these groups of Fulani implied complete disconnection from the region and people they left behind. Little connectivity was established, and life on the fringes of urban and rural economies seemed to be very isolated. Recent developments in communication technology, such as mobile phones, have enabled a drastic change in this situation. This development is rather new; the mobile phone only became effective as a communication tool for the poor and for those living in remote rural areas after 2009 (see for instance Keïta et al. 2015; Seli 2014; De Bruijn 2019). Evidently, connectivity is not only brought about by mobile telephony. In this article we explore technology of connectivity also as an interaction between different techniques of connectivity such as mobile phones, travelling and people, and in this case the specific person of the researcher. However, the presence of the possibility to connect does not necessarily mean that people become visible. In this chapter, we explore a preliminary hypothesis that the wandering nomads stay invisible, even though new technologies of connection theoretically increasingly enable them to reconnect with the people they left behind long ago.

Through an analysis of former research, recent research with invisible nomads in Chad, Cameroon, Mali and Niger, and the biographical approach, this chapter tries to understand the agency of the wandering nomad. Are they a mere proletariat, working for the better off? Are they consciously developing a strategy in which they unfold strong decisions and agency, akin to what Scott has labelled 'the art of not being governed' (Scott 2009), or are these Fulani mere victims of circumstances, in the absence of good governance that denies them a decent life? How complex are the lives of invisible mobile people? Within their trajectories of mobility, we can discern certain moments of invisibility in the relational sphere, for instance vis-à-vis their family members. Can this be considered strategic invisibility, and if so, what would be its purpose? We will shed light on these different aspects, supported by a reconstruction of the biography of Amadou, a Fulani man who 'vanished' for several decades and was reunited with his family in 2016. We followed Amadou between October 2008 and January 2009 when he was in Bamenda, and we had several encounters with him between 2010 and 2016 in Yaoundé, and in Lomé in June 2016, April 2017 and March 2019, during which we carried out in-depth interviews about his life.

Biographies have 'proven to be an excellent way of making theoretical sense of social phenomena' (Apitzsch and Siouti 2007: 3) and 'biographical choices are shaped by the cultural, socio-economic and historical factors that impact [informants'] lifeworlds' (Buitelaar 2014: 31). Hence authors like Fabian (2003, 2007), who introduced the notion of memory work as an active process in constructing a biography, and Jackson (2008), who took the biography in context as his central methodology in understanding the phenomenon of migration, have inspired our method. It is especially interesting to zoom in on an individual case, and Amadou's mobile life path is exemplary for a vast group of people who are not only hardly visible vis-à-vis institutions like the state, but also often overlooked in the literature about migration and displacement. Like so many people, Amadou's mobile life path is dispersed over different countries within the African continent. In order to situate Amadou's biographical narrative, we will first explore our own relationality with the research theme and with Amadou.

Fulani mobility and the researcher as technology of connectivity

It seems difficult to understand any African society without taking into account the high level of mobility of its inhabitants, which has been a reaction to certain circumstances and a basis for millions of Africans to make a livelihood. Although there are many forms of mobility, rural–urban migration has extensively been studied because of its massive and transformative character (De Bruijn et al. 2001). However, for many groups and individuals, mobility is a way of life, and does not necessarily imply a unidirectional, intentional process in which people move from one well-defined place to another. Semi-nomadic Fulani groups in West and Central Africa have been moving around with their cattle, even though many have become more settled over the past centuries. A few male family members go on transhumance with the cattle during the dry season, whereas their village is more or less bound to a geographical location. The mobility of individual family members is high from childhood onwards; from children in search of Koranic or 'modern' education to spouses moving through marriage; to adolescents trying their luck in the city, or fleeing regions because of drought. In one lifetime these different reasons to be mobile are lived through successively or even at the same time.

The mobile life paths of the Fulani lead to emotional stories and narratives of displacement and disconnection. One such story is recounted by co-author Adamou, and is about his father-in-law. Adamou's father-in-law is a Fulani man who had come from Niger to Cameroon in his adolescent years, just like Amadou, the protagonist in this chapter. Unlike Amadou, Adamou's father-in-law has married and has raised his children in Cameroon. In several conversations, he seemed to lament the fact that he had no contact with his son he had left behind in Niger ever since he had come to Cameroon. Every time that Adamou tried to trace the 'vanishing' of his father-in-law, the old man replied in the same vein: 'If you find yourself under the big trees at the central market of Niamey and you say my name, ask some people whether they know me, and they will surely know who I am.'

Adamou, Roos and Mirjam discussed the scientific interest of actually going to the central market and filming the search for re-connecting a lost Fulani with his family. And so it happened that one day in November 2011, Roos was filming at the central market in Niamey, where she did not succeed in finding acquaintances of Adamou's father-in-law. Not only had the central market burned down several times since the departure of the old man, which had made it impossible to locate 'the big trees', his name also appeared to be a general name for shepherd in one of the local languages. Even though his photo went from hand to hand, no one seemed to recognize the man. Several people in the market replied that it would be much easier if they knew the village of birth of the old man. At a certain stage, a Fulani woman spontaneously left a message for her brother called Ibrahim, who had left Niger decades ago. She thought he might be in Cameroon, so she talked to the camera, asking her brother to come home. Roos contacted Adamou and asked him to insist that his father-in-law provide at least the name of his village of birth, but the old man avoided giving more details, saying it was such a long time ago. Remembering Niger and the relation to his child is an example of how the father-in-law 'worked' his memory to serve mainly his own emotions. We do not know what we did by discovering that the memory of the old man no longer had any link to the present in Niger. Did it increase his invisibility?

While Roos was in Niger, she also lived up to a promise we had made to Amadou, the man whose biography will be unfolded below. We will present his life history and then come to an analysis of the possible motives and factors of his mobility. His case might be special, but at the same time in many ways it is exemplary for this and related phenomena of a perpetual mobility in geographic, imagined, embodied and spiritual directions (Jeannerat 2009; Lentz 2013; Nyamnjoh 2005). A special relationship developed over the years, which we will first discuss in order to situate the case.

In October 2008, Roos met Amadou in a roadside restaurant in the centre of Bamenda, Cameroon, where he had only recently arrived to try his luck. Upon hearing that Roos carried out a study about a Fulani group in town,[1] he was eager to share his own story, actively seeking visibility. Roos introduced Amadou to Mirjam and Adamou, and from October 2008 onwards, several interviews and informal conversations followed, mainly between Amadou and Roos, but also with Adamou and Mirjam.

In 2011, Roos and Amadou met again in Yaoundé, and like he had done in Bamenda, he again gave her the phone numbers of the two sons of his older brother Boukari, Moussa and Husseini, who were living in Niger. When she was in Niamey later that year, she called Amadou to say that both numbers did not pass, and he gave her the name of a wealthy cousin, whom he also described as his enemy, to which we will return later. In order to locate the cousin, Roos visited a Fulani association in Niamey and mentioned the name of the cousin. One of the persons immediately offered to accompany her to the place where she could find him. This underlines the idea that information technologies are never more important than the people who make use of them (Keja forthcoming). However, at the same time their impact is clear; without mobile phones and without the researchers as technologies of communication, Amadou's more recent years would have looked very different. From the moment that Roos passed her phone to Amadou's cousin for them to talk, and the cousin immediately started to say 'Amadou, war, warte' [come], Amadou's return started to materialize. The intention solidified when Roos accepted the invitation of the cousin to travel to their village of birth, and when she passed on Amadou's greetings in a room packed with about forty men and one woman – Amadou's sister Zeinabou. Roos improvised a speech, in which she said that she would do her best to bring Amadou home. After this meeting, Roos filmed his village, and the video included spontaneous messages from the imam, his brother Boukari, sister Zeinabou, dozens of children of his village, yelling 'Amadou come, Amadou come', and his nephew Moussa. When she was back in Niamey, Roos called Amadou to tell him about her trip to his village, and to ask him whether he wanted to return home. He replied that he could leave tomorrow, as his bags were already packed, and Roos offered him her support for the journey.

In the months and years that followed, Roos and Amadou kept in touch through the mobile phone on an infrequent basis, and Adamou sometimes visited Amadou in Yaoundé. They kept on verifying whether Amadou still wanted to return home, and he always confirmed this. During one of these visits, Adamou showed the video to Amadou in Yaoundé. Upon seeing his family members, including all the children that had been born in his absence, Amadou cried. Seeing the images increased his already existing wish to see all of the people in real life, which was stronger than his shame for his poverty and childlessness.

The ethics surrounding the envisioned intervention in Amadou's life was a point of discussion between us. We had clearly influenced Amadou's wish to return to his village, not only by going there in person, but also by making a video in the village and showing it to him. Even though this had never been the intention, the meaning attached to these actions was shaped accordingly, and transformed into being intentional. Whenever we discussed these issues with Amadou, he invariably replied not to worry, adding that everything would happen according to God's plan. Nonetheless, this divine responsibility does not invalidate the discussion about the responsibility of a researcher towards 'protecting' her 'informants'. At the same time, Amadou is far from being a research object; his agency is apparent. This fits in a changed world in which the boundaries between researcher and researched have become increasingly blurred, not least because of the mobile phone, as was also expounded upon by Pelckmans (2009). The fact that Amadou called Roos once every few months made Roos' disengagement less probable. For Amadou, this particular unfolding of 'co-creation' of not only the research about his life, but also of his life story itself, has given him several chances that otherwise would have been difficult to reach.

The plan evolved to make a documentary of Amadou's return, which did not (yet) materialize. Whenever Roos apologized for not taking any action, he told her not to worry, as he was patient and understood her family duties, and he told her to have faith in God. In February 2015, Amadou got a Cameroonian passport with the help of a friend, for which Roos made a transfer via Western Union. In August 2016, when Roos was in Togo for another research, she finally asked Amadou to accept a flight from Yaoundé to Lomé. She also asked Moussa, the son of Amadou's brother Boukari, to join her in Lomé, to pick up Amadou at the airport, which he and the family readily accepted. Some days later, Amadou and Moussa took a bus to Niamey (see Figure 11.1). They first stayed in Niamey for ten days, and then, on 28 August 2016, after thirty years of absence, Amadou returned to his village.

The wandering of Amadou

Within the past decade, Amadou has shared his life history with us on several occasions. During our last encounter in Lomé, in March 2019, he recounted his life history once more. His different versions do not have great variations, although in earlier stages, he gave more details about what had pushed him to leave. In this last version, he was very detailed, which is why the narrative of his life that is given here is based on this version, at times almost verbatim. As he was suffering from a headache and fever, he was laying on the couch in a villa rented by Roos, and Roos sat by his side taking notes, interrupting Amadou from time to time to verify some details.

Figure 11.1 Amadou and Moussa buying a bus ticket to Niamey

Amadou was born in 1961 in present-day Niger, in an area that was, at the time, part of Burkina Faso, where his parents had settled after having moved from Mali. He started frequenting the Koranic school in his village at six years old. When he was ten years old, his older sister married, and he followed her and her husband to northern Burkina Faso, where he continued his Koranic education, but he did not like it, so he returned home after a year. By the time he was thirteen years old, a marabout from his village who had gone to Mali paid a visit to the village, and Amadou insisted with his father that he wanted to follow the marabout. His father was reluctant at first, because he had heard that people there killed children to use their body parts in their charms, but Amadou managed to convince his father, and he spent five years with the marabout. They left the village by foot and for their survival, Amadou and the other Koranic pupils went door to door to beg for food, as has commonly been the case throughout the sub-region (Cissé 1992).

After having read the Koran from beginning to end, and then back again from the end to two-thirds of the way through, Amadou left his marabout along with four other pupils. The long-haired teenagers stayed for a year in Ouagadougou, 'wasting time' while begging for food and clothes, smoking cigarettes and doing nothing. When he was nineteen, Amadou decided to return home, and he walked the last part from Dori to the village. He arrived in the afternoon, and went up to the well outside the village where he asked some girls for water. He stayed under a tree until evening; having spent so many years away, he could not just walk into the village at any time. Around sunset, he walked towards the village, where his older sister Kadiatou was preparing food, while his mother was praying. When Kadiatou saw him, she cried out: 'Amadou warte, Amadou warte!' You have come! His mother could not stop asking: 'Is it you, is it really you?'

Amadou stayed in the village for a year, wanting to return to Mali to continue studying the Koran, but the opportunity did not present itself. His cousin, a close friend and cousin insisted that Amadou should marry his sister, until Amadou asked his father to go to their father to ask for her hand. In 1979, the marriage between Amadou and Ramata was tied, and she gave birth to a boy in 1980 which was, as Amadou adds, the year that my troubles began, the troubles that bother me up to today'.

In 1981, Amadou (Figure 11.2) left for Ivory Coast, and his older brother Boukari came to visit him in Abidjan some months later, begging him to return home. He replied that he would come soon, and Boukari left, but Amadou never followed him. A year later, Boukari travelled to Abidjan once more to ask him to come back, and stayed with him while he had a small job for three months. They left together, and he bought a cow in Boké and sold it before he returned home. Amadou did not mention this, but upon their return home, migrants often invest their money in something like a cow or a motorbike, which might be a safer way of transporting the income earned abroad.

Amadou was reunited with his wife in the village, and in 1984, she gave birth to a girl. As the year was a very harsh one, they decided to dismantle the village.

Figure 11.2 Amadou in 1981

Amadou went south with his wife, sister, mother and the children, whereas Boukari moved north with the cattle. During the severe droughts in 1985 and 1986, Amadou's children both died. In 1985, he left the village for Niamey to sell a cow and, as he explains, 'there was nothing in Niamey that interested me, I could not stay, I just wanted to leave'. This urge pushed him to find a means of transport to Malanville in Benin, at the border with Niger, leaving with only 100 Francs in his pocket. In Malanville, he negotiated with some cattle traders to take him to Lagos, where he got one Naira for his 100 FCFA: 'I bought a cup of tea and a piece of bread, and my Naira was gone'. The owner of the cafeteria gave him an old mat, which he put in front of a mosque. He stayed there for a month, and he recalls: 'The suffering, without anyone I know, without understanding the language, this is suffering'.

His luck was that a Fulani man gave him some coins every day, and he started to gain some money 'writing the Koran', doing some *maraboutage*. He left to Ogbomosho, a city in Oyo State in south-western Nigeria, where he stayed with a Fulani trader from Burkina Faso for seven months, until he left again for Lagos. The trader was from the Diallo family, cousins to his family. During this time, he had linked up with the network of this trader who became his client for his *maraboutage*, and he often stayed in Cotonou for one or two months. In the nine years that followed, he travelled between Cotonou, Lagos and Ibadan; he would move each time he earned some money from his *maraboutage*. In 1990, he decided to travel to the harbour in Tema, 30 kilometres east of Accra, in order to meet up with a close cousin from his village, whom he managed to find after asking around with several Fulani people at the mosque, mentioning his cousin's name. The cousin was amazed that Amadou had found him.

After having spent some days with him, Amadou left again to Cotonou, where he had rented a room at the time, until he left for Lagos in 1992, aged thirty-one. Towards the end of Ramadan, he coupled up with two Malian Fulani men who wanted to go eastwards, towards Cameroon. They took several minibuses until they arrived in Calabar, where they took a pirogue. The boat stopped on a small island, and left again in the middle of the night, filled with people and goods. However, the motor gave up during a thunderstorm, and in the pouring rain, surrounded by high waves, the pirogue had great difficulty returning to the island. The next evening, the endeavour was successful, and they arrived in Limbé on the Cameroonian coast around six in the morning. The Cameroonians he encountered at the beach were not easy going, as he summarizes: 'We're being made like sheep'. A Hausa man took him and his travel companions to Douala in his small car, and after some days, the other two men moved on to Gabon. Amadou did not want to continue, as he had found other Fulani who 'did the Koran'. He started earning some money, and when he had accumulated 300,000 FCFA, he paid for a small studio in Douala, where he stayed for about twenty years. He went to Yaoundé two times, in 2005 and 2007, but he did not stay there.

In 2008, two Nigerien friends, among whom one was from his own village, urged Amadou to come to Bamenda. He stayed there for eighteen months, but even though both friends had more or less convinced him to go to Bamenda, they never came to meet him or to settle in Bamenda themselves, something he was somewhat bitter about. This is where Amadou and Roos met, and Roos introduced Amadou to Adamou and Mirjam. At that time, his *maraboutage* did not yield much revenue, and he travelled back to Douala in 2010 and on to Yaoundé, as a wealthy Fulani man from Guinea had invited him there to work with him. However, this did not go as Amadou expected, as they did not really collaborate; on one occasion Amadou earned 600,000 FCFA, but apart from that, he was only asked to write Koranic texts from time to time. Amadou remarks: 'This is not work, he has millions. All the big people in Yaoundé are in his hands, the ministers, ancient and new. The bastard, he will convince you. He is a friend, but often he is not nice. Life is like that'.

Throughout this period of his travelling, Amadou hardly had any contact with his family members. He did not pay taxes in any of these countries. *Maraboutage* is an informal popular circuit. Hence, we can say that Amadou was invisible to his kin, and also to the official circuits of the state. Solitude and loneliness transpire through his story. What did this do to Amadou emotionally? His resentment towards people who failed him, and the events that followed in our interaction with Amadou, shows a form of despair, but at the same time an art of survival; the art of not being governed as an individual.

Remaining invisible while reconnecting?

In today's interconnected world, it has become increasingly complex to disappear and become completely invisible vis-à-vis one's family members and vis-à-vis authorities. People have to develop new strategies to disconnect in their newly acquired connectivity. While it comforts them to feel more connected to their family members and miss them less, it also brings stress; the stress of hearing the worries and problems of their family members and not being able to do anything, and the stress of having to conceal their own problems and pretend as if everything is going well. This, again, has to do with shame. It is tempting to ask the question whether Amadou himself is better off in Niamey than he was in Yaoundé, which, throughout his trajectory, has been a recurring point of discussion between us researchers.

For Amadou and many migrants alike, remaining invisible comes with high emotional costs, but so does greater visibility. Invisibility, as well as connectivity, are most often coupled with ambivalence. In this sense, the question of whether a man like Amadou is more 'in place' among his family members than in a faraway city would miss the point of what invisibility and mobility actually mean – which is exactly the point that this chapter makes.

Amadou's displacement has nearly been an invisible displacement; after he left Ghana, where he had some family members, his family did not hear from him for several years. After he reached Cameroon, he encountered some Fulani from Niger, and also one person from his village. Through this person, he finally got the phone numbers of two sons of his older brother, and the contact was more or less re-established.

Figure 11.3 People greeting Amadou upon his return to his birth village

However, it was only when someone physically moved to Niger to actively search for his family that the contact gradually materialized. In this respect, the researchers themselves are a certain technology of connectivity, as we discussed earlier. On several occasions, Amadou emphasized that he had met other people from Niger, even from his village, but that in all those years, no one had ever travelled up to his village to convey his greetings. He did and does not cease to express his gratitude to Roos for this.

When he was sixty-five years old, after thirty years of absence, Amadou returned to his village, at the prayer of *makthoub* at sunset, and found the house crowded with people (Figure 11.3). He related:

> Men, women, children … I only cry! You, you who are old, how do you cry now, I am someone who has left for thirty years. I left when I was young. When I left, Zeinabou had only one child! Just before we arrived, Moussa told me 'don't cry', but I only cry. So, this is my life, until today, I have not had the chance, I have been harmed. Since I was ten years old, I have never had the chance to stay in the village for more than two years.

After having spent some weeks in the village, Amadou visited his two older sisters who had moved to other villages, and then he settled in Niamey. The climate change did not improve his weak health situation, and he fell ill for about six months. In 2017, a marriage was tied with a girl from his village who was 'given' to Amadou by her father, and she gave birth to their son in 2018.

Being reunited with his closest family members did not only bring joy; they also expressed their expectations of him. When he and his brother Boukari visited their eldest sister, she assured Amadou that he would be dead to the family if he ever disappeared again. What could be interpreted as a warning, or possibly her fear of another extended period of his physical absence, appeared to be not so far from the truth. As his *maraboutage* does not yield many results, it is difficult for Amadou to let go of the idea of travelling. He mainly gets by with the support of his nephews Moussa and Housseini, and with a casual gift from other family members. In one of the many audio exchanges on WhatsApp with Roos in the past years, Moussa talked about the pressure of feeding so many family members on the basis of his earnings, and explained that they do have wealthy family members to whom Amadou could turn in theory. In practice, this does not happen, as Amadou has too much pride to ask for their help, something for which Moussa respects Amadou. Not long after his return, Amadou was ill at ease with his situation, and between 2017 and 2019 he often sent Roos voice messages through WhatsApp in which he spoke of leaving for a few months to 'find something'.

In March 2019, Roos invited Amadou and his nephew Moussa to spend a week with her in Lomé, and Amadou revealed his plans to her to find a room to rent and stay in Lomé for some months, visit his cousin in Accra, and earn some money before returning to Niamey towards the end of Ramadan. Moussa expressed his unhappiness with Amadou's wish, even though Amadou insisted that he could never stay out of Niamey for more than two or three months, especially because he felt the desire to be close to his child. Like Moussa, other close family members had been opposed to his plan. In one of their private conversations, Moussa told Roos that upon hearing that they would meet Roos in Lomé, Amadou's sister Zeinabou had exclaimed that Amadou would certainly go back to Douala.

However, once again, Amadou's plans did not materialize. Because of his worries about how to make a decent living and his decision to 'find something' in another country yet again, Amadou did not sleep the night before his travels to Lomé. After the long bus ride from Niamey to Lomé, he fell ill after his arrival. When he felt somewhat better, he headed towards a mosque in a certain neighbourhood to meet a Fulani from Niger who could help him with a room. However, on the way, he fell ill again, which pushed him to decide to call off the plan altogether and return to Niamey with Moussa. When he explained that he would go back to Niamey with Moussa, he was full of sadness, but as a recurrent theme in all his conversations, he vowed: 'This is how God has wanted it to be'.

Reasons for vanishing: adventure, shame and '*mauvais sort*'

Amadou's story has captured our interest for many different reasons, and, as has become clear, it has also become intertwined with our own lives. Therefore, a reflection on the role of the researchers cannot be omitted, to which we return below. However, Amadou is one among thousands of people who leave their home as a coping strategy. Even though Amadou introduced himself in 2008 as a 'tourist on the

African continent', which resembles the adventurer presented by Bredeloup (2013), there are also other reasons and motives for his extreme mobility, which are more subtle. As also mentioned above, there are indications that many people do not want to return home, because they have not succeeded in life (Collyer 2007; De Bruijn and van Dijk 2003); instead of having to deal with feelings of shame and dependence on a daily basis, people prefer to continue a life in relative isolation. By considering such mechanisms, we do not want to argue that this is necessarily the case for Amadou, but these factors are not negligible in his life.

Amadou attributes his long exile from his village to the 'work' of his enemy. His narrative of exile is similar to what a character in Ekwensi's novel *Burning Grass* (1962) experienced, and described as 'the wandering disease' or *sukugo* in a Nigerian dialect of the language of the Fulani, Fulfulde. Amadou believes that one of his cousins has prevented him from returning home. Since his time in Ivory Coast, he has been having dreams about this cousin, and once he was in Douala, he saw his suspicion confirmed in a dream in which the cousin carried a handgun. This dream made him understand that this was his enemy, and he immediately realized that this was also the reason for his long absence from home.

Whereas the context of socio-economic, political and climatic hardships are factors in the constant mobility of individuals like Amadou, mobility is influenced by many more factors, like the practice of adventure seeking as a normality in the process of growing up. Moreover, a feeling of shame seems to guide people in their choices of mobility and immobility; they sometimes prefer to live in isolation from their families, staying invisible, instead of having to face the fact that their own living conditions are well below those of the people around them.

Amadou's state of deprivation was explained by his nephew Moussa. Moussa judged that Amadou's refusal to turn to his wealthier cousins for help did not make things easier for Amadou. Moussa described this as *yaage*, which means shame in Fulfulde.

Although shame is not confined to Fulani groups, it is certainly a principal 'marker' that plays a large role in interactions and relations among Fulani groups in the Sahel region that we have been following for several decades. Shame is a deep emotion in Fulani life. It guides taboos on social relations, and it guides where a person can go. As De Bruijn and van Dijk (1995) have analysed, it is also related to wealth and not having wealth in Fulbe society. Being poor is shameful. This deep emotion, that may lead a Fulani woman or man to deny her or his own identity, can inform decisions to leave their kin in order not to reveal their poverty.

Nevertheless, even though we may be uncomfortable with the inexplicable, Amadou's own analysis of his 'troubles' needs to be recognized here. When he met with his cousin, who had difficulties recognizing him at first, the cousin exclaimed: 'It is only God who has brought you here'. According to Amadou, this was once again an implicit confirmation that the cousin had never believed that Amadou would return home. As mentioned earlier, according to Amadou, the '*mauvais sort*' or bad luck that was given to him by his cousin is the source of his prolonged exile.

It remains an unanswered question whether this cousin has been the driving force of Amadou's mobility from the beginning, and there are no answers as to the extent to which Amadou has experienced his mobility as a life in exile throughout his different life stages. What is intriguing in Amadou's mobile life path is the way in which he has presented and represented his life throughout the years, and his personal narrative to come to grips with his own story, in other words his 'memory work'. Clearly, at this moment in his life, he considers that he has not been able to achieve what he had wanted to achieve from the onset, and he has lived a hard life. He is grateful that he has been reconciled with his family after so many years, and his close family members are also grateful for the chance to have him in their midst. However, the (emotional) suffering continues; even though it seems to be consoling for Amadou to be close to his family members, it seems to be upsetting to continuously face his situation of economic deprivation vis-à-vis the people with whom he grew up, and who are better off today. It gives him a feeling that he does not really count, and that his life has not yielded what it should have.

Reflections on invisibility

Despite being increasingly connected, highly mobile persons like Amadou remain invisible. When Amadou fell ill in 2018, Moussa complained in a voice message to Roos that Amadou stays in his room in Niamey for most of the time. By doing this, he more or less chooses to be invisible to his kin. According to Moussa, the fact that Amadou hardly ever moves his body harms his physical health. The feeling of shame that renders migrants invisible can be coupled with an invisibility from within; the internal reason for this invisibility is encapsulated in the feeling of shame that one has not yet reached one's aims.

The more obvious layer of visibility is related to recognition as a citizen. States might consider individuals such as Amadou as non-citizens, but this is not the whole story. In his life story, we can discern different levels of visibility, first of all vis-à-vis state actors: he was born in the borderlands between Burkina Faso and Niger, and he has moved throughout several West African countries for three decades. Of course, he came into contact with authorities on several occasions; in Cameroon, he carried a Cameroonian identity card like most others. He went through the process of acquiring a Cameroonian passport, which allowed him to travel by air, but also incited the border police to make him pay for not having the right stamp upon his travel from Lomé to Niger in 2016 – a hassle which Moussa was spared, who travelled with his Nigerien identity card. It goes without saying that Amadou's Nigerien identity card was produced in Niamey shortly after his return.

Even though Amadou might exist in the administrative layers of two countries, he is probably foremost part of communities that have no borders but relate to other social circles – in the case of Amadou that of the Muslim world. As a marabout, Amadou does exist in a religious world that has no frontiers. However, we can question his visibility in this non-state community as well. As became clear from his life story, he did not really have success as a marabout, in that it has not given him lasting economic success, and hence did not give him visibility in that sense.

Adding a more psychological layer, it is worth considering whether a person like Amadou is visible in his own view. Who is he? He has taken on a personal narrative in which he explains to himself why he is displaced. For Amadou, back in 2008, the narrative of adventurer or tourist was attractive, whereas in 2019, his life of mobility is much more framed as being caused by a '*mauvais sort*', the work done by his cousin. Moreover, he is part of a cultural system in which shame plays a central role, which, in its extreme form, can destroy individuals, and even lead people to commit suicide, the most extreme form of invisibilization (De Bruijn and Van Dijk 2003).

In this chapter, we have attempted to understand invisibility not only in an instrumental way, but also in emotional and spiritual ways. As we have seen in Amadou's story, there are cases when invisibility is partly imposed by the person himself. This mixture of shame, the exterior context and the cultural frame, works like a vicious cycle, and can in some ways also be considered '*mauvais sort*'. This 'cultural' invisibility is partly people's own choice, but it is also partly inherent to their cultural context that pushes them to become invisible. In this search of 'lost' Fulani, there are some who really disappear, others who become successful and others who remain poor, and halfway connected. These mobile lives, however, are temporary situations, always in transit.

Amadou's story and its contribution to the debates on mobility in the Sahel

Migration and mobility are not new phenomena. In line with age-old practices in West African societies, where young people have little opportunities to start making a living, they leave their homes in search of wealth and adventure, building up wealth before returning home and settling down (Dougnon 2008; Klute and Hahn 2007; Nyamnjoh 2010). Whereas their stories, and the story of Amadou, can be put in the frame of adventure (Bredeloup 2013) and initiation (Dougnon 2008), they can simultaneously be framed as coping mechanisms in times of duress (De Bruijn and Van Dijk 2003). De Bruijn and van Dijk noticed that the semi-nomadic Fulani families with whom they worked in northern Mali 'dissolved' during times of extreme drought. As a coping strategy, the extended families fell apart in ever smaller units, down to individuals going their own way.

Some of the people who migrate reach their destination and find the wealth and well-being that they were looking for. Their stories travel far, and serve as inspiration for others to also undertake the journey in search of better pastures. Whereas in the past, people moved to regional centres such as Abidjan or Lagos, the scope of current migration is larger; people travel greater distances, trying to reach Europe, the Middle East or other parts of the world, which is partly influenced by technological innovation and a proliferation of means and possibilities. Moreover, the intensity of information sharing is denser, and ambitions are also higher to reach the life that is displayed through different media channels (Pelican 2016; Bredeloup 2013; Buggenhagen 2012; Ferguson 2006). It is also a lot easier to stay in touch with the ones left behind. This connectedness can contribute to people's emotional well-being, but it has also made it more complex to leave one's old life behind and start anew. The connection with home can be established within minutes, implying that people are 'only a phone call away'.

The majority of people who leave their home do this so the intention of returning one day. However, there are many people who never return home from their journey, in some cases because they do not survive, in other cases because they 'get stuck'. On their way to Europe, many Africans stay in Morocco or Turkey and phone home every once in a while, to explain that all is going well, asking for a little patience before they can send money home (Collyer 2007; Schapendonk 2011). Shame and pride seem to play a large role in their considerations of which information to share with 'home'. Moreover, admitting to oneself that one has failed to achieve an aim might break one's spirit, which might as well be the same as not surviving the journey. For the moment, these people have 'failed' economically, and as they return, they would not bring back the wealth they and their families had hoped for, and invested in. This brings with it a set of challenges; for instance, upon returning, migrants who have been deported can be met with ambivalence or even overt disappointment by their social environment (De Latour 2001; Lecadet 2016). So, as much as economic and administrative boundaries can be an obstacle for migrants to return, mental and mystical boundaries also play a role in situations of immobility, as we have also seen in Amadou's story.

Authors like Loftsdóttir (2004) and Boesen (2007), who have studied former nomadic pastoralist Fulani in urban areas in Niger, including Woodaabe groups, have provided interesting insights into these people's ways of interweaving their mobile mind-set with their city life. For instance, Woodaabe urban workers considered their stay in the city as a temporary interruption, necessary for rebuilding their herds in a later stage of their life. They did not seem to construct houses, but rather dwelled in provisional places before moving on. Even though the idea that one's settlement in a new environment is provisional is common for migrants throughout the world (De Bruijn et al. 2001), this 'temporariness' is constant for the individuals and families on whom this chapter is based. The image of temporariness can serve to bridge people's hopes and imaginations, and the harsh reality of their everyday lives. Amadou also has a mobile mind-set. Although his family members complain, they did accept his leaving; apart from the first years when his brother looked for him in Ivory Coast, serious attempts have never been made to reach out to him, until the mobile phone arrived.

Amadou's story adds to our understanding of the reasons to be mobile, giving space to both the agency of the migrant and the constrained circumstances in which this happens. His itinerary, his life history is exemplary as it reveals the experiences and personal narratives of those people who have not achieved what they aspired for. They live a life in the margins, and their invisibility is not only imposed by the state or society in which they live, but is also, to a certain extent, self-imposed. Considering this in relation to notions of shame and dignity, spelling out Amadou's journey contributes to a better understanding of people's agency in seeking invisibility, a necessarily constrained form of agency in the frame of an enduring experience of hardship (De Bruijn and Both 2018). For Amadou to deal with crises, his personal crises but also the general societal crises like the droughts, his feelings of duress were translated into mobility. This mobility functioned not only as a strategy to survive, but also to become invisible. His invisibility would leave him as a human being, and would allow him a decent identity. It seems that he has accepted at the end of his life to give in to that identity. Is this because he has no choice, or is it that after all, he does want to be among his own people, have a son and be remembered among his kin?

Note

1 Roos did her fieldwork for her MA thesis 'Moving in and into the Urban: Mbororo Generations Finding and Creating a Place in Bamenda, Cameroon', supervised by Mirjam, who joined her in Bamenda in December 2008.

References

Amadou, Adamou (2018) 'Bonee and Fitina: Mbororo nomads facing and adapting to conflict in Central Africa', *Conflict and Society*, 4(1): 245–258.

Apitzsch, Ursula and Irini Siouti (2007) 'Biographical analysis as an interdisciplinary research perspective in the field of migration studies', Frankfurt am Main: Goethe-Universität, working paper.

Boesen, Elisabeth (2007) 'Des localités nomades: les "maisons" Wodaabe en brousse et en ville', in Elisabeth Boesen and Laurence Marfaing (eds), *Les nouveaux urbains dans l'espace Sahara-Sahel: un cosmopolitisme par le bas*, Paris: Karthala, 209–231.

Bredeloup, Sylvie (2013) 'The figure of the adventurer as an African migrant', *Journal of African Cultural Studies*, 25(2): 170–182.

Buggenhagen, Beth A. (2012) *Muslim Families in Global Senegal: Money takes care of shame*, Bloomington, IN: Indiana University Press.

Buitelaar, Marjo (2014) '"Discovering a different me": discursive positioning in life story telling over time', *Women's Studies International Forum*, 43: 30–37.

Cissé, Seydou (1992) *L'enseignement islamique en Afrique Noire*, Paris: L'Harmattan.

Collyer, Michael (2007) 'In-between places: trans-Saharan transit migrants in Morocco and the fragmented journey to Europe', *Antipode*, 39(4): 668–690.

De Bruijn, Mirjam E. (2019) 'Digitalization and the field of African studies', Carl Schlettwein Lecture 12, Basler Afrika Bibliographien.

De Bruijn, Mirjam E. and Jonna Both (2018) 'Introduction: understanding experiences and decisions in situations of enduring hardship in Africa', *Conflict and Society: Advances in Research*, 4: 186–198.

De Bruijn, Mirjam E. and Han van Dijk (1995) *Arid Ways: Cultural understandings of insecurity in Fulbe society, Central Mali*, Amsterdam: Thela.

De Bruijn, Mirjam E. and Han Van Dijk (2003) 'Changing population mobility in West Africa: Fulbe pastoralists in central and south Mali', *African Affairs*, 102: 285–307.

De Bruijn, Mirjam E., Rijk Van Dijk and Dick Foeken (2001) 'Mobile Africa: an introduction', in Mirjam de Bruijn, Rijk Van Dijk and Dick Foeken (eds), *Mobile Africa: Changing patterns of movement in Africa and beyond*, Leiden: Brill, 1–7.

De Latour, Éliane (2001) 'Du ghetto au voyage clandestin: la métaphore héroïque', *Autrepart*, 19: 155–169.

Dougnon, Isaïe (2008) *Etude comparative des tendances migratoires des Sonraï et Dogon vers le Ghana*, Oxford: IMI.

Ekwensi, Christopher (1962) *Burning Grass*, London: Heinemann .

Fabian, Johannes (2003) 'Forgetful remembering: a colonial life in the Congo', *Africa*, 73(4): 489–504.

—— (2007) *Memory against Culture: Arguments and reminders*, Durham, NC and London: Duke University Press.

Ferguson, James (2006) *Global Shadows: Africa in the neoliberal world order*, Durham, NC: Duke University Press .

Jackson, Michael (2008) 'Between biography and ethnography', *Harvard Theological Review*, 101(3–4): 377–397.

Jeannerat, Caroline (2009) 'Of lizards, misfortune and deliverance: Pentecostal soteriology in the life of a migrant', *African Studies*, 68(2): 251–271.

Keïta, Naffet, Seydou Magassa, Boukary Sangaré and Youssouf Ag Rhissa (2015) *Téléphonie et mobilité au Mali*, Mankon: Langaa Research and Publishing Common Initiative Group.

Keja, Roos (forthcoming) *Intimate Information Flows in Hardship: Mobile phones and the civic-ness of connectivity in Sokodé, Togo*, Berlin: De Gruyter.

Klute, Georg and Hans Peter Hahn (2007) 'Cultures of migration: introduction', in Georg Klute and Hans P. Hahn (eds), *Cultures of Migration: African perspectives*, Berlin: Lit Verlag, 9–27 .

Lecadet, Clara (2016) *Le manifeste des expulsés: Errance, survie et politique au Mali*, Tours: Presses Universitaire François Rabelais .

Lentz, Carola (2013) 'Pushing frontiers: the social organization of mobility', in *Land, Mobility and Belonging in West Africa*, Bloomington, IN: Indiana University Press, 28–81.

Loftsdóttir, Kristín (2004) 'When nomads lose cattle: WoDaaBe negotiations of ethnicity', *African Sociological Review*, 8(2): 52–76.

Nyamnjoh, Francis B. (2005) 'Images of Nyongo amongst Bamenda grassfielders in whiteman kontri', *Citizenship Studies*, 9(3): 241–269.

Nyamnjoh, Henrietta (2010) *'We Get Nothing from Fishing': Fishing for boat opportunities amongst Senegalese fisher migrants*, Bamenda and Leiden: Langaa and African Studies Centre.

Pelckmans, Lotte (2009) 'Phoning anthropologists: the mobile phone's (re-) shaping of anthropological research', in Mirjam de Bruijn, Francis B. Nyamnjoh and Inge Brinkman (eds), *Mobile Phones in Africa: The new talking drums in everyday life*, Bamenda/Leiden: Langaa RCPIG/ASC, 23–49.

Pelican, Michaela (2016) 'Les migrants camerounais à Dubaï: stratégies d'insertion socio-économique et relations transnationales', *Al Irfan 2: Revista de humanidades y ciencias sociales*, Dossier 'Repensar el multiculturalismo': 91–114.

Schapendonk, Joris (2011) 'Migrants' im/mobilities on their way to the EU: lost in transit?', *Tijdschrift voor economische en sociale geografie*, 103(5): 577–583.

Scott, James C. (2009) *The Art of Not Being Governed: An anarchist history of upland Southeast Asia*, New Haven, CT and London: Yale University Press.

Seli, Djimet (2014) *(Dé)connexions identitaires hadjeray: les enjeux des technologies de la communication au Tchad*, Mankon: Langaa Research and Publishing CIG.

12 | Fugitive emplacements: mobility as discontent for *wahaya* concubine women with slave status in the transnational borderlands of Niger–Nigeria, 1960–2016

Lotte Pelckmans

Introduction: voting with one's feet

This chapter analyses the flow – or 'undercurrent' – of forced displacement of low status women from central-south Niger who are contracted as 'concubines' in northern Nigeria.[1] While these displacements are small scale, highly individual and low density in terms of quantity, I take a special interest in them for their ignored *longue durée*, intergenerational and qualitatively disruptive impact on families and more specifically women, with slave status.

The practice of what I will call 'concubinage' can have different connotations and is valued differently by different individuals in the predominantly Islamic Sahel and beyond. While some strands in Islamic ideology describe 'concubinage' as the most honourable and dignified chance to marry up for slave women, legally offering viable ways to emancipation, reality seems to not always conform to this ideal to the women themselves, or to their offspring. Indeed, on the other side of the spectrum, some human rights and anti-slavery activists have framed some contemporary concubines as part of the industry of 'human trafficking' or even 'prostitution', because being 'married' as concubines rather than as official wives seems to increasingly be tied up with specific forms of sexual abuse and forced labour, stripped of any norms, rights and dignity. In view of this highly conflicting landscape of affects, opinions and ideologies surrounding the practice, I propose a focus on how the women themselves visibilize their own opinion about concubinage through their movements. In other words, they *vote with their feet* to render rupture with social norms visible.[2] Flight becomes a medium for the message that this concubinage is unacceptable for the woman involved. Independent of the opinions spread by activists, their fellow concubines or Islamic ideology, it is thus the fugitive movements that voice how the women themselves appreciate their condition. In order to map fugitive mobilities, I focus on a corpus of interviews with concubines in these borderlands as recorded by activists from Niger, thereby not so much analysing the women's oral life *his*tories – which are highly mediated – but rather the descriptions of their fugitive movements as their *stories*.[3]

Several (legal) scholars (of Islam) have described the institution of concubinage matter-of-factly, but rare are the interviews and contacts in contemporary academic work that give insights into the views 'from below', that is the emic perspectives of the concubines themselves about their situation, their status, their past and future aspirations for themselves and their families.[4] For many different reasons, not least those related to ambiguous attitudes in public opinion, secrecy and taboo, but also issues of access in terms of religion, gender and regional insecurity, the opinions and voices of these women have thus remained scarce in both historical and contemporary empirical source material. I engage with two types of sources, the first one a documentary film focusing on the court case of one concubine woman in Niger, the second one a report based on interviews with 165 concubines in both Niger and Nigeria, as recorded by a Niger-based anti-slavery organization called Timidria (Tidjani Alou, 2000). Most of the narratives in this report reflect situations and experiences that took place sometime between the 1960s and 2000s, in the borderlands between Niger and Nigeria. My focus is on references to actual or wished-for fugitive movement in these narratives.

After the first – often forced – move towards the compounds of their new husband-masters, some of the women describe in the narratives how after many years/decades of exploitation in Nigeria, they wish they could flee. Others describe how they actually managed to flee back to Niger. I argue that it is these 'inverse' fugitive movements that make these women's discontent visible. Indeed, their affects and emotions confirm the idea of exploitation and disagreement over their condition, starkly contrasting with the benign, even honourable condition concubines ideally and legally could and indeed did inhabit, as demonstrated with the story of Fatma by McDougall (1998).

The main argument is that while the forced displacement for 'marriage' from Niger towards Nigeria renders the anomalous suffering related to their concubine status invisible and spatially out of reach to their kin and social networks, it is the reverse process of their flight away from the concubinage in Nigeria, their fugitive emplacement, that makes their suffering visible.

The text starts with a first section giving the necessary (historical) background to the phenomenon of concubinage in the Sahel and then discusses ways in which concepts are a normative minefield surrounding these female displacements and their union with men. The methodology and the notion of narratives to describe the archival material (NGO report and visual documentary material) are also introduced. The final section zooms in on concubine mobility and the processes of in/visibility related to their initial forced displacement and eventual fugitive emplacement. These 'fugitive emplacements' are explained as roads to visibility and potentiality, however limited and even when inscribed in ongoing experiences of duress.

Understanding contemporary concubinage in the Sahel

Since the abolition of domestic slavery in French African colonies in 1905, concubinage 'ought to be' non-existent. The practice is definitely illegal in the realms of national constitutional and international law. Nevertheless, certain mixed customary-Islamic worldviews continue to promote the practice in specific regions. In what follows, I briefly explain how and why.

In the West African Sahel, 'the justifications for enslavement, and the institutions were those given by Muslim law and ideology, so we may label this as Muslim slavery in Africa' (Manning 1990: 128; see also Miller 1992). This 'Muslim slavery' was described extensively in Islamic texts, also by several scholars from the Sahel region who specialized in legal prescriptions from the fifteenth century onwards. However, it was also continuously blended with customary ideas and notions of personhood, family and power. The main legal strand used to be and is to date the Malikite doctrine of Islamic Law, which clearly distinguishes between two categories of persons: those born free and those who are not free (Hurault 1994: 91; Brunschwig 1960: 30).

The Malikite doctrine contains the most elaborate body of rules concerning the (non-)rights of unfree slaves (Lydon 2007: 391) and it allows for only one accepted legal form of 'mixing' free and slave groups: concubinage. This is the practice whereby a man of high status, or at least sufficient wealth, can take more women than the legally established limit of four freeborn wives, by adding 'foreign' slave women, or concubines. McDougall (2007: 173) indicates how 'In Islam, concubinage is completely acceptable. Honourable even. However, only slaves can be concubines'. Stillwell (1999: 157), in his analysis of royal slaves in the nineteenth century Kano Caliphate (Nigeria), describes how although royal slave concubines in some ways could become respected, their ties to their husband-master were not as formal and did not give them access to the same rights as his freeborn wives (McDougall 1998). Indeed, today, many concubines continue to be categorized on the basis of their slave status, as 'moveable' property and have less rights than freeborn wives.

It is part of the Islamic possibilities for freeborn men to take as concubines those women who are poor and/or unfree/slaves (Gausset 2007). Lovejoy (1988: 245) indicates how: 'Slavery had been an important instrument for the recruitment of women, through capture and purchase, from outside the Sokoto Caliphate'. And he also explains how in northern Nigeria's Sokoto caliphate, under colonial rule the powers of the aristocracy were enhanced and colonial administrators accepted the status quo of the practice of concubinage (Lovejoy 1988: 245): 'Women in general held an inferior position in society, both legally and in fact. Concubines and slave women were even worse off than free women. For the British, the treatment of women was not an important issue … Concubinage was allowed to continue'.[5]

The practice of concubinage can only be understood in the broader context of the slow death of the internal (West) African slavery, which has been explained, documented and described by several historians and anthropologists alike (Rossi 2017;

Bellagamba 2017; Hogendorn and Lovejoy 1993). Slave women were more valued than men in African slave systems, and 'the death of slavery' in Africa has been and continues to be much slower for women than for slave men (Robertson and Klein 1997; Gausset 2007).

In the Sahel region, with variations through space and time, rather large groups of people were unfree/slaves. Scholars like Meillassoux (1975) have estimated their proportion in the twentieth century to be between 30 and 50 per cent of the total population, some even higher. People with slave status remain numerous, mainly because slave status is hereditary; the category to which one belongs is almost perpetually defined by the parents' status and bloodlines (Thioub 2012), resulting in so/called 'classificatory slavery' (Rossi 2009: 4). Therefore, despite the legal constitutional abolition of slavery, high numbers of people in specific regions and ethnic groups in the Sahel continue to be considered as having slave status and can be stigmatized and excluded from various vital realms of social life on that basis (Rossi 2009; Lecocq and Hahonou 2015; Pelckmans and Hardung 2015).

Several concubines together constitute a 'harem', a term denoting the pool of women available to more or less influential freeborn men, ranging from established traders to emirs and sultans. Melman (quoted in Sinderud 2013: 2) has defined the 'harem system' as 'the combination of the seclusion of females with polygamy and concubinage'. In view of the 1904 and 1905 (re-)abolition of slavery, specifically for the British and French colonial West African territories, one could presume that this 'historical' phenomenon of concubinage and harems is legally something of the past. However, different Muslim constituencies in the Sahel continue to use a blend of customary and Islamic Law in everyday life, especially with regard to the rights and duties of women.

The norms, numbers and practices vary across space and time. So while the regional rulers of the Fulani in northern Cameroon in the 1950s had about 300 concubines within the palace, with a clear division of tasks and hierarchy among them (Sinderud 2013), in other places like northern Nigeria, the Kano emirate (subject to the Sokoto caliphate) of the nineteenth century was very well known for even bigger harems, but simultaneously also commoners could resort to buying slave concubines, but usually did not cumulate more than three or four in total. Arguably, this democratization of the practice of concubinage in combination with colonialism, patriarchy and neo-liberalism seems to have opened up the practice for different forms of abuse and non/respect of the legal prescriptions and religious norms (McDougall 1998). Poverty leads to some families handing out their daughters without being able to control their actual treatment once 'married' off.

Despite a large body of constitutional and international laws forbidding classificatory slavery, human trafficking and early marriage, it is the tension between different legal traditions and normative frameworks and worldviews that accounts for why the institution of concubinage is ongoing in the contemporary context and can even be considered and defended legally in certain places and social circles of southern Niger and northern Nigeria (and beyond).

> [L]egal pluralism makes possible the simultaneous and tense coexistence of abolitionist ideologies, on the one hand, and worldviews in which slavery is seen as integral to the constitution of society, on the other. In such contexts we should try to explain the co-presence of slavery and post-slavery, and not the transition from the former to the latter. (Rossi 2015: 304)

Indeed, in the worldviews of some, concubinage and/or the exploitation of a poor woman of slave status, remained perfectly legal, desirable even (Abdelkader and Zangaou 2012: 5), personified for example by the husband-master in the documentary film *Hadijatou*, described in more detail below. Anti-slavery activists like Abdelkader and Zangaou (2012: 5) counter this perspective by emphasizing that, '[t]his cannot, however, be used to justify present practice, in particular because Wahayu [i.e. concubines] are Muslim and Islam states that a Muslim cannot enslave another Muslim'.

People inhabiting the Niger–Nigeria borderlands have a strong preference for dealing with issues related to marriage, inheritance and so on, by consulting local scholars, who often base their arguments on a mix of customary and Malikite legal provisions. Against this, there is of course a national constitution in Niger, banning slavery and even turning it explicitly into a criminal offence, voted in parliament on 5 May 2003 and called law 2003-5, reforming the penal code of 1961. Furthermore, there is an international body of anti-slavery legislation, which allows for condemning 'fake marriages' and concubine practices, such as the 1998 session of the United Nations Working Group on Contemporary Forms of Slavery, where a recommendation was adopted stating that: 'cross-border trafficking of women and girls for sexual exploitation is a contemporary form of slavery and constitutes a serious violation of human rights'. Nevertheless, despite law 2003-5 being in place for about two decades now, less than five cases have resulted in actual conviction and sentencing. One of these cases was enforced through interregional ECOWAS law enforcement, namely the case of Hadijatou Mani, which has received some international attention, by academics (Allain 2009; Duffy 2009) and various media outlets (e.g. the *Time* top 100 award of 2009).[6]

Transnational *wahayu* concubines in the Niger–Nigeria borderlands

As in other parts of the Sahel, the borderlands between Niger and Nigeria have high levels of permeability and historical exchange between traders, nomads and so on. Historically, the circulation of women in the Sokoto caliphate (1804–1903) was dense and slave women were given as gifts, both among rulers and subjects, but also to travellers, guests and so on. The cross-border region under study remains an important and coherent unit, for example with a lot of seasonal migration and pastoralist nomadism occurring in these borderlands. In the report by Abdelkader and Zangaou (2012: 24) a woman called Bouweye Tabalole indicates how her family moved with the herds from Niger to Nigeria, and while in Nigeria, she was given to the Sultan's daughter, probably in the 1960s, in a time period way beyond the time of the Sokoto caliphate, colonial rule and the official abolition of slavery.

The contemporary continuation of concubinage in the social landscape of Niger–Nigeria is – according to the Timidria report – numerically especially affecting women in the region of southern Niger and northern Nigeria, both formerly part of the Sokoto caliphate. However, other studies demonstrate how concubinage and exchange of women also takes place in other Sahelian borderlands, such as the one between Mali and Mauritania/Morocco (McDougall 1998), and the one between Mali and Niger (Temedt 2014).

Today, it is a public secret that high-status men from Hausa communities in northern Nigeria continue to seek out concubines across the border in Niger, mainly in the Tahoua region, where Hausa and Tamacheq-speaking communities dominate and where concubines are called *wahaya/wahayu*. To do so, the man in question usually contracts the services of an intermediary or fixer, who seeks out a girl across the border, negotiates for her 'sale' and transports her in the Niger–Nigeria borderlands. Through their social networks, middlemen seek out (the families of) poor illiterate women in faraway places and solicit them for a marriage. This cross-border networking has the double advantage that the displacement will both impede the woman's flight or the easy possibility to return home, while at the same time re-enforcing resocialization through social and cultural isolation, by severing the woman from any linguistic and social skills and networks. Upon arrival in their new husband-masters compound, most *wahayu* are secluded and solicited for sexual services by him, as well as for domestic labour and childcare by his legal wives.

Practices vary from one location to another, some purchase a concubine nearby, while others purchase them across the border. In some cases, the girls spends some years as a domestic worker, before moving on to another compound where she is sold as a concubine. Importantly, not all of them are exploited abusively without mercy. But, as I will demonstrate in the following section, it is precisely the plurality of laws, norms and discourses that seems to allow for some to fall between the holes of the security net otherwise reserved to their honour.

Fragmentation: the plurality of laws, norms and discourses

Besides legal pluralism, there is also a strong normative pluralism (Hahonou 2015) in the Sahel region, in which 'the discursive regimes on categorical slavery and social status are not unified' (Rossi 2015: 304). Words, vocabularies and languages are important to contextualize in the face of such a complex and highly fragmented field of norms, laws and practices. The production of invisibility takes place in the interstices of these fragmented landscapes of affects.

Those practising concubinage to date know very well that it became a taboo practice that has been condemned as an unwanted legacy of historical forms of internal African slavery. This is well-documented in the person of the husband-master in the documentary film *Hadijatou*. This husband-master balances his words delicately towards the camera and the anti-slavery activists that confront him, by continuously sharing his conviction that Allah is on his side and will have the last word. In view of the religious and political power of many husband-masters like him who continue the practice to date, it is difficult, if not outright dangerous, to criticize them for such practices. A *wahaya* who is still living with her husband-master, mentions how it is only because her husband is travelling that the interviewees have managed to get access to her to talk. She concludes: 'otherwise the guard would be in trouble. He [i.e. her husband-master] is a fanatical man' (Abdelkader and Zangaou 2012: 22).

The different parties involved conceal the practice by talking about it in euphemistic, symbolic or cryptic language, referring to it as the 'acquisition/ownership of an animal'.[7] The comparison of people with slave status with goats or donkeys occurs often and is current across the Sahel, for example in Mali (Pelckmans 2011: 223). The comparison of a runaway concubine to a goat constitutes the opening scene of the documentary film *Hadijatou* described below.

In academic analysis, the *wahayu* practice in the Sahel region has been studied using the concepts of 'concubinage', 'conjugal slavery' and 'harem domesticity' (Mack 1990; Cooper 1994; Gausset 2007; Sinderud 2013; Jeppie et al. 2010; Rossi 2015). I here adopt the word concubinage to respect the Anglophone nature of this text, and as it probably comes closest to an English translation for the term *wahaya/wahayu* in the Zerma dialect of Niger. Using these categories directs the focus to the alternative 'marriage' arrangements which concubinage entails, coming with a different set of rituals, expectations and modalities when compared to traditional marriage arrangements. I use the term husband-master to distinguish from a traditional husband, because the transaction for concubines is considered a payment for all-in property rights, and more than a husband, the new male figure is above all the owner of the concubine.

The trajectory from Niger to Nigeria, as well as full names of places and persons the women are brought to, are often concealed to the women and their families in order to avoid flight, evasion and denunciation. The terminology for the movements of slave concubines towards their new husband-master, can range from 'marriage migration' to 'forced displacement' to 'forceful abduction' (Sinderud 2013: 7) and even the vocabulary of being 'exiled' (Abdelkader and Zangaou 2012: 9) has been used.

In contemporary NGO and human rights discourses, the terms 'abduction', 'human trafficking', 'prostitution' or 'sex slavery' are usually used (Dottridge 2005) to describe (aspects of) the practice of concubinage. In vernacular emic languages, different terms are used, depending on the context and the speaker's positionality. Words referring the legal prescriptions in Koranic texts are the Arab term *Umm al-Walad* (the manumission of a slave women having a child with her master). In the Hausa language, which is the lingua franca in the borderlands between Niger and

Nigeria, the practice is popularly referred to as *sa daka*, which – according to the Timidria report – literally means 'put in the bedroom' or 'shove her in the bedroom!', with the intention to have sexual relations being implicit (Abdelkader and Zangaou 2012 :5).

Since the women are often chosen in direct relation to their low class and classificatory slave status, their displacement can occur without their own or their families' full consent. Their initial displacement is often framed as being for (innocent) marriage purposes, sometimes it is a full abduction (secret and without any consent from any family member), but more often it is part of a transaction in which family members or at least some local middlemen of the community are involved and have gotten some financial benefit or share. People in these regions function in economies where little cash circulates. Therefore, most people's livelihood depends on social relationships, making it difficult to discern and qualify the boundary between freedom and exploitation, between consent and free will, especially for women in such highly patriarchal societies.

The scant attention to ongoing forms of concubinage can be linked directly to practices of categorization, whereby it is very easy to describe these displacements as common forms of 'early marriage' mobility and therefore a traditional and 'innocent' practice of kinship connections, which should not in any way be problematized on a political level (cf. Dottridge 2005).

Sources and access For many different reasons, not least those related to the above-mentioned fragmented and ambiguous attitudes in public opinion, but also issues of access in terms of religion, gender and regional insecurity, the opinions and voices of these women, have remained scarce in both historical and contemporary empirical source material. Studies from the perspective of female slaves and concubines themselves, have not only been difficult in terms of access, but seem also to have been a rather neglected topic of research (Sinderud 2013). At least historically, data on this phenomenon are generally scarce in conventional colonial and anthropological written sources, because of the assumption that the lives of these women were of little importance to politics and the general course of history. Today, difficult access to secluded female spaces, as well as the illegality and consequent secrecy surrounding the practice does not help matters either. Because conducting first-hand interviews in Niger or Nigeria myself is virtually impossible, given the current security situation in these borderlands, I rely on source material collected by others. Since my aim is not about mapping the exact number of women who are concubines (an impossible endeavour), nor about in-depth detailed testimonies, I base my analysis on two mediated sources to give insights into the actual or wished-for fugitive mobilities of some contemporary concubines.

The first one is a report by anti-slavery organization Timidria, the second one is a documentary film called *Hadijatou*, made by independent Spanish filmmaker Lala Goma in cooperation with a Nigerien cameraman. Both sources are explained in more detail below. I compare and triangulate this material with a range of historical and anthropological writings, but also put my own experience with interviewing people with slave status/concubines among Fulani in Mali (Pelckmans 2011, 2012) in the balance. I have two decades of experience working with slave status in the Sahel, including interviewing and working with regional anti-slavery associations, such as Timidria-Niger, Temedt-Mali and IRA-Mauritania (Pelckmans and Hahonou 2011; Pelckmans and Hardung, 2015).

THE TIMIDRIA REPORT: TRANSNATIONAL CONCUBINAGE NARRATIVES The quotes I use are from the Timidria report and they are certainly not without bias, as they are based on ten narratives, published by Timidria, the oldest anti-slavery organization from Niger, edited by activists Abdelkader and Zangaou (2012).[8] The data can therefore certainly be suspected of having an activist bias, underlining and seeking to prove the 'exploitation' and 'victimhood' of the persons interviewed. The narratives Timidria chose to publish have been selected from a total corpus of 165 interviews, mainly with (ex-)*wahayu* themselves in Niger (Tahoua region) and Nigeria (Kano, Sokoto, Kaduna and Zaria state). Out of the 165 women interviewed, 129 have slave status. The narratives have been recorded by local researchers, recruited by the association Timidria in Niger and co-financed by Anti-Slavery International and the Department for International Development (DfID), based in the UK. For my work on anti-slavery movements in the subregions (see Pelckmans and Hahonou 2011; Pelckmans and Hardung 2015) I have discussed this study and report with both female and male members of the staff of Timidria, in 2011 in Niamey.

In what follows I will use the concept of 'narratives' (Eastmond 2007) rather than the concept of 'testimonies', which is used by Timidria. The women themselves being illiterate, a lot of translation steps in the process from oral interview to written publishing have been made. Indeed, apart from the 'activist' bias, the positionality of the interviewer (status, language and gender) must have influenced the data, even more so when those who transcribed and translated the interviews were not the same persons as the interviewers. A third likely bias is the changes in the nuances of the stories in their translation from local languages (Hausa, Tamacheq and Zerma) into French and from French into English. The English quotations used in this text, are thus likely to have been the furthest removed from the literal statements of the women involved. In short, the concept of narratives is used to recall that the narratives referred to here have been recorded, edited, aligned and organized by authors other than the respondents/informants/interlocutors. The authors – and in many ways authorities – of these narratives are anti-slavery activists who have been involved in decisions on how, to what extent and on what basis the original oral life histories have been corrected, selected, edited, represented and circulated.

The resulting report, published in both French and English, consists of nine stories of *wahaya* women, with the tenth being the story of a *wahayu* owner. Out of nine published female narratives, five are from ex-*wahayu* who have fled, while four are from *wahaya* still serving their husband-master, or having obtained their freedom through flight or otherwise. Out of those who fled, three are living in a kind of 'freedom village' and two others live elsewhere. Their ages range from seventeen to eighty years. In the last narrative in the report, a male *wahayu* owner expresses how his goal in life is to have 100 children and explains why he needs *wahaya* to reach such a goal. This last story is very revealing on different levels, not least about the importance of fertility and reproduction in Niger (see Cooper 2019) and on the ways in which gendered paternalist perceptions of women (and slaves) as reproducers is a common moral view, in spite of the post-abolition era.

I argue it is possible to move beyond these positionalities, and the quest for any objective 'truth' these narratives might or might not represent, by focusing not so much on what these women say they experienced, but on what they actually and undeniably did in terms of movement.

HADIJATOU, THE DOCUMENTARY Compared to the women of the report, most of whom are from Niger and became concubines in Nigeria, the case of Hadijatou, central to the documentary movie, is exceptional, in the sense of her physical closeness to her home community, and the fact that she has been picked up by the anti-slavery organization to pursue her ex-husband-master in court (Allain 2009; Duffy 2009), Nevertheless, Hadijatou also comes from roughly the same region as the fugitive ex-*wahayu* of Zongon Ablo (see below).

Fugitive emplacements: flight as visibilization in the Niger–Nigeria borderlands

This final section focuses on the dialectics between visibility and invisibility culminating in the act of 'fugitive emplacement', namely the reversed displacement in the form of flight whereby the woman moves away from her husband-master's compound as a tactic of resistance and a road towards re-visibility.

While the *wahayu*'s displacement trajectory to northern Nigerian families is worth a study in itself, my focus here is on another set of less common, reversed cross-border movements, namely the ones where *wahayu* take flight and move away from their hardships as 'slaves' in their Nigerian husband-masters' households. Summarizing from their 165 interviews, the Timidria report singles out the following elements explaining why some *wahayu* want to flee: repeated sale and switching husband-masters, because they can always be given away, resold or rebought at any given moment, especially when they have no children yet. Furthermore heavy physical labour, humiliation and insults based on their status as well as that of their children, jealousy and mistreatment by the legal wives of their husband-master and strong alienation from one's own family, language and home.

In view of these hardships, there are those women who express the wish to flee, versus those who actually fled. A *wahaya* who is still living in with her husband-master says at the time of the interview (A & Z 2012: 22): 'As soon as I get the chance, I'll leave. We're kept like prisoners'.

Tadant (A & Z 2012: 23), also a *wahaya* who is still living with their husband-master, mentions the impact of the flight of another *wahaya*:

> There was also another *wahaya* … abused by the master, she later fled back to her parents … Before Tantout's escape, us three *wahayu* all lived together in one room, but now we have our own rooms. The legal wives' rooms are all decorated up to the ceiling, with beds and other furniture. My room just has an old, dirty mattress.

The *wahaya* called Tabalole Bouweye (A & Z 2012: 24) escaped from her third husband-master back to her first master, because that was the only place she had ever known to be somehow 'home':

> At that time, there were three other *wahayu* … who all went on to escape. I also ended up escaping seventeen years ago. I returned to live with the late Aïlale III of Sokoto [i.e. her first master], which was the only home I knew because I had been raised there. I didn't know any of my own family. I was sold young.

As mentioned in the introduction, for some women, their 'sale' came before their actual engagement as a concubine. For several of them, they first did household chores here and there and were then finally handed over or sold off to someone as a concubine.

The documentary *Hadijatou* allows us to listen to several voices bespeaking Hadijatou's repeated flights from her husband-master, which was possible thanks to his proximity (only about 10 kilometres) to her family. Her brother indicates how she came back time and again after abuses by her husband-master. He also indicates how Hadijatou pleaded to at least give birth back home with her mother, without success. Her ex-husband-master complains about her flights and it is only because her case became so mediatized and has been followed up so closely that Hadijatou is left in peace by her former husband-master today.

In what follows, some women describe how they actually managed to flee.

Out of the five narratives of *wahayu* who fled in the Timidria report, three live currently in the village of Zongon Ablo and two other ex-*wahaya* fugitive women went to live elsewhere. What kind of tactics of refuge and flight do women in the freedom village of Zongon Ablo share?

Tabas Aborak recounts (A & Z 2012: 13):

> I had to look after the children of the mistresses and the four *wahayu* … I dreaded it when they travelled, because it was my role to prepare a horse for them and to follow behind on foot, carrying the child they were nursing on

> my back, both on the outward and return journeys. That always made me want to find a way out … Before I was transferred to my third master, my parents managed to have me back for a while. I then managed to get together a little money, which I kept with me. This money let me plan my escape. One day I decided to run away, though I was very scared. It took days and nights of absolute anxiety, passing through villages and hamlets and asking where the black Touareg lived. I can't recall all the villages I went through, only that I held on to the name of Zongon Ablo. Zongon Ablo is a village where 80 per cent of the inhabitants, mostly women, are originally from other places. I focused all my attention on getting there. I know I went through Guidan Iddar. Zongon Ablo! I had finally arrived.

Tebarkot Adarfor, today living in the village of Zongon Ablo, explains (A & Z 2012: 15) how the way in which she and her children were treated was unbearable and she underlines her failing motherhood as the most unbearable:

> It became unbearable for me and for my children. They needed protection and affection from me but all they got was this kind of treatment. I could never show them any moral support, which I'm sure they needed from me. With the children increasingly aware of my inability to be a mother to them, I began preparing a plan to get us out of our worsening situation. I wanted to escape with my children. But it wasn't possible. So when Peulh cattle-herdsmen arrived from Niger, I took the opportunity to flee, abandoning my children.

Most *wahayu* indicate how they fled without being able to bring along their own children and with the village name of Zongon Ablo as their only point of orientation. These central tropes vary in detail across the different cases, but what many of them have in common is the haphazard flight.

Not all forms of flight are successful though. The report and the documentary give us some insights into those *wahaya* who successfully managed to flee, although always without their children. Many *wahaya* were sold at a very young age and do not at all remember or only have vague memories of their homes. Those who do have such memories and continued to be in touch with their families might opt for returning to their parents, but according to the report by Timidria, and as illustrated by the particular case of Hadijatou in the documentary film, once returned home, either the parents themselves, or the husband-master will most likely return the woman to her husband-master, because that is where she officially 'belongs'.

Of course, there are always exceptions and not all women shared similar fates. So those who had more supportive families, could return 'back home' after they fled, not least because their families had not realized just how different some parts of northern Nigeria's Hausa culture is when it comes to these '*wahaya*' marriages, with, for example, the prohibition or discouragement of family visits being deemed too much. The following story gives us some insight into the pride and also possibility to resist the suffering. It is the story of Akarat Idimi (A & Z 2012: 20):

> My parents recognized the abuse that my family and I had suffered at Sarkin Koudou's [i.e. husband-masters] house and didn't send me back. And while my so-called 'husband' was counting on my master to send me back, the latter no longer had any control over me because he had already sold me. I didn't have to answer to him anymore. That's what the Hausa from Sokoto didn't understand. In their view, the slave is part of a human herd that the master can draw on as he wishes. So that is how my so-called marriage ended, because I categorically refused to return to it.

It is interesting to note how in this quote, Akarat refers to some elements of cultural difference in the borderlands of Niger–Nigeria: it is the Hausa of Sokoto who did not understand what real marriage is, they only lure people into a 'so-called marriage'. In saying this, she confirms that her flight and subsequent refusal to return is a way to say no to excessive suffering and treatment 'like an animal in a herd', rather than a human being in a concubine arrangement.

Other options for those who flee and cannot return home consist of trying to make a living in small towns and cities, but in these very patriarchal societies, where women are supposed to be protected through marriage, many of the fugitive *wahayu* – according to Abdelkader and Zangaou (2012: 7) – end up as prostitutes. Several others, and especially those who have fled from Nigeria to Niger, took refuge in the village of Zongon Ablo (district of Konni), where there is a significant fugitive ex-*wahayu* population. As the section below outlines, Zongon Ablo has become their place of refuge and a place where they can start a new life.

Zongon Ablo: making home in a place of refuge

Zongon Ablo is geographically situated close to the border with northern Nigeria, north of the contemporary Nigerian town of Sokoto, in the Nigerien district of Konni. It is a village known for its significant fugitive ex-*wahayu* population. Hardly any of the fugitive ex-*wahayu* living in Zongon Ablo have returned to or are in contact with their original families and/or their natal villages. Some express feelings of fear and resentment towards both their ex-husband-masters and/or their own families who 'sold' or at least 'betrayed' them, others want to avoid being 'recaptured' or looked down upon for their disrespect of 'tradition' when fleeing.

The documentary visualizes at the end how Hadijatou visits some of the fugitive ex-*wahayu* inhabiting the village of Zongon Ablo to encourage them to also take their case (of abuse) to court, following her example. The film shows us some excerpts of a kind of group discussion Hadijatou has with these women about their experiences/suffering as *wahayu*. Quite a number of the interviews that form part of the corpus of the 165 narratives recorded by Timidria have been recorded in this village as well. Both the film and the report mention how one of its founders, a fugitive ex-*wahaya* called Tassourabat, living in southern Niger, in the meantime has the name and fame that inspired others to come over as well. She is also known as the 'wise woman' and her name and that of the village itself have been mentioned by several *wahayu* as their – only – point of orientation/navigation for their flight. In this section, even though the material is neither very detailed nor rich, I analyse how some women living there reflect on this village as a place of refuge and comment on the status of this village in the eyes of other Nigerien citizens.

In the report, fugitive ex-*wahayu* Talak Azgar (A & Z 2012: 14), currently living in Zongon Ablo, indicates:

> In my view, Zongon Ablo is the ideal village. Most of the women, men, old people and young people are like me. Everyone knows everyone else's past. No one mocks anyone else – at least, not in my neighbourhood – because everyone has had a tragic past. Zongon Ablo is a village of tragedies: everyone who lives here came unexpectedly, and all of us, especially the women, share a low former social status [sic]. About 80 per cent of us, the women of Ablo, are fugitives. That's why we get on and help each other without any difficulties.

While these women have managed to cross back over the international Nigeria–Niger border, their fugitive displacement has not made them overcome internal boundaries of social and economic segregation. Many continue to struggle hard both when it comes to economic survival, but also social recognition. In most narratives, references to continued poverty, loss of many children and discrimination based on their low status are mentioned. Many – including Hadijatou – indicate how they often have a workload similar to before and poorer husbands than before, but they underline that the main difference is that they now work for their own family and future and they can keep property or earnings to invest these in their children, whom they dream of saving from the same destiny as theirs. Indeed, in a society where individual freedom is least possible for women with slave status (McDougall 1998), these women indicate how they aspire to and 'desire to inhabit a position of relational worth from which people may engage in a positive sociality' (Bjarnesen and Vigh 2016: 11).

This village of refuge is not comparable to its historical counterpart: the so-called 'freedom villages' (in French: *villages de liberté*) established by colonial officers in an effort to support runaway slaves after the abolition of slavery. While in the past freedom villages used to be funded and erected by the colonial state (Bouche 1950, 1968), Zongon Ablo has been initiated by fugitive *wahayu* themselves and is currently being 'taken care of' by the funds of activists of Timidria. Since the name of the village and the status of its inhabitants is known in the wider surroundings, the fugitive women who settled there are thus paradoxically in plain sight and cannot hide their status as slaves and *wahayu*. The help and regular presence of members of the organization Timidria give them some protection from husband-masters who want to reclaim them, which was not the case in colonial freedom villages.

It is the intense disruptions and dispersals of families with slave status that make Zongon Ablo into a new place of belonging and connection and a refuge for those who have nothing to return to. In many ways, it is a kind of frontier village, functioning at the edges of the broader societal norms of belonging and being.[9]

Here I propose to introduce the concept of 'fugitive emplacement' as the aspiration to a dignified life through flight. Emplacement is here equated with windows of hope and future aspirations towards a new life, and for the women discussed here, this means mainly a dignified life in terms of kinship, as both wife and mother. I thus define emplacement in line with Bjarnesen and Vigh (2016: 13) as 'a conceptual move away from place as location toward place as a process of socio-affective attachment, as a point of valued or tenable being'. Emplacement is not to be seen here 'in the sense of a physical location, but rather the striving towards being positively related in a social landscape' (Englund 2002: 263). By moving to a specific village of refuge, several ex-concubines indeed manage to establish such a position of relational worth and more positive sociality, even though they remain poor and stigmatized by outsiders. Their fugitive emplacement 'articulates a social positioning that enables the pursuit of existentially meaningful life-making, but as an ongoing struggle for access, rather than a fixed position or status' (Bjarnesen and Vigh 2016: 14).

Conclusion

Mobility as a strategy of emancipation for slaves has been explored historically,[10] but much less so when it comes to women who continue to be defined by their classificatory slave status today. The broader argument made here, about invisibility of these women's movements and suffering cannot be disconnected from the invisibility of contemporary slavery practices in so-called 'post-'slavery societies. This is so because concepts like post-abolition and post-slavery uphold the linear idea that legally abolishing slavery equals ending local norms and conceptions of social hierarchies. Also, ideas and ideologies of freedom have been diverse, but often only defined and rendered visible and intelligible in the Western liberal individualistic tradition, thereby overshadowing and silencing other more subtle forms of emancipation. This issue is even more central in the lives of women with attributed slave status today. For most women in the Sahel region, their freedom lies in social recognition as a mother and wife, not in becoming an individual with freedom of movement at any time. Paradoxically, however, it is precisely when these freedoms to connection and belonging are constantly undermined, that flight and the individual ability to move seems to be the only way out.

The invisibilization central to this text is that of concubine – locally called *wahayu* – suffering. While only some of these concubines are physically mistreated, all of them are expected and sometimes forced to do hard physical labour and provide sexual services. In terms of class, gender and racial characteristics, concubinage is only inhabited and thus experienced by a specific category of citizens in the borderlands of Niger–Nigeria, namely poor females of slave descent, who according to local ideologies are also often considered as 'black'. In view of their double historical and contemporary marginalization and stigmatization, it is a category of citizens and women, who due to their low status have a very long history of invisibility. This invisibility was and continues to be upheld up to the present through the use of euphemistic language and a fragmented landscape with multiple opinions and voices reflecting legal, religious and normative pluralism.

The invisibilization of their suffering not only follows from their low status as both slaves and women, but it is exacerbated by transnational border crossings, whereby the ideology of concubinage is used to lure families into accepting concubinage for their daughters, but without having any influence over their actual treatment once they have been displaced and forced to live with their new husband-masters.

Their involuntary spatial and social displacements remained not only hidden for (inter-)national actors due to regional insecurity, border crossings, the invocation of 'marriage' as an innocent social practice and anti-slavery legislation (unintelligible /) illegible and otherwise inaccessible due to the vulnerability of its main 'targets', but what is more, even their own kin and children often remain in the dark about their precise whereabouts. So if the practice is highly invisible in an international research or activist context, it is almost as invisible or at least unspeakable in the social environments where it takes place. There is not much room for objection, revolt or resistance. But for those who take the opportunity, fleeing has been the main way out with all the risks it entails, including that of leaving one's children behind, knowing that a similar, or worse fate than the one they are fleeing from, awaits them. Flight then renders an invisibilized process of suffering visible through mobility.

My micro-level examination of historical continuities in forced mobilities of slave concubines is based on a focus in wished-for or actual flight in the narratives of the concubines assembled by activists from Niger. I thus argued for looking into how certain qualities of movement – fugitive and forced – produce in/visibilization in significant ways. Their suffering remains invisible and thus not recognized by families, communities, activists or state authorities. It is only when fleeing that the unacceptable living conditions become visible. These women as such 'vote with their feet' showing their opinion, namely that they no longer support their 'concubinage' by leaving the place where they are kept as concubines. Indeed, in a society where individual freedom is not possible for women with slave status (McDougall 1998), these women indicate how they aspire to and 'desire to inhabit a position of relational worth from which people may engage in a positive sociality' (Bjarnesen and Vigh 2016: 11).

Refuge/flight is a form of displacement directly related to an important tipping point in the woman's self-awareness about the invisibility of her or her children's suffering. Many women are aware of their suffering but do not realize that they have the right not to be exposed to it. The fugitive movement is thus the productive moment that leads to visibility. The choice for flight – in spite of its high risk and emotional costs – renders concubinage visible as an institution that marginalizes and alienates these women from the basic rights, expectations and norms for accessing human dignity available to women in the Sahel: that of marriage and motherhood (Cooper 2019). Maybe with the described exception of the village of refuge called Zongon Ablo, these women have become a 'diaspora without a homeland', a term evoked by Gaibazzi (2013) in the context of men with slave status among the Soninke in The Gambia.

Fugitive mobility thus ultimately visibilizes the personal discontent of the women affected by concubinage. It is fugitive emplacement that renders the trajectories out of suffering and towards freedom from below visible, possible and memorable. Clearly, there are many risks involved in fugitive emplacement. But when succeeding, fugitive emplacement of the concubines gives insight into the long history of emotions, affects and vernacular understandings of violence that undergird the small-scale but nevertheless ongoing *longue durée* displacements of generations of concubines with slave status.

Finally, I tried to write the largely non-written freedom narratives of contemporary concubines with slave status in northern Nigeria–Niger borderlands. Their fugitive narratives, or in other words their bodily mobility in the form of flight, bear witness to the protracted histories of suffering that concubines of slave status continue to experience today.

Notes

1 More specifically the Tahoua region of Niger and northern Nigerian provinces formerly belonging to the historical Sokoto Caliphate (1804–1903) (see also Lovejoy 1990).

2 I have adapted the definition from www.collinsdictionary.com/dictionary/english/to-vote-with-your-feet to fit with the context of this chapter. The original definition is: 'If you vote with your feet, you show that you do not support something by leaving the place where it is happening or leaving the organization that is supporting it.'

3 I am inspired here by the way in which McDougall (1998) analyses and describes the methodological differences between life *his*tory and life *story* for female slave narratives. However, the outcome of the particular mobility stories in my text reveal a sense of not belonging, rather than the sense of belonging expressed by concubine Fatma central to her article.

4 Notable exceptions describing voices of concubine lives in the mid and late twentieth century in West Africa are McDougall (1998), Sinderud (2013) and Mack (1990). I have interviewed a concubine among the elite of the village where I have worked in central Mali, but have never published about it.

5 Moreover, as demonstrated by Rodet (2011) and others for the French colonies in the Sahel, concubinage was also practised by the colonial officers themselves.

6 www.antislavery.org/time-magazine-top-100-award-hadijatou/.

7 See e.g. the opening scene of the documentary film *Hadijatou*, by Lala Goma.

8 In the remainder of this chapter, and to enhance readability, I will use the

abbreviation A & Z 2012 when referring to the report.

9 For a similar example of such a village where all kinds of low-status outcasts of other areas in the vicinity have gathered and started a new village society, but this time in Mali, see De Bruijn and Pelckmans (2005).

10 To name but one example for the West African context, see Klein and Roberts (1980) and specifically for the history of women fleeing slavery, see Rodet (2009).

References

Abdelkader, G.K. and M. Zangaou (2012) *Wahaya: Domestic and sexual slavery in Niger*, Report by Association Timidria in cooperation with Anti-Slavery International. Retrieved from: www.antislavery.org/wp-content/uploads/2018/10/Wahaya-report.pdf.

Allain, J. (2009) 'Hadijatou Mani Koraou v. Republic Of Niger. Judgment No. ECW/CCJ/JUD/06/08', *American Journal of International Law*, 103(2): 311. doi:10.2307/20535154.

Bellagamba, A. (2017) 'Freedom from below', *Journal of Global Slavery*, 2(1–2): 1–9. doi:10.1163/2405836x-00201013.

Bjarnesen, J. and H. Vigh (2016) 'Introduction: the dialectics of displacement and emplacement', *Conflict and Society: Advances in Research*, 2(1) (06): 9–15.

Bouche, D. (1950) *Les villages de liberté en Afrique occidentale française*, Paris: Mouton.

—— (1968) *Les villages de liberté en Afrique noire française, 1887–1910*, Paris: Mouton.

Brunschwig, R. (1960) '`Abd', *The Encyclopedia of Islam*, 2nd edition, Leiden: Brill.

Cooper, B.M. (1994) 'Reflections on slavery, seclusion and female labor in the Maradi region of Niger in the nineteenth and twentieth centuries'. *The Journal of African History*, 35(1): 61–78. doi:10.1017/s0021853700025962.

—— (2019) *Countless Blessings: A history of childbirth and reproduction in the Sahel*, Bloomington, IN: Indiana University Press.

De Bruijn, M.E. and L. Pelckmans (2005) 'Facing dilemmas: former Fulbe slaves in modern Mali', *Canadian Journal of African Studies* 39(1): 69–96.

Dottridge, M. (2005) 'Types of forced labour and slavery-like abuse occurring in Africa today', *Cahiers d'études africaines*, 45(179–180): 689–712. doi:10.4000/etudesafricaines.5619.

Duffy, H. (2009) 'Hadijatou Mani Koroua v Niger: slavery unveiled by the ECOWAS Court', *Human Rights Law Review*, 9(1): 151–170. doi:10.1093/hrlr/ngn041.

Eastmond, M. (2007) 'Stories as lived experience: narratives in forced migration research', *Journal of Refugee Studies*, 20(2): 248–264. https://doi.org/10.1093/jrs/fem007.

Englund, Harri (2002) 'Ethnography after globalism: migration and emplacement in Malawi', *American Ethnologist*, 29(2): 261–286.

Gaibazzi, P. (2013) 'Diaspora without homeland: slave descendants and the cultural politics of ancestry in the Upper Gambia River Valley', *Revue européenne des migrations internationales*, 29(1): 23–43. doi:10.4000/remi.6253.

Gausset, Q. (2007) 'Women, gender and slavery: sub-Saharan Africa', *Encyclopedia of Women and Islamic Cultures: Economics, education, mobility and space*, Leiden: Brill, 4: 510–513.

Hogendorn, J.S. and P.E. Lovejoy (eds) (1993) *Slow Death for Slavery: The course of abolition in northern Nigeria 1897–1936*, Cambridge: Cambridge University Press.

Hurault, J. (1994) 'Les noms attribués aux non-libres dans le lamidat de Banyo', *Journal des Africanistes*, 64(1): 91–107.

Jeppie, S., E. Moosa and R. Roberts (eds) (2010) *Muslim Family Law in Sub-Saharan Africa: Colonial legacies and*

post-colonial challenges, Amsterdam: Amsterdam University Press.
Klein, M.A. (1998) *Slavery and Colonial Rule in French West Africa*. Cambridge: Cambridge University Press.
Klein, M.A. and R. Roberts (1980) 'The Banamba slave exodus of 1905 and the decline of slavery in the western Sudan', *The Journal of African History*, 21(3): 375–394.
Lecocq, B. and E.K. Hahonou (2015) 'Introduction: exploring post-slavery in contemporary Africa', *International Journal of African Historical Studies*, 48(2): 181–192.
Lovejoy, Paul E. (1988) 'Concubinage and the status of women slaves in early colonial northern Nigeria', *The Journal of African History*, 29(2): 245–266. doi:10.1017/s0021853700023665.
—— (1990) 'Concubinage in the Sokoto caliphate (1804–1903)', *Slavery and Abolition*, 11(2): 159–189. doi:10.1080/01440399008575005.
Lydon, G. (2007) 'Islamic legal culture and slave-ownership contests in nineteenth century Sahara', *International Journal of African Historical Studies*, 40(3): 391–439.
Mack, B.B. (1990) 'Service and status: slaves and concubines in Kano, Nigeria', in R. Sanjek and S. Colen (eds), *At Work in Homes: Household workers in world perspective*, Washington, DC: American Anthropological Association Monograph Series, 14–34.
Manning, P. (1990) *Slavery and African Life: Occidental, Oriental and African slave trades*. Cambridge: Cambridge University Press.
McDougall, E.A. (1998) 'A sense of self: the life of Fatma Barka', *Canadian Journal of African Studies*, 32(2): 285–315. doi:10.2307/486151.
—— (2007) 'The practice of rachat in French West Africa', in K.A. Appiah and M. Bunzl (eds), *Buying Freedom: The ethics and economics of slave redemption*, Princeton, NJ: Princeton University Press, 158–178.
Meillassoux, C. (1975) *L'esclavage en Afrique précoloniale*, Paris: Éditions François Maspero.
Miller, Joseph C. (1992) 'Muslim slavery and slaving: a bibliography', *Slavery and Abolition*, 13(1): 249–271, doi:10.1080/01440399208575060.
Pelckmans, L. (2011) *Travelling Hierarchies: Moving in and out of slave status in a central Malian Fulɓe network*, Leiden: African Studies Centre.
—— (2012) '"Having a road": social and spatial mobility of persons of slave and mixed descent in post-independence Central Mali', *Journal of African History*, 53(2): 235–255.
Pelckmans, L. and C. Hardung (eds) (2015) 'Post-esclavage et mobilisations', *Politique africaine* (special issue), 140(4): 5–22.
Pelckmans, L. and E.K. Hahonou (2011) 'West African antislavery movements: citizenship struggles and the legacies of slavery', *Vienna Journal of African Studies*, (20): 141–162.
Robertson, C.C and M.A. Klein (1997) *Women and Slavery in Africa*, Portsmouth, NH: Heinemann.
Rodet, M. (2009) *Les migrantes ignorées du Haut-Sénégal (1900–1946)*, Paris: Karthala.
—— (2011) 'Sexualité, mariage et esclavage au Soudan français à la fin du XIXe siècle', *Colonisations*, 33: 45–64.
Rossi, B. (2009) *Reconfiguring Slavery: West African trajectories*, Liverpool: Liverpool University Press.
—— (2015) 'African post-slavery: a history of the future', *International Journal of African Historical Studies*, 48(2): 303–324.
—— (2017) 'Freedom under scrutiny', *Journal of Global Slavery*, (1–2): 185–194. doi:10.1163/2405836x-00201014.
Sinderud, M.B. (2013) 'Royal Concubinage in Ngaoundere, Northern Cameroon, ca. 1900–1960', *The International Journal of African Historical Studies*, 46(1): 1–25.
Stillwell, S. (1999) 'Culture, kinship and power: the evolution of royal slavery in nineteenth-century Kano', *African Economic History*, 27: 137–175.

Temedt Association (2014) *Esclavage au Mali: Des victims témoignent*, Paris: Editions L'Harmattan.
Thioub, I. (2012) 'Stigmas and memory of slavery in West Africa: skin color and blood as social fracture lines', *New Global Studies*, 6(3). doi:10.1515/1940-0004.1188.
Tidjani Alou, M. (2000) 'Courtiers malgré eux. Trajectoires de reconversion dans l'association Timidria au Niger', in T. Bierschenk, J.-P. Chauveau and J.-P. Olivier de Sardan (eds), *Courtiers en développement. Les villages africains en quête de projets*, Paris: Karthala, 279–304.

Documentary film

Goma, L. (2016) *Hadijatou*. See for more: https://leslan.org/hadijatou/.

13 | The paradoxes of migrant in/visibility: understanding displacement intersectionalities in Bobo-Dioulasso, Burkina Faso

Jesper Bjarnesen

Introduction

In the early 2000s, the advent of armed conflict in Côte d'Ivoire changed the outlooks and trajectories of the country's considerable Burkinabe diaspora. More than 800,000 Burkinabe citizens are estimated to have left Côte d'Ivoire during the first decade of the new millennium, as their livelihoods and personal safety were threatened by their increasing stigmatization as 'strangers' in Ivorian political rhetoric (see Dembélé 2002). This politicization of immigration in a country that had famously welcomed labour migrants in the post-independence era marked, if not a clean break, a dramatic deterioration of what was popularly known as '*le contrat*': the contract, or mutual understanding between sending and receiving populations in the long history of circular labour migration between Burkina Faso and Côte d'Ivoire.

This chapter considers the settlement histories of Burkinabe families, displaced from Côte d'Ivoire during this turbulent decade. The overall purpose of the analysis is to explore the paradoxes of migrant in/visibility in contexts of displacement. Through the attention to migrant in/visibilization, the analysis emphasizes the complex distribution of vulnerability in displacement within seemingly homogenous migrant communities as well as within households. The chapter thereby analyses the intersectionality of migrant vulnerabilities in the context of war-related displacement and urban resettlement. The following section elaborates this conceptual framework by briefly reviewing a selection of readings on (mis)recognition and invisibilization, with particular emphasis on intersectionality and the paradoxes of displacement.

The ethnographic material on which the analysis builds has been recorded in dialogue with resettled families in an informal settlement in Bobo-Dioulasso over the course of ten years, during which I have relied primarily on migration and resettlement histories and extended participant observation. The chapter's ethnography is structured into two sections, reflecting the chronology of the armed conflict and its aftermath, but also emphasizing two distinct phases in the resettlement of Burkinabe migrants who were forced to leave Côte d'Ivoire during the Ivorian crisis. The first section explores the intersectionalities of vulnerability in the initial resettlement in Burkina Faso, while the second analyses the paradoxes of displacement as most families, despite their hardships, were reaching a sense of emplacement. Finally, the conclusion highlights the paradoxes of migrant in/visibility, as migrants faced the possibilities and limitations of longer-term assimilation or integration.

Understanding migrant in/visibilities

When activists or testimonies or, on the rare occasion, social scientists, claim recognition for a cause or a group of people, such claims are often stated and understood as claims for voice. Demands that the powerholders listen; the disenfranchised be given the chance to speak (out); and that these words not fall on deaf ears. At the same time, recognition has a decidedly spectral connotation: it involves seeing or being seen, and on the basis of that seeing, of being accepted, or understood. However, both the auditive and spectral understandings of recognition tend to evoke strictly binary positions, one is either heard or not heard; either seen or not seen. This book's approach to the complex production of in/visibility serves to illustrate that, upon closer inspection, being seen and not being seen are not as simple matters as one might assume. Coming into view of the authorities may be the last thing an undocumented migrant wishes, even as she works under appalling conditions somewhere in the European shadow economy. Even the well-intended recognition of someone's particular needs for protection may render vulnerable groups or individuals more exposed to persecution and resentment, as B Camminga's contribution to this volume painfully illustrates through the story of Julia's experiences as a transgender refugee in the Kakuma refugee camp in Kenya. In these ways and more, the effects of recognition by states or other institutional actors are not as straightforward as they may seem.

Furthermore, recognition is not only or always about acceptance or understanding. In her reflections on strangerhood, Sara Ahmed asks, 'How do you recognise a stranger?' The question seems counterintuitive; a stranger might be said to be someone you do not recognize. But in the context of everyday interaction, Ahmed insists that perceiving someone as a stranger implies an act of recognition: 'we recognise someone *as a stranger*, rather than simply failing to recognise them' (Ahmed 2000: 19, emphasis in original). Implicit in this reflection on strangerhood are the power dynamics that inevitably become central when analysing the question of recognition as a contestation of rights, as evoked earlier. This question brings us closer to the theme of the present book. As Polzer and Hammond (2008) have argued, invisibility is 'fundamentally relational; its impacts depend on the power relations and interests connecting those who see and those who are to be seen (or not)' (Polzer and Hammond 2008: 417). These power relations, furthermore, cannot be reduced to a unidirectional, or even a binary, relationship between one and the other:

> power does not rest univocally with seeing or with being seen. Rather, it is the style in which seeing and being seen takes place that carries the most important

consequences. The exercise of power is always an exercise in activating selective in/visibilities. (Brighenti 2007: 339)

In this chapter, I explore the dynamics of (mis)recognition in the context of the resettlement of displaced migrants from Côte d'Ivoire in urban Burkina Faso. In the context of an informal settlement in the town of Bobo-Dioulasso, I build on Ahmed's assertion that '[s]trangers are not simply those who are not known in this dwelling, but those who are, in their very proximity, *already recognised as not belonging*, as being out of place' (Ahmed 2000: 20, emphasis in original). Rather than emphasizing ascriptions or experiences of strangerhood, however, I apply this analytical perspective to understand the (mis)recognition of migrant vulnerability among neighbours and within families. This approach to analysing the dynamics of (mis)recognition, I argue, enables an intersectional understanding of intimate power dynamics in the context of displacement.

By thinking about migrant vulnerability through the notion of (mis)recognition, the analysis aligns with a growing anthropological literature on subjective experiences of displacement (e.g. Lubkemann 2008; Jansen and Löfving 2009; Bjarnesen 2016). In these studies, the unequal distribution of vulnerability in displacement is understood in holistic terms, in the context of everyday life, which runs counter to the tendency of seeing displacement as a more categorical disruption of normality, implied in the popular understanding of mass displacement. Reinserting our understanding of displacement into the flow of everyday life enables an analytical approach that, firstly, opens up to the 'politics of mobility and access' (cf. Massey 1993) through which, 'the distribution of both voluntary and involuntary forms of (im)mobility are structured according to contextually specific hierarchies of gender, generation, and class' (Bjarnesen and Vigh 2016: 14). Secondly, such an approach ascribes neither agency nor causality to the effects of displacement, bringing into view 'the paradoxically productive dynamics of displacement' (Hammar 2014: 8).

Involuntary returns and the intersectionalities of vulnerability

This section introduces the two primary empirical examples of the chapter, the first being the experiences of the Kabré family and the second those of young adult resettled migrants. The ethnography centres on the unequal distribution of vulnerability in displacement, evoking the concept of in/visibilization to account for the persistence of such unequal distributions in what may otherwise seem to be a fairly homogenous social setting.

Invisible displacements The Kabré family was one of the first families I encountered during my initial fieldwork in Bobo-Dioulasso in 2009, and during the eleven months I spent in Bobo-Dioulasso in 2010 as well as in my shorter visits in 2017 and 2018, I have kept up with all members of the household, which includes five, by now adult, children and their parents. I first came to know Mme Kabré, or Fatou, who, in

2009, was doing everything she could to make a living for herself and the children while her husband, Oumar, remained in Côte d'Ivoire searching for work. At the age of forty-seven, Fatou had never expected to be rummaging the outskirts of Bobo-Dioulasso for firewood in order to feed her family. Before the war, she was a successful trader in Abidjan, and her husband worked as a security guard for an American NGO. They had lived in a two-bedroom house in a neighbourhood where migrants and Ivorians lived side by side and running water and electricity could be taken for granted. The small house in mud bricks they had built back home in Burkina Faso, in what had since then become a vibrant and densely populated informal settlement (*quartier populaire* in local parlance), was meant as an investment in their old age, not as their only home. But Fatou was not one to complain, and she always made an effort to appear smiling and jovial in front of her neighbours. She rarely fell asleep without weeping, though. Her husband had been struggling to find work in Côte d'Ivoire for the past two years and hardly ever called home out of embarrassment, she believed. The family received support for the children's schooling from an international NGO, but the several hundred thousand people displaced by the Ivorian crisis were generally left to their own devices for their survival in Burkina Faso. 'We are the repatriates', Fatou stated emphatically on our first meeting, 'we are everywhere but no one sees us', referring to the official use of the term 'repatriate' by the Burkinabe authorities to designate its citizens returning from Côte d'Ivoire due to persecution and insecurity during the Ivorian armed conflict. She felt that her experiences of flight and disenfranchisement were being ignored by the authorities, and to some extent by the other residents in the area. And she was probably particularly set on stating her sense of misrecognition and loss towards an unknown European who might be able to help somehow.

Although Fatou was justified in her feeling that the challenges of her family's self-settlement were rendered relatively invisible, the Burkinabe authorities did recognize the mass arrivals of Burkinabe citizens since Ivorian president Laurent Gbagbo's controversial electoral victory in 2000. But neither the official 'rescue mission' to bring back Burkinabe citizens from Côte d'Ivoire, *Opération Bayiri*,[1] nor the 'National Assistance Strategy for the Socio-Economic Reintegration of the Repatriates' (Action-Sociale 2003), reached more than a few thousand recipients (Riester 2011b: 192). Contrary to the negligible impact of these government initiatives in terms of assistance, the Burkinabe authorities were more successful in fuelling resentment against repatriates at the local level. In a context where local communities were put under pressure by the mass influx of involuntary returnees in need of housing and livelihood options, the authorities made matters worse by stating publicly that the repatriates' superior capabilities and experience as migrants set them apart from the local non-migrant population (see also Riester 2011a: 175).

Despite this unwanted exposure, the self-settlement of repatriates to dense urban neighbourhoods in particular went relatively unnoticed by local authorities, which in itself was no surprise in a context were state presence is only felt on rare occasions.

What weighed heavily on the Kabré family was the sense that their displacement histories went relatively unseen by their neighbours. The neighbourhood had received migrants from other parts of Burkina Faso since the 1980s, as well as returning migrants from Côte d'Ivoire prior to the armed conflict, and longer-term residents were not particularly inclined to appreciate the possible differences in these migrant trajectories. Importantly, rather than exhibiting her vulnerability, Fatou contributed actively to this invisibilization by making an effort to conceal her hardships from public view; in part out of pride, and in part in an attempt to present herself as an asset to potential collaborators. As a former trader, she believed that impression management might pave the way for future success, even at the modest level of petty trade at the local street corner. Finally, as I have elaborated elsewhere (Bjarnesen 2016), Fatou's predicaments were relatively invisible even to members of her own family. Her oldest son, Ibrahim, had been able to continue his studies at the University of Ouagadougou, thanks to his parents' conviction that their children's schooling was their most important investment, and to the willingness of Fatou's older brother to take Ibrahim in while he was at school in the capital. However, when Ibrahim visited his mother during the holidays in August 2010, he was shocked to find her living on the edge of starvation, with barely enough to feed his siblings more than once a day.

Much as her insistence on keeping up appearances towards her neighbours, Fatou had been set on managing her household in Bobo-Dioulasso without involving her older brother or Ibrahim more than necessary. Ibrahim needed to keep his mind on his studies, she told me, and worrying him about the family's plight would not change anything anyway. The Kabré family's experiences of displacement and resettlement bring out several aspects of migrant invisibilization that are not usually part of conversations around displacement – whether in public debate, political rhetoric or academic analysis. In this example, Fatou's own assessments and priorities played a central role in managing her own in/visibility as a newly self-settled war refugee.[2] Although she berated the lack of recognition towards the repatriates by local authorities, her appeal for outside assistance was mostly rhetorical in meeting a European researcher with possible links to humanitarian actors. Her main preoccupation was to bear the burden of displacement on her own shoulders as far as possible in order to, on the one hand, present herself to her neighbours as an equal rather than someone in need of charity or pity. On the other hand, she was intent on allowing her son to focus on his studies in the capital, rather than have him worry in vain about her plight.

These dispositions reflect several significant power relations implicit in the social dynamics of in/visibilization, but not in a simple dyadic relationship between those who see – assumed to possess the power of the selective gaze to either recognize or not recognize – or those who are seen. In Fatou's case, she was the primary architect of her own invisibilization. Her vulnerability in displacement and resettlement were not immediately readable in the context of the urban informal settlement, where state presence was minimal, and most residents were making the best of difficult circumstances. In addition to these personal choices, in a situation that may otherwise seem as being relatively deprived of choice, Fatou's predicaments reflect several social differentiations in displacement, at intimate social levels such as the neighbourhood or even within households. On the one hand, her position as female head of household in the absence of her migrant husband was a transnational family structure that was well-known in a context where generations of labour migrants to Côte d'Ivoire had followed similar paths (see e.g. Cordell et al. 1996; Amin 1967; Bjarnesen 2013). On the other hand, however, Fatou's burden in this transnational arrangement was, obviously, highly gender specific, firstly, because it would have been much less accepted in this socio-cultural context for a woman to take on the role of labour migrant while her husband took care of the children and household in Burkina Faso. Secondly, despite their historical precedents, female-headed households were perceived with some suspicion, as a potential source of promiscuity as well as the culturally dubious empowerment of women as primary breadwinners and decision-makers. As a further source of differentiation, Fatou was negotiating new circumstances for handling intergenerational relationships within the family. In the absence of her husband, her son Ibrahim could easily be seen as the *de facto* head of household, as was the case in other repatriate families. By prioritizing Ibrahim's studies in the capital, however, Fatou ensured herself the space to manage the visibility of her own vulnerability, while also investing in her oldest son's future prospects. The effects of these choices were that the generational differentiation of vulnerability within the family became even more articulated, Ibrahim more or less oblivious to the hardships that his mother bore on a daily basis.

Negotiating visibility While Fatou and her family were coming to terms with these unequally distributed vulnerabilities, and their relative invisibility in relation to both local authorities, their neighbours and to some extent to each other, displacement from Côte d'Ivoire also had highly visibilizing effects. Especially to young adults, born in Côte d'Ivoire to Burkinabe parents, arriving to Burkina Faso not only meant resettling in a place they generally only knew from their parents' accounts and from negative Ivorian stereotypes (see Newell 2012), but also an unexpected confrontation with the ambivalent perceptions that many Burkinabe hold towards Côte d'Ivoire. On the one hand, Côte d'Ivoire remains the preferred destination for most aspiring migrants in Burkina Faso. The southern plantation sector and the informal urban economy in Abidjan, until recently one of the subregion's most dynamic cities, have attracted regional labour migrants for generations. In addition to the higher standard of living, Côte d'Ivoire has also gained a status as being more cosmopolitan and globally connected, particularly because of its vibrant music and fashion industries, which are consumed across the French-speaking parts of West Africa. On the other hand, while many Burkinabe still admire this Ivorian cosmopolitanism, they tend to perceive Ivorians as arrogant and superficial, in contrast to their own perceived moderation and integrity.[3]

Young adult migrants arriving from Côte d'Ivoire to Burkina Faso were confronted with this ambivalence in their encounters with local authorities as well as with their new neighbours. They were given nicknames and treated with suspicion and distance (cf. Bjarnesen 2014). To local youths in particular, seeing the newcomers dress in hip-hop or designer-style clothing inspired admiration but also envy and suspicion, and gave them the impression that these young 'Ivorians', or 'diaspos'[4] as they were commonly called (see Bjarnesen 2014), were showing off their affluence. While young repatriates were generally self-aware in their choice of aesthetics, however, their performative style of dressing and loud banter in the public spaces of the neighbourhood told a more complicated story. As Sasha Newell has argued in his ethnography of urban youth culture in Abidjan, investing in clothing and appearances was primarily a way for lower-class urban youths to challenge their exclusion from the elaborate lifestyles of the elite through what he calls 'the modernity bluff'. Rather than simply a form of deception, Newell reads 'the bluff' as social 'performances that produce meaningful fictions' (Newell 2012: 247) intended to emphasize the *aspirations*, rather than the lived circumstances of the majority of urban youths in this context. In practice, to the young repatriates in Bobo-Dioulasso, this meant buying second-hand clothes with their generally modest means and doing their best to repair them and make them look 'fresh', rather than buying locally produced shirts or cheaper fabrics, which were, stereotypically, associated with Burkinabe youths in this juxtaposition of culturally specific aesthetics.

This confrontation between youth cultural styles, however, left little consideration for the predicaments facing repatriate youths in their displacement and resettlement. As in Fatou's case, repatriate youths actively contributed to concealing their hardships, for example by preferring to meet and hang out away from their homes. This difference was first noticeable to me as a methodological challenge, as the young repatriates generally hesitated in exposing too much of their circumstances and insisted on keeping up appearances. The first time I met Pascal's parents, for example, seemed excruciating to him, as his father openly confessed to the family's hardships, while Pascal had, over the course of several months, chosen to steer our conversations towards the collective mobilization of repatriate youths and other themes that concerned young repatriates in general, rather than dwell on his own circumstances. A similar sense of reservation or 'impression management' (cf. Goffman 1959) was felt by local youths, which added to the sense that these 'Ivorians' were untrustworthy and superficial.

Although the young repatriates generally took such hostility in their stride, resettlement in Burkina Faso did expose them to a sense of combined exposure and isolation akin to the experiences of migrants in many other settings around the world. Donald Carter, for example, describes the position of West African migrants in Europe as living 'in a subterranean world that cuts them off from full social personhood, and yet their presence maintains a kind of hypervisibility as the issue of immigration has become one of the permanent features of national discourse' (Carter 2010: 12). In Bobo-Dioulasso, immigrants were not targeted by national discourse to the same extent, but the young migrants were, rather, negotiating their visibility at the level of the neighbourhood, and coming to terms with their relative social isolation. To paraphrase Sara Ahmed, they were persistently recognized as not belonging in their new surroundings. This sense of social exclusion, ironically, was not dissimilar to the identity politics at the heart of the Ivorian armed conflict, which had led to their displacement to begin with. In Côte d'Ivoire, one of the central fault lines of the armed conflict was the contestation over the citizenship rights of people perceived by the regime to be 'strangers' (see Dembélé 2002; Banégas and Otayek 2003; McGovern 2011). This socio-political category was gradually extended during the 1990s to include not only immigrants and people of immigrant decent, but also Ivorian citizens whose family names and local dialects were associated with the country's northern regions, reflecting the tendency found across the globe of essentializing notions of autochthony through politically contentious rhetoric (Geschiere 2009).

From the perspectives of young repatriates in Bobo-Dioulasso, the experience of facing different versions of exclusionary identity politics on both sides of the border resonated with the song by Ivorian *zouglou* artists Yodé and Siro, 'Quel est mon pays?' (Which is my country?) which was played on stereos and mp3 players repeatedly in 2009–2010. The song describes someone of mixed heritage, with parents of different West African nationalities, travelling the region in search of their roots, and facing suspicion and hostility wherever they go. As if addressed to the young repatriates in Bobo-Dioulasso, the chorus summarizes, 'In Burkina they say, there's an Ivorian / In Côte d'Ivoire, there's a Burkinabe / All around I am recognized but not as such / Which is my country? The country of mixage [mestizo]'.[5] To many young repatriates in Bobo-Dioulasso this feeling of betwixt-and-between resonated with their own experiences, first of being persecuted as 'strangers' in Côte d'Ivoire and eventually as 'Ivorians' in Burkina Faso. I have explored these experiences elsewhere at some length (Bjarnesen 2015, 2017) but here I want to emphasize what they might tell us about the paradoxes of migrant in/visibility. Although the lyrics to 'Quel est mon pays?' were usually interpreted to me as being about marginalization, about not being accepted, in light of the conceptual reflections above, I would argue that it is more precise to say that the lyrics evoke misrecognition; of being recognized but not on one's own terms. The phrase, 'All around I am recognized but *not as such*' (emphasis added), in fact, seems to reflect Sara Ahmed's notion of 'recognising strangers' (2000), of a recognition that does not entail the acceptance or inclusion commonly associated with the term, but rather an identification that is squarely premised on the predilections of the host population, reproducing an unequal power relationship between those with the power to see and those being seen, as Polzer and Hammond suggested above (2008).

The differentiation of migrant in/visibilization Although I only met the involuntary returnees in Bobo-Dioulasso several years after their displacement from Côte d'Ivoire, most interlocutors described experiences of misrecognition in their encounters with longer-term residents in the informal settlement where I conducted most of my fieldwork in 2009–2010. To Fatou, and other migrants of her generational position, assimilation was relatively effortless because they had generally left Burkina Faso in their youth, and were returning to a setting with which they were still quite familiar. Their sense of misrecognition, however, concerned the effects of their displacement from Côte d'Ivoire, which had left most families destitute and looking to build their lives 'from zero' as people would often say. The ensuing vulnerability in terms of a general lack of livelihood options and social connections to rely on left many repatriates struggling for a daily meal, but without the extent of their hardships being known, or exposed, to their neighbours.

For young adults, who were generally born and raised in Côte d'Ivoire, assimilation was far more challenging, and despite their feeling of being labelled as strangers on both sides of the border, they generally preferred to emphasize their distinctness as 'Ivorians' rather than invest in adapting their aesthetics and language to the new context. Behind the façade of this 'modernity bluff', however, many youths struggled initially to make ends meet.

While the overall experiences of misrecognition and vulnerability may have shared some features across generations and other social markers, it is important to emphasize the unequal distribution of vulnerability within and across these categories. In one sense, the informal settlement attracted families who were intent on resettling in the city but generally lacked the means or connections to invest in housing in the formalized residential areas, which gave the impression of a relatively homogenous population of low-income households. Across different households, however, idiosyncratic variations in income levels; the extent to which families had close social ties nearby; as well as the abilities of especially the parent generation to establish good relations with their neighbours were all contributing factors to the extent of their vulnerability.

Even within repatriate families, as parents put the needs of their children first, or as adult children were able to take charge of their own needs through work, patronage or schooling, the effects of displacement were rarely distributed equally across generations. In a context of relatively rigid gender norms, furthermore, adult men felt the pressure of wanting to be seen as the main breadwinners of the household, while adult women faced the risk of being labelled as sexually or socially promiscuous, while also carrying the sole burden of providing for their family in cases where their husbands had remained in Côte d'Ivoire.

Despite such trying circumstances, much emphasis was placed on not exposing a family's or individual's hardships in public. These efforts were, to the best of my understanding, not necessarily grounded in a cultural master narrative about keeping up appearances or avoiding shame, but were enacted as strategies of invisibilization to manage relationships to neighbours, and even towards other members of the same household. In the Kabré family, much as Fatou was left guessing about her husband's plight and whereabouts in Côte d'Ivoire, Ibrahim had little insight into the duress that his mother bore in order to provide for her children. These intimate differentiations in the context of displacement and resettlement rarely register on humanitarian radars or academic analyses, as they are meant to be kept out of sight, but they are, I would argue, crucial for appreciating the intersectionalities of vulnerability, and the in/visibilization strategies migrants enact to cope with such difficult circumstances.

Paradoxes of displacement

Clearly, the return of Burkinabe families from Côte d'Ivoire was not a straightforward homecoming but rather, at least in the cases considered above, a resettlement process with significant elements of displacement, albeit with considerable variations across and within families. Not surprisingly, the longer-term effects of these displacements were equally varied and unpredictable. This section considers the shifts in the distribution of vulnerability over time, and connects these shifts to the conceptualization of displacement as an open-ended and paradoxical process of mobility-related disenfranchisement.

Ambiguous family reunification As I discussed in the previous section, many repatriate families chose a resettlement strategy in which the male head of household remained in Côte d'Ivoire to look for work opportunities, while his (first) wife would take over the primary responsibilities for the family upon resettlement in Burkina Faso. Fatou Kabré was one such female head of household when I first met her in 2009. In the Kabré family, Fatou was able to gradually improve her standing in the neighbourhood and invest her modest earning in small-scale trade. While other families struggled with intergenerational conflicts due to the new family composition, or to changing roles within the household following resettlement, the relationship between Fatou and her oldest son, Ibrahim actually improved in Burkina Faso. Having witnessed the sacrifices his mother had made to provide for the family in the absence of his father, Ibrahim admitted that he had gained a new kind of respect and admiration for Fatou, and that this realization had challenged him to reevaluate his unarticulated ideas relating to gender roles within the family. He had no intention to contest the position as head of household, although he was aware that other young men had gained, or indeed been handed, such a responsibility in their fathers' place.

When Fatou's husband, Oumar, eventually joined his family in Burkina Faso, this equilibrium was thrown into disarray. Following the reescalation of armed conflict in Côte d'Ivoire in the aftermath of the presidential elections held in December 2010, Oumar had been destitute and he had survived by the generosity of his neighbours until he decided, in late 2014, that there were no viable prospects for him in Abidjan.

But his resettlement in Burkina Faso was not as straightforward as he had hoped. While Fatou had established close connections to her female neighbours, Oumar found himself socially isolated and with few options for finding work in a city he only knew through his brother-in-law, who had since then moved to the capital. During a joint conversation with Oumar and Fatou in 2017, I was struck by the parallels between Oumar's way of expressing his concerns as a (relatively) recent arrival to the neighbourhood, and Fatou's narrative when I first met her in 2009. Oumar talked about the lack of employment opportunities and of social ties, and his sense of isolation and lack of recognition by the authorities, while Fatou was now preoccupied with her daily activities as the main breadwinner, planning her next trip to the city centre, and making sure that her two youngest children were doing their chores. While Oumar mostly stayed around the house, tending to a sore knee, Fatou spent most days sitting with a group of female traders, chatting and laughing, and small-talking with her neighbours as they passed by. During our conversation, Fatou was articulate and hopeful in her reflections on the family's future, while Oumar struggled to see beyond his current hardships. Once he settled more into the conversation, he rehearsed familiar narratives about the hardships of life 'here in Africa' and the lack of opportunities, to the point that Fatou fell asleep in her chair beside him.

Remembering Fatou's destitution during the first years after her arrival to Burkina Faso, one might have expected the arrival of Oumar to be a relief, the source of support that Fatou had longed for, and the reestablishment of a household composition that corresponded more clearly to societal norms. In fact, Oumar's arrival to Burkina Faso had been more of a burden, as Fatou would state in no uncertain terms. She had no patience with his sense of despair and isolation, and wanted him to make more of an effort in reaching out to neighbours and other potential collaborators. Once again, the unequal distribution of vulnerability within the Kabré family was striking. While Fatou had undergone the journey of gradual and difficult integration in the informal settlement, she seemed to inflict a similar misrecognition upon her husband as the one she had endured in the early stages of her own resettlement. Now she was the one who found the specific circumstances of a newcomer's displacement history uninteresting, while Oumar struggled with the sense of isolation and hopelessness.

By now, Ibrahim had made the most of his move from Côte d'Ivoire to Ouagadougou, benefitting from the more stable political climate and the patronage of his maternal uncle to finish his degree in history in 2013. He was able to gain a teaching position at a private college in Bobo-Dioulasso before the popular uprising of 2014 that eventually ousted president Blaise Compaoré after twenty-seven years in power (see Hagberg et al. 2018) and marked the beginning of a tumultuous two years of political transition, a failed coup and a general standstill in public administration at the local and municipal levels. These broader circumstances entrenched employment opportunities in Burkina Faso even further, but Ibrahim praised his luck in finding work at the right moment, and had rented a house in the adjacent, formalized, residential area to his parents' neighbourhood. Given his father's troubles, and the tense atmosphere between his parents, however, Ibrahim kept his distance. He and his fiancée had their first child in 2015 but they rarely visited his parents, and, as his father told me begrudgingly, they had never been invited to see his new home. In this way, Fatou's sacrifices had paid off in securing Ibrahim a university degree and steady employment but since his father's arrival, Ibrahim had chosen to more or less ignore the implicit obligations to reciprocate by contributing to his parents' upkeep, what Claudia Roth has called 'the intergenerational contract' (Roth 2008).

Paradoxically, then, Fatou's displacement had eventually led her to an empowered position in the family, as she had gradually taken over and lifted the burden as the main breadwinner. At the same time, Oumar's trajectory, following his failed attempts to secure a profitable livelihood option in Côte d'Ivoire, paralleled the experiences of Fatou, but at a seven-year delay, leaving him weakened and despairing by the side of his industrious wife. Ibrahim, as the oldest son, had complied with his parents' wishes that he complete his degree in Ouagadougou, but had since then decided not to become too involved in the quarrels between his parents, and to ignore their appeals for financial support. In all these ways, the differentiated distribution of vulnerability within the Kabré family shifted significantly over time, leading to Fatou's social visibilization in the neighbourhood; Oumar's sense of misrecognition in relation to his neighbours as well as, to some extent, his own family; while Ibrahim chose a strategy of avoidance towards his parents, to their great concern.

From misrecognition to social branding While the Kabré family were coming to terms with the shifting configurations of vulnerability, repatriate youths also experienced considerable transformations in the implications of their (mis)recognition as strangers in the neighbourhood over time. While this exposure had initially led to a sense of isolation and exclusion, their upbringing in Côte d'Ivoire turned out to carry some advantages in negotiating access to employment opportunities in Bobo-Dioulasso. To the young repatriates I have followed the closest, the realization that their social exposure might carry an advantage was facilitated by their attempt to mobilize collectively in order to claim more recognition in relation to the municipal authorities. The attempts to set up a 'diaspo' association to this end eventually failed. But the sense that young repatriates had something to offer led a smaller group to approach the local youth wing of the (then) ruling party, the CDP, and offer their services as musicians and '*ambianceurs*',[6] an Ivorian slang word for someone who creates the right atmosphere at social gatherings. Such connections paved the way for closer ties to the local political elite and, for a select few, a backdoor into the attractive world of public sector employment.

Furthermore, Ivorian dialects of French were widely seen as more cosmopolitan than their Burkinabe counterparts, and these linguistic advantages led some young repatriates to careers in radio broadcasting and journalism, or for those who had obtained the relevant diploma to teaching positions or other jobs in which communication skills were central. These opportunities obviously did not benefit all repatriate youths, but the remarkable achievements of the select few did not go unnoticed and public perceptions towards them gradually shifted, to the extent that the common term, 'diaspo', became a label that repatriate youths would reappropriate, and present as a common denominator for their particular capabilities. As I have argued elsewhere (Bjarnesen 2014), in fact, the term 'diaspo' eventually became an important collective marker; a social brand, signifying all that Burkinabe admired about Côte d'Ivoire. In this way, while remaining visibilized as outsiders, the signification of this exposure shifted dramatically over time, to the explicit benefit of a select few, who gained employment opportunities and important connections, but also to the advantage of repatriate youths more generally, as their visibilized differences were resignified and became an enabler of, rather than a hindrance to, local integration.

Conclusion

This chapter has analysed the differentiated, and sometimes paradoxical, distribution of vulnerability in the context of displacement and resettlement in Bobo-Dioulasso during the Ivorian crisis and its aftermath. Through the experiences of the Kabré family, I have illustrated how even the closest social ties, within the immediate family, may be characterized by 'selective invisibilizations' (cf. Brighenti 2007), and how these intersectionalities may shift over time. To the parent generation of repatriates, resettlement in Bobo-Dioulasso entailed a sense of misrecognition premised on the arrival of newcomers as an unspectacular event in an informal settlement characterized by steady in-migration since the 1980s. Although the experience of social isolation may apply to immigrants in many contexts across the globe, the misrecognition of repatriates in Burkina Faso carries some important differences. Rather than being excluded on the basis of racialized or cultural difference, Fatou's experience of not being recognized as 'repatriate' – which meant that her neighbours generally displayed unawareness or indifference towards her displacement history – implies that she was taken for a non-stranger, to evoke Sara Ahmed's work on strangerhood; of being seen as a neighbour among other neighbours. Misrecognition here lies in not being recognized as being different; in this case as having endured displacement from Côte d'Ivoire and living through precarious resettlement in Burkina Faso. From the perspective of migrant 'integration', this misrecognition may seem counterintuitive; the repatriate experience of misrecognition was not one of exclusion, of being labelled a stranger or a misfit but, on the contrary of being seen as yet another newcomer, as any other migrant. The repatriate experience of invisibilization, in other words, was one of *involuntary integration*, of being seen as operating on a par with residents with less acute displacement histories.

This sense of misrecognition was shown to be generationally specific, and differed significantly from the experiences of repatriate youths. While the parent generation may have wished to stand out more, in order to claim some recognition of their plight, young adults were hypervisibilized through their clothing styles and demeanour, exposing them to the resentment of local youths in particular. These generational differences align, however, in the overall sense of misrecognition; of being recognized, but not on one's own terms.

What adds significantly to the complexity of these dynamics of migrant in/visibilization is their changeability over time. In fact, the very traits that exposed young repatriates to the resentment of local youths eventually became their greatest assets, as the select few were able to enter local labour markets and social networks, thereby resignifying their differences in positive terms. Even Fatou's initial destitution eventually gave way to her integration into more viable livelihood options, and more enduring social ties in the neighbourhood. While her husband may have been expected to benefit from local ideals of gendered access to influence and privilege within the family, moreover, Fatou's role as the main breadwinner further challenged the gendered distribution of vulnerability within the family.

Notes

1 *Opération Bayiri*, or 'Operation motherland' from the Mooré word *bayiri*, was launched in December 2002 by the Burkinabe authorities to repatriate Burkinabe citizens living in Côte d'Ivoire (Banégas and Marshall-Fratani 2003: 10, see also Bredeloup 2006; Banégas and Otayek 2003). Despite its stated intentions of coming to the aid of the Burkinabe diaspora in Côte d'Ivoire, the operation was only able to repatriate approximately 10,000 citizens – a negligible percentage of the total population of Burkinabes in Côte d'Ivoire, which exceeds 3 million (Action-Sociale 2003: 8; SP/CONASUR, UNICEF and PAM 2004).

2 I use the term 'war refugee' knowingly, to evoke the parallels of the Kabré family's experiences with those of other empirical examples of people displaced by armed conflict, but I do not use the term to claim that Burkinabe nationals in such a situation would qualify for the legal status as refugees under humanitarian law.

3 The name 'Burkina Faso', after all, famously translates as '*le pays des hommes intègres*' – the land/country of the honourable/respectable men.

4 As I have elaborated elsewhere (e.g. Bjarnesen 2014), the term 'diaspo' became the most common appellation of repatriate youths, referring to their origins in the Burkinabe diaspora in Côte d'Ivoire (see also Zongo 2010).

5 My translation. The original lyrics in French read as follows, 'Au Burkina, on dit voilà ivoirien / en Côte d'Ivoire, voila burkinabé / De part et d'autre je suis reconnu mais pas en tant que tel / Quel est mon pays? Le pays du métis'.

6 The term 'ambianceurs' has a longer history in connection with the Congolese 'La Sape' movement. While the word 'sape' refers to fashionable clothing in French, the acronym stands for 'Société des Ambianceurs et des Personnes Élégantes'.

References

Action-Sociale (2003) *Plan d'appui à la réinsertion socio-économique des rapatriés*, Burkina Faso: Gouvernement de Burkina Faso.

Ahmed, Sara (2000) *Strange Encounters: Embodied others in post-coloniality*, London: Routledge.

Amin, S. (1967) *Le développement du capitalisme en Côte d'Ivoire*, Grands Documents, Paris: Les Éditions de Minuit.

Banégas, Richard and Ruth Marshall-Fratani (2003) 'Côte d'Ivoire, un conflit régional?', *Politique Africaine*, 89: 5–11.

Banégas, Richard and René Otayek (2003) 'Le Burkina Faso dans la Crise Ivoirienne: effets d'aubaine et incertitudes politiques', *Politique Africaine*, 89: 71–87.

Bjarnesen, Jesper (2013) 'Diaspora at home? *Wartime mobilities in the Burkina Faso–Côte d'Ivoire transnational space*', *PhD Thesis, Uppsala Series in Cultural Anthropology no.* 53, Uppsala: Acta Universitatis Upsaliensis.

—— (2014) 'Social branding in urban Burkina Faso', *Nordic Journal of African Studies*, 23(2): 83–99.

—— (2015) 'The ambivalence of neighbourhood in urban Burkina Faso', *Anthropology Southern Africa*, 38(3–4): 331–343.

—— (2016) 'Between labor migration and forced displacement', *Conflict & Society*, 2: 52–67.

—— (2017) 'Zouglou music and youth in urban Burkina Faso: displacement and the social performance of hope', in Nauja Kleist and Dorte Thorsen (eds), *Hope and Uncertainty in Contemporary African Migration*, London: Routledge, 58–75.

Bjarnesen, Jesper and Henrik Vigh (2016) 'Introduction: the dialectics of displacement and emplacement', *Conflict & Society*, 2: 9–15.

Bredeloup, S. (2006) 'Réinstallation à Ouagadougou des "rapatriés" burkinabè de Côte d'Ivoire', *Afrique contemporaine*, 1: 185–201.

Brighenti, Andrea (2007) 'Visibility: a category for the social sciences', *Current Sociology*, 55(3): 323–342.

Carter, D.M. (2010) *Navigating the African Diaspora: The anthropology of invisibility*, Minneapolis, MN: University of Minnesota Press.

Cordell, D.D., J.W. Gregory and V. Piché (1996) *Hoe and Wage: A social history of a circular migration system in West Africa*, Boulder, CO: Westview Press.

Dembélé, Ousmane (2002) 'La construction économique et politique de la catégorie "étranger" en Côte d'Ivoire', in M. Le Pape and C. Vidal (eds), *Côte d'Ivoire. L'année terrible 1999–2000*, Paris: Karthala, 123–171.

Geschiere, Peter (2009) *The Perils of Belonging: Autochthony, citizenship, and exclusion in Africa and Europe*, Chicago, IL: The University of Chicago Press.

Goffman, Erving (1959) *The Presentation of Self in Everyday Life*, London: Penguin.

Hagberg, Sten, Ludovic Kibora, Sidi Barry, Siaka Gnessi and Adjara Konkobo (eds) (2018) *'Nothing Will Be as Before!' Anthropological perspectives on political practice and democratic culture in 'a new Burkina Faso'*, Uppsala: Uppsala Papers in Africa Studies.

Hammar, Amanda (ed.) (2014) *Displacement Economies in Africa: Paradoxes of crisis and creativity*, London and New York: Zed Books and Nordic Africa Institute.

Jansen, Stef and Staffan Löfving (2009) *Struggles for Home: Violence, hope and the movement of people*, New York: Berghahn Books.

Lubkemann, Stephen C. (2008) *Culture in Chaos: An anthropology of the social condition in war*, Chicago, IL: The University of Chicago Press.

Massey, Doreen (1993) 'Power-geometry and a progressive sense of place', in J. Bird, B. Curtis, T. Putnam, G. Robertson and L. Tickner (eds), *Mapping the Futures: Local cultures, global change*, New York: Routledge, 59–69.

McGovern, Mike (2011) *Making War in Côte d'Ivoire*, London: C. Hurst.

Newell, Sasha (2012) *The Modernity Bluff: Crime, consumption, and citizenship in Côte d'Ivoire*, Chicago, IL and London: The University of Chicago Press.

Polzer, Tara and Laura Hammond (2008) 'Invisible displacement', *Journal of Refugee Studies*, 21(4): 417–431.

Riester, Andrea (2011a) 'Failure of a national construction of belonging: social integration of Burkinabe migrants displaced from Côte d'Ivoire', *African Diaspora*, 4: 185–206.

—— (2011b) 'Migration and conflict: the integration of Burkinabe migrants displaced from Côte d'Ivoire', PhD Thesis, Der Philosophischen Fakultät I der Martin-Luther-Universität Halle-Wittenberg.

Roth, Claudia (2008) '"Shameful!" The inverted intergenerational contract in Bobo-Dioulasso, Burkina Faso', in E. Alber, S. van der Geest and S. Reynolds Whyte (eds), *Generations in Africa: Connections and conflicts*, Berlin: Lit Verlag, 47–69.

SP/CONASUR, UNICEF and PAM (2004) 'Analyse des données sur les rapatriés de Côte d'Ivoire', Ouagadougou.

Zongo, Mahamadou (2010) *Les enjeux autour de la diaspora burkinabé. Burkinabé à l'étranger, étrangers au Burkina Faso*, Paris: L'Harmattan.

Afterword: the times of invisibility

Loren B. Landau

Goffman (1959) long ago distinguished between self-representation and the self. His account explicitly recognizes how fear, opportunity and situational ethos shape people and groups' outward expressions. In all social interactions there is an audience and one being watched, but it is emergent, dialogical interactions that shape understandings of the other and personal possibilities. Subsequent works on semiotics and resistance firmly emplace seeing and being seen (or not) as core constituents of social and political engagement. Being seen means being coded and categorized. Labelling others is at once an act of power, but also a means of potential self-deception and misdirection that generates schema that shroud peoples, places, and processes behind conceptual curtains. Conscious or unconscious, done to others or to oneself, the preceding chapters leave no doubt that guise, disguise, revelation and anonymity deserve continued attention in scholarly and interventionist accounts of human migration.

Of the many to choose from, my reflections centre on three themes at the intersection of (in)visibility and mobility. The first is to prompt scholars and activists to explicitly recognize how the benefits of visibilizing may accrue far more substantially to them than to those they study. Even when well meaning, the telling of particular stories can transgress commitments to 'do no harm' (see, for example, Tammas 2019). Second, it draws connections between visibilizing and the ethics of welcome. Particularly, it asks how invisibility, intentional self-authorship or 'flickering' recognition of the other challenges the bases of hospitality and accommodation. Lastly, I explore temporal revelation and uncertainty. My concern goes beyond questions of waiting and delays – in camps, in processing applications, in accessing services – to comprehending how situating competing or parallel locations in temporal streams helps better understand migrant behaviour. Moreover, how the difficulty of seeing futures reshapes agency and socio-political interactions. I end by considering how scholarship and the humanitarian community, with which it is closely intertwined, regularly code time in ways with implications for understanding and engagement.

I present this trio of reflections as empirical, epistemological and ethical provocations. They build on an extended period of engagement with migration as an object of study and the scholars who conduct these inquiries. Perhaps equally important,

I draw on almost two decades bridging migration scholarship with activism and policy making at multiple scales. There is little conclusive here apart from the almost self-evident recognition of complexity. I hope it can nonetheless further discussions of positionality and the research process.

Visibilizing as academic and humanitarian impulse

Displacement is increasingly conspicuous in humanitarian operations and scholarship. With the numbers of refugees and displaced persons evidently higher than at any time since World War Two (UNHCR 2016), its prominence is understandable. European politicians and citizen's anxiety about real and potential arrivals across the Mediterranean has translated into significant resources dedicated to understanding African mobility (see Curzi 2016). These include migration observatories and investments in research projects designed across a range of fronts from tracking migration patterns to determining the psychology behind Africans' migration design-making. With millions of euros behind their efforts, they have generated a potentially pernicious form of visibilization with the power to make any one writing on African migration or displacement complicit in a concerted containment campaign (Landau 2019a).

Europe's interest in Africans' migration movements and motivations complements the 'visibilization' meta-trend within studies of displacement: to identify and expose the vulnerabilities of varied groups and define them in terms that make them suitable objects of humanitarian action and inquiry (see Lubkemann 2010; Polzer and Hammond 2008). This impulse to reveal populations, processes and patterns of marginalization not only informs, but energizes and legitimates the study of displacement. As David Turton (1996: 96) asked years ago, how does one ethically justify researching other people's suffering if alleviating that suffering is not an explicit objective? Demonstrating vulnerability and offering solutions reveals and codes people and processes, making them visible to other scholars, activists, organizations and policy makers (see Jacobsen and Landau 2003). Many scholars' financial reliance on the humanitarian community – particularly those working on displacement at sub-Saharan institutions – only exacerbates these tendencies.

From early inquiries into camp-based refugees, scholarship has expanded to include various categories of the displaced (especially those 'internally displaced'). More recently, scholars have added studies on people involuntarily held in place, those left behind, returnees and other groups. My own work on displacement to and within urban areas follows this arc (Landau 2006). While visibilization and novelty increases researchers' academic currency, it too is not politically neutral. As Polzer and Hammond (2008: 421) note, this process of visibilization must be situated within complex sets of power relations: 'Invisibility is a relationship between those who have the power to see or to choose not to see, and on the other hand, those who lack the power to demand to be seen, or to protect themselves from the negative effects of imposed visibility'.

Despite strong voices for policy-irrelevant research (Bakewell 2008; Rodgers 2004), displacement work rooted solely within the disciplines often stays on the margins of 'displacement' scholarship. Malkki's (1995) work on Burundian refugees in Tanzania and Weiner's (1996) studies connecting displacement with foreign policy are rare exceptions. To be sure, there are many researching migration and displacement who do not follow this pattern, but they often speak so explicitly to home disciplines that their work remains corralled within them. Work gaining attention across the 'displacement' field tends to reproduce variations on sometimes contradictory, dyadic scripts that usefully bolster other scholars and humanitarian action. The first concerns the failure of international humanitarianism or solutions for improving humanitarian practice. The second speaks of displacement heroism or, more commonly, their vulnerability. The latter is informed by a humanitarian imperative, driven both by efforts to permanently remedy the unfortunate conditions of those in need and, perhaps more immediately, by the imperative to legitimize humanitarian assistance or asylum (see, for example, debates over 'survival migration' (Betts 2013)). This is clear in Behrends' chapter on the Chad–Sudan borderland where humanitarians make visible the need for their presence while hiding elements of the humanitarian infrastructure. This includes the right to identify, or legibilize, its needy subjects.

The more confident people are in the apparati they have constructed to monitor, observe and quantify – and the more desperate they are for institutional or personal recognition – the less likely they are to challenge tropes by revealing people, places or processes that destabilize ethical and cognitive schema. The consequence includes forms of scholarly invisibilization where researchers fear their accounts might be mobilized against those being described. These include discussions of smuggling, abuse at the hands of migrants, or refugees' ingenious ways of gaming the system. These fears are legitimate as anti-immigrant activists regularly mobilize such accounts to demonstrate and illustrate Africans' unsuitability for life in Europe while justifying more exclusionary policies (see Landau 2019b). Such (in)visibilization weakens scholarship, ironically excluding from the frame the displaced in their full humanity less their faults be used against them.

This book moves beyond such self-silencing. Its authors situate visibility within an overt recognition of the politics surroundings displacement and knowledge produced about it. This means at once acknowledging the legal frameworks and their impact on the construction of socio-political realities, without reifying them or allowing them to structure the narrative. It explicitly recognizes that the social categories produced by laws and policies are potentially oppressive, but also offer opportunities. The displaced, as others, can exploit their position along legal frontiers and the multiple audiences potentially interested in them. As multiple authors in the book attest, migrants too play a role in visibilizing themselves strategically, reframing or dissimulating, or remaining remarkably invisible (see also Ticktin 2011).

Seeing, othering and welcome

Beyond the ethics of research, the book's chapters raise fundamental questions about the ethical foundations of asylum, sanctuary and accommodation. As overt acts of hospitality, these demand modes of recognition largely disabled by invisibility or the uncertainty associated with blurred or flickering recognition. The master–slave dialectical, central to Hegelian thinking, operates on the basis of interactions through which all parties come to recognize themselves and understand 'the other'. Such demands for recognition as visibility are central to theoretical and practical foundations of welcome, accommodation and conviviality. The unseen or invisibilized cannot be recognized. As Boeyink notes (quoting Honneth 2001), mutual recognition is at the basis of justice and welcome. Similarly, Derridean or Kantian understandings of welcome and hospitality depend on recognition (see also Arendt 1951: 301). Walzer's (1983: 60) work points us to an important and relevant realization: for people to claim rights, they must be 'recognized' or legible to others with whom they share space. Within such ethical frameworks, displaced people claim rights and recognition only when they come to recognize, and be recognized by, the communal other. At heart here are distinctions between insider and outsider, guest and host, arrivant and resident.

Purdeková's piece subtly surfaces tensions around 'integration' and invisibility and how the act of integrating requires visibilizing difference. Camminga's work similarly speaks to fear of recognition and the simultaneous need for it. The form of self-authored representation many authors describe may temporarily enable a semblance of acceptance, but only when that representation disciplines and shapes its author can the engagement be sustained. Without the ability to recognize the other, it then becomes almost impossible to recognize one's self. If Bulley (2006) is right, that 'hospitality requires some notion of an "at home" for its possible performance', then on what basis is political community likely to emerge in spaces where people maintain multiple points of orientation and where people appear and disappear? If one cannot self-consciously be a host, then one cannot voluntarily offer welcome. Derrida (2010) proffers the term 'hostipitality' to connote the hostility such situations of coerced hospitality tend to generate. The results may be a kind of shallow acceptance of others but without some common set of rules or recognition of others' rights to share space amid thrown togetherness resulting from displacement (see Sandercock 2003), even such shallowness may prove elusive. Recognition may itself be a form of disciplinary power, but the possibility of strategic invisibility or invisibility rendered through divergent temporalities, geographic movement or social diversity demands a novel ethics of acceptance.

The times of mobility

Underlying many of the chapters are concerns with invisibility that go well beyond bureaucratic categorization, gender, nationality or legal status. While these remain enduring concerns for many – as they should – questions of temporality surface in the text in at least two closely connected ways. First, as a subjective but empirical phenomenon that helps explain orientations to place, people and institutions. Second, as an epistemic one.

As an empirical phenomenon, temporalities are a central part of migration and displacement, but ones often hidden from scholars by their focus on the present and materiality of displacement. This book helps to address that. This stands in contrast to the migrant-centrism often informing scholarly accounts of geographic mobility. Take, for example, Xiang and Lindquist's (2014: 124) proposal to, 'systematically interlinked technologies, institutions, and actors that facilitate and condition mobility'. Their holism draws attention to five dimensions of migration infrastructure in an important attempt to unify multiple fields of scholarship (e.g. migration law and policy; labour brokering; supply chains and markets; or the material and strategies of exclusion and incorporation. See Løvgren and Turner 2019; Iskander and Lowe 2013; Sassen 2014; Landau et al. 2017). While offering a heuristic for exploring migration, the structures and outcomes they discuss are also largely material. Moreover, they are almost all structural and external to migrants. Despite mention of social networks, there is little emphasis on the sociality of networks or their connections to space, desire or mobility (cf. Kathiravelu 2012).

Visibilizing the non-material, as so many of these chapters do, furthers understanding of the patterns, consequences and meaning of displacement across multiple geographic and temporal scales. Only by including social subjectivities that frame migrant and 'host' objectives and perceptions is it possible to make sense of mobilities and their implications. Entrenched gender and generational structures, conceptions of community appropriateness, political and social loyalties, and social definitions of value enable, limit and shape movement as much or more than any material or formal incentive and regulation (cf. Lubkemann 2008). These include conceptions of self that are both spatial and temporal that transform (see Levitt 2015; Mitchell 1991) and generate continually emergent infrastructures of meaning (see Sibeon 1999; Lukes 1997; Latham 2000).

It is precisely the connection between temporality and meaning that so many of this book's chapters help visibilize (see, also, Sorokin and Merton 1937; Geertz 1973; Turton and Ruggles 1978; Baas and Yeoh 2018). For societies reliant on exporting or importing migrant labour, future expectations often demand assistance from outside and shape how people react to varied groups in their midst. This comes through clearly in Richter's engagement with hodological space – a kind of imagined spatio-temporal journey that remains almost entirely invisible for those relying on Cartesian maps or material metrics of vulnerability and success. Others explore temporal disruptions associated with structural forces (e.g. economic precarity), violence (domestic, criminal or military) or institutional incapacity (see also Oldfield and Greyling 2015; also Jeffrey 2010; Katz 2004; Appadurai 2002; Bayart 2007; Mains 2007; Katz 2004). Embedded in much of this work are discussions of structures that work to invisibilize people's futures. In an era of precarious work, extra-legal detentions and almost interminable containment in temporary spaces, it becomes almost impossible for people to see their futures with any certainty.

Nowhere are the possibilities of being stuck in space and time more evident than in the archipelago of global refugee settlements and detention centres, a distinct form of global humanitarian urbanism (see Siddiqi 2017; Corthouts 2016). Within these varied sites, people often experience a distinct sense of 'stuckness'. As Jefferson et al. (2019: 3) note (see also Turner 2015; Ramakrishnan 2013: 755):

> To be existentially and socially stuck is not just a question of being stuck in place but equally about being stuck in time. It is the sense of not making progress, of not seeing a future, which leads to a sense of stuckness that may linger.

Elsewhere, displacements occur because people are unable to move (cf. Lubkemann 2008), a kind of enforced immobility often overlooked by migration scholars (see Polzer and Hammond 2008).

These temporalities are critical components to the subjectivities shaping mobility. They help determine the desire and expectations for movement, reaction to others who have arrived or departed, and the metrics individuals and collectives employ to evaluate migration success. Disrupted life courses also become solvents that potentially erode long-held beliefs and practices as people seek meaning in their novel space-times. To some extent, these divergent temporalities also account for the kind of recognition, justice and inclusion people seek.

Temporality – particularly the presentism of many studies of displacement – also works epistemically as a means of visibilization and invisibilization both presentist and historical. In many of the book's account, there are origins and subjectivities that speak to entanglements and histories themselves often forgotten or untold. It requires careful scholarship to understand how the history of slavery shapes contemporary responses to African migrants in Libya as Cepero does in the preceding pages.

The close connection between displacement scholarship and immediate application – policy formation, critique or humanitarian assistance – often necessitates a presentism that shrouds historical legacies and bequests. Instead, discussions of emergency, crisis and solutions tend to visibilize certain processes and generate linear historiographies and teleologies. Much as in individual recounting of particularly meaningful events makes such occurrence appear inevitable and reinforces specific aetiologies, histories of displacement are often overly deterministic. An emphasis on solutions also tends to reinforce efforts to restore the status quo ante or introduce linear temporalities in which people move from displacement forward to durable solutions. If nothing else, scholarship increasingly demonstrates the illusion of durability, and how displacement often occurs in the context of far broader socio-political and economic reconfigurations such as urbanization, precaritization, changing gender norms or networked connectivity.

Work driven by the humanitarian imperative often shrouds continuities and these longer cycles of change situating refugees outside of local and global time. As Gibney notes, scholars and policy makers often understand the displaced as those who have not only 'lost the protection of [their] basic rights', in a legal sense, but more broadly as those deprived of their social worlds (Gibney 2015: 13). Such framing establishes a problematic in which 'solutions' restore, replicate or at least approximate the status quo ante through the provision of legal rights and the reconstruction of place-bound socialities. While often elusive, the global humanitarian apparatus and much humanitarian scholarship draw lines beneath the displacement period when the displaced, alone or with assistance, achieve such goals (see Long 2014; Black and Koser 1999). Even while recognizing that displacement, like other movements, is part of irreversible change (see Lubkemann 2010), discussions of durable solutions nonetheless evoke a sense of permanent resolution: a return to predictability, solidity and solidarity. The emphasis on reunification, a return to families' mechanical solidarity whether in sites of origins, sanctuary or elsewhere, is perhaps the most visible illustration of this (see UNHCR 1993).

Visibilizing multiple temporalities beyond crisis helps understand how 'solutions' may be premised on actively and selectively evading particular forms of connections and recognition. For some who have been displaced – as for many others living amid economic, political and environmental precarity – there can be little sense of site-specific durability, but rather a future imagined as continual mobility accompanied by tactical connections and disengagements. Visibilizing processes beyond crisis can help understand, as so many of the authors in this book do, that what may first appear as the (self-)reservation of social marginalization and vulnerability in the form of alienation from family, kin and community represents tactical agency: a quest for protection and durability amid the structural uncertainty of contemporary urbanism.

In concluding, it is worth reflecting on one final form of visibility and invisibility: that of people studying displacement within a broader scholarly field. This book actively seeks to erode various categories inherited from policy related studies. This is sound, valuable and builds on a broader effort to do so. The question remains whether the boundaries around migration or displacement studies also form a means of producing invisibility across the conceptual membrane separating the field from other forms of social inquiry. This book clearly demonstrates that this membrane is permeable. Unlike many previous works on displacement, this one explicitly absorbs and integrates from across the social sciences: psychology, studies, anthropology, sociology, queer and urban studies, and area studies. The lingering question remains as to whether our collective efforts to discuss and visibilize displacement speaks back to our home disciplines and departments. If nothing else, the book illustrates that studies of displacement, and Africa, clearly should.

References

Appadurai, A. (2002) 'Deep democracy: urban governmentality and the horizon of politics', *Public Culture*, 14(1): 21–47.

Arendt, H. (1951) *The Origins of Totalitarianism*, New York: Meridian Books.

Baas, M. and B.S. Yeoh (2018) 'Introduction: migration studies and critical temporalities', *Current Sociology*. https://doi.org/10.1177/0011392118792924.

Bakewell, O. (2008) 'Research beyond the categories: the importance of policy irrelevant research into forced migration', *Journal of Refugee Studies*, 21(4): 432–453.

Bayart, J.F. (2007) *Global Subjects: A political critique of globalization*, Cambridge: Polity Press.

Betts, A. (2013) *Survival Migration: Failed governance and the crisis of displacement*, Ithaca, NY: Cornell University Press.

Black, R. and K. Koser (1999) 'The end of the refugee cycle?', in R. Black and K. Koser (eds), *The End of the Refugee Cycle? Refugee repatriation and reconstruction*, Oxford: Berghahn Books.

Bulley, D. (2006) 'Negotiating ethics: Campbell, ontopology, and hospitality', *Review of International Studies*, 32(4): 645–663.

Corthouts, L. (dir.) (2016) *The Invisible City: Kakuma* (Documentary).

Curzi, C.L. (2016) 'The externalisation of European borders: steps and consequences of a dangerous process', *Open Migration*, 12 July.

Derrida, J. (2010) 'Hostipitality', *Angelaki*, 5(3): 3–18.

Geertz, C. (1973) 'Person, time, and conduct in Bali', in *The Interpretation of Cultures*, New York: Basic Books.

Gibney, M.J. (2015) 'Refugees and justice between states', *European Journal of Political Theory*, 14: 448–463.

Goffman, E. (1959) *The Presentation of Self in Everyday Life*, New York: Anchor Books.

Honneth, A. (2001) 'Recognition or redistribution?', *Theory, Culture & Society*, 18(2–3), 43–55.

Iskander, N. and N. Lowe (2013) 'Building job quality from the inside-out: immigrants, skill, and jobs in the construction industry', *Industrial Labor Relations Review*, 66(4): 785–807.

Jacobsen, K. and L.B. Landau (2003) 'The dual imperative in refugee research: some methodological and ethical considerations in social science research on forced migration', *Disasters*, 27(3): 95–116.

Jefferson, A., S. Turner and S. Jensen (2019) 'Introduction: on stuckness and sites of confinement', *Ethnos*, 84(1): 1–13.

Jeffrey, C. (2010) 'Timepass: youth, class, and time among unemployed men in India', *American Ethnologist*, 37(3): 465–481.

Kathiravelu, L. (2012) 'Social networks in Dubai: informal solidarities in an uncaring state', *Journal of Intercultural Studies*, 33(1): 103–119.

Katz, C. (2004) *Growing Up Global: Economic restructuring and children's everyday lives*, Minneapolis, MN: University of Minnesota Press.

Landau, L.B. (2006) 'Protection and dignity in Johannesburg: shortcomings of South Africa's urban refugee policy', *Journal of Refugee Studies*, 19(3): 308–327.

—— (2019a) 'Capacity, complicity, and subversion: revisiting collaborative refugee research in an era of containment', in J. Young and S. McGrath (eds), *Reflections on a Decade of the Refugee Research Network*, Calgary: University of Calgary Press, 25–44.

—— (2019b) 'A chronotope of containment development: Europe's migrant crisis and Africa's reterritorialization', *Antipode*, 51(1): 169–186.

Landau, L.B., K. Bule, A. Malik, C.W. Kihato, Y. Irvin-Erickson, B. Edwards

and E. Mohr (2017) *Displacement and Disconnection? Exploring the role of social networks in the livelihoods of refugees in Gaziantep, Nairobi, and Peshawar*, Washington, DC: Urban Institute.
Latham, R. (2000) 'Social sovereignty', *Theory, Culture & Society*, 17(4): 1–18.
Levitt, P. (2015) *Artifacts and Allegiances: How museums put the nation and the world on display*. Berkeley, CA: University of California Press.
Long, K. (2014) 'Rethinking durable solutions', in E. Fiddian-Qismeyeh, G. Loescher, K. Long and N. Sigona (eds), *The Oxford Handbook of Refugee and Forced Migration Studies*, Oxford: Oxford University Press.
Løvgren, R. and S. Turner (2019) '"Winning life" and the discipline of death at Iwawa Island', *Ethnos*, 84(1): 27–40.
Lubkemann, S. (2008) 'Involuntary immobility: on a theoretical invisibility in forced migration studies', *Journal of Refugee Studies*, 21(4): 454–475.
—— (2010) 'Past directions and future possibilities in the study of African displacement', Unpublished scoping study for the Nordic Afrika Institute.
Lukes, S. (1997) *Power: A radical view*, London: Macmillan.
Mains, D. (2007) 'Neoliberal times: progress, boredom, and shame among young men in urban Ethiopia', *American Ethnologist*, 34(4): 659–673.
Malkki, L. (1995) 'Refugees and exile: from "refugee studies" to the national order of things', *Annual Review of Anthropology*, 24: 495–523.
Mitchell, T. (1991) 'The limits of the state: beyond statist approaches and their critics', *American Political Science Quarterly*, 85: 77–96.
Oldfield, S. and S. Greyling (2015) 'Waiting for the state: a politics of housing in South Africa', *Environment and Planning A*, 47(5): 1100–1112.
Polzer, T. and L. Hammond (2008) 'Invisible displacement', *Journal of Refugee Studies*, 21(4): 417–431.
Ramakrishnan, K. (2013) 'Disrupted futures: unpacking metaphors of marginalization in eviction and resettlement narratives', *Antipode*, 46(3): 754–772.
Rodgers, G. (2004) '"Hanging out" with forced migrants: methodological and ethical challenges', *Forced Migration Review*, 21. Retrieved from: www.fmreview.org/return-reintegration/rodgers.
Sandercock, L. (2003) *Cosmopolis II: Mongrel cities of the 21st century*, London: Bloomsbury.
Sassen, S. (2014) *Expulsions*, Cambridge, MA: Harvard University Press.
Sibeon, R. (1999) 'Agency, structure, and social chance as cross disciplinary concepts', *Politics*, 19(3): 139–144.
Siddiqi, A. (2017) 'Architecture culture, humanitarian expertise: from the tropics to shelter, 1953–93', *Journal of the Society of Architectural Historians*, 76(3): 367–384.
Sorokin, P.A. and R.K. Merton (1937) 'Social time: a methodological and functional analysis', *American Journal of Sociology*, 42(5): 615–629.
Tammas, R. (2019) 'Refugee stories could do more harm than good', *Open Democracy*, 19 November. Retrieved 20 February 2020 from: www.opendemocracy.net/en/refugee-stories-could-do-more-harm-good/.
Ticktin, M. (2011) *Casualties of Care: Immigration and the politics of humanitarianism in France*, Berkeley, CA: University of California Press.
Turner, S. (2015) '"We wait for miracles": ideas of hope and future among clandestine Burundian refugees in Nairobi', in D. Pratten and E. Cooper (eds), *Ethnographies of Uncertainty*, London: Palgrave Macmillan, 173–193.
Turton, D. (1996) 'Migrants and Refugees', in Tim Allen (ed.), *In Search of Cool Ground: War, flight, and homecoming in northeast Africa*, Trenton, NJ: Africa World Press, 96–110.

Turton, D. and C. Ruggles (1978) 'Agreeing to disagree: the measurement of duration in a southwestern Ethiopian community', *Current Anthropology*, 19(3): 585–600.

UNHCR (1993) *UNHCR Guidelines on Reunification of Refugee Families (July 1983)*, Geneva: UNHCR.

—— (2016) 'Global forced displacement hits record high'. Retrieved from: www.unhcr.org/news/latest/2016/6/5763b65a4/global-forced-displacement-hits-record-high.html.

Walzer, M. (1983) *Spheres of Justice*, New York: Basic Books.

Weiner, M. (1996) 'Ethics, national sovereignty and the control of immigration', *The International Migration Review*, 30(1): 171–191.

Xiang, B. and J. Lindquist (2014) 'Migration infrastructure', *International Migration Review*, 48(1).

Index

Note: Page numbers in italic indicate figures/photos; page numbers followed by *n* indicate an endnote with relevant number.

www.ingramcontent.com/pod-product-compliance
Lightning Source LLC
Chambersburg PA
CBHW071351220926
51613CB00008B/91

* 9 7 8 1 7 8 6 9 9 9 1 9 1 *